AF394387

UTTERLY LAZY AND INATTENTIVE

Martin Parr in Words and Pictures

PARTICULAR BOOKS
an imprint of
PENGUIN BOOKS

For George Parr, the second coming. MP.

For Solly. And Joanna Scanlan, with thanks. WJ.

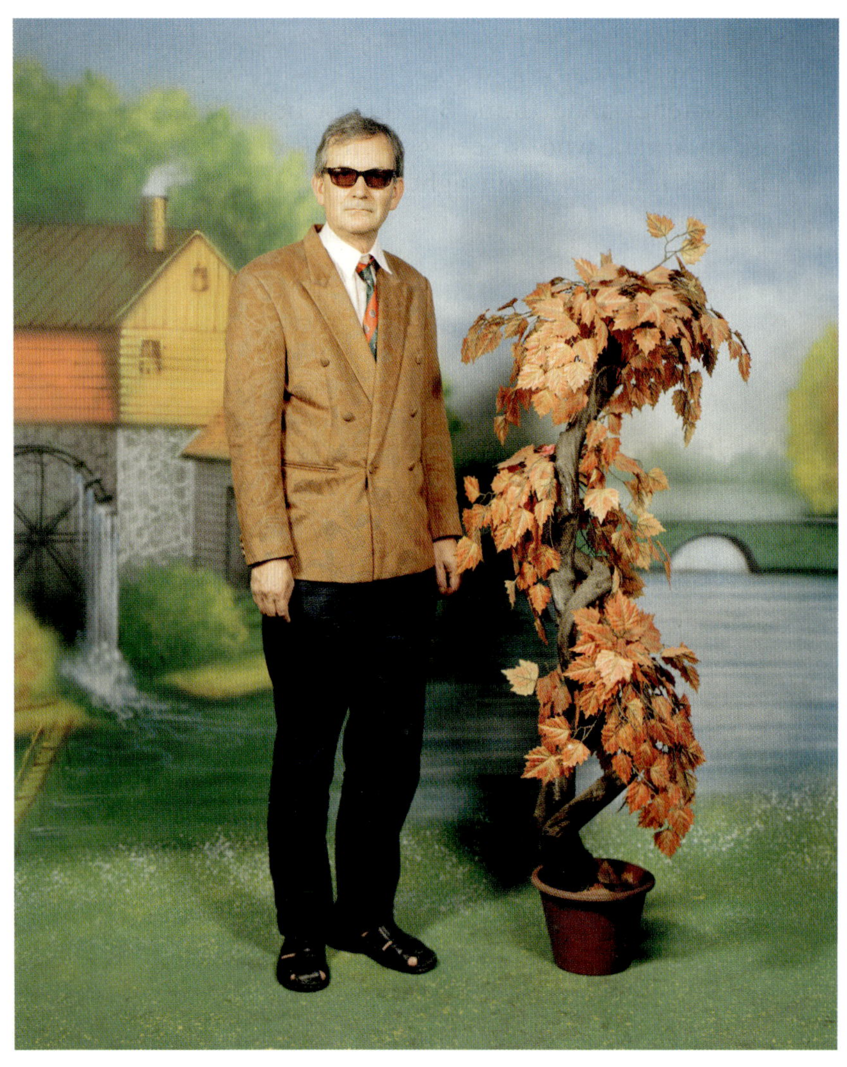

NEW MING CHUN PHOTO STUDIO
FROM *AUTOPORTRAIT*
SINGAPORE, 2007

Introduction

If you saw Martin Parr and didn't know who he was, you would barely notice him. He is Mr Invisible and Mr Normal rolled into one, in his sensible jumper – probably from Marks and Spencer – and sensible socks and sandals. He has a neat side parting and neatly cut hair. He has a mild and conventional manner and a mild and conventional appearance. There is something of the naff birdwatcher about him. But do not be fooled. This is the disguise of a man who is seeing far more than most of us ever see, and he's hiding in plain sight. He may even have taken your photo without you realizing – many people in this book have no idea they are here. He's clever, very clever, and knows how to get access; how to be mistaken for an amateur, a keen and harmless photographer. He is a genius who has changed photography. He is one of the great artists of our time.

So who is Martin Parr? And what would he say if we listened?

Martin Parr's life is, in many ways, an Everyman's life: He's born into a family made of a mix of characters and classes; he has a devoted grandparent; he is undistinguished at school – perhaps he's not having the happiest of childhoods; he's a silly boy; he goes to college; mucks around, tries new things, gets a girlfriend, has some holiday jobs. He enters adulthood in an inauspicious way, works hard, sees something of the world; gets married, becomes a father, builds up his career, travels; has conflict, success, illness, recovery; becomes a grandfather, gains wisdom and respect. An ordinary life that follows an ordinary arc.

Martin Parr's life is also a life of its century. He was there in the Great Freeze of 1962 – he records it with his first photo. He's a grammar-school boy who train-spots the last steam engines, then a hippy student with long hair in the 70s. He's in Ireland during the Troubles, then, in the 80s, he's capturing fashion, luxury, consumerism and British Conservatism. He sees the fall of Communism in the 90s, the rise of McDonald's and the explosion in international tourism. In the new millennium, he watches India transforming, industry dying in the Black Country, the traditional English village enduring; he sees South Africa after apartheid and the growth in the standard of living worldwide. He lives through the arrival of digital photography, mobile phones, and selfies. He sees Gay Pride marches and Black Lives Matter protests, meets the elderly Queen and survives the pandemic. And he photographs it all. He's like a photographic Forrest Gump.

Yet Martin is one individual man living one unique life, someone who, with a gift, encouragement, assiduous unrelenting hard work and absolute focus, has achieved greatness. This is the life of an artist whose work is so powerful his name is an adjective: Parr-esque. There is hope for many young people in the experience of the utterly failing pupil who becomes one of the world's most successful photographers. His was no glorious and gilded path, but one with failures, working hard on his own in backwater towns, in a DIY darkroom, without a telephone, doing it his own way, none of which seemed to be at all successful for a long time.

Then, in the mid-80s, like the film of *The Wizard of Oz*, his work burst into colour, not in a wonderland like Oz but in a downtrodden, dirty, unglamorous seaside resort near Liverpool called New Brighton. He photographed gulls, litter, people sunbathing on cement walkways, babies crying and chip shops. Not for him the luscious aesthetic of 1930s seaside posters. This was a working-class day out, and Martin displayed it in vibrant, flash-induced, saturated colour. In New Brighton, Martin became the photographer we know him to be now – vivid, demanding our attention, socially aware and pulling us in like a magnet.

With the publication of *The Last Resort*, Martin made his mark. But Magnum Photos, the most prestigious photography agency in the world, and Henri Cartier-Bresson, perhaps the most prestigious photographer in the world, didn't want him. They argued that this upstart recording crude modernity was undermining the serious purposes of documentary photography. The old guard at Magnum fought hard and bitterly to keep him out. It was said he sneered. But sneering and cynicism don't make for long-lasting art – it's too easy. If he was sneering, Martin's work would have been one dimensional, and his photographs wouldn't hold the sway over us that they do. Martin, with characteristic lightness of touch, perhaps hurt, let it wash over him. He knew the value of a controversy.

A fight with Magnum wasn't going to stop him. He began travelling everywhere, all the time, to take photographs – he still does. If it's colourful and lively, has crowds and queues and beaches and junk food, you'll find Martin has been there. If it's modern and exciting, Martin has photographed it. If it's on the tourist trail, Martin will have tried to take a photo of it. Like the martin, the bird he is named after, he is swift, agile and travels far. He has, by his own admission, taken millions of photos. When we began this book, we had 48,000 to choose from.

'Which ones shall we choose, Wendy? Which one do you think?' Martin would ask.

It was like being in a sweetshop of art. 'This photo or this one?' I was often speechless, and would reply, 'You choose, Martin, you know best.'

I said, 'Oh, I *love* that one,' so many times that it was embarrassing, for I am a keen, enthusiastic and hugely admiring biographer.

This is because, one day, when I was a student sitting on the nylon carpet in front of an enormous, wooden-boxed television, a programme came on. Normal people were talking about their sofa and ornaments, their wallpaper, their furniture, the tiles in their bathroom, and why they decorated their houses as they did. Nothing could be more boring, really. It hardly seemed worthy of a television programme, but I was riveted. It was *Signs of the Times*, a five-part BBC series about British style in 1992, directed by Nicholas Barker, with still photographs taken by Martin Parr.

All of which was lost on me. Yet, for the first time in my life, I was watching exactly what I knew – suburbia, normal people talking about their normal houses. I was astounded, shocked; I remember it very clearly. It was the moment I came across art made from the normal, known world: art made alive. Not that I would or could have said anything like that then. I just knew I was amazed, but didn't know why. I woke up during that television programme. My world was taken, shaken, shot, cut and presented back to me on a screen, and exposed. This was what art was: it was what you knew, but you saw it, instead of being blind to it.

Years passed. Then, in 2008, I was chatting to a friend in his kitchen in London, when he said to me, 'I met Martin Parr in a queue' – which is a very Martin Parr place to meet him.

'Who's Martin Parr?' I asked.

'He's the photographer. He did that programme *Signs of the Times*.'

'*Signs of the Times*? I remember that! About houses!'

So I approached Martin, and asked if I could write his

biography. He said yes. We tried, we failed. I asked Martin questions; he replied quickly and briskly. I asked the same questions again, I tried to dig deeper. I failed. I wanted to write something analytical, deep, full of myth, id and ego. Martin talked about birdwatching and regularly said the worst phrase a biographer can hear: 'That's all I've got to say about that.' How could I write a book with so few words? I couldn't. I thought and thought about it, and how I could do it this way or that, but Martin was – almost – a closed book. All of Martin, or nearly all of Martin, is in his pictures, not words.

Fifteen years later, I went back to him and said, 'How about you tell your life story through photographs and you talk about your photos?' And he said yes, because Martin is someone who says yes.

He talked through his past. I watched him as we talked. Physically, he has kindly eyes, sensible square glasses and a soft look. He's exact: 'Correct,' he says often. 'Therefore' and 'That's not right' pepper his speech. He's funny – a dry funny. Listen carefully, and he's making jokes. He's gentle, under a bruff exterior. He has a quiet kindness in keeping with his quiet nature, and he is quietly compassionate. I've seen him full of excitement to meet photographers nowhere near as acclaimed as he is.

When I go to the Martin Parr Foundation in Bristol, Martin sits contentedly in the corner, looking at books, looking at photos, calling out questions, getting up to reach another book, then offering to make everyone tea, as his skilled and professional staff work around him with an air of respect. Visitors come to the gallery. Patrons of the Foundation come for tours. They nod readily, speak politely, embarrassed by the chatty toddlers they've had to bring with them and to whom Martin's assistant gives the *Martin Parr Colouring Book*. At lunch, the visitors sit next to Martin's collection of space-dog ephemera and Saddam Hussein watches and eat soup that his wife, Susie, has made. There are books and photos everywhere. It's warm and light, a modern-day, techy monastery where pictures and photobooks, those modern illuminated – and illuminating – manuscripts, are made.

To see Martin at the Martin Parr Foundation is to sense that he is enjoying life and enjoying being himself. He's deeply, quietly and appreciatively in love with Susie. You could say Susie Parr is Martin Parr's wife, but it would be more accurate to say Martin Parr is Susie Parr's husband. He is interested in the now. When he couldn't come to our meetings, it was because he was photographing a world-famous pop star, or in Athens, or doing a photo shoot for *Vogue*, or was being celebrated at Photo London. The photographs he's taking today are the ones our great-great-grandchildren will be looking at. He's interested in the latest tech and in photography's latest fad – the selfie – but he was there forty years before everyone else, with his *Autoportrait* project. He saw that taking a portrait of oneself, the obsession with our own image above all else, was the future. And he's interested in the future: the iPhone 15 has a new lens, he tells me, and he wants to explore using it because it's better at seeing in half-light than the human eye. Yet Martin has an eye that is better than the iPhone 15 – better than any camera at noticing. Martin's great gift is to be someone who notices. And we can see too, when he shows us.

Martin is older now, a statesman in his world. He commands respect, he has much to give, and he's more fully acknowledged. He's very different from the Martin Parr I met in 2008, when he was more dynamic in his movements, upright in stance and constantly travelling. Now he's slower, the result of an illness, and has the air of someone who's seen everything – which, in a way, he has. By his own admission he's one of the most travelled people in the world. But he's still at it. He recently held an exhibition of his photos on smoking – *No Smoking* – exploring the contentious, difficult borders between comfort and discomfort. Martin has work to do, an ever-changing world to document, boring things to find that he's going to make us interested in. He sees history where we see someone just hanging around in an electric car showroom. So if you see a mild-mannered man walking along and he points his camera at you – especially if you're doing something unremarkable, such as standing at the checkout, having a cup of tea, taking a selfie or even just waiting in a queue – you may have been Parr-ed.

Wendy Jones
London
January 2025

UTTERLY
LAZY
AND
INATTENTIVE

1. Beginnings

Well, I was born on 23 May 1952. I was born in Epsom Hospital in Surrey, England, to Donald Parr, and my mother was called Joyce Doreen Watts. I was brought up in suburbia, initially in Chessington, then in Ashtead, Surrey. And I have a sister, Vivien, who is seven years younger. My paternal grandfather, George Parr, would have taken this photograph. He took many photos of me. He was an amateur photographer.

MARTIN PARR, AGED FIVE
PHOTOGRAPH BY GEORGE PARR
ENGLAND, 1958

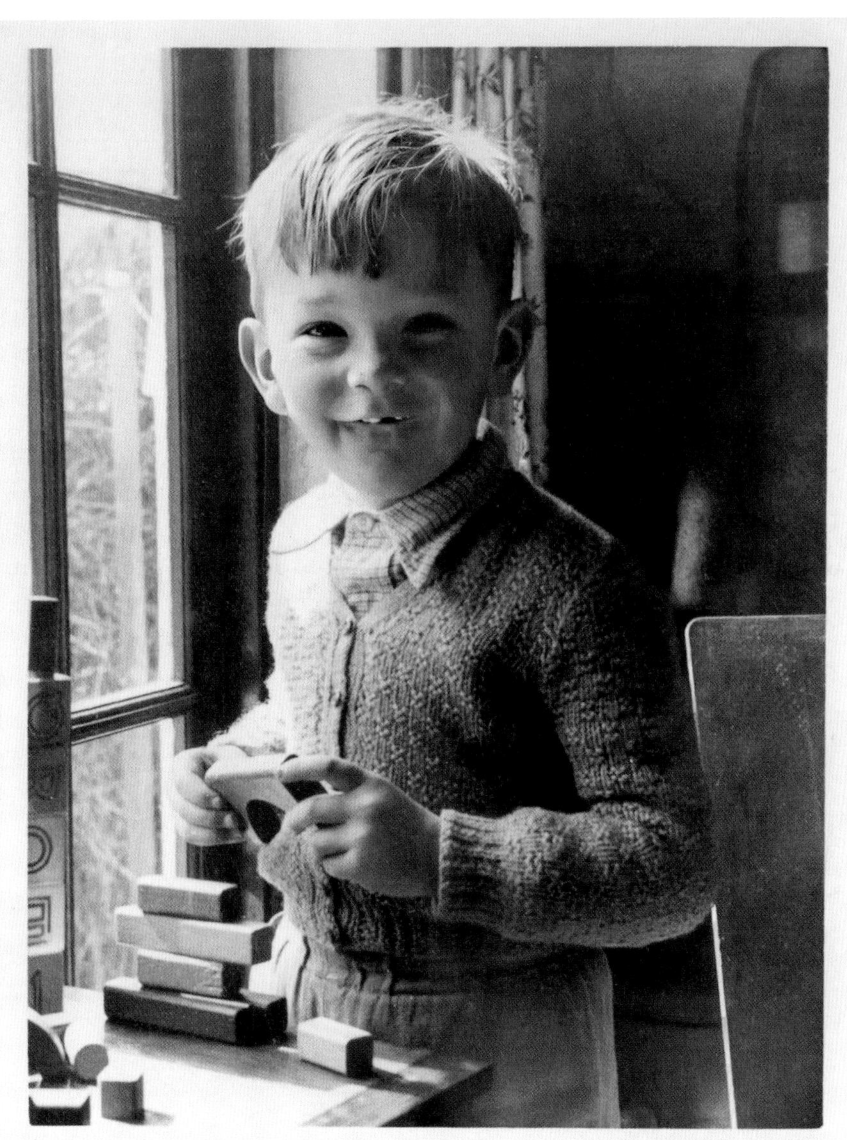

2. My Family

They were very different people, my parents. My mum was very bright and was brought up as an only child in Sharpness, in Gloucestershire. Her father was a headteacher. Her mother – my granny – didn't work. She was a real Cheltenham lady, Granny: she was really quite posh, so I suppose my mum was initially from something posher than middle class. She was brought up very strictly. I don't know whether Granny approved of my mother marrying my father, Donald, because he was a very bluff Yorkshireman, but I think she was won round by his genuine personality. My father was brought up as a Methodist in Yorkshire. He did National Service during the war in the communications department – he used to do Morse code. My mother was in the Royal Signals, doing telecommunications. After the war, my father was a civil servant in the Department of Environment and my mother was a part-time typist, then a teacher. I think they must have met in the Civil Service.

This photo was taken when we drove to the Pyrenees on holiday. We visited the caves at Lascaux. I was very impressed by the caves at Lascaux. I remember we had hazelnut ice cream. I was more impressed by the hazelnut ice cream than the caves.

PARR FAMILY HOLIDAY
PYRENEES, FRANCE, 1962

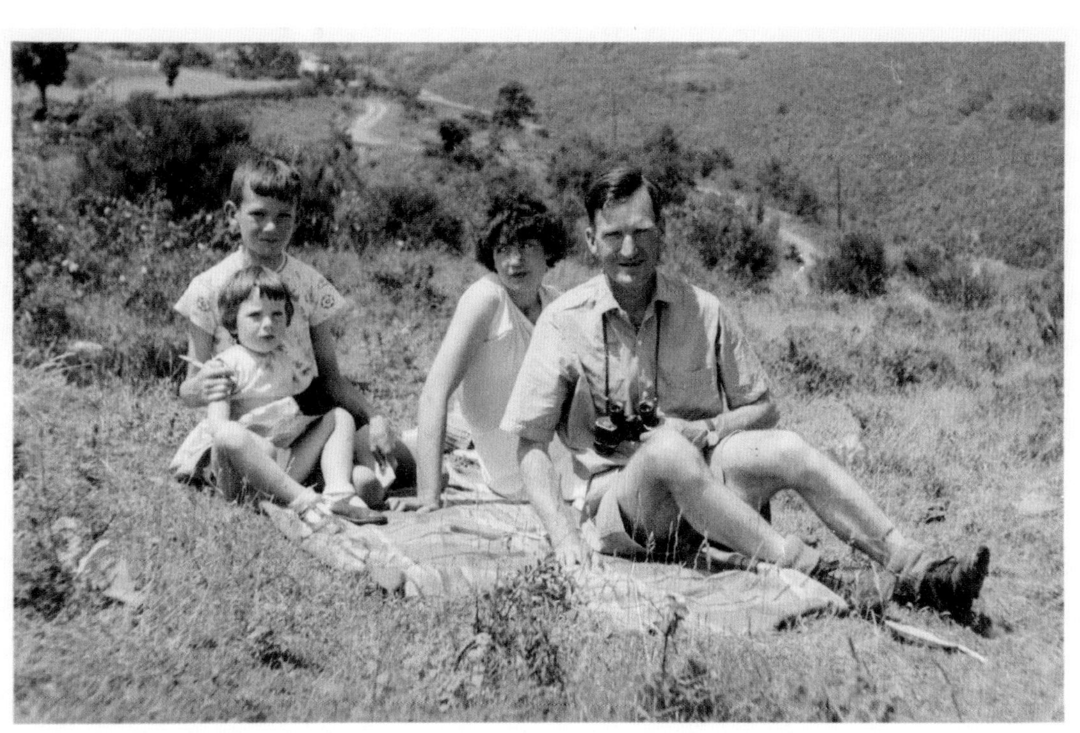

3. Grandfather

My grandfather was a very nice, very attentive, very gentle, soothing bloke. He set this picture up and took it: an old man showing a young boy how a camera works. That was Wilf, one of his cousins, acting as the grandfather-type figure. I'd be about nine or ten here – I was taking photos at this time, but not many. He would lend me a camera, we'd go out shooting, process the film and make prints. He had a darkroom, and that was really exciting. Part of the magic of photography was visiting my grandfather and going into his darkroom and seeing the prints come out of the developer. I'd go up in the summer holidays and stay on my own with my grandfather in Calverley in rural Yorkshire. It was a lot more fun in Yorkshire than in Surrey.

When he retired from working as a printer, he took up photography much more. He was a Fellow of the Royal Photographic Society and a member of the Bromoil Circle, where the fifteen or so members would send each other their bromoils – that's a photographic print, where the image is bleached out, then re-inked using brushes to alter the tone. The members wrote comments on the back of each other's prints, criticizing what was wrong, admiring what was right.

My grandfather was a Methodist lay preacher. He was quite religious. As were my parents. They attended the Methodist chapel in Surrey, where I went to Sunday school. I remember always arguing with the Sunday school teachers about religion. I was quite combative; I wouldn't just accept the generalizations about Christianity even then. I'm an atheist now. I probably was then, but didn't realize it.

MARTIN AGED TEN, WITH UNCLE WILF
PHOTOGRAPH BY GEORGE PARR
CALVERLY, ENGLAND, 1962

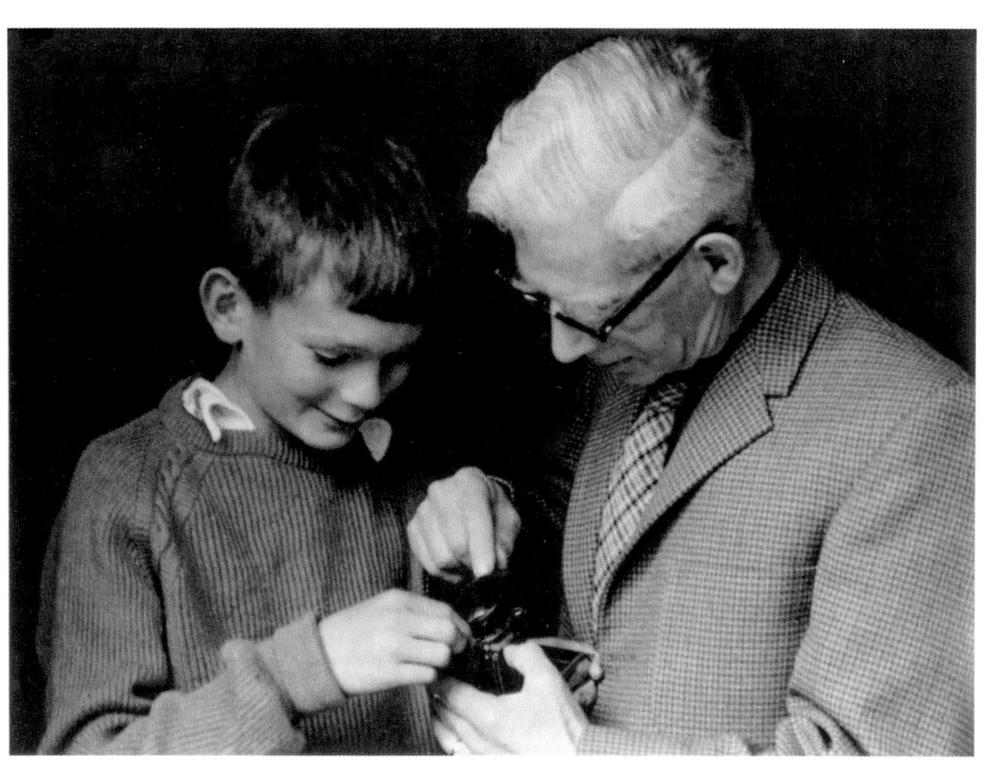

4. Museum in the Cellar

It might have been my grandfather who took this photo of my father emerging from the cellar in 20 Filby Road in Chessington. My father's got a blanket in his hand – perhaps he's preparing for a picnic. My dad was really quiet: he wasn't a chatterer. He was a really lovely man, like my grandfather.

The cellar was the site of my first museum, when I was eight or nine. As you went down into the cellar and turned left, there were tables on which I displayed my natural history collection of bird pellets – which is when birds of prey regurgitate bones and things that they can't eat – as well as birds' nests and fossils. And a stuffed mole. I had a wonderful mole that my father had stuffed with cotton wool. He'd found a dead mole and thought he'd stuff it. You know, why not? What else do you do with a dead mole? He was always collecting dead birds, too. People would come and visit my museum; I would encourage visitors. My parents came, my friends came. I would show them my bird pellets, my dead birds, a bird's nest, fossils – and the stuffed mole.

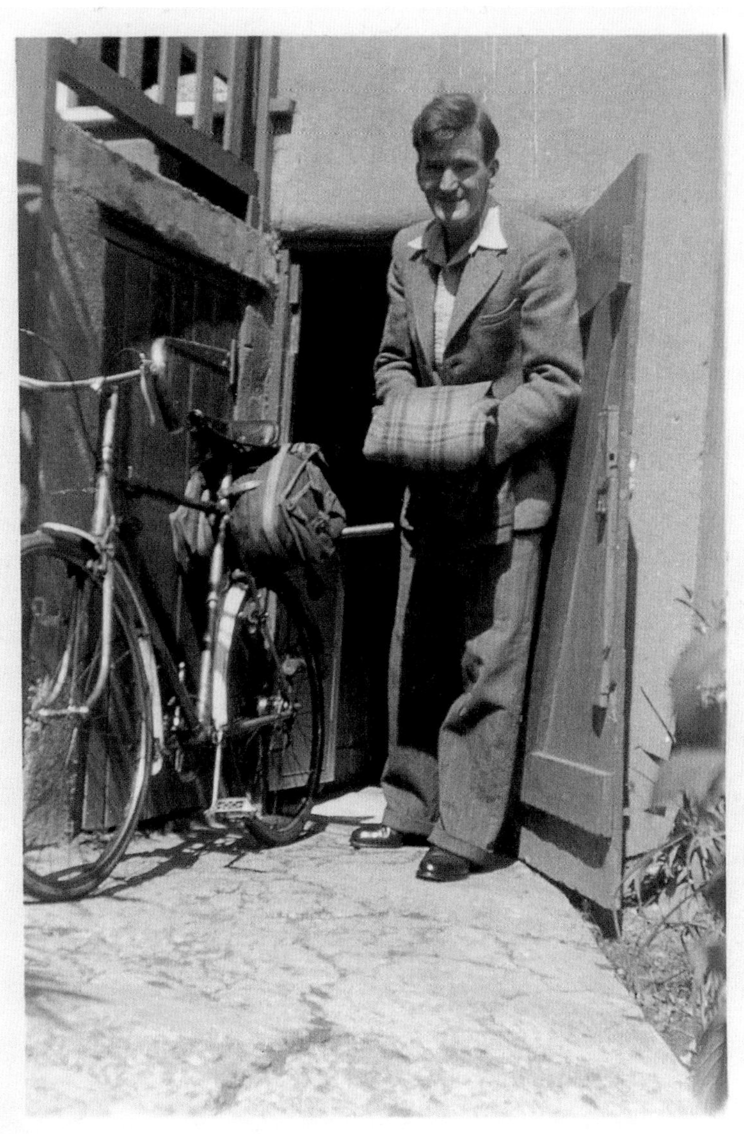

5. The Great Freeze

The first photo I remember taking is this one, of my father on a frozen stream. I used to play here, next to our house in Chessington. I would have been ten when I took this picture during the Great Freeze, that very cold winter of 1962–3. I remember helping my father to sweep the snow outside our house, and people thanking us – everyone was going about being nice to each other because it was a very bad, very cold winter.

You can see my father's got his binoculars on. He was a very great birdwatcher, as was my mother, which meant all our trips out were to birdwatching places – to Thursley Common to see the Dartford warbler, and down to Pagham, looking for waders. We would go to Hersham Sewage Works, where I spent many Saturdays looking for migratory birds. We would put up mist nets, which are two poles with netting between, and the birds would fly into the nets and get tangled, then we'd untangle them and put rings on their legs to trace their migration. We went to the sewage works because a lot of birds came there to feed. It was smelly and we wore Wellingtons. There were tomatoes growing. We used to pick green tomatoes that had literally grown in human shit. All you needed was one seed to fall onto the manure-like sewage and the tomatoes would grow. It was like a field of green tomatoes. They would never ripen; they were always green. We'd pick them, and my mother used to make green tomato chutney.

FROZEN STREAM
MARTIN'S FIRST PHOTOGRAPH
CHESSINGTON, ENGLAND, 1962-3

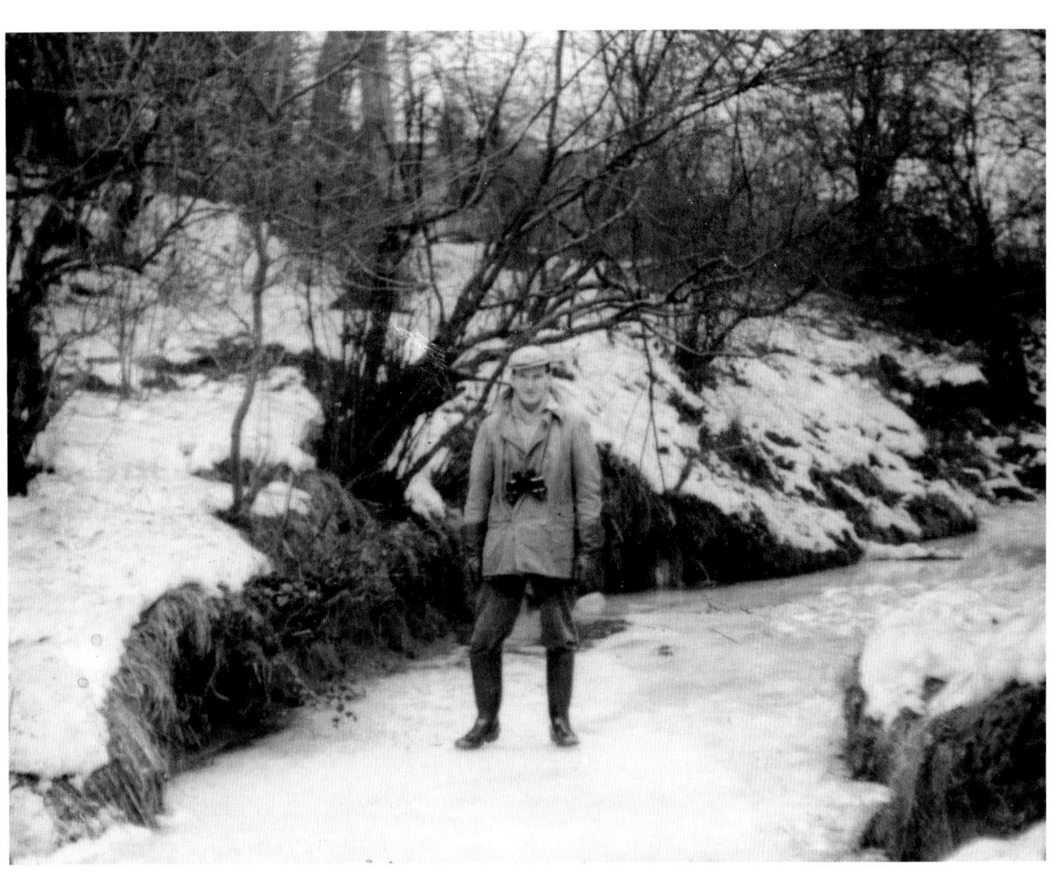

6. Granny

Oh, there's Granny. Granny was full of life and fun. And very eccentric. Granny had gone to Pate's Grammar School for Girls. She was quite wealthy. Her family were from Gloucestershire for generations. My mother was much more closed down. I was very fond of my gran. She talked non-stop. She could go out of the room talking, be out for five minutes, and come back in talking. Still talking. She was just a fantastic person. And very tall.

MARTIN WITH GRANNY WATTS
LYNMOUTH, ENGLAND, 1962

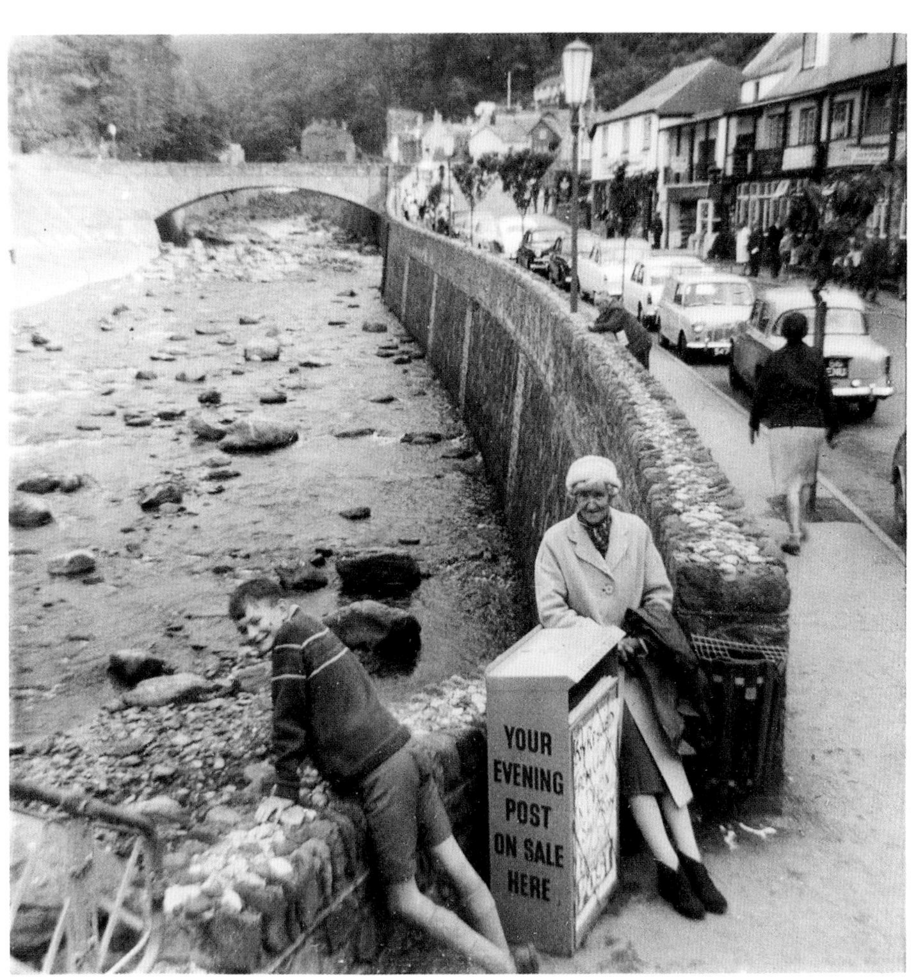

YOUR
EVENING
POST
ON SALE
HERE

7. Two Buses, Then a Train

I didn't really enjoy school. I was never very academic. The teachers thought I would fail the eleven-plus exam. I don't know how I passed it, no one expected me to; I just did, and I got into Surbiton County Grammar School in Thames Ditton.

We moved to Ashtead when I was eleven, where we got a bigger house – I guess it was upward mobility. So I had a long journey of two buses, then a train, to get to grammar school. I had to get the bus to Leatherhead, then the bus to Surbiton and get the train to Thames Ditton, and I had to leave at 7.30 a.m. to do all that. I didn't work once I got there, not much.

MARTIN, AGED 13
SURREY, ENGLAND, 1965

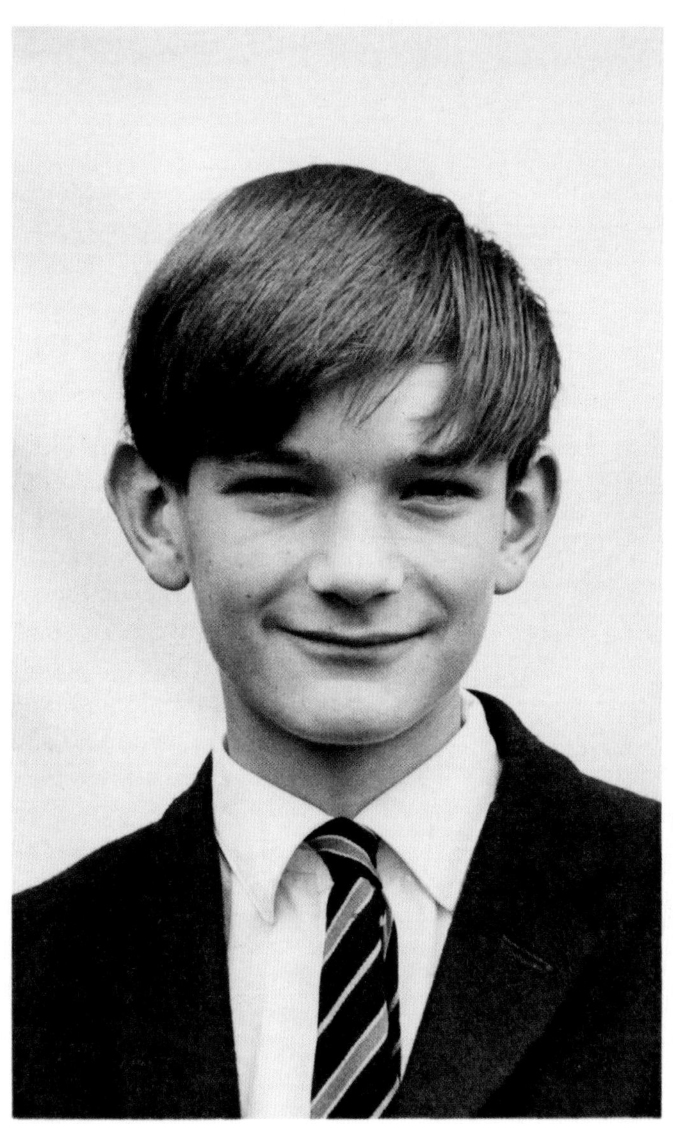

8. Steam Engines

I'd taken up trainspotting when we were living in Chessington, because the main Waterloo to Bournemouth line ran alongside Hersham Sewage Works. I would get a bit bored there; imagine going to the sewage works every Saturday. It wasn't good news, really. I started trainspotting to relieve the boredom of it all. I collected the numbers on trains. That's what you do as a train-spotter – you collect numbers. Steam trains were still going strong, amazingly, in 1963. They must have been phased out three or four years later. The highlight would be seeing the Bournemouth Belle and the Pullman Service.

Later on, as a teenager, I used to go up to London to the steam sheds, like Old Oak Common Engine Shed near Paddington.

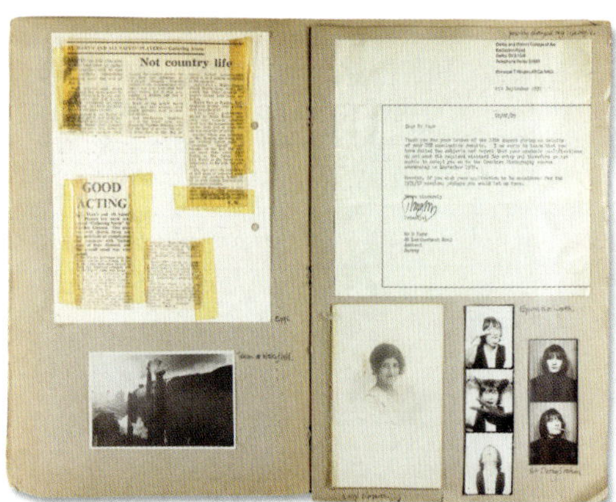

There was a guidebook about how to get inside the sheds where all the steam trains were kept, and you could sneak in. You weren't really allowed to. I'd also go to King's Cross station and remember being propositioned once by some old guy who was obviously trying to pick up young boys. I had my Ian Allen Locomotive listing book where I ticked off all the train numbers, and I had the *Ian Allen Combo* – that's the spotters' Bible, where you underline the engines you've seen, and if you put a '*c*' by a train, it means you've been in a cab, or you've cabbed it.

Trainspotting was much more to my liking than birdwatching. Birds were my father's obsession. But it's all collecting, isn't it? It's all looking and gathering things together. From an early age I was collecting and organizing and thinking about things in groups.

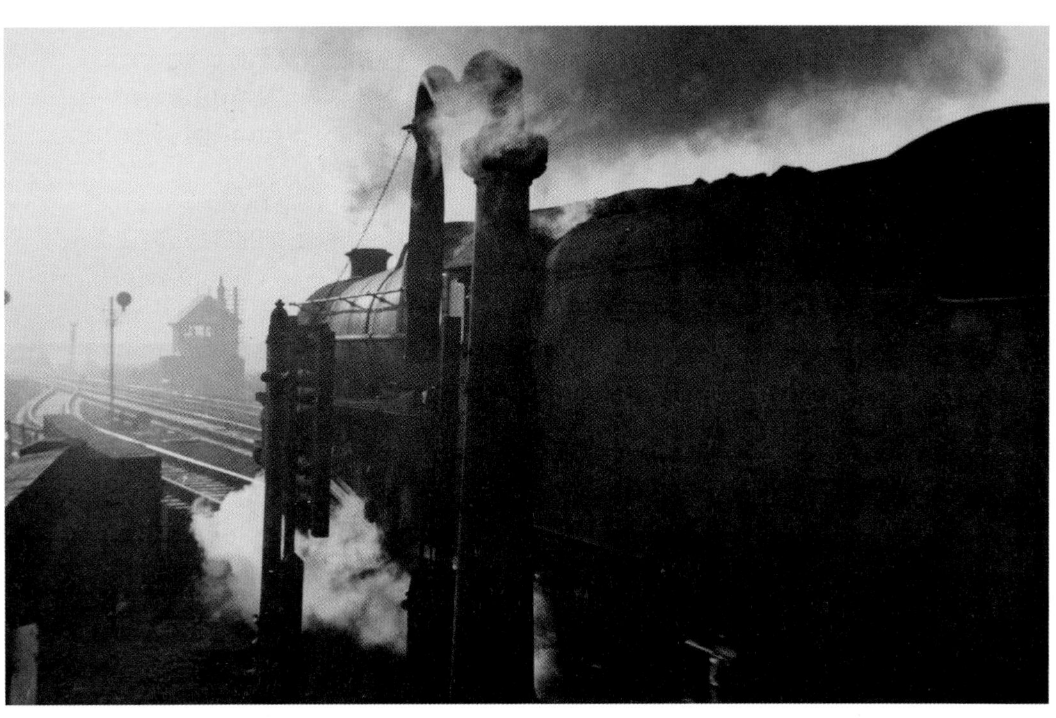

9. Humour

I must have been around thirteen when I discovered Tom Lehrer. He was an American maths professor and satirist who wrote the most brilliant, cutting songs. I loved Tom Lehrer. When I was fourteen or so, I went up to London on my own for the first time to go to Foyles Bookshop and buy his songbook. It was the very first book I ever bought. Lehrer lived to the age of 97, actually, which is amazing.

The point I'm trying to make here is that I studied humour very carefully from a very early age. Even when I was 10, I got special permission to sit up and watch *That Was the Week That Was*, David Frost's Saturday-night satire programme. I also loved Tony Hancock and his programme, *Hancock's Half Hour*. He was good at pricking the pomposity of the English. That's something which, in a sense, I do, too. I've always been very keen on satire and humour. This is where my interest in it began, through song and comedy, not photography. I take it very seriously.

THE TOM LEHRER SONGBOOK
PUBLISHED BY ELEK BOOKS, 1958
MARTIN'S COPY BOUGHT IN 1966

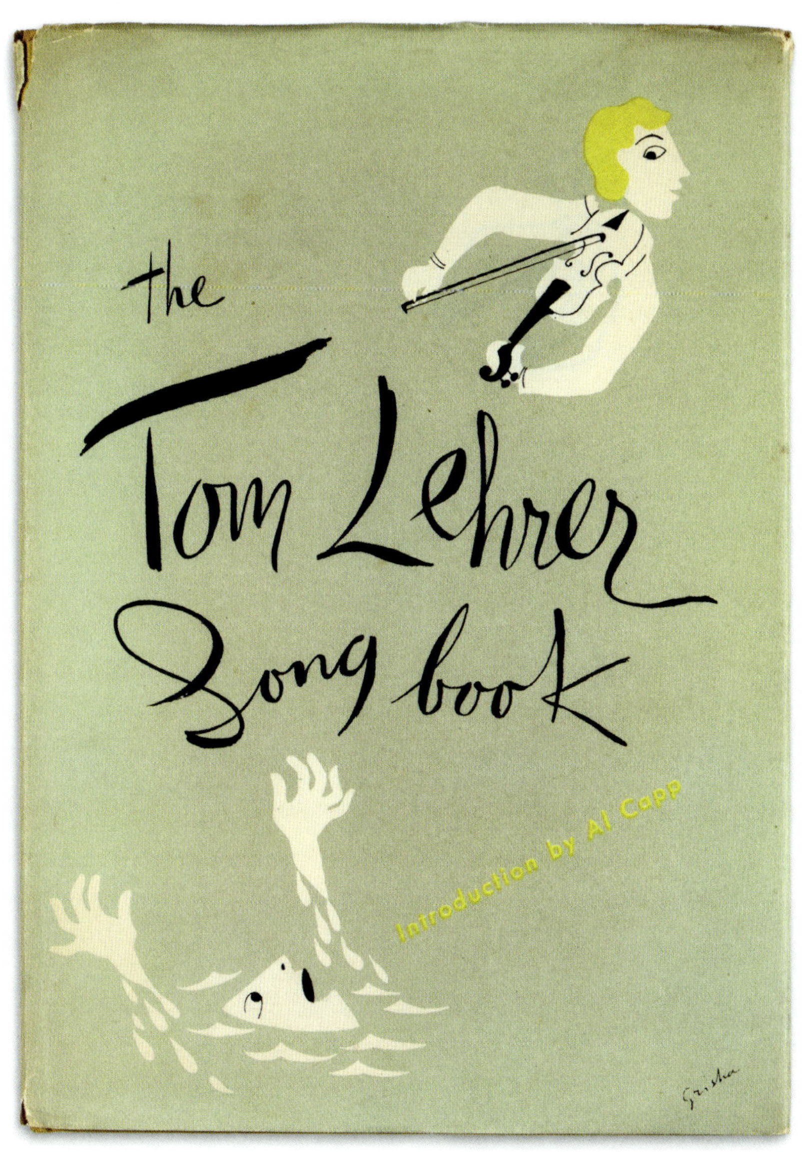
the
Tom Lehrer
Song book
Introduction by Al Capp
Grisha

10. Winogrand

I didn't get on particularly well at Surbiton Grammar School. It just wasn't the right atmosphere for me. Well, it was probably me to blame, wasn't it? Being bored by the lessons. I just wasn't that interested. Nothing interested me, really, apart from trains and photography. I didn't have people to connect with. The only connection I made was with the craft teacher, Phil Reed, who brought a camera into the lessons, so that was very exciting for me. He liked photography and had copies of *Creative Camera* magazine in his classroom, which I would look at. It was exciting to see the photography from America – to see pictures by Garry Winogrand and Robert Frank.

Garry Winogrand became one of my heroes. He only worked in the street, never in the studio, and his ability to shoot and make sense of chaos was quite remarkable. Later, when I saw films of him working, he was clicking away like a madman. In fact, when he found out that he'd got cancer, he went completely bananas and shot thousands of rolls and never had them processed. Winogrand showed me what was possible on the street, and how a photograph can be created out of nothing much.

There was one picture of his that I loved because it was unpredictable. It had a kid silhouetted against the garage, a tricycle knocked over, then a very beautiful sky and mountains with shadows on the top. It is such a strange and compelling photograph. Why it works is still a mystery to me, but it is sheer brilliance because it's so unexpected. Everything about it is perfect.

By the age of fourteen, I decided I would be a photographer. I said, 'It's what I will do for the rest of my life, until I drop dead.' I knew when I was very young. It was a definite decision. Don't ask me why. I just knew it was the right thing.

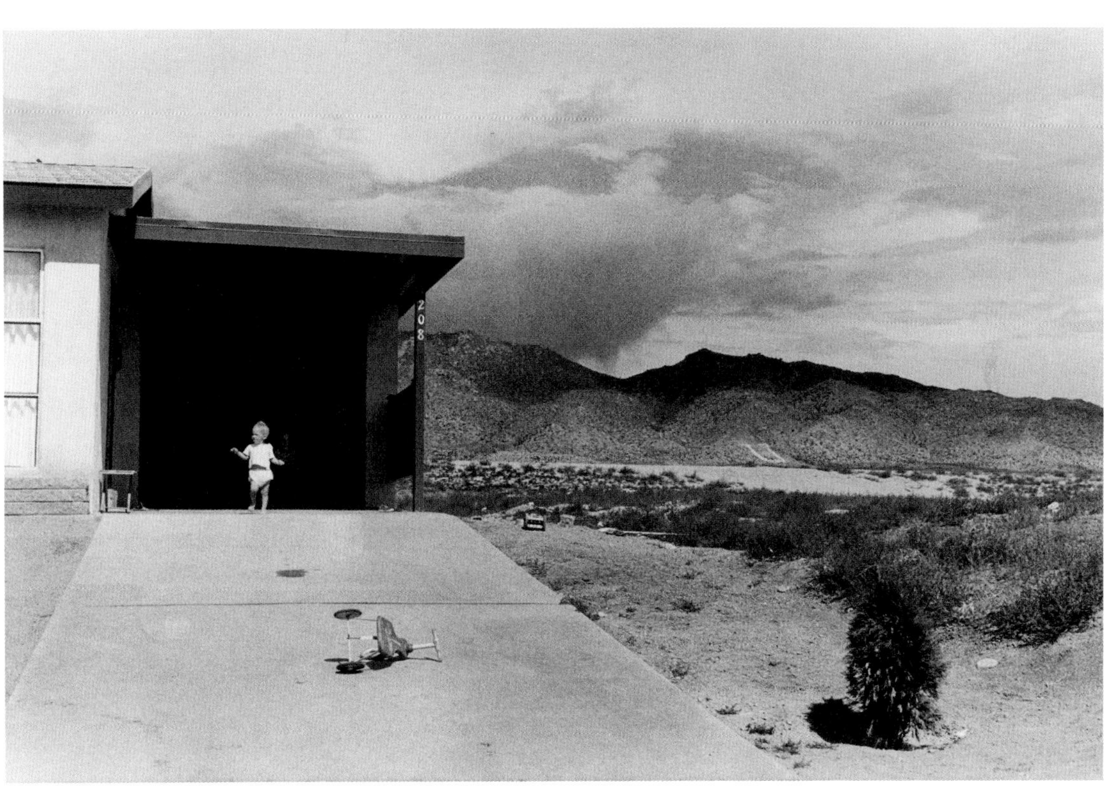

11. Utterly Lazy and Inattentive

I wasn't interested at all, academically. I thought, I'm not doing it. If I wasn't interested, I didn't pretend to be. This is my school report from Surbiton Grammar School in the summer of 1966. My mother saw it and just tore it up in front of me. Perhaps she was so disappointed by my school reports because her father, my grandfather, had been a headmaster. The memorable one was French. I got DD: *'Utterly lazy and inattentive.'*

My later school reports didn't get any better. Art: 'Very little work achieved.' English Lit: 'Shows hardly any interest in class and written work. He makes no effort.' Photography offered a glimmer of hope: 'Martin has a certain flair and amount of ability for photography. But there seems to be little chance of realizing his ability if he doesn't do any work.' 'I wish I could understand his temperamental difficulties,' wrote Earnest Waller, the headmaster. If only Mr Earnest Waller could see me now! I've become very proud of 'utterly lazy and inattentive'. It's a badge of honour.

SURBITON COUNTY GRAMMAR SCHOOL

REPORT for _Inter_ 2nd Half-year, 19 66.

NAME _Martin Parr._ FORM _4.M._

No. in Form _34._ Order in Form _21_ Times Absent _6_ Times late _4_

SUBJECT	CLASSWORK		ASSESSMENT or EXAMINATION		Supplementary Remarks	Master's Initials
	Effort	Stand-ard	Mark P'cent	Form Posn.		
RELIGIOUS INSTRUCTION	B	B	56	11	Improved.	_EG._
ENGLISH	C+	C	34	24	Weak in exam.	_Mac_
HISTORY	B	B	55	8	With care he can do well.	
GEOGRAPHY	B-	B	42	23=	Signs of laziness. He has ability.	_RGH._
LATIN						
FRENCH	D	D	21	29	Utterly lazy & inattentive.	
MATHEMATICS	B-	B-	28	22	Has ability but makes little effort.	
PHYSICS / GENERAL SCIENCE	B-	C+	21	26	Too easily satisfied.	
CHEMISTRY	B	B	55	6=	Steady progress	
BIOLOGY	B+	B+	52	8=	Pleasing result.	
ART	B	B	—	—		
CRAFTS / ENGLISH LIT.						
TECHNICAL DRAWING	B	B	55	16	Considerable improvement	
GERMAN						
PHYSICAL EDUCATION						
EXTRA – CURRICULAR ATTAINMENTS						

EFFORT SYMBOLS :—
Very Good — A
Satisfactory — B
Weak — C
Culpable — D

STANDARD SYMBOLS :—
Exceptionally Good — A
Good — B+
Satisfactory — B
Mediocre — B—
Weak — C
— D

NEXT TERM WILL BEGIN
PARENT-TEACHER INTERVIEWS }
ON _Sept. 6th_ 19 66

Not without ability, but there are danger signs.

R.G. Major. Form Master

SPECIAL COMMENT

Tutor
House Master

A very mixed report.

E. Walls M.A., Head Master

To: Mr. & Mrs Parr
20. Filby Road
Chessington.

12. A Horse, an Old Lady, Some Trees

When I was staying with my grandfather in Yorkshire, we would go to Scarborough and on drives across the Dales. I liked the Dales. I used to think when we drove through Skipton that it had the best of both worlds, because it was near the Dales, but it was a town as well. Before I'd decided to become a photographer, I'd imagined myself as a teacher in the Dales for some reason. I had this fiction of being a teacher in Skipton.

It was on one of those drives that I took this picture. It's an image of a horse, an old lady, some trees, and those are the Dales. I remember taking it and thinking, this is really exciting, getting the juxtaposition between the tree and the horse. This is the first picture I took where I felt, oh, here's something happening. This is exciting.

This was in 1967, so I'd have been fifteen. It's quite an advanced picture for a fifteen-year-old. I had a hunch I was good at photography. I knew I was better than the other boy in my craft class. My grandfather must have seen this photo and had a sense I had potential. I was excited by this photograph – everything about it felt radical.

AN EARLY PHOTOGRAPH BY MARTIN, AGED FIFTEEN
THE YORKSHIRE DALES, ENGLAND, 1967

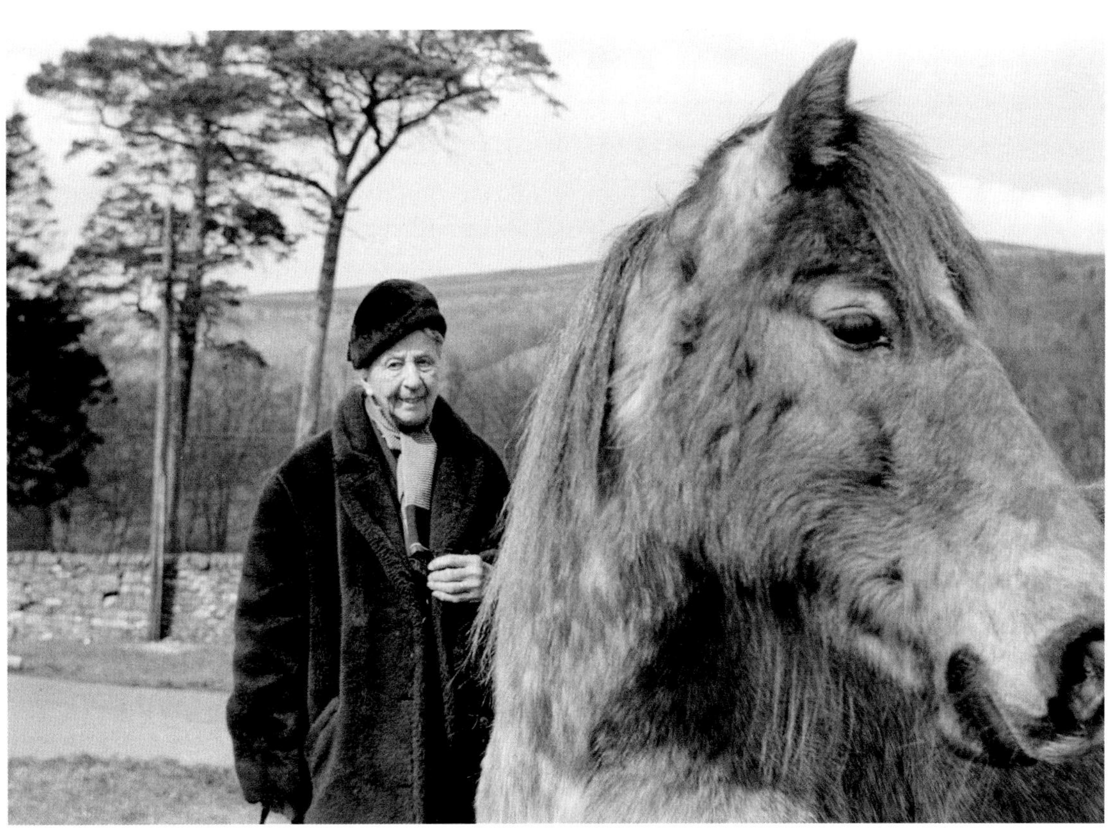

13. Harry Ramsden's Fish and Chip Café

When I was staying with my grandfather in Yorkshire, my parents would come up and visit and take me for fish and chips. We went to the posh one – Harry Ramsden's in Guiseley. I did my first photo essay on Harry Ramsden's when I was sixteen. I was going around trying to record things with my first camera, which my grandfather had given me, and I did the photo essay for myself, for no particular purpose. I photographed the chandeliers, and the waiters and waitresses in black-and-white uniforms. Next to the restaurant was a very basic café where they did takeaway fish and chips. I did a photo essay on that café too. Well – it was two photos plus some writing. It says: 'Yorkshire men flock to Harry Ramsden's at the slightest excuse, whether it be a wedding reception, celebrating Flossie's birthday or even that the gas cooker's broken down!'

MARTIN'S FIRST PHOTO ESSAY, ABOUT
HARRY RAMSDEN'S FISH AND CHIP CAFÉ
GUISELEY, ENGLAND, 1967

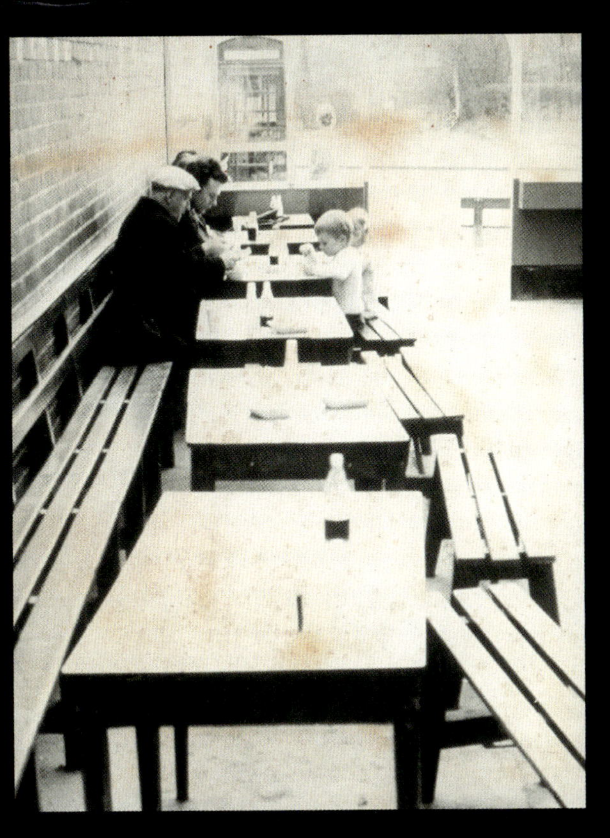

HARRY RAMSDEN - A FISH AND CHIP PARLOUR

Yorkshire Bus Limited offer coach trips to Fountains Abbey, Ilkley Moor, York Minster and to finish the day "an enjoyable meal" at Harry Ramsden's.

Yorkshiremen flock to Harry Ramsden at the slightest excuse, whether it be a wedding reception, celebrating Florence's birthday or even that the gas cooker's broken down. Harry Ramsden is situated in Guiseley, about ten miles from Leeds and queues for free fish and chips (a stimulus offered by the real Mr. H.R. when he opened the parlour between the wars) were allegedly nearly into Leeds and anything up to an hour staring at a choice of non-fish and faded postcards should not be dismissed as unusual.

However glamour and yesterday's newspapers are well separated in Harry Ramsdens. On the one side there's deep carpet, chandeliers and Jack Payne's music with the option of a visit to 'Harry's Fun Parlour' afterwards while on the other side sit the lonely and hungry on hard seats at dirty tables listening to the music of frying cod.

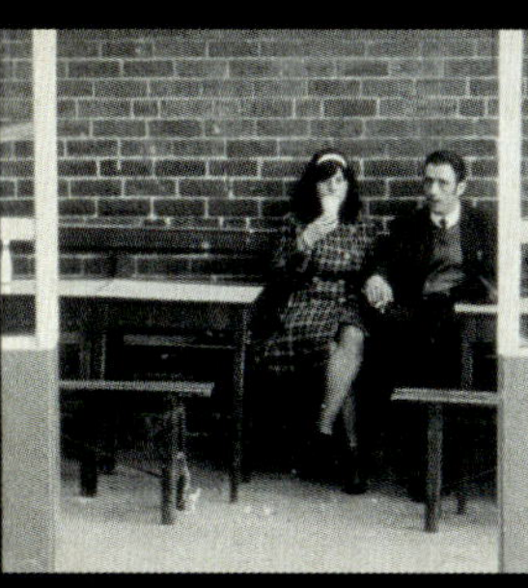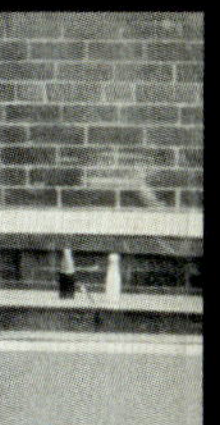

14. Robert Frank

The Americans by Robert Frank is perhaps the greatest photo essay ever made by any photographer on the planet. It's got eighty-three pictures, and there's not one duff one. All of the images became iconic. It's a very famous book. It's a brilliant book. It's regarded in photography as one of the absolute classics. And it's got a fantastic introduction by Jack Kerouac. It was the very first photographic book that I bought – I wrote inside it that it was 1969 when I got it. I came to know the pictures so well they were etched onto my consciousness.

Robert Frank was a Swiss Jew who emigrated to New York in 1947. In the mid-50s, he toured around America taking photos, funded by a Guggenheim Fellowship. He must have been on the road for a couple of years putting the whole project together. The pictures show the tension in mid-century America; they're very beautiful pictures to look at, but the message was that America was a bit of a shabby place. If you look at the cover photo, the black people are at the back of the bus while the white people are at the front. It's probably a segregated bus, isn't it?

I don't think many people would dispute that *The Americans* is the best photography book in the world. Robert Frank structures a picture so brilliantly. You don't often have photographers of this skill, and he inspired a whole generation of photographers, including me.

THE AMERICANS BY ROBERT FRANK
PUBLISHED BY GROVE PRESS, 1959
MARTIN'S COPY BOUGHT IN 1969

THE AMERICANS

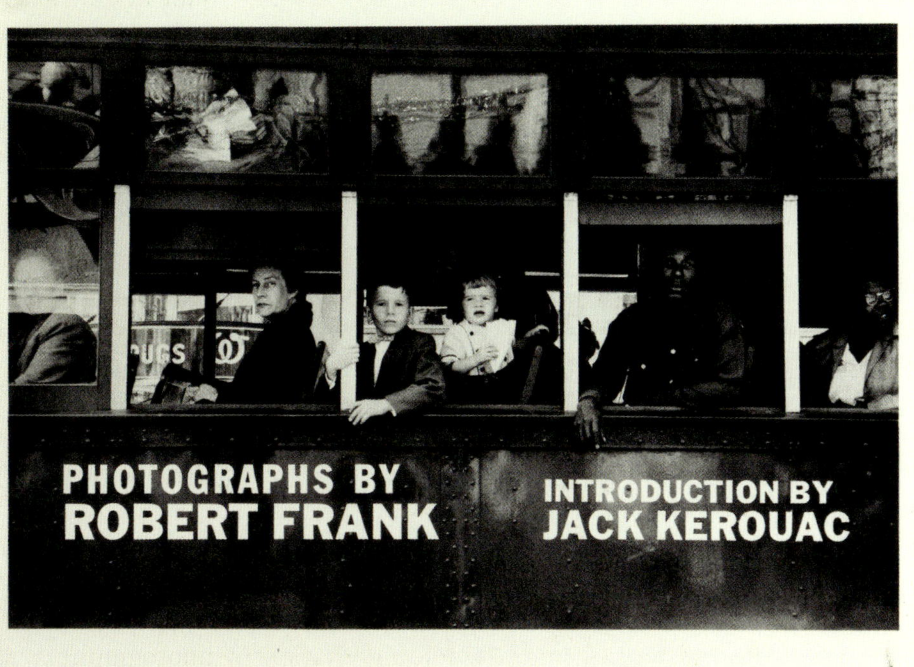

PHOTOGRAPHS BY ROBERT FRANK

INTRODUCTION BY JACK KEROUAC

15. The Surbitonian

The first pictures I had published were in *The Surbitonian*, our school magazine, in 1969. I was doing photography classes and the art master got us to go around Thames Ditton taking pictures. The text says: 'Less than 5,000 souls inhabit the three quaint streets and the urban byroads and factories that constitute this sprawled watering place.' Someone else wrote the text. It's not an industrial area, really. It's a posh village.

SPREAD FROM *THE SURBITONIAN* SCHOOL MAGAZINE
WITH PHOTOGRAPHS BY MARTIN
SURBITON, ENGLAND, 1969

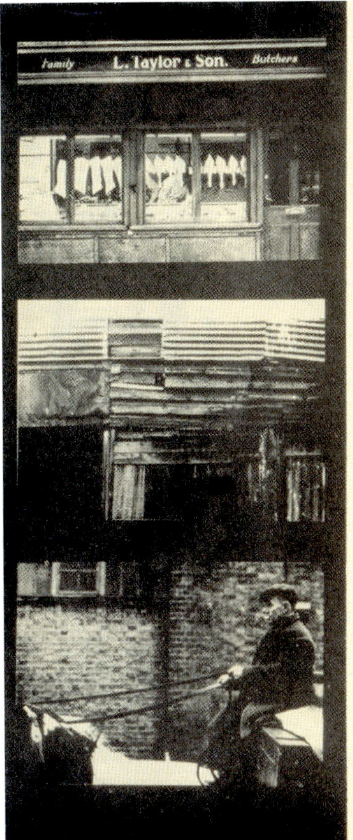

VOICE OF A GUIDE BOOK

Less than five thousand souls inhabit the three quaint streets and the urban by-roads and factories that constitute this sprawled watering-place which may, indeed, be called a 'backwater of life' without disrespect to its natives who possess, to this very day a gritty individuality of their own. The High Street consists, for the most part, of humble, two storied houses, some of which seem to be in a sad state of repair. Though there is little to attract the hill-climber, the healthseeker or the weekending motorist, the contemplative may, if sufficiently attracted to spare it some leisurly hours, find, in its antique shops, its dark santanic ironworks and its little cafe (which, incidently provides inexpensive meals for those who have no fear of putting on weight), some of the picturesque sense of the past so frequently lacking in towns and villages which have kept more abreast of the times. The one place of worship, with its neglected graveyard, is of no architectural interest. (With apologies to Dylan Thomas.)

Admittedly the primary function of modern Thames Ditton is to house the middle class commuter and his family, but it is the estab-lished section of the Thames Ditton community which gives it its character. One resident when asked what she thought of the people of Thames Ditton said that they like to pretend to be affluent and are very conscious of the industrial side of the village.

M. Trevett and M. Parr
Photographs by M. Parr

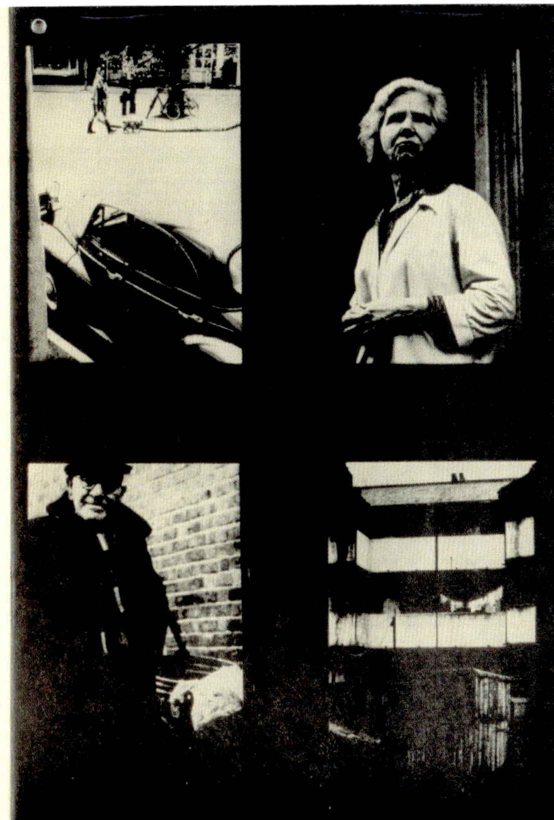

16. Den in the Attic

I had my den in the attic of our bungalow in Ashtead. I don't know who took this; it must have been my father. I'd have been about sixteen or seventeen. Those things on the shelf look like fossils and bird pellets – more evidence of my collecting gene. That's a display of some of my art in the Art Corner: montages and pen and ink. And look at my paisley shirt. I was into . . .

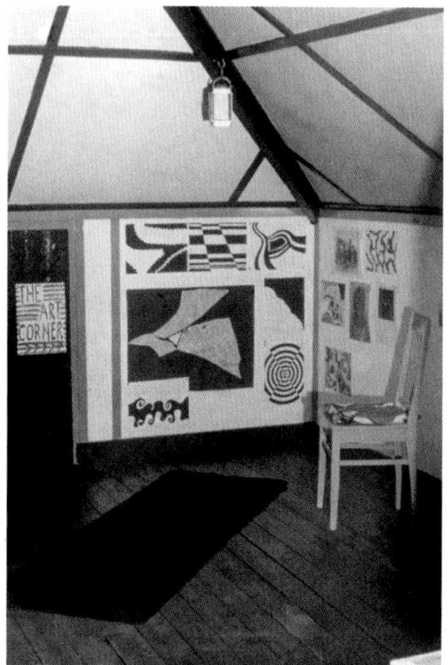

what were they called? That big band? Very melodic, orchestral-type music. Pink Floyd. I used to have my friends from the Methodist Youth Club around, I'd entertain them, and listen to music. And I would hang out in my den, having my own life in my own world.

I was just waiting for the opportunity to go and study photography at college – which I did, but only by the skin of my teeth. I applied to three colleges, Manchester, Derby and Farnham. I went for interviews and got offered places at all three. Derby and Farnham would only take me if I had two A-levels, whereas Manchester Polytechnic would take me with one. Derby was the coolest, because when you were in the third year, you got a shared darkroom with another pupil and you could smoke in there. I thought that was the height of coolness, having your own darkroom and being able to smoke in it, even though I had a 'No Smoking' sign up in my den. I remember touring Derby College and thinking, 'Wow! This is something else, this is great.'

But that's not the point. I took three A-levels and failed two. I only got Art, which was the easiest one. When I think back, I always think it's very lucky I failed most of my A-levels, and that, therefore, the only college that would take me was Manchester. It meant the rest of my life unfolded in the way it did.

MARTIN'S 'ART CORNER' (ABOVE)
ASHTEAD, SURREY, ENGLAND, 1969

INSIDE MARTIN'S DEN
PHOTOGRAPH BY DONALD PARR
ASHTEAD, SURREY, ENGLAND, 1969

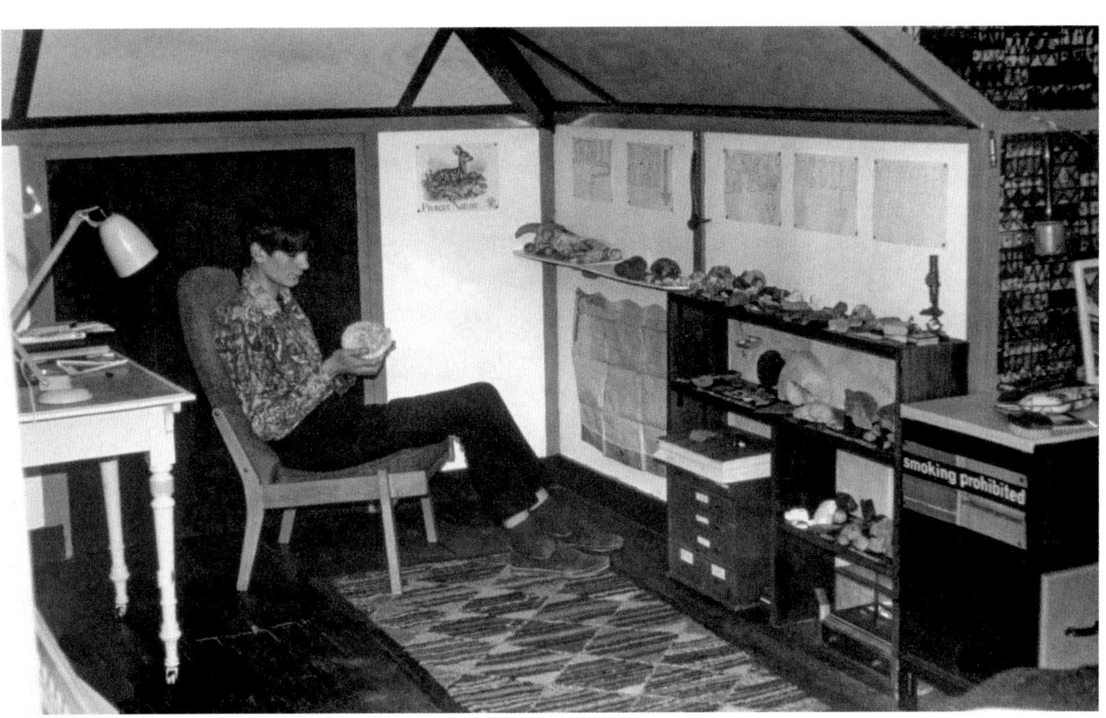

Pocket Nature
smoking prohibited

17. Last Year of School

Back in those days, there was no independent photography scene, and photography wasn't really taken seriously in Britain as an art form, compared to the US. The first photography gallery – the Photographers' Gallery – didn't open until 1971. Even so, I wanted to be a photographer. It was what I wanted to do, but I hadn't thought about what genre, or how to make a living from it. I just knew I wanted to do it.

I remember in 1970, in my last year of school, going to see the London Salon of Photography exhibition, and the International Photography Exhibition at the Royal Photographic Society. My grandfather's bromoils were shown in that. That year I also went to the Bill Brandt show at the Hayward Gallery and the Henri Cartier-Bresson exhibition at the Victoria and Albert Museum. It was great to see those two shows, of two very important photographers, and see their work. I was more influenced by Cartier-Bresson's exhibition because I liked the relationship he created between people and their environment.

MARTIN AS A TEENAGER
SURREY, ENGLAND, 1970

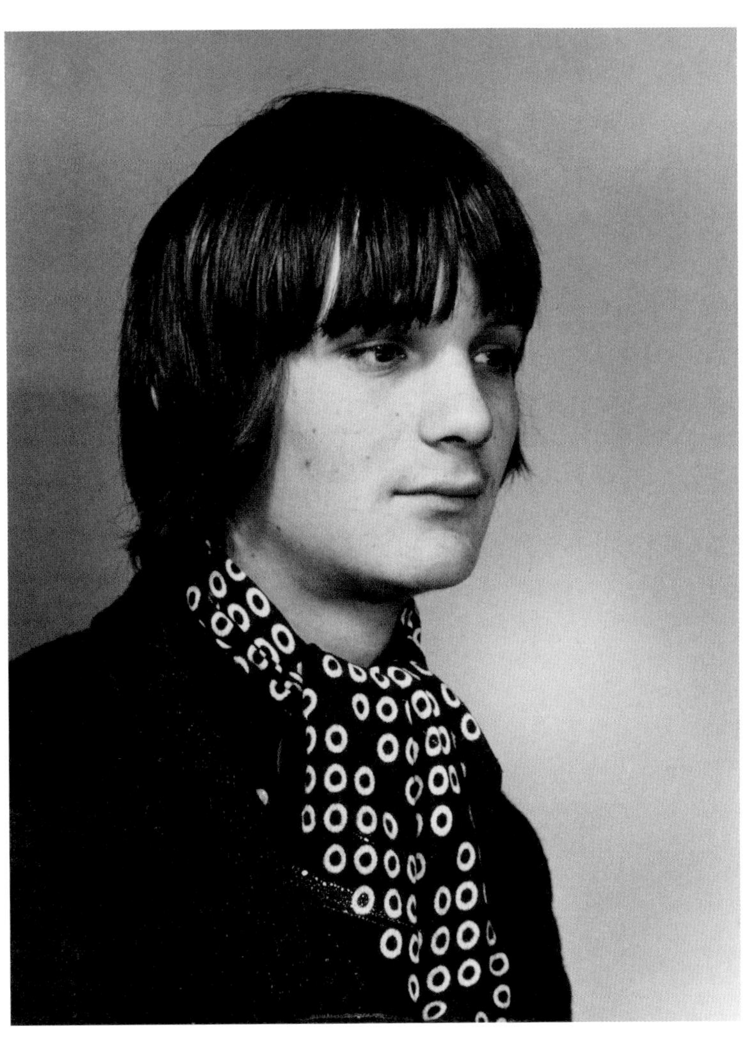

18. College Days

I left home at eighteen to go to Manchester Polytechnic. I was very happy to get out. I had friends in Surrey, but it was very normal and suburban. It was exciting to go up north. It was exciting to leave home. My home life wasn't fun, not really. Manchester was a big city and had plenty going on; it had a big scene. As soon as I got to college, I felt very comfortable. No longer was I at the bottom of everything. I was taking photos and doing quite good practical work.

I had a lot of fun in Manchester. A lot of fun. I was sharing a room in a house with a guy called Ray. We had two single beds in the same room. We had a TV – we were absolutely glued to *Monty Python*. It was one of the highlights of the week and the touchstone of our humour. I didn't just mingle with photographers at poly, I mingled with painters, sculptors, fine artists. As did Susie. She was bored with the students on her English degree at Manchester University, and she found art students a lot more exciting. She was living opposite us in a student house. Eventually, we met.

I had long hair, then. I was pretty tall and thin. I suppose jackets were just normal. I can't believe my hair was that long.

MARTIN AS A STUDENT
PHOTOGRAPH BY JOHN GREENWOOD
DERWENT WATER, LAKE DISTRICT, ENGLAND, 1973

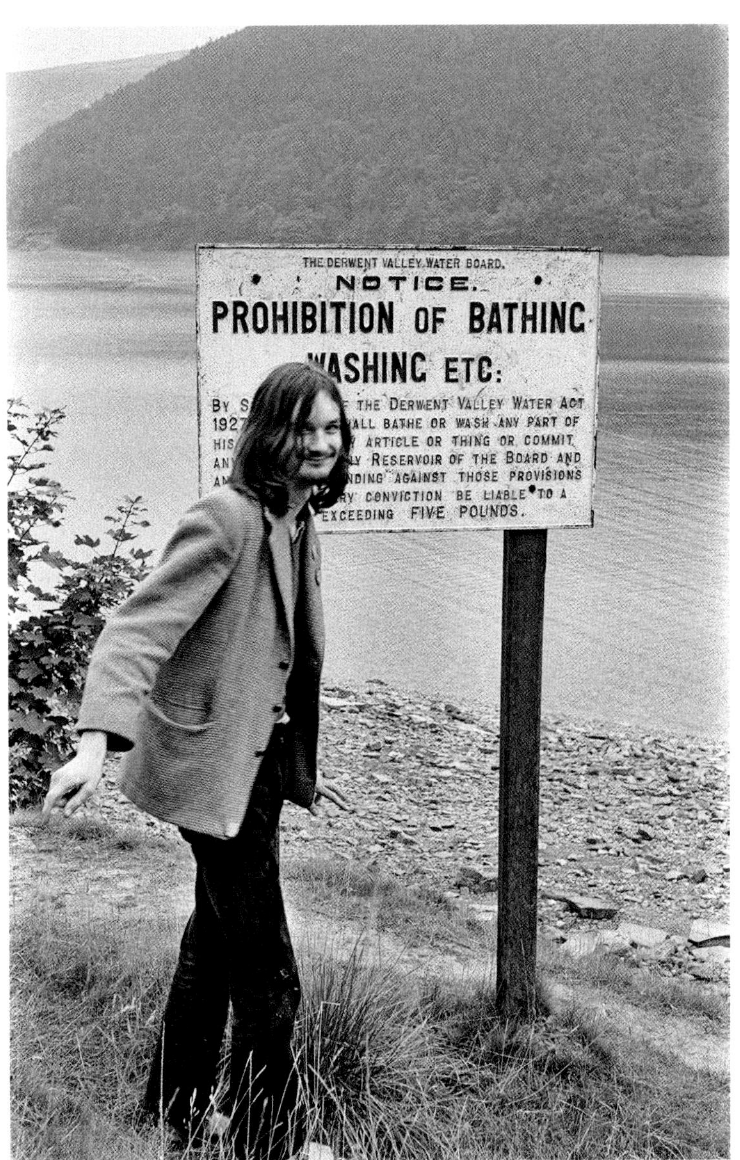
THE DERWENT VALLEY WATER BOARD.
NOTICE.
PROHIBITION OF BATHING
WASHING ETC:
BY S   THE DERWENT VALLEY WATER ACT
1927   ALL BATHE OR WASH ANY PART OF
HIS   ARTICLE OR THING OR COMMIT
AN   RESERVOIR OF THE BOARD AND
AM   AGAINST THOSE PROVISIONS
              CONVICTION BE LIABLE TO A
EXCEEDING FIVE POUNDS.

19. The Young Decorators

The course at Manchester Polytechnic was very much geared towards becoming a photographer's assistant. The classic system was that you became an assistant to a photographer and then, eventually, you took over from the photographer. In those days, there wasn't much opportunity to do editorial work on your own. The Sunday newspaper colour supplements had started appearing in the 1960s, and they'd commission photographers to do original photographic projects, but it was difficult work to get. College wanted us to be commercial photographers working in studios, doing weddings, portraits, fashion, advertising – whatever. Commercial work meant using photography to sell things. I was against that. I thought, I'm not going to be a commercial photographer, I'll just take my own pictures. I was rebelling.

I didn't do well at college. They tried to throw me out after the first year because I failed my theory exam on technical know-how. Then, my first-year tutor, Alan Murgatroyd, said, 'This guy's good, we have to keep him.' He managed to keep me on the course. I owe him a great deal.

MARTIN AND HIS FRIEND NOEL HOLDING PAINTBRUSHES
PHOTOGRAPH BY MARTIN'S GRANNY WATTS
CHELTENHAM, ENGLAND, 1970

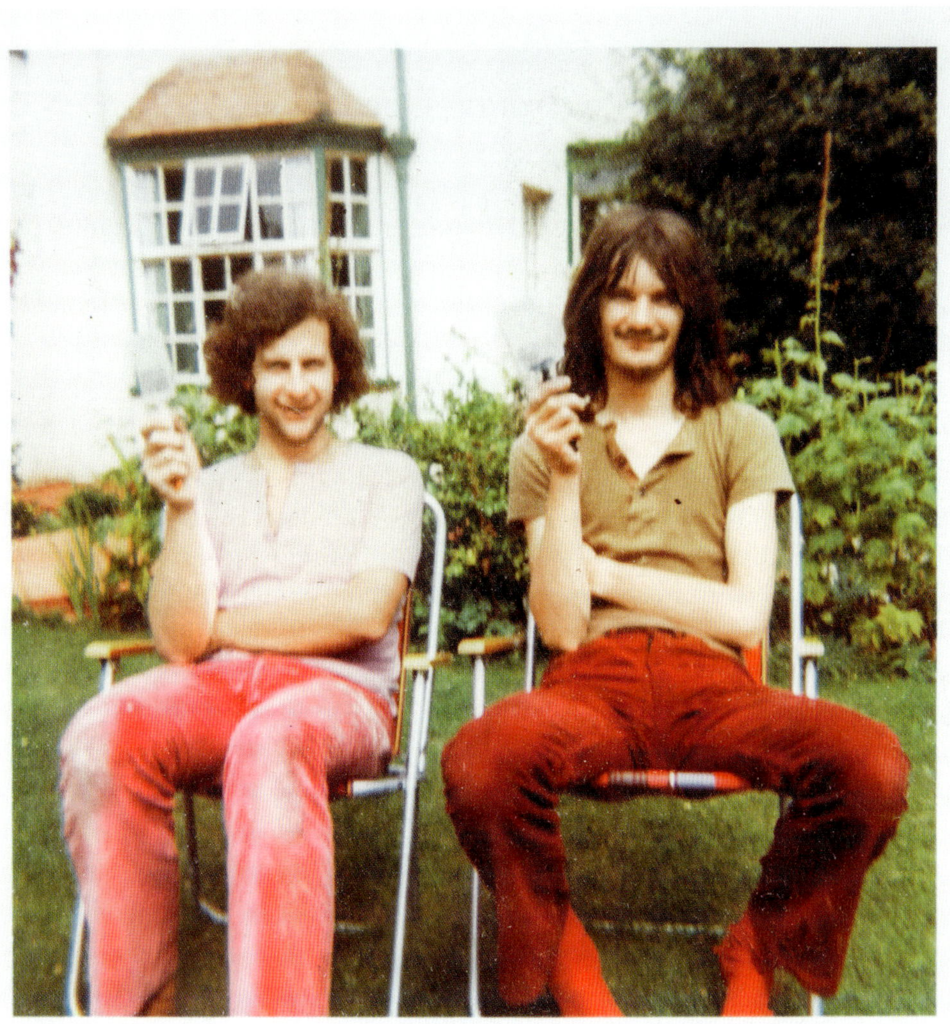

20. Tony Ray-Jones

In 1971, the editor of *Creative Camera* magazine, Bill Jay, gave a talk at Manchester Polytechnic in which he showed us work by Tony Ray-Jones. It had a profound influence on many of the students, but probably most of all on me.

Tony Ray-Jones was a great photographer who died very young, aged thirty, in 1972. He studied graphics at the London College of Printing. Then, in 1960, he went to America for five years, where he became part of the vibrant photo scene. He met people like Robert Frank, Garry Winogrand and Lee Friedlander and started to understand how American photography worked. In Britain, we'd been dominated by photography magazines like *Picture Post*, where the subject was usually bang in the centre of the picture. Tony Ray-Jones began to explore the edges and the whole frame. It was to do with the spaces between things, not just the narrative.

So, look at this picture here. Everything about *Ramsgate 1967* is immaculate. To get that is a great achievement, really, for any photographer. This guy's good, coming in. Then the kid clapping her hands. The dog – a brilliant silhouette, couldn't be better. A couple with a pram. And a couple looking into the photo. Even these two people in the corner by the shop. The kid climbing on the window ledge. Everything about it is brilliant. It has many stories.

Tony Ray-Jones taught me how good a photo taken in England could be. He had the intuition and knowledge to be able to spot the scene. When I was at college, I'd look at his pictures and constantly be amazed at how good they were. As I am now.

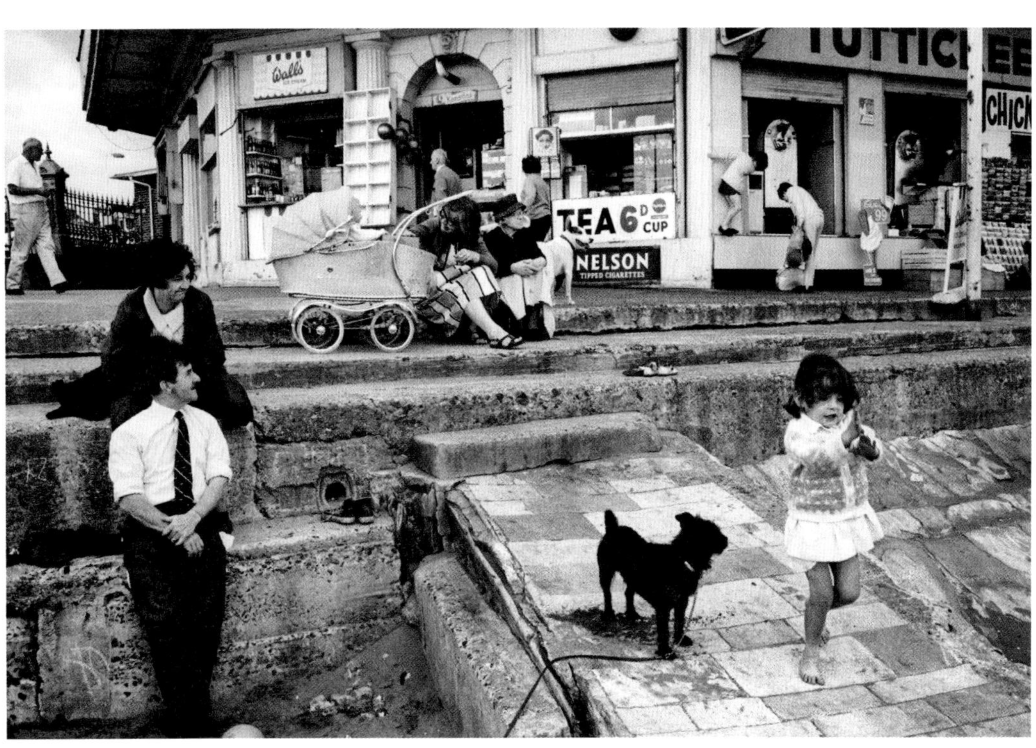
Wall's
TUTTI
CHICK
CHICK
TEA 6 D CUP
NELSON
TIPPED CIGARETTES

21. Birdwatchers

When I went home during the college breaks, I'd take pictures of my father's birdwatching trips with the Surrey Bird Club – my father was the president of the Surrey Bird Club. He made lists of the birds, and the Dartford warbler was his specialism.

This picture was taken when the bird club was having its picnic lunch. I guess this photo works because you've got these two couples, both with binoculars, so it looks quite surreal. They look like owls themselves. I was beginning to look at scenes that were familiar in a slightly remote way. And there's humour in it – it was the first photo I could clearly see the humour in.

SURREY BIRD CLUB
SURREY, ENGLAND, 1972

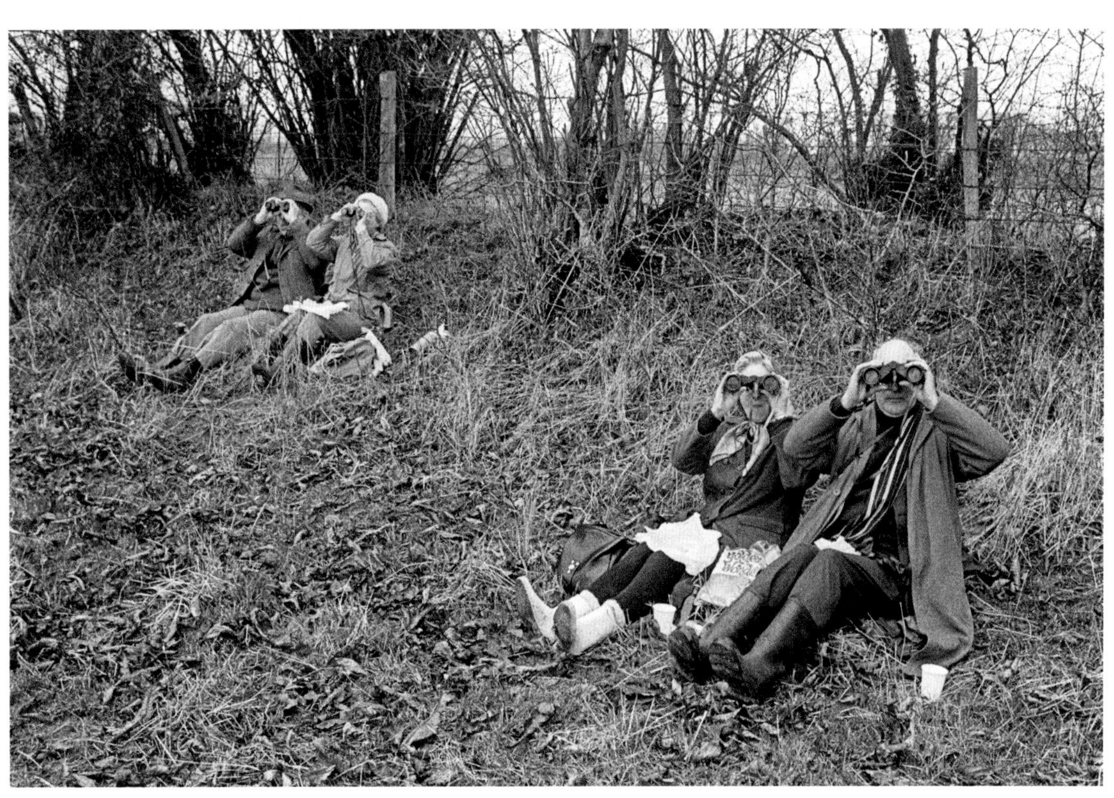

22. Prestwich Mental Hospital

A friend of mine had a brother who was in Prestwich Mental Hospital, and one day we went to see him. I was completely struck by the visual narrative of the hospital, so I decided I'd do a photography project on it. Back in those days I didn't need long, complicated permissions. I just talked to the chief nurse and said, 'Let's do some photos here.' She said, 'Come in whenever you want. Would you be able to start now?'

I spent ten weeks photographing the hospital and had a very productive time. But college didn't like it. They said I was spending too long on one project. I had to fight to justify the fact that I wanted to keep on doing it. I was there three or four times a week, going around different wards and making a whole set of social documentary pictures. It was the first photography project where I got really involved.

The hospital was totally fascinating to photograph. The people there were very friendly, very sociable, and I could just wander around and do anything I liked. You'd never be able to do that now, would you? The building looked like a stately home, but it was grim and it had a smell – a bleach smell. There must have been hundreds of residents there. There were wards with maybe forty people on, and at least twenty wards. And there were activities like football and dancing. In this photo, I like the way this guy's looking around. I seem to remember him being someone who would pester people, get in the way. He was very chatty. Interfering. Pestering's the word. The other man's watching telly. Trying to, anyway.

And here's a picture of me taken by one of the patients. It's out of focus, which, in fact, adds to its quality.

PRESTWICH MENTAL HOSPITAL (TOP)
MARTIN PHOTOGRAPHED BY A PATIENT AT THE HOSPITAL (BELOW)
PRESTWICH, ENGLAND, 1972

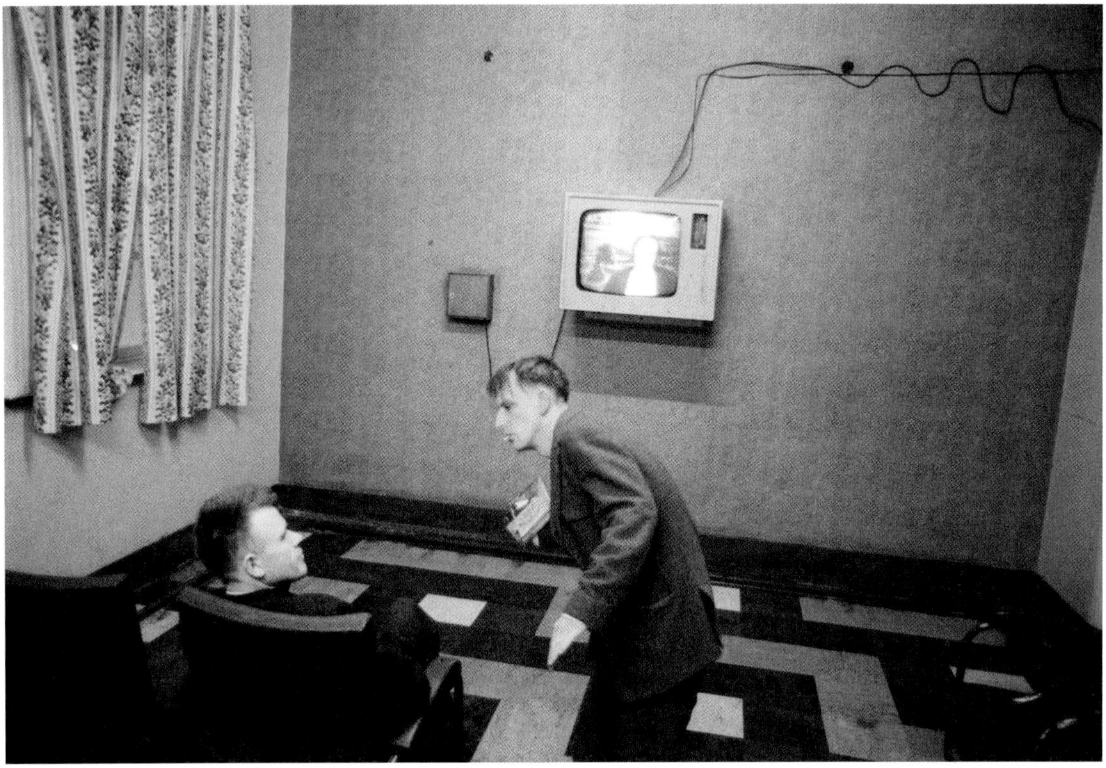

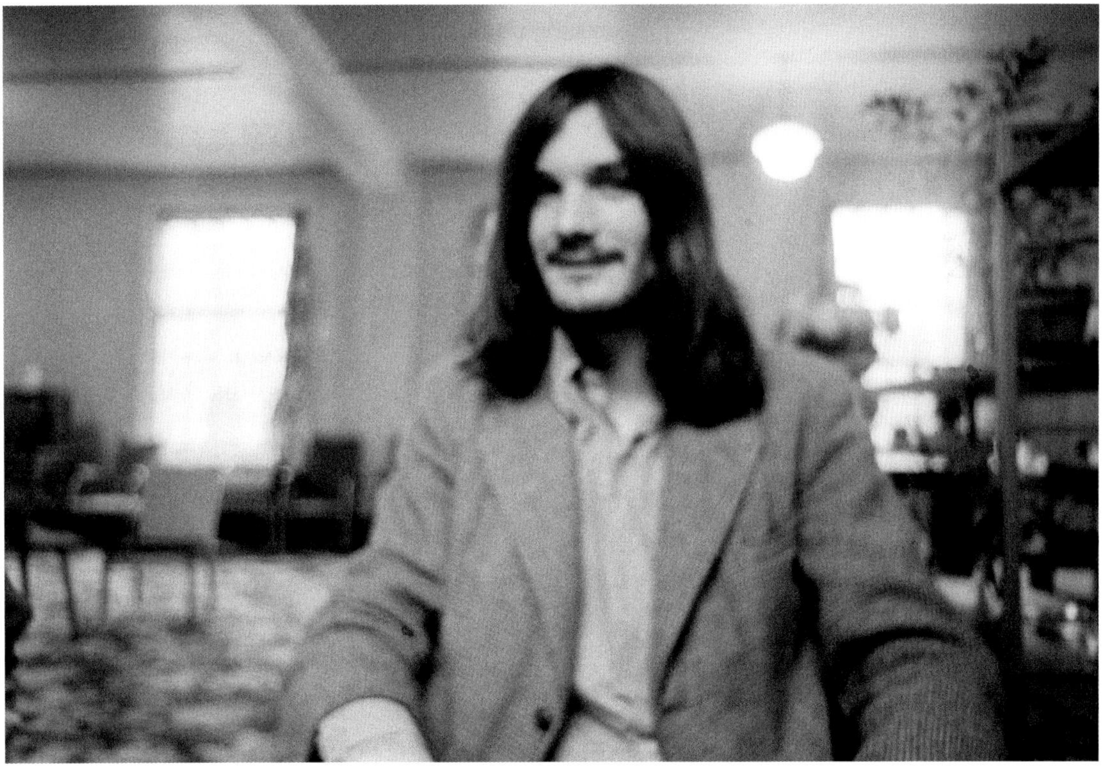

23. Bolton Abbey

This is one of the first interesting photos I took. There's a priest in Bolton Abbey, holding a Bible. He's got sunglasses on as well. He looks quite smug, doesn't he? He looks quite swish. The other guy's head is bowed as if he's guilty, as if he's been given a talking-to. With that pose, you don't really need to see a face. The relationship between these two people is awfully illustrative, with the humour coming out.

When I took the picture, I didn't notice the grass line between the priest and the guy standing in front of him – it was one of those things I picked up afterwards, when I developed it. It's a straightforward composition, with two people in the middle and the abbey behind them decaying, falling apart – I wouldn't call it pioneering, but it's an interesting picture.

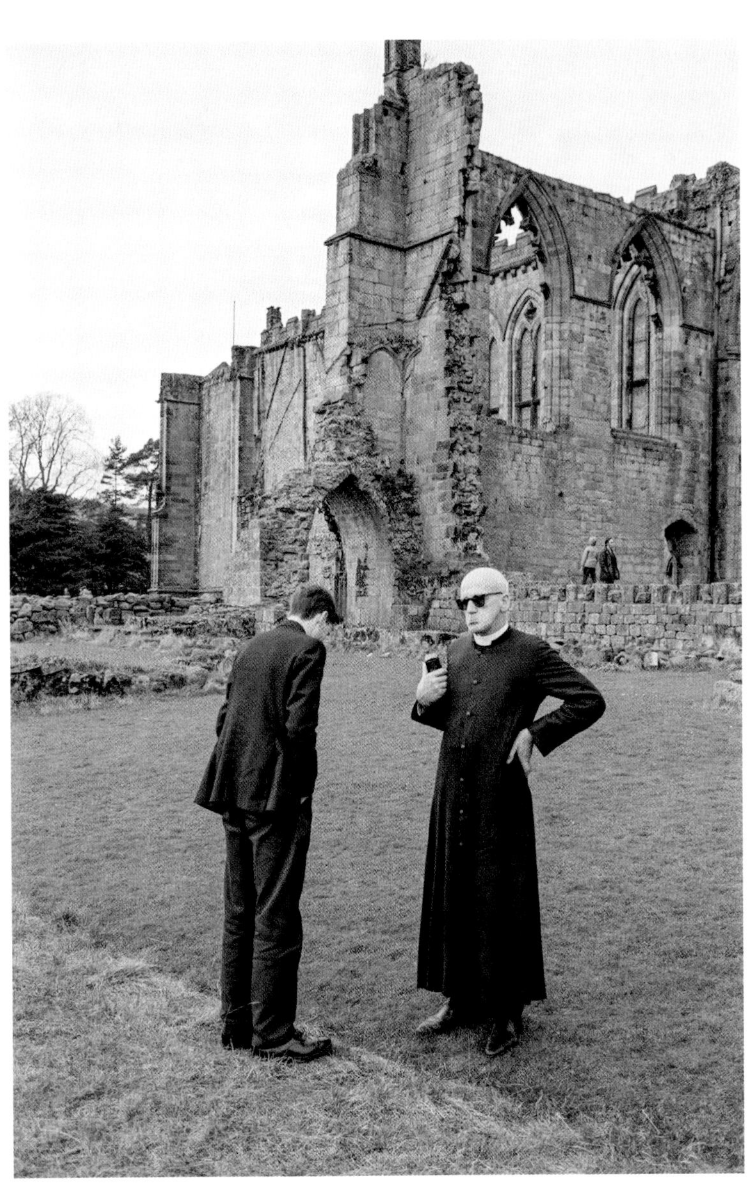

24. June Street

In my final year at college, I collaborated with my friend Daniel Meadows on a project about June Street in Salford where we went about photographing people in their living rooms. June Street was one of the streets where they used to film the soap opera *Coronation Street*, before they built their own set in Granada Studios. It was in a working-class area near Manchester, with twenty houses, ten on each side.

We would go with a tripod into each house, replace the lightbulb in the ceiling with a much brighter bulb, and take the picture. At first, only a few people on the street said yes to having their portrait taken, but by the end 75 per cent agreed. This is one of the better pictures. I like all the dogs. I like the fact that the tights are on the mantelpiece drying. And I like the decor and those brasses on the wall above the fireplace. Are those guns on the wall? I think that they liked this project at college, too.

This might be Daniel's photo, though: it was a collaboration, so we didn't individually credit pictures. I was very happy to work with him – I've always enjoyed collaborations.

JUNE STREET, SALFORD
COLLABORATION WITH DANIEL MEADOWS
SALFORD, ENGLAND, 1973

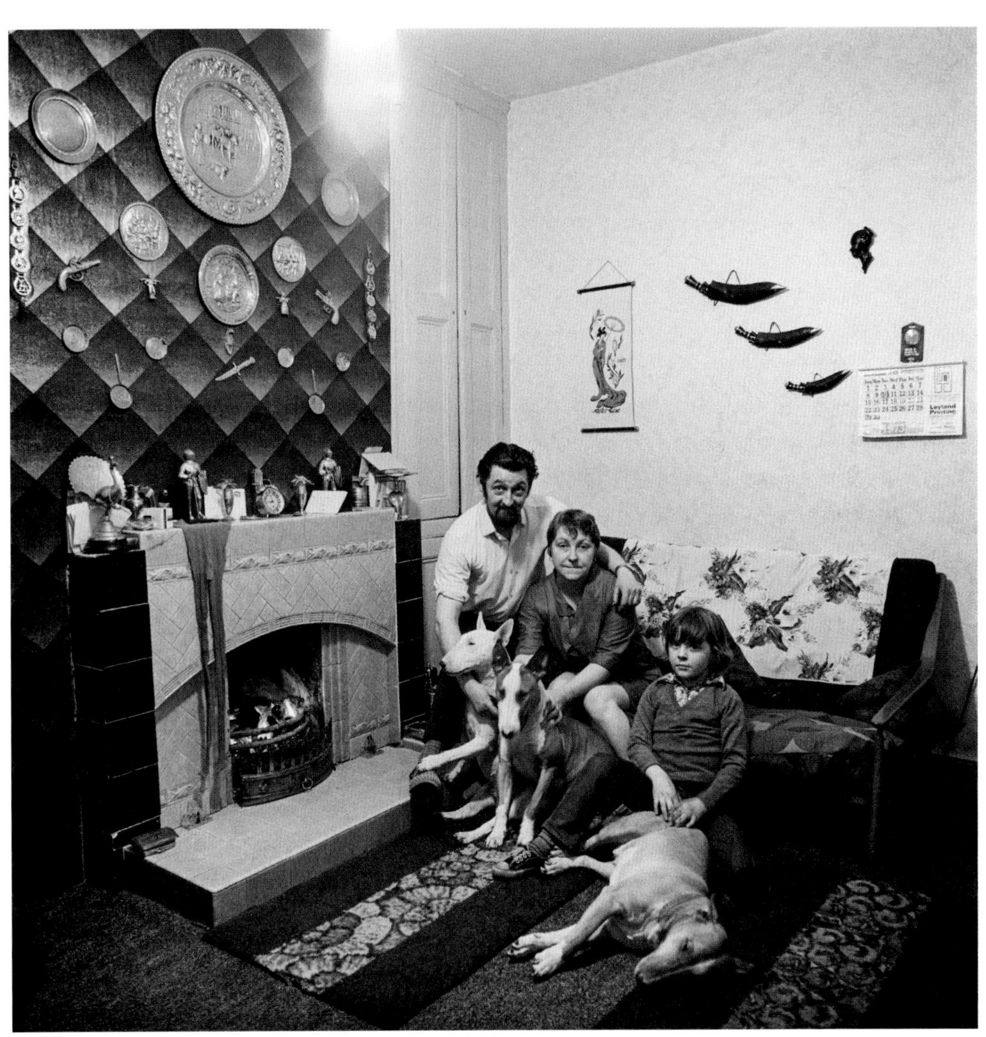

25. Letter from My Father

Ashtead,
20th May 1973

Dear Martin,
Your 21st birthday is something of an occasion. It marks more so, I think, than your 18th birthday, your attainment of adulthood. Although I am not given much to lecturing or sermonizing, having suffered a great deal from that myself in bygone years, I think I can perhaps allow myself a few words to you on this special day.

Firstly, I will say how we have been very pleased at the way you settled into your photographic course. We were somewhat sceptical when you first started that you would stay the course. But it seems to me we need not have worried and it is to your credit that you have got down to it and soon bringing it to a successful conclusion with some notable achievements already notched up.

Secondly, we are noting steady growth in your maturity. Whereas you set forth to Manchester nearly three years ago a very new, very raw, immature youth, you will be returning considerably assured and a man, no less. Although you couldn't expect us to applaud all your ideas and understand all your ideas and although you have not generally 'officially' endorsed the faith we were nurtured on we do recognize and admire the ideas of integrity with which you have said you hope to go forward. We can only hope and wish that you will maintain them. Success in life, as I need hardly say, cannot be measured in worldly goods.

Ashtead
20. 5. 73

Dear Martin

Your 21st birthday is something of an occasion it marks, more so I think than your 18th birthday, your attainment of adulthood. Although I am not given much to lecturing or sermonizing (having suffered a good deal from that myself in byegone years), I think I can perhaps allow myself a few words to you on

You have, we are sure, something of value and benefit to give to society and we trust you will discharge whatever you judge yourself to be best fitted for with honesty and consideration of others. Whatever you choose to do, you will be assured of our love and support.

Well, I don't want to frighten you off and perhaps it is better to change key and come down to more mundane things. Your mother told you about my Portuguese trip. It's still on but not until the 18th June. When do you break up? David Mance is going with me and perhaps Alan Chapman. I am now trying to finalize details. It should be an interesting trip if we survive the mosquitoes! We will await news from you before doing anything about your presence. Do you remember borrowing a small rucksack from me? I forgot to mention it at Easter but I want it for my Portugal trip so could you send it down if you can find it? Your mother is back at 'school' but she is a little bit below par at the moment. However, half term is just around the corner so there will be a break for all then.

Write sometime.

Love,
Dad.

26. Home Sweet Home

For my diploma show, I built an installation – a free-standing room called *Home Sweet Home*. I recreated my bedroom in Manchester and decorated it with various pictures I'd taken. I photographed the view from my window, blew that up, and stuck it on the wall. There was a picture of my eccentric granny in a 1930s frame. Around the walls, I had my photos in naff frames from Woolworths. Those silver things on wedding cakes that say, *'good luck'* – I stuck them on the frames. I visited an old lady in June Street and photographed her telly while Princess Anne was getting married, and framed that, too. There were real curtains, rose perfume and a permanently playing tape of *The Sound of Music*.

Why did I do a room? Why not? No one else had done an installation like it in Manchester Polytechnic. It was, I guess, truly original. The staff looked at it, didn't know what to make of it and gave me a 2:2. They thought it was too wacky. Other people's diploma shows were more traditional. Then the external assessor came, thought it was absolutely brilliant and insisted I get a First. So I ended up with a First-Class Honours Diploma in Creative Photography. It shows that the powers that be in the college were never quite behind me, with the exception of my first-year tutor and the external assessor. That gave me a certain amount of pride, I guess. Along the way, the odd person believed in me.

Then the director of the Impressions Gallery in York saw the installation, and said, 'We're going to offer you a show of *Home Sweet Home*.' So that was my first solo public exhibition, in 1974.

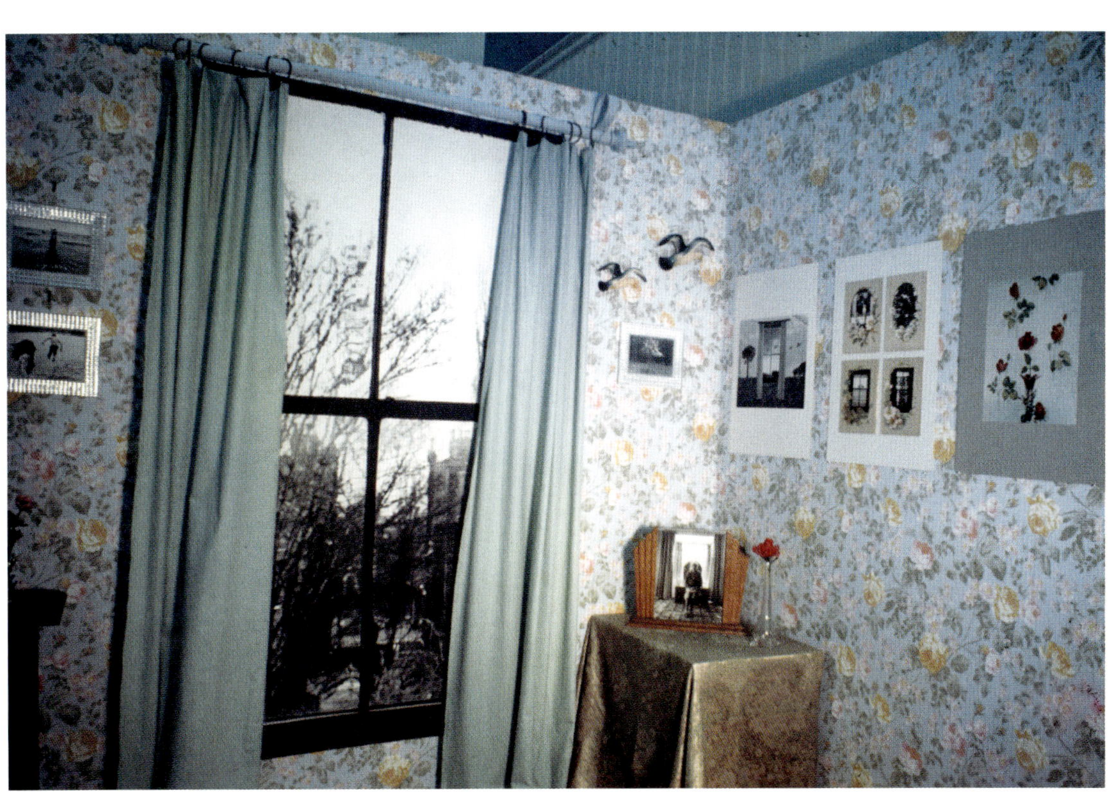

27. Butlin's Holiday Camp

I worked at Butlin's Holiday Camp in Filey, Yorkshire, after my second and third years at college. The first summer, I went as a black-and-white walkie, which meant I walked around taking black-and-white pictures. I'd go into the dining rooms and take pictures of people eating their dinner. Then, in the evening, I'd wander around the bars, taking more pictures. The photos were displayed on a board the following day, and people could buy them. Someone else did the developing – there was a whole laboratory working on that. People would ask me, 'What happens to the pictures if we don't buy them?' I'd say, 'We just throw them away.' That motivated people to buy them – they didn't want them destroyed. When Susie first met me, in a pub in Manchester, I was wearing my Butlin's jacket.

The summer after I graduated, I became a colour walkie. I got access to the Caribbean-themed Beachcomber Bar, the most prestigious bar in Butlin's Filey. Every half hour there was a tropical storm, with thunder and lightning, and water falling from the ceiling. I was inspired by John Hinde, who did a famous photo of the Beachcomber Bar. John Hinde was an English guy who ran a circus in Ireland, which failed, so he set up a company producing postcards and introduced the use of vivid colours. These were an instant hit with American tourists, who were coming into Shannon Airport to discover their Irish roots, and he became the biggest manufacturer of postcards in Europe. He did postcards of holiday resorts, including postcards of Butlin's holiday camps. I used to love them. At the time, even though I was buying and collecting his postcards, I didn't know who he was.

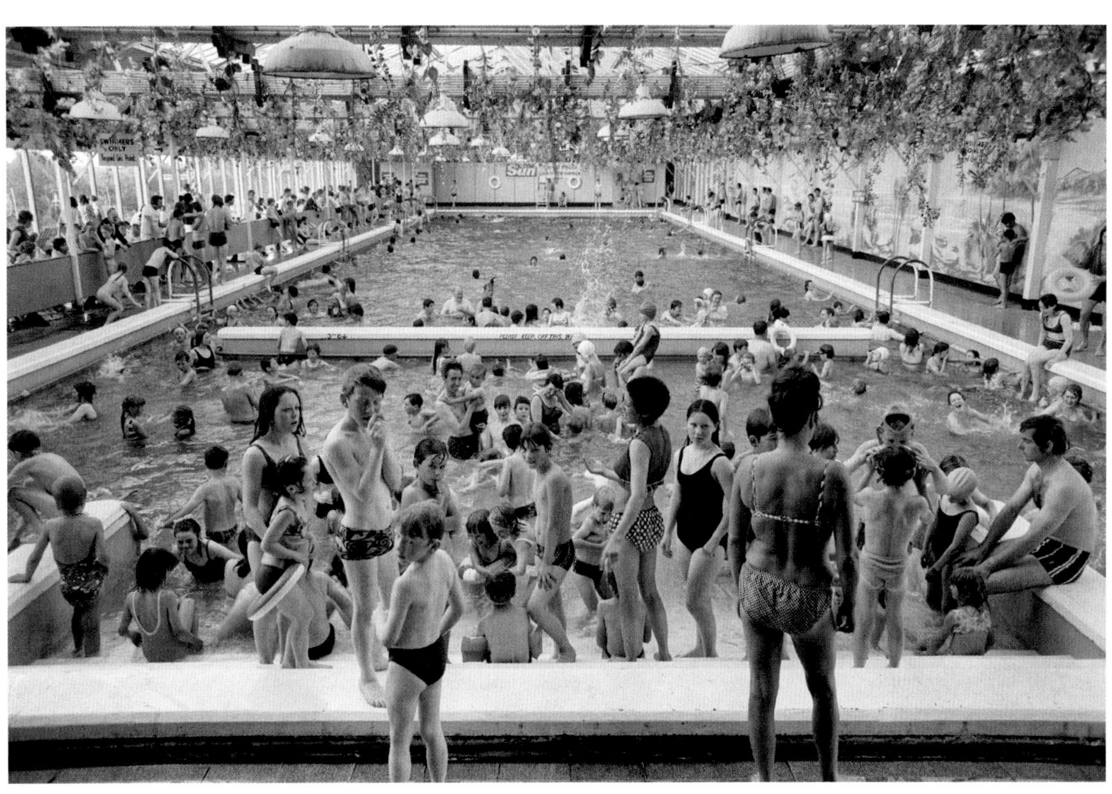

28. Bilberry Picking

A bilberry is quite hard, sharp and unlike a blueberry. You can't buy bilberries in a greengrocer because they are too small and fiddly to cultivate, so that helps give them their mystique. It's a real tradition to go collecting the wild bilberries from Brimham Rocks, which are very dramatic rock formations near Harrogate in Yorkshire. It's one of my favourite places.

These people in their nice, smart clothes were picking bilberries for bilberry pie. I like that they are integrated into the bracken and the bushes, and I like that this lady's just got one leg showing. Bilberries make a delicious pie. I have great memories of my grandmother from the Yorkshire side making bilberry pie and me declaring it delicious.

BILBERRY PICKING AT BRIMHAM ROCKS
HARROGATE, ENGLAND, 1974

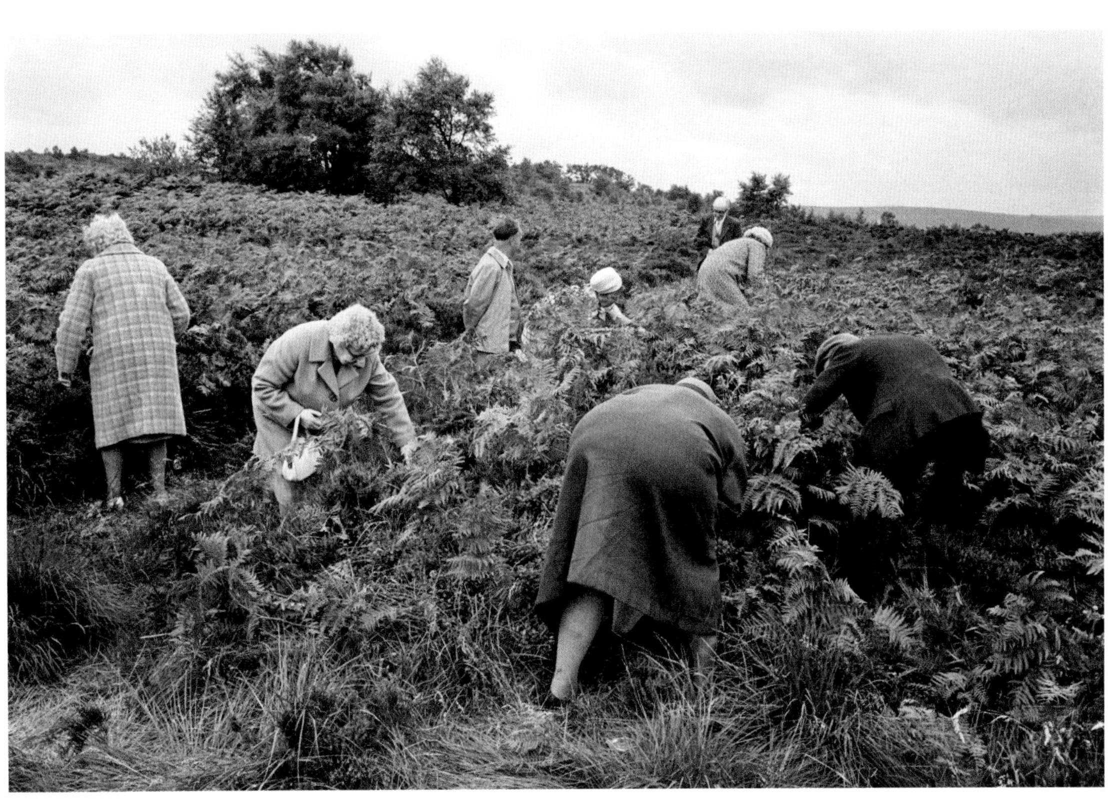

29. Steep Lane Baptist Chapel

After I finished at college, I was briefly on the dole. Then I got some money from the Arts Council to document the town of Hebden Bridge in Yorkshire when I was twenty-three. So, Susie and I moved to Hebden Bridge with some friends from Manchester. We rented a small shop and turned it into a gallery called the Albert Street Workshop, where we showed photographs, paintings and ceramics.

To the outside person, Hebden Bridge would not have looked promising to photograph, although it was a very picturesque, traditional mill town in decline. I was doing classic documentary photography, so there was nothing radical about it, but before long I knew I was onto something. I was honing in on the chapels in Hebden Bridge for a project called *The Non-Conformists*.

Steep Lane Baptist Chapel was in decline: its heyday was seventy-five years earlier, when it would have been really swinging. By 1977, it was all older people. Lay preachers would travel around to different chapels – as my grandfather, who was a Methodist lay preacher, would have done. That's why it was so appealing to me. I was very focused on exploring this world, which was familiar to me in one way, but completely different in another.

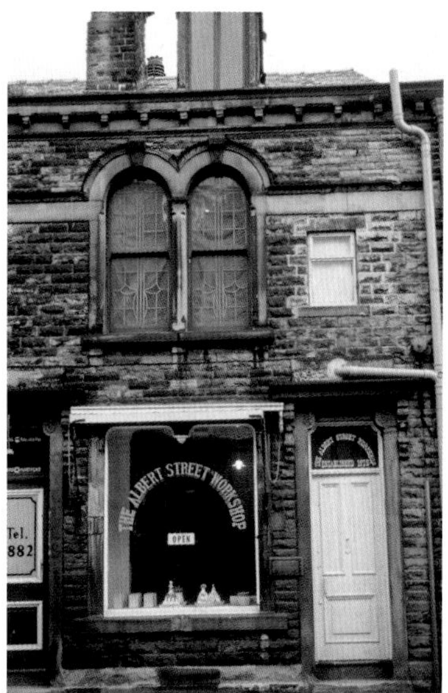

This was the morning service at Steep Lane Baptist Chapel, and they let me take photos during the service – I wasn't using flash, and it was a very quiet camera, a Leica. When this picture was in the Albert Street Workshop someone wanted to buy the top half of the print because they didn't know the people in the bottom. I thought that was quite amusing. I just gave them the whole picture. I left it for them to cut off whatever they wanted.

THE ALBERT STREET
WORKSHOP (ABOVE)
HEBDEN BRIDGE, ENGLAND, 1975

STEEP LANE BAPTIST CHAPEL
FROM *THE NON-CONFORMISTS*
WEST YORKSHIRE, ENGLAND, 1977

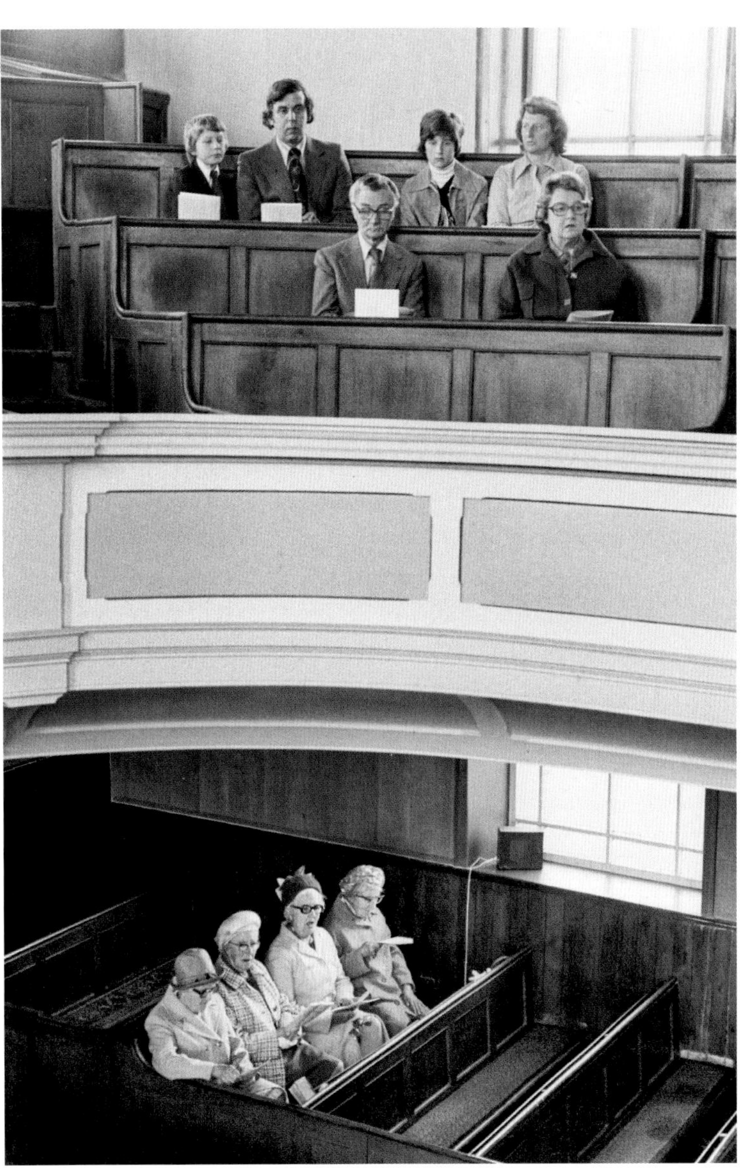

30. Charlie and Sarah Hannah Greenwood

Charlie Greenwood was one of the most eccentric members of the congregation at Crimsworth Dean Methodist Chapel. He lived with his sister, Sarah Hannah, in the last farm in the valley, six miles from Hebden Bridge. They were probably born in that house. He's hanging up the lace curtains in their front room because it was the chapel anniversary. It was the only time they put the curtains up, otherwise they didn't bother. They thought curtains were too fancy. They also only had a rug in front of the fire for special occasions. Look how raggy Charlie's clothes are at the elbow, they're worn away. Before Charlie learnt to drive, he travelled on a pony and trap, so on his first driving lesson he thought that he had to pull on the steering wheel to stop the car.

Every summer, Crimsworth Dean Methodist Chapel had an anniversary service to celebrate the chapel's birthday, and after the morning service they would provide an afternoon tea, which was very photogenic. Charlie Greenwood came to church every Sunday, but Sarah Hannah only came for the anniversary service, and she had a special coat and hat she only wore for that occasion.

Charlie Greenwood and Sarah Hannah trusted me. We were good friends. When Susie and I knew they were snowed in, we used to walk six miles with fresh milk and bread for them. I was fascinated by Charlie and Sarah Hannah because they were of another age, and being able to photograph them with their curtains was the sort of hidden detail that really inspired me. I wanted to capture it because it was something in decline that no one else was documenting, and because it was absolutely extraordinary.

CRIMSWORTH DEAN CHAPEL ANNIVERSARY
FROM *THE NON-CONFORMISTS*
HEBDEN BRIDGE, ENGLAND, 1976

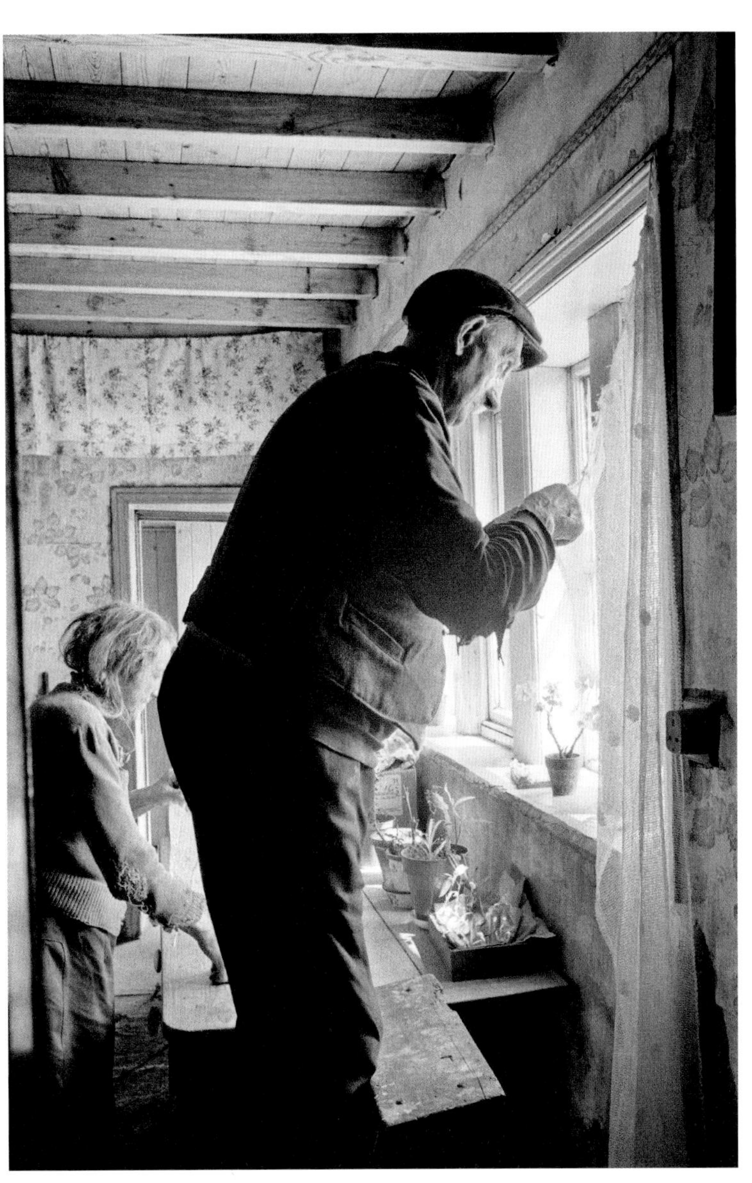

31. The Ancient Order of Henpecked Husbands

To say you're henpecked is quite daring, isn't it? The Ancient Order of Henpecked Husbands' Annual General Meeting took place every Easter Monday at Nazebottom Chapel in Hebden Bridge. Obviously, they're all men, and obviously, this is one great big joke. The rules of the Order said that henpecked husbands are slaves for 364 days, but that one day a year, Easter Monday, was their own to have a jovial time.

Back in 1977, I wasn't married, so they only let me in to the beginning of the meeting, so when the meeting agenda began, I had to leave. Photographing meetings is difficult because they tend to be boring. They're not very visual. But I liked this room. I loved the lights on the ceiling and the walls, the sun-blessed chairs and people smoking. Back in those days, people would smoke in meetings. Even I think it is quite an achievement to get a vaguely interesting picture out of a meeting. It's all to do with the narrative. The caption for this photo is crucial. They all look very ancient and very obedient. The Ancient Order of Henpecked Husbands eventually closed down. Probably it was regarded as not quite of its age. I'm sure these men are all dead now, which is a bit sad. I often look back at the Hebden Bridge images and think, they'll all be dead.

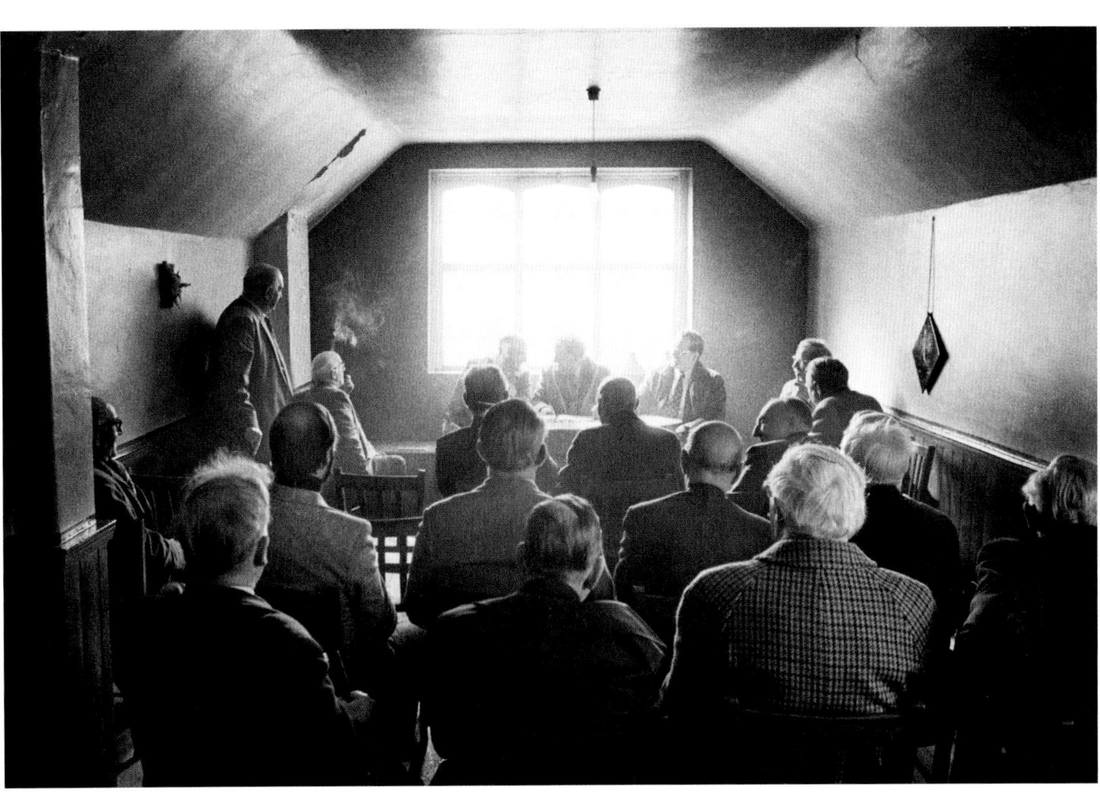

32. Living with Susie

Susie and I spent five years living in Hebden Bridge. Susie
did cleaning and teaching jobs, and God knows what else, to
keep body and soul together. She also ran the Sunday school
in Crimsworth Dean, even though it's unusual for an atheist
to do a Sunday school – but they were desperate because they
were all ancient. Then she thought, Right, I've had enough of
this, and decided to become a speech therapist, and went back
to college to study. Meanwhile, I carried on photographing. *The
Non-Conformists* didn't get published; the newspaper picture
editors weren't interested. It was shown in the Albert Street
Workshop, and in Halifax, then Camerawork in London, though,
so it did okay.

MARTIN AND SUSIE AT HOME
PHOTOGRAPH BY BRIAN GRIFFIN
HEBDEN BRIDGE, ENGLAND, CHRISTMAS 1979

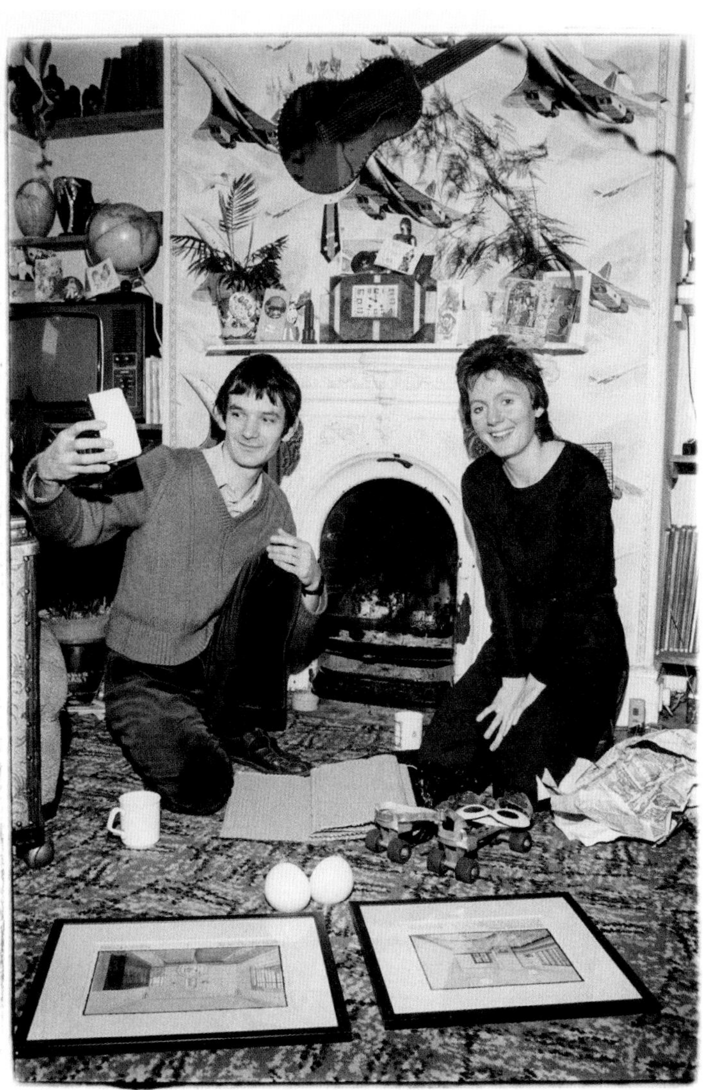

33. Yates's Wine Lodge

While I was in Hebden Bridge, I began a project going around every Yates's Wine Lodge in the country. There were about thirty-two of them, all in the north, and I photographed every single one. They had wooden floors, the beer was cheap, and they used to serve a drink called a Blob, a fortified sweet wine with lemon, sugar and hot water. The biggest one was in Blackpool: they did champagne on tap. They also sold brown flour, sardines and tea. The original founder of Yates's in 1884 wanted to make sure the working class had an opportunity to buy good, wholesome food so people could make bread, eat sardines and drink tea. It was to make sure that people didn't just survive on drink.

Yates's Wine Lodges were a bit rough. I remember getting into trouble in the one in Nottingham. This guy followed me into the toilet and began threatening me because I was taking pictures. Someone spotted what was happening and pulled the guy away. It's the nearest I've ever been to being physically accosted as a photographer – accosted as anything! People do sometimes turn on photographers. It's an occupational hazard. Some people think you haven't got the right to photograph them, and they get very protective. Some people think it's illegal, which, of course, it's not. Some people might be worried they'll get caught doing something they shouldn't. I'm often accused of being sent from the Department of Health and Social Security to check if people deserve their benefits. I'm accused of spying on people, although I don't think the DHSS employ photographers.

YATES'S WINE LODGE, GREAT CHARLOTTE STREET
LIVERPOOL, ENGLAND, 1983

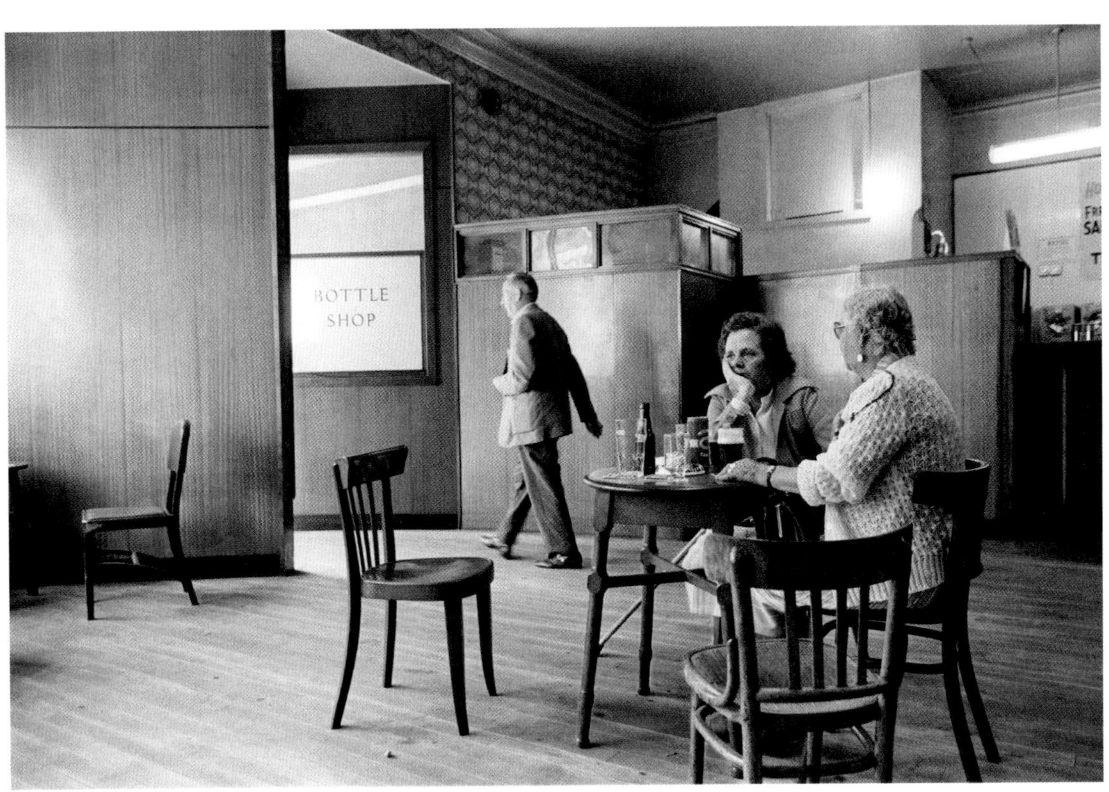

BOTTLE
SHOP

34. Susie in Paris

Despite being utterly inattentive and lazy in French at school, in the late 70s I began to go on trips to France. I went to see Jean-Claude Lemagny, who was in charge of the photography collection of the Bibliothèque Nationale de France in Paris. He bought many early black-and-white prints from me – for bargain prices, but it was a great thrill to feel that the work was being bought, and appreciated, and going into a big French institution. You can't get much better than the Bibliothèque Nationale. The trips were very exciting and helped build up my reputation in France. And Susie came along, because she could speak French.

This was taken in one of those classic French bistros. Susie didn't like being photographed by me at all. She'd put her hand up in front of her face. She has always said she looks awful, which is absolute rubbish. She doesn't look awful here. Not at all. Her skin is beautiful. She still puts her hand up now. It doesn't stop me taking pictures, so it's a bit useless, really. I can easily outwit her. I mean, I've got lots of photos of Susie in the archive.

SUSIE MITCHELL
PARIS, FRANCE, 1978

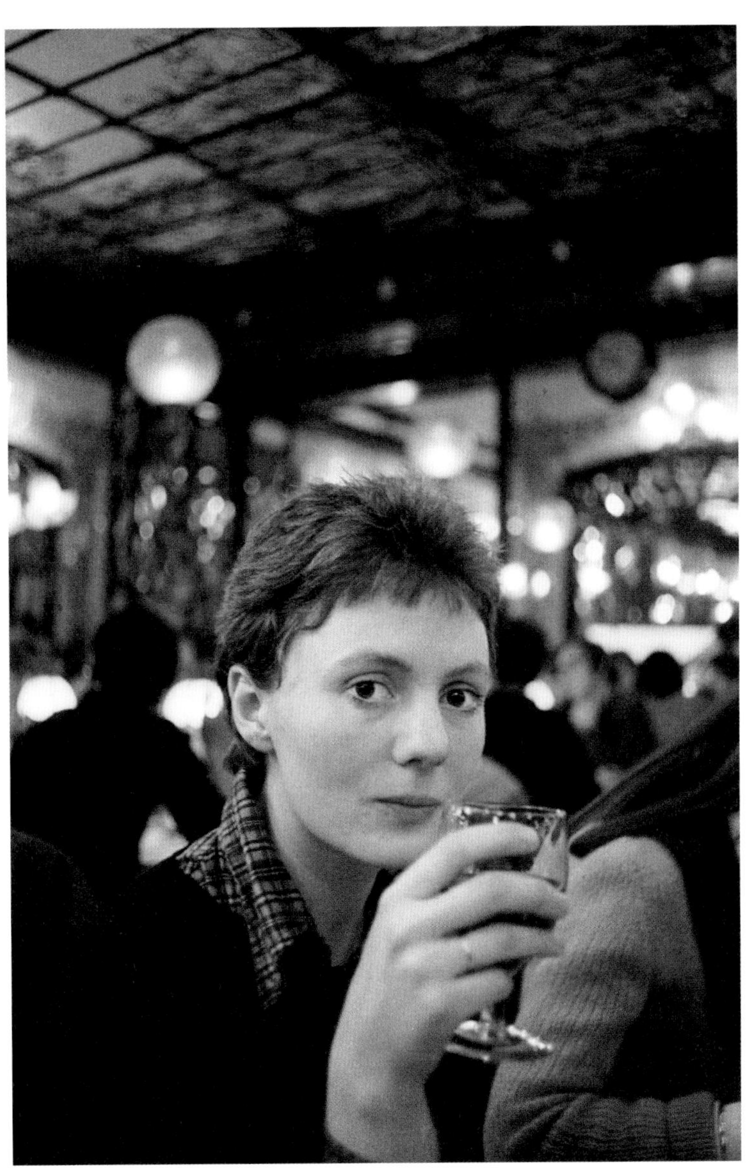

35. Evidence

In the mid-70s, two American photographers – Larry Sultan and
Mike Mandel – went around US government agencies, police
departments and research institutions, got their files of photographs out, selected fifty-nine anonymous photographs they
thought were most interesting, and published them in a book
called *Evidence*. I remember seeing this book just after it came
out and thinking, 'This is the craziest book I've ever seen.' It
really is one of the most beautiful, dense and puzzling photobooks in existence, an endless visual box of tricks.

What was so thought-provoking about the book to my generation of photographers, was that all these pictures were taken by
anonymous people who were just recording what was in front
of them, rather than taking photos for any artistic purpose. It
completely overturned the idea that the only way to get a good
picture was to have a good author. I remember thinking, if an
anonymous photographer can do this, and it's better than the
pictures being taken by famous photographers, what's gone wrong?
Well, nothing much, really, had gone wrong. It just introduced me
to the power of vernacular photography. Vernacular photographs
– snapshots, postcards, commercial photography, scientific and
governmental photography – are photographs with a job to do,
which is to record what's in front of them. In a sense, vernacular
photography reinvented itself when this book was published.

Everything about this photograph, for instance, is extraordinary. It has surprise and energy. Don't ask me what's going on – the
whole point is we never know what is going on. We don't know
who these three men are, although we assume they're scientists.
We don't know what they're testing, or where. There are no
captions. There's no description of what's happening, because it
would take away the magic of the image. It's a completely myster-
ious, wonderful image taken by an unknown photographer, as
evidence, to prove something. Prove what? We do not know. And
it doesn't matter.

FROM *EVIDENCE* BY LARRY SULTAN AND MIKE MANDEL
PUBLISHED BY MANDEL/SULTAN
SANTA CRUZ, 1977

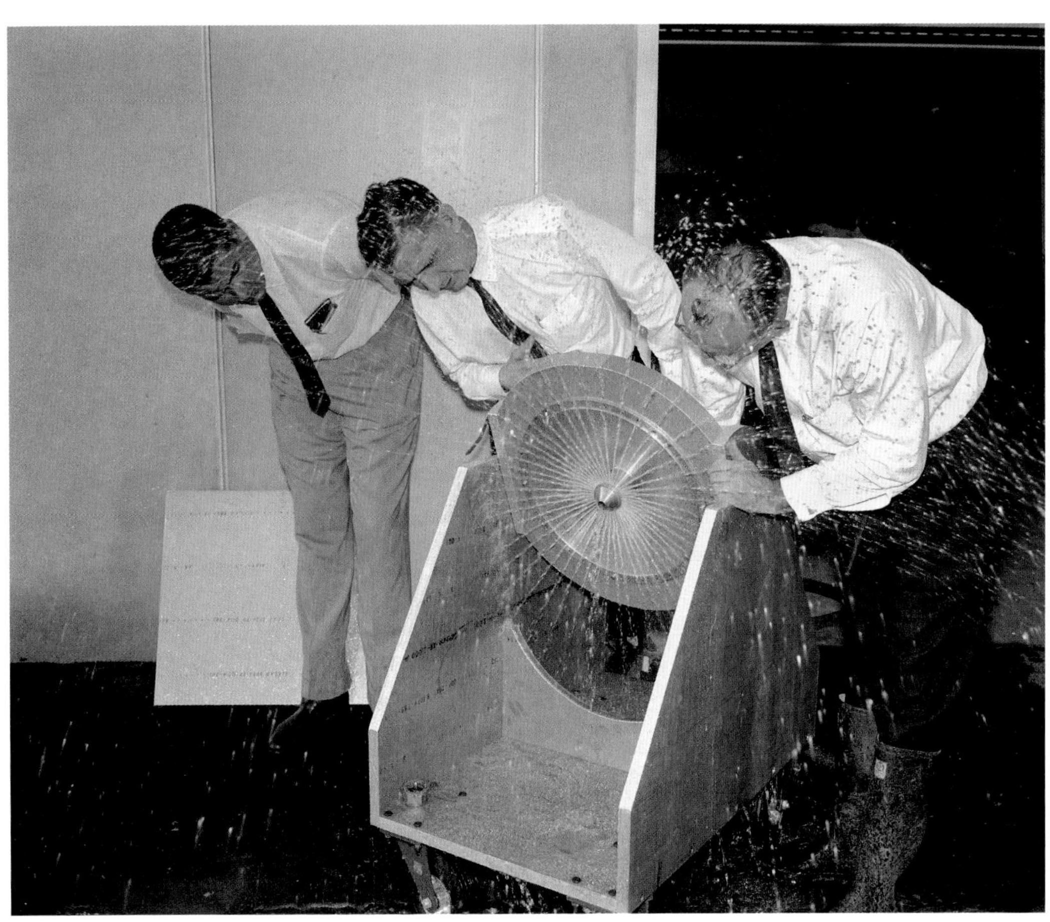

36. Bad Weather

Bad weather is so British. There's an obsession with talking about the weather all the time because it's so changeable. I liked the idea of doing a project around a theme that people are obsessed with. So one day, while I was still in Hebden Bridge, I bought an underwater camera and an underwater flash gun, even though I'm a non-swimmer. They told me in the shop that I was the only non-swimmer who had ever bought an underwater camera. With this combination, I started to take pictures for my *Bad Weather* project. I'd go around different towns, looking for situations to photograph in bad weather.

Here, a man in a coat is walking down a hill in the rain. It was taken during what we call the magic hour, when the light is fading. By using the flash, I got blobs on the images – they were raindrops on the screen. The blobs were the most interesting thing about the picture, so I started to use this as a technique and incorporating them into photographs. Sometimes I'd even put water on the lens to give that slightly out-of-focus look.

The *Bad Weather* project gave me a chance to do the opposite of what I was doing in Hebden Bridge, which was involving myself very closely with the local community. With *Bad Weather*, it was more of a conceptual approach: I could go anywhere and take photographs. In fact, when the weather was bad, I would take myself to the dullest places – motorway service stations, super-market car parks, inner cities, suburbia – to challenge myself to see if I could take an interesting photo in a very boring place. I proved to myself that I could.

FROM *BAD WEATHER*
HALIFAX, ENGLAND, 1978

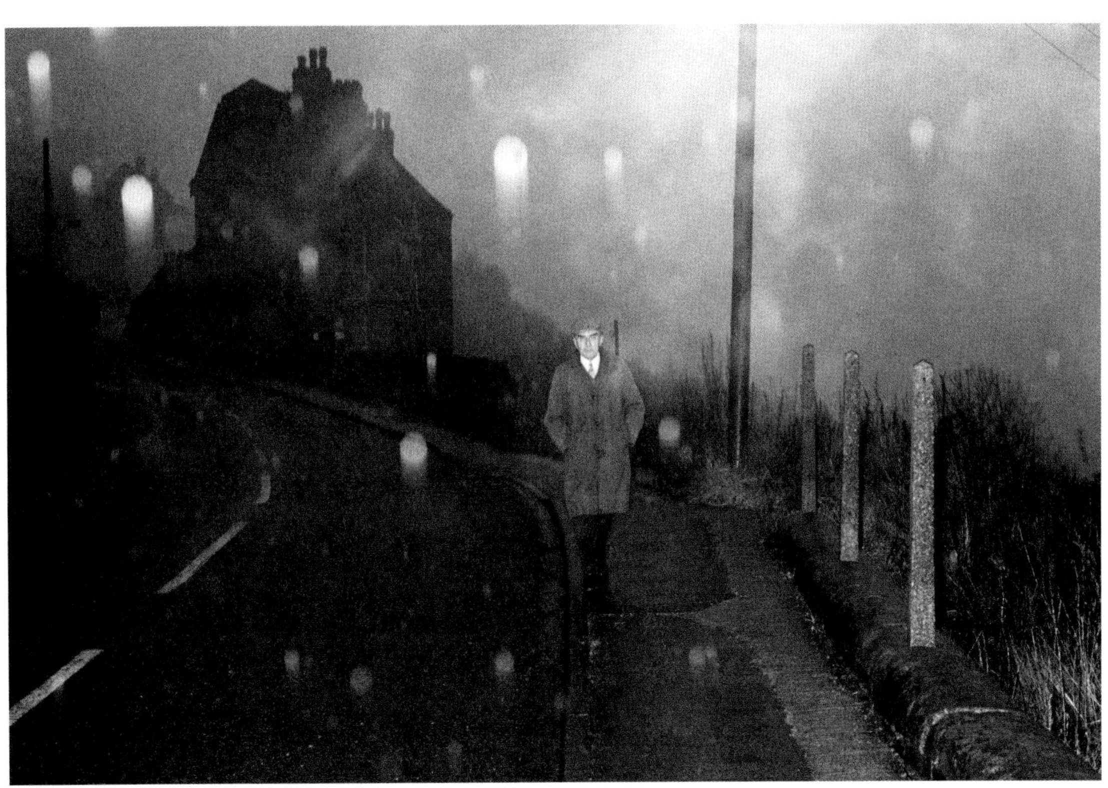

37. Cobblestones

I've always loved the feeling of cobblestones when they are wet and, therefore, reflecting light. And this is a cobbled street in Bacup, on a rainy day.

To me, what's amazing looking at this picture now is that there are no cars parked in the street at all. I assume this street is still standing and I'm sure now there'll be cars parked all the way down. What is also amazing is the pointing between the bricks: obviously, one person pointed their house and then everybody else did the same. And the bins outside – that's all they've got outside: bins. In hindsight it is a very beautiful, immaculate street.

FROM *BAD WEATHER*
BACUP, ENGLAND, 1980

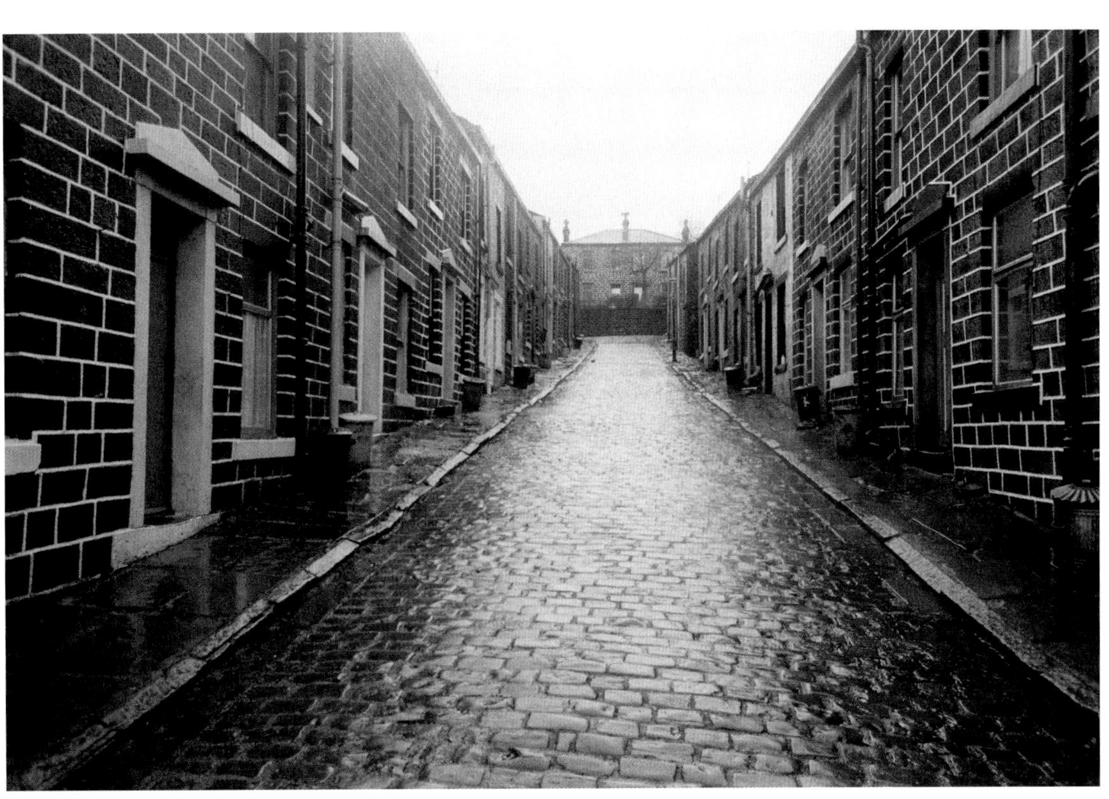

38. Bubble Car

Bubble cars are quite interesting. They have three wheels, two at the front and one at the back, so they're less stable than cars with four. You don't see them on the road at all now. Back in the 70s they were still around, but they had stopped making them in 1966, and by the 80s they had faded away. They're incredibly dangerous, because a bubble car is like a motorcycle, but with a sort of cover over it – like a covered tricycle. You can only fit one small person in a bubble car. How brilliant that this car is parked in front of a bush and appears to be exploding. This simple juxtaposition makes the photo work.

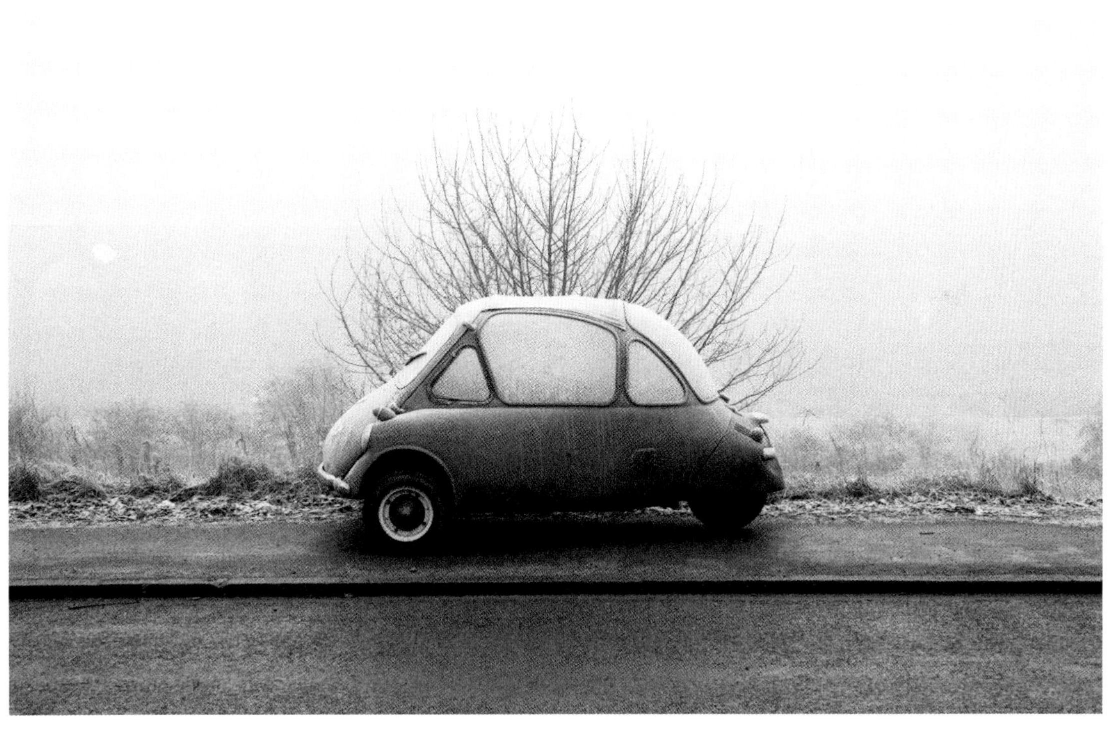

39. With Daniel and Philip

In the early part of my career, teaching was my main income, and, in 1978, my friend Daniel Meadows and I assisted Philip Jones-Griffiths at a photography workshop at Lumb Bank Writing Centre. Philip Jones-Griffiths was a very famous Welsh photojournalist. His most important book was *Vietnam Inc.*, which had a big impact in America, when it was published in 1971, to zip up the anti-war campaign. He was also a member of Magnum, which is probably the most prestigious photographic agency in the world. It only has about forty members. It has always been very hard to get in – in those days, about seven hundred people applied to join every year.

Back then, Philip Jones-Griffiths liked my work – we had great communication. The point is, we got on extremely well. However, when I applied to join Magnum, fifteen years later, he led the conservative brigade that said, 'Martin Parr must never become a member of Magnum,' which sparked off the most heated debate they've ever had about voting in a photographer. According to him, I was a spawn of Thatcher and a fascist because of my later colour work. He said, 'I have great respect for him as the dedicated enemy of everything I believe in and, I trust, what Magnum still believes in. Martin Parr would destroy Magnum if we let him in.' You'd have to ask him why he thought I would destroy Magnum, not me, and he's dead.

PHILIP JONES-GRIFFITHS, MARTIN PARR, DANIEL MEADOWS (L–R)
LUMB BANK WRITING CENTRE
YORKSHIRE, ENGLAND, 1978

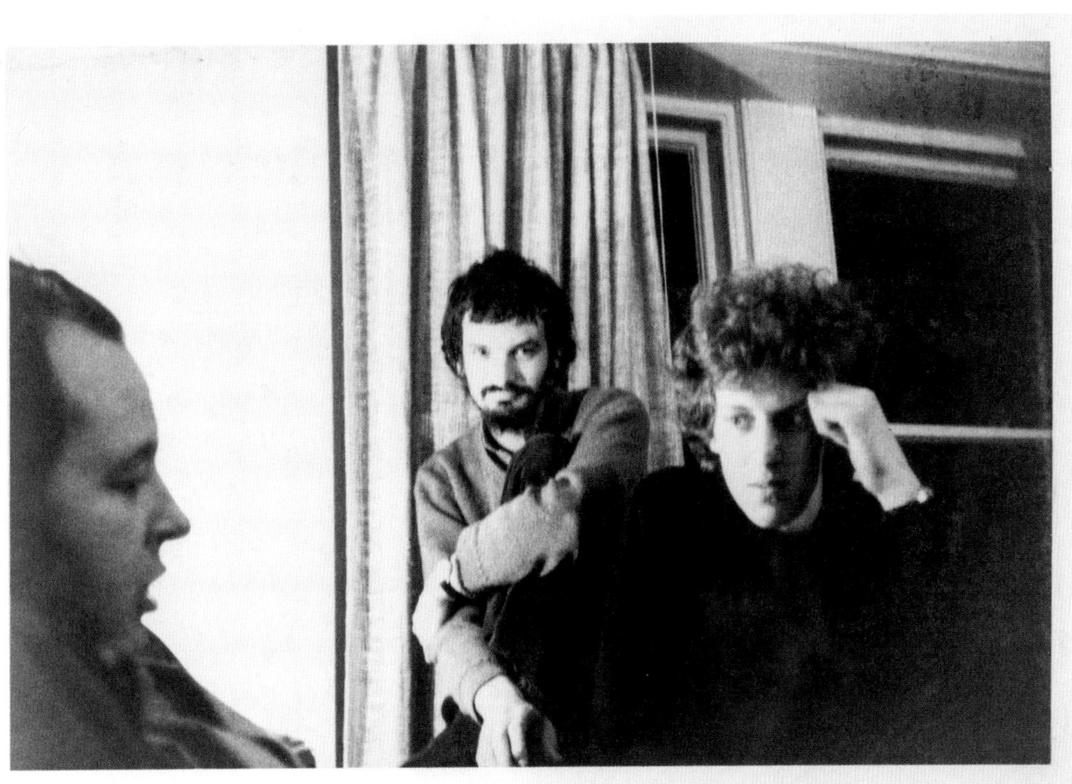

40. A Mass Mass

When Pope John Paul II visited Ireland in 1979, two and a half million people – out of a population of around three million – went to see him. I travelled over for the visit, and photographed him in Phoenix Park, Dublin, where there was a Catholic Mass – literally, a mass Mass. Then the Pope went to the Sanctuary of Our Lady in Knock, the big religious shrine in the west of Ireland, so I went to Knock as well. The train was absolutely rammed. There were hundreds of people pushing in, getting on. I remember being desperate for a wee and being unable to get to the toilet because there were so many people.

These are some of the 450,000 people in Knock waiting for Mass to start. They can't attend Mass because there's no space, so they have found a way of watching it by breaking down – or sawing off – the top of a hedge so as to see. I like that a couple of the men have got a suit and tie on to see the Pope, even though they're behind a hedge.

THE POPE GIVES MASS IN KNOCK
FROM *A FAIR DAY*
COUNTY MAYO, IRELAND, 1979

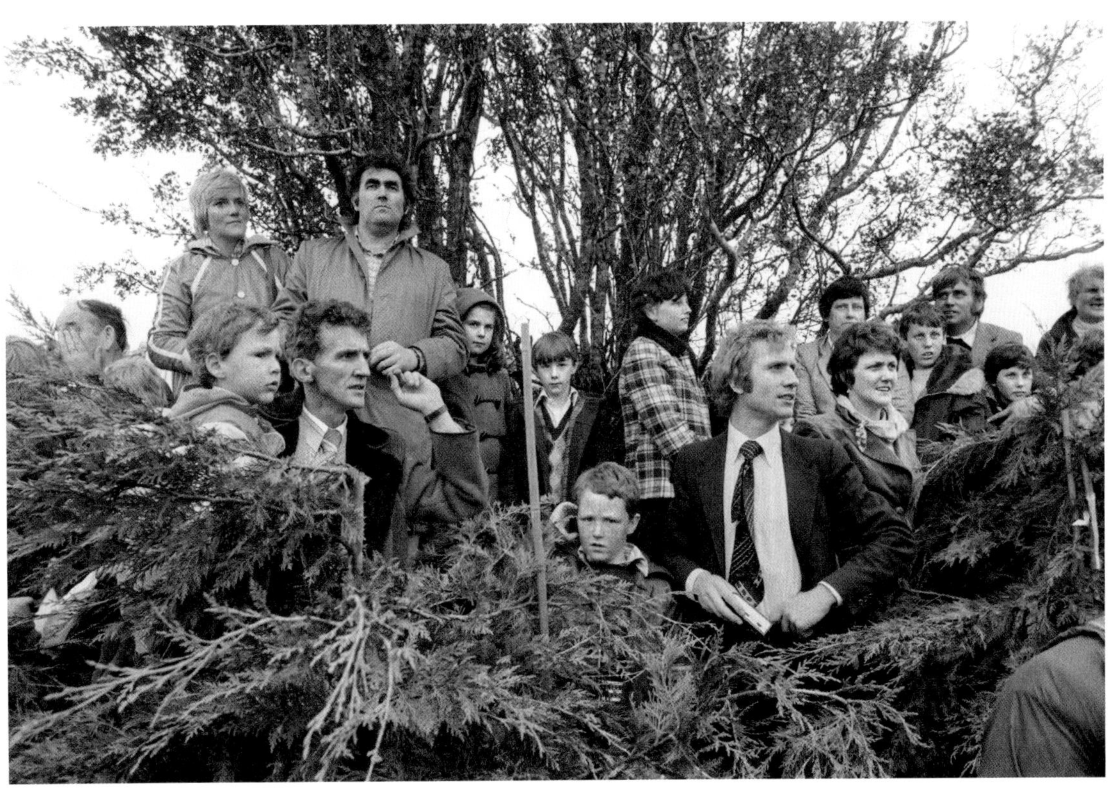

41. Magical Mystery Tour

I still had the mole my dad stuffed – the one I'd displayed in my museum – when I met Susie, and she hounded me about this creature. She threatened not to marry me unless the stuffed mole went. I couldn't understand. She said, 'You've got to choose between the stinky mole or me. It's me or the mole.'

We got married in 1980. We were moving to Ireland for Susie's work, and we thought that, since Ireland was such a Catholic country, it might be a problem if we showed up as an unmarried couple. It turned out to be unnecessary, but I was very happy to get married anyway.

For our wedding, Susie and I hired a double-decker bus and had a magical mystery tour. We all met in Hebden Bridge station car park at 10 a.m., and our rather hippy-ish looking invitees got onto this bus with us. Susie looks like she's distributing lemonade.

No one knew where we were going. The first stop was Wainhouse Tower, which is a very interesting tower in Halifax, not normally open to the public. We got it to open up, and had cake at the top, with an extraordinary view over the Calder Valley. Next stop was Brimham Rocks, where people pick bilberries. As we arrived, lunch was laid out, and a string quartet was playing, and everyone had a great time. Then we went to Undercliffe Cemetery in Bradford and had a treasure hunt. That was very successful. People were getting a bit tired, but we then went to a curry house in Bradford and had our evening meal. We were going to have a disco that night, and Susie and I turned up – but no one else came because they were completely shattered. Everyone had had lots of drink at lunchtime and had sobered up with a Bradford curry and just wanted to go home. And these are young people. Can you imagine?

MARTIN AND SUSIE'S WEDDING DAY
YORKSHIRE, ENGLAND, 1980

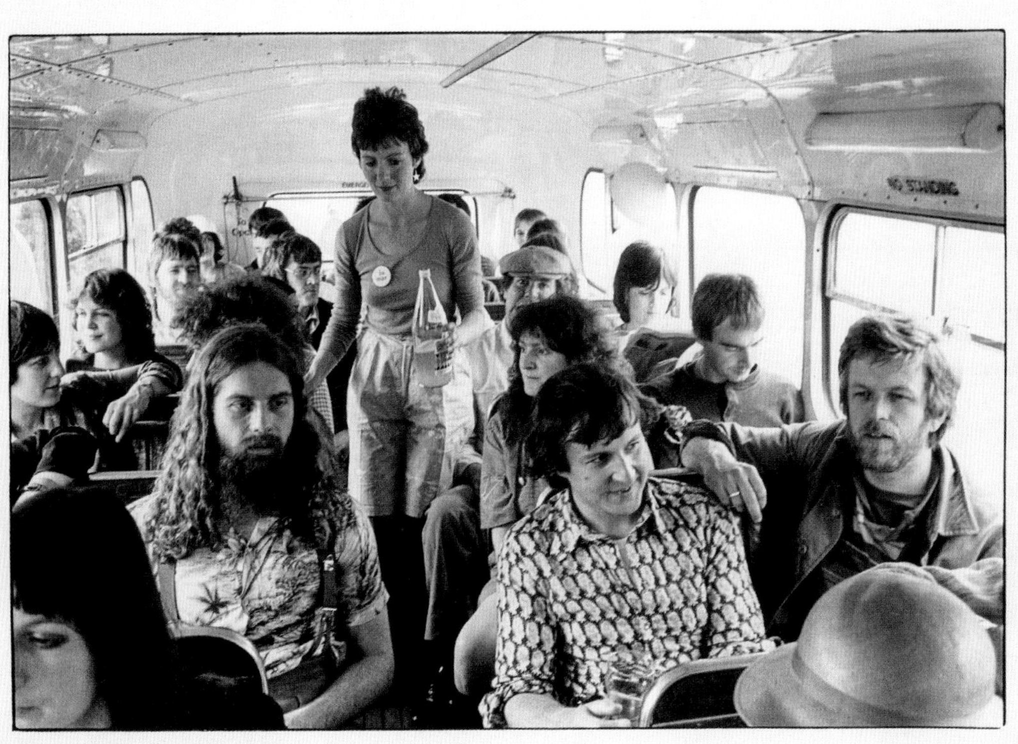

42. Just Married

On our wedding day, Susie wore a badge that says JU-MAR and my badge was ST-RIED. My friend Daniel Meadows took this photo of us holding our badges together. It was published on the front cover of *New Society* magazine for an article about marriage and young people.

SUSIE AND MARTIN ON THEIR WEDDING DAY
PHOTOGRAPH BY DANIEL MEADOWS
YORKSHIRE, ENGLAND, 1980

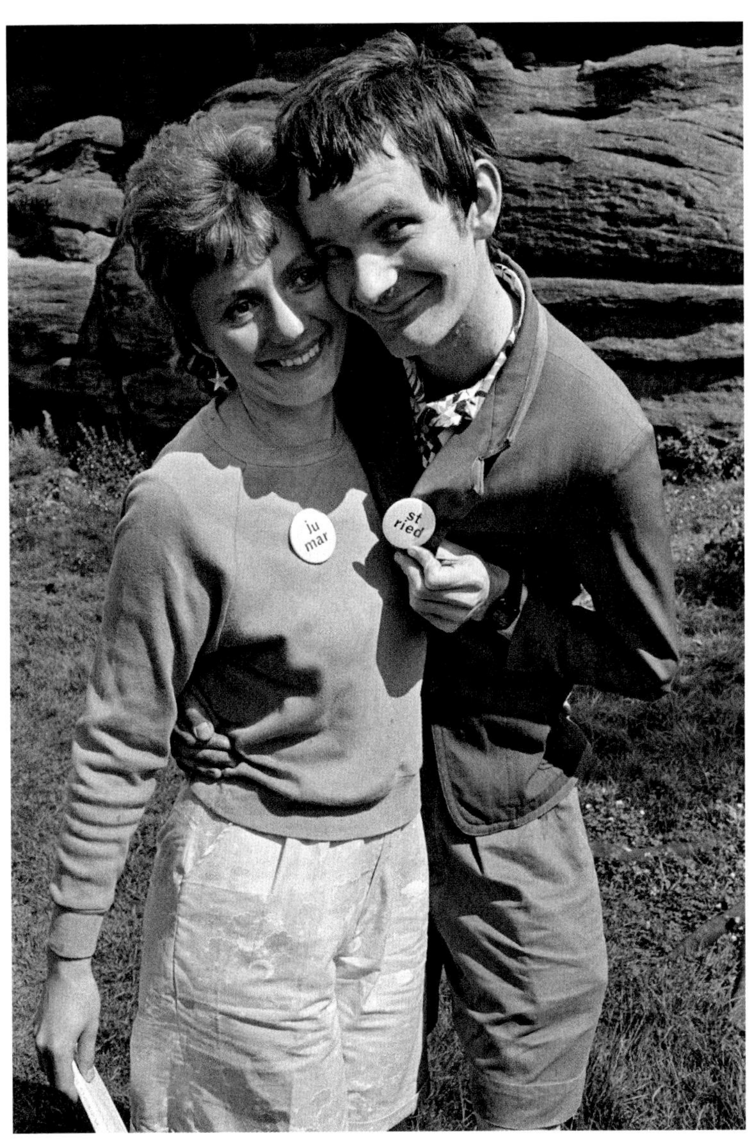
ju
mar
st
ried

43. Bungalow Bliss

When we first moved to Ireland, I photographed the new-build bungalows and houses that were springing up everywhere. We could see the first signs of what is now called the 'Celtic Tiger' emerging. Ireland had done very well from joining the European Union in 1972, and money was coming into the country in a way it hadn't before. One of the first things that the farmers of the west of Ireland did was to replace their shabby, damp, thatched cottages with new bungalows. There was a book called *Bungalow Bliss*, which was published every year from 1971 to the late 80s, that had two hundred designs for different bungalows and houses in each issue. You said to a builder, 'I'd like the one on page 42,' and they would build it. This one, *High Chaparral*, is a more extreme – but very good – example of that aspiration coming through in the early 80s. The links between Ireland and America were much stronger than between Ireland and the UK at the time.

HIGH CHAPARRAL
FROM *A FAIR DAY*
COUNTY MAYO, IRELAND, 1981

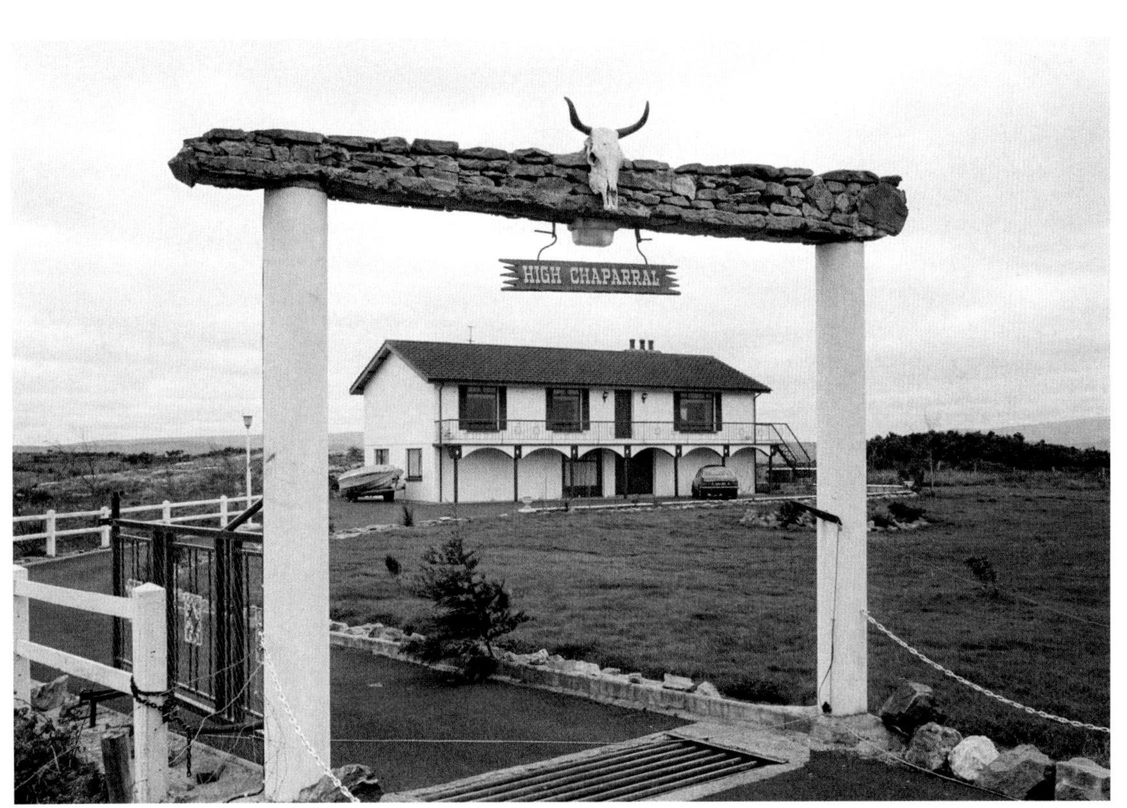
HIGH CHAPARRAL

44. The Mayflower Ballroom

The Mayflower Ballroom in Drumshanbo, County Leitrim was one of many ballrooms in the west of Ireland in the 80s. These ballrooms would open at about 11.30 p.m. on a Saturday, after the pubs shut. You couldn't buy alcohol in them; they only served soft drinks and had country and western acts like Big Tom and the Mainliners playing. I would venture in to take photos, but, oh my God . . . it was painful. I felt like a complete interloper, an outsider – which, of course, I was. I just felt very uncomfortable sitting and watching, observing. It was men and women trying to find partners. There would be a set of three dances. The women would stand around the edge of the ballroom, and the men would circulate and invite someone to have a dance. After that, the man would let the woman go. The Mayflower Ballroom was ramshackle, but it must have felt very glamorous to these young people. This was the middle of rural Ireland. Around that time, my dad came to visit us to do some bird ringing in the countryside. I remember him reaching into his pocket for something, and he brought out a dead pipit he'd forgotten about. He said, 'Oh, that bloomin' pipit.' He was still collecting dead birds.

Susie and I actually saw the Supremes in all their gear at a ballroom in County Mayo. A nuclear bomb could have gone off and it wouldn't have stopped them. They absolutely blasted through their set. They were very glamorous compared with Big Tom and the Mainliners.

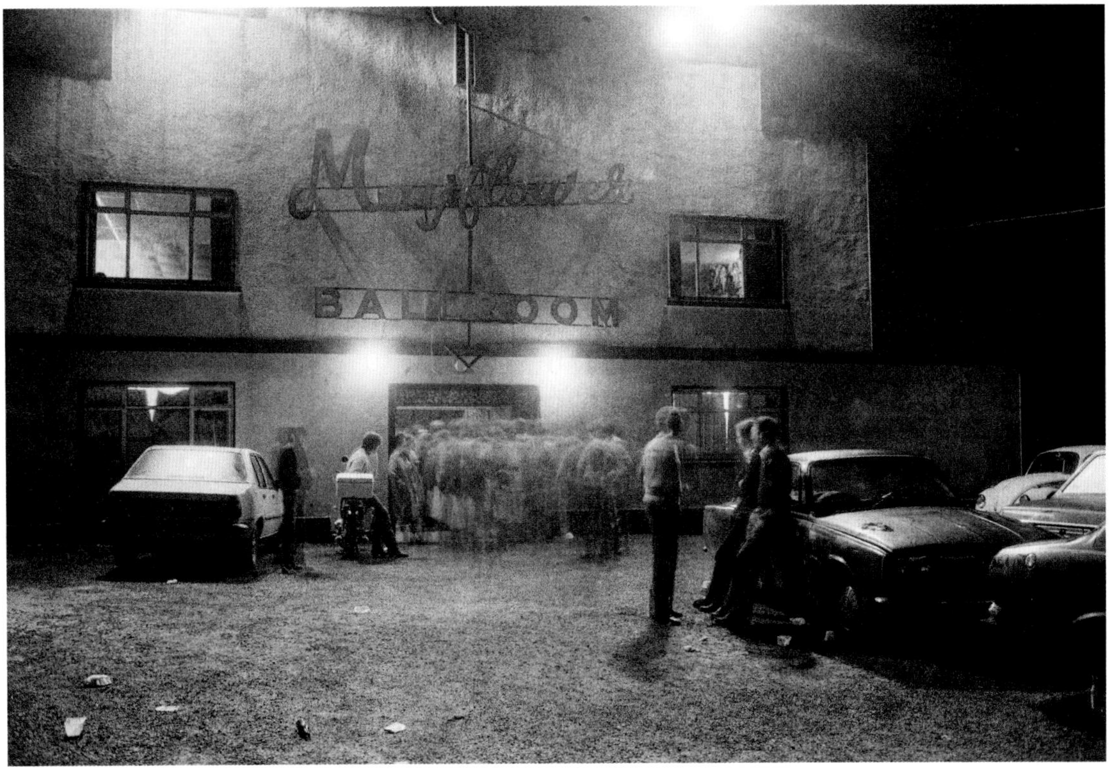

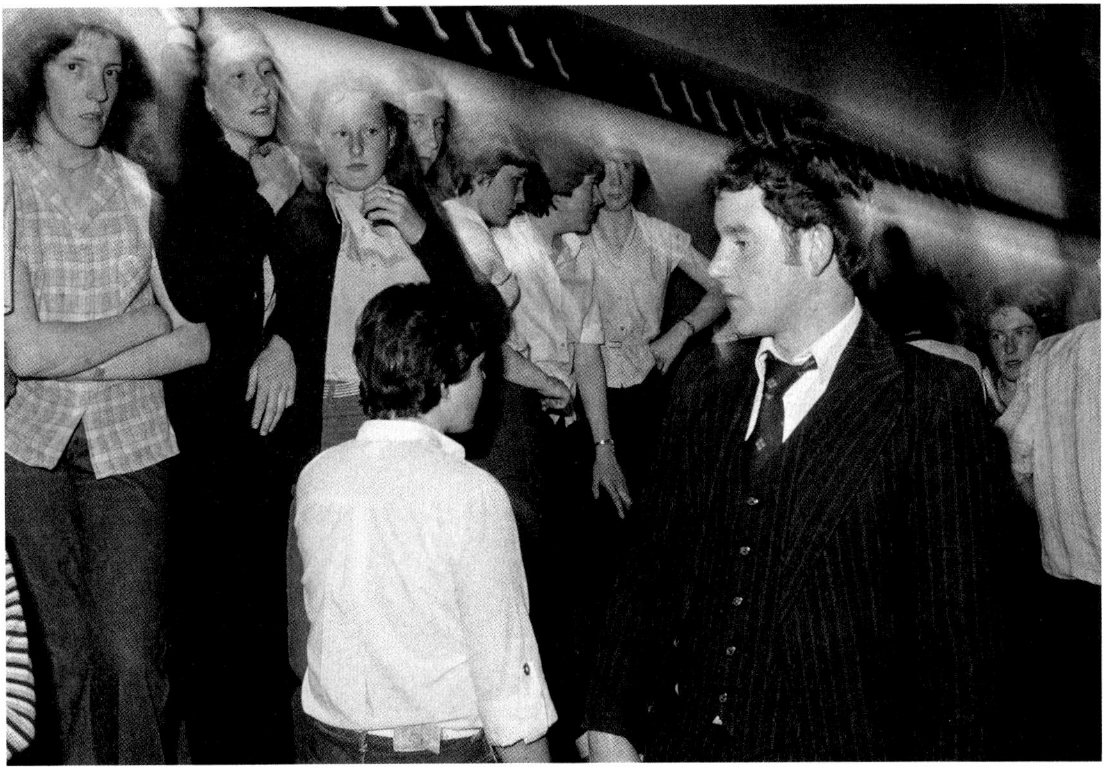

45. Puck Fair

It was quite amazing to see five people fast asleep on the pavement at 5 a.m. This was during Puck Fair in Killorglin, Ireland. Susie and I used to go to Puck Fair every July. Puck Fair was amazing. On the first day, cattle would be sold in the street. On the second day, horses and ponies would be sold in the street. On the third day, they would get a feral goat and put it up in Puck Tower and it would be proclaimed King Puck. He'd have a crown and some hay and he'd stay up there for three days. Now, because of animal rights, they only put the goat up there for two hours.

Back then Puck Fair was really an excuse for drinking. I got up very early one morning to take pictures. And there you go. I was lucky enough to find this sort of scene. It looks uncomfortable sleeping on the streets. They haven't exactly got pillows, they don't have enough space, some of them haven't even lain out properly. It's funny that they've all joined together: strength in numbers.

I'm sure now if you went down to the street at 5 a.m., you wouldn't see a scene like this. Puck Fair used to feel really wild. It has completely transformed in recent years, and now it's civilized. It's a tourist event. There are coffee shops selling cappuccinos and fancy sandwiches. A theme in my photography is how things have changed. And they've really changed.

PUCK FAIR
KILLORGLIN, COUNTY KERRY, IRELAND, 1981

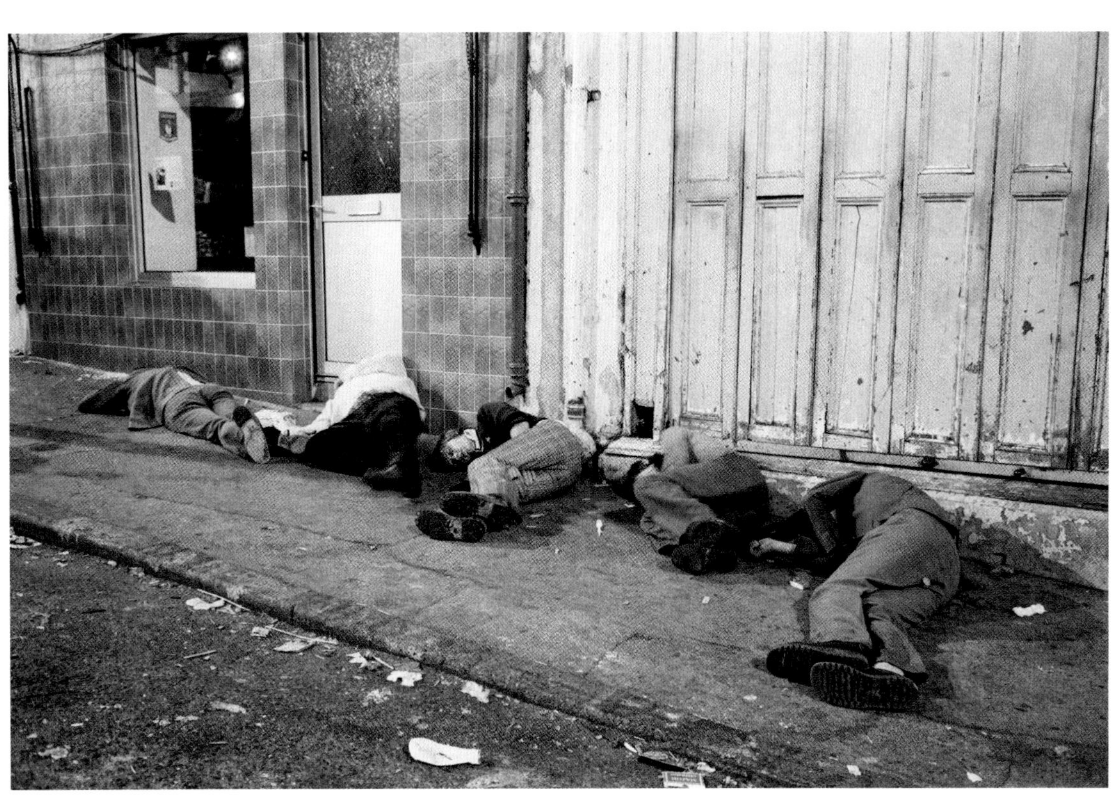

46. Not Much Happening

This is a picture I missed first time around. Then, when I looked through the contacts forty years later, I found a whole lot of new pictures that I hadn't spotted in the first instance. And this is one such picture.

I like the arrangement of the people. The way this guy in the middle is walking into the post. The guy sat on the window – couldn't be better. The guy next to him, just standing there. The girl walking out of the picture on the right-hand side – she balances the picture and keeps it even. The shadows are good, aren't they? It's just an empty corner. It would happen quite a lot in Ireland that people would hang around at the crossroads in a town, meet each other and chat. There's nothing significant about the corner in and of itself. I guess I'd say it's a non-event, where nothing of importance is taking place.

In a way, all my photography is of non-events. I never know when these non-events are going to turn into an interesting photograph. And I don't know why I missed this picture in the first instance. I took it there and then, and therefore I achieved it, but I didn't recognize it. I guess I have got better at recognizing photographs over the years. It's very difficult to describe how and when I like a picture. There's something about it that intuitively works. That's the magic of photography; I can't tell you what the magic is.

CROSSROADS
KILLORGLIN, COUNTY KERRY, IRELAND, 1981

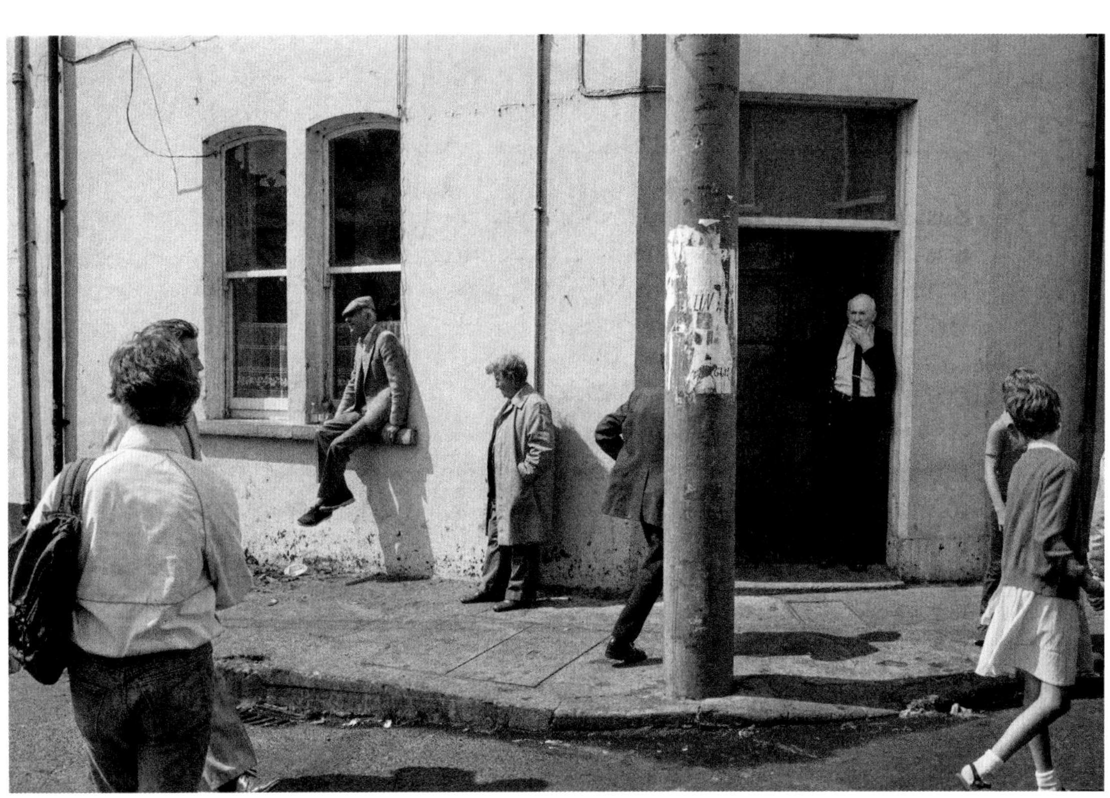

47. Black Flag

Susie and I were in Ireland during the height of the Troubles. Susie was employed to set up the first speech therapy service in County Leitrim, and she worked in Republican hotspots during the hunger strikes. Everywhere we went, to show sympathy for the hunger strikers, there were these black plastic flags made from bin bags, often hanging from the crosses on Catholic shrines. The hunger strikers were Republican martyrs who'd been imprisoned for their politics. Bobby Sands was the first of ten hunger strikers to die in 1981, which made him a hero for the Republican movement. The whole atmosphere was very oppressive. We never had any problems, or saw any violence, but we kept our heads down. It was a very political atmosphere with this absolutely charming veneer over the top.

BLACK FLAG
FROM *A FAIR DAY*
COLLOONEY, COUNTY SLIGO, IRELAND, 1983

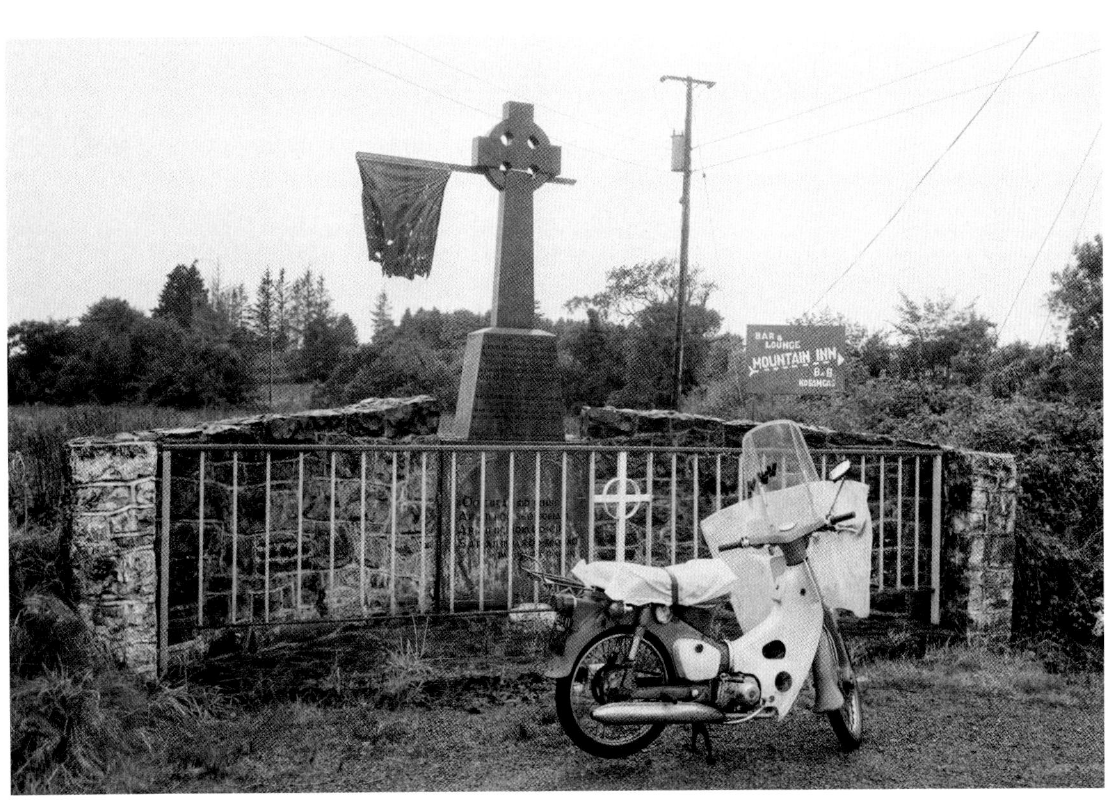

48. Dingle Races

Race meetings in Ireland were a very good ground for taking photographs, so I went to many of them. When I saw this stand in this old-fashioned racecourse at the Dingle races in County Kerry, I could hardly believe how good it was. This is one of my favourite photos from Ireland.

I was trying to be a freelance photographer and get commissions from newspapers and magazines, but we couldn't get a telephone put into our place. To get around this, I had notepaper printed with the telephone numbers of the places where Susie worked during the week. On Monday, it was Manorhamilton 26. If you wanted to get a hold of me, you had to phone Susie at work, talk to Susie and leave a number to call, and then that night, I would go to the local phone box with a bundle of 5p pieces – it was 70p to phone the UK – and feed them into the phone. Thursday was Mohill 5. That was a convent. Susie would be working in the convent, and so a nun would come in and say, 'There's someone on the phone for you,' and it would be someone trying to contact me about a commission. It was really hopeless. You'd have to be pretty bloody determined to get hold of me through those tortuous phone routes. I didn't get any work to speak of. I didn't earn much money, so Susie was supporting me.

DINGLE RACES
FROM *A FAIR DAY*
COUNTY KERRY, IRELAND, 1983

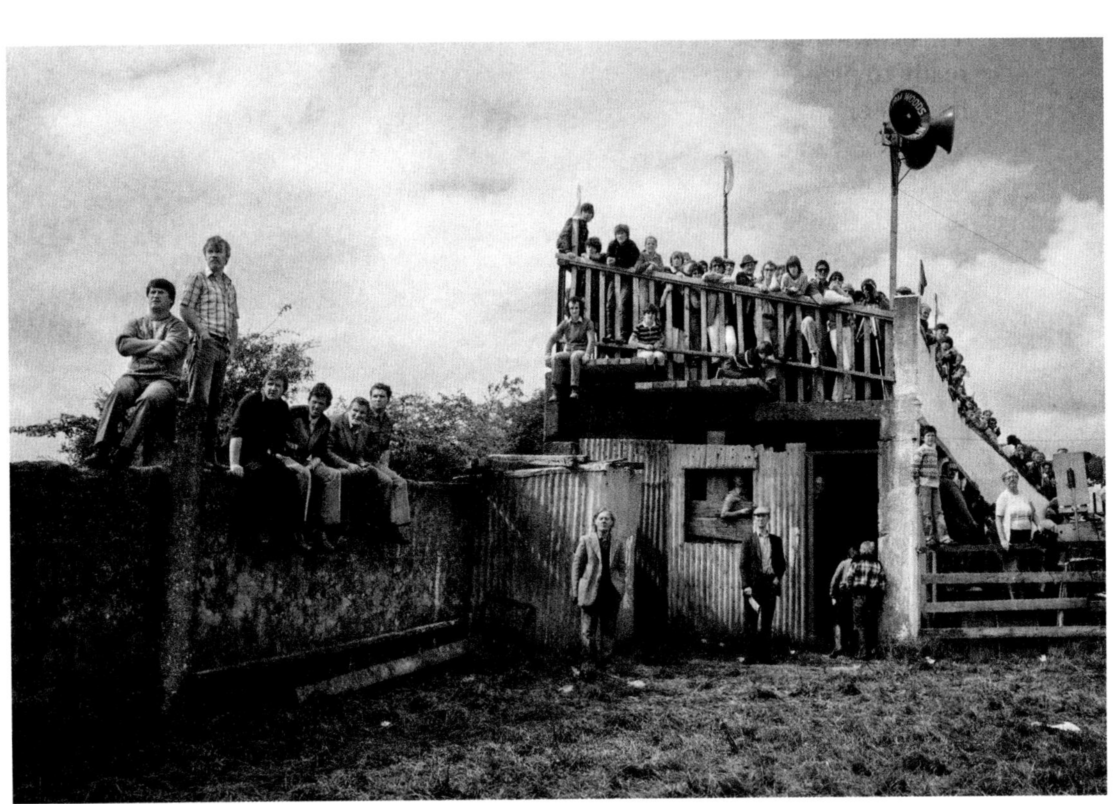

49. Cabbage Plants

Ballaghaderreen is a very traditional town in County Roscommon, Ireland, and it had a fair – all these towns had fairs. Further down this street, they were selling horses and cattle and vegetables. This is where they are selling cabbage plants with their roots on, ready to plant. I might have taken ten photographs here. It might have been five. Might have been fifteen. I just don't know – I stay with an event until it's expired. I knew there was a real possibility here because the lady's got her cabbage plants, so I was waiting for something – the dog, the man – just hanging around in that particular place. And then things started to happen. That's very much one of my techniques: just hang around. Loitering with intent. Slowly, slowly catch a birdie.

The guy walking through makes it. He's necessary to make the picture work. I like all the different people in the frame, even the guy's head on the bottom right which balances it out. The chained-up bikes and dogs by the lampposts are nice. The old lady is looking ahead. The cabbages look better because they're sticking out into the centre of the picture. Everything's in the right place. When I'm taking photographs, I look for the space between things, the relationship between components of the picture; not the thing itself, but how they relate.

I was shooting in black and white because I could develop it myself. I turned a bedroom in our house near Boyle into a darkroom, painted it black and put up blinds, and that was the last time I had my own darkroom, processed the film and printed all my own pictures. I self-published my photos of Ireland a couple of years later, in a book called *A Fair Day*. I wanted to show a society caught between the past and the twentieth century.

IRISH LADY WITH CABBAGE PLANTS
COUNTY ROSCOMMON, IRELAND, 1982

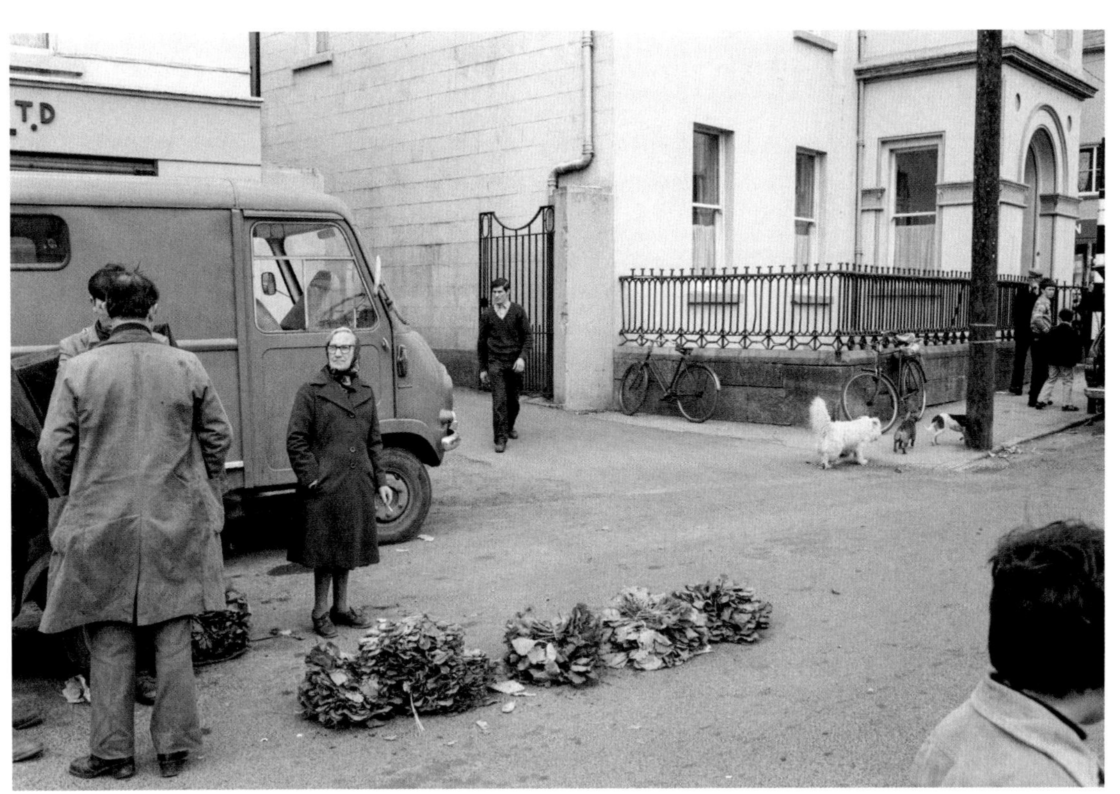

50. New Brighton

Susie and I both wanted to move, and in 1982 Susie got a job in Liverpool. We found a house overlooking the Mersey, in the Wirral. I knew that the seaside resort, New Brighton, was a mile down the road, and that it would be a great place for me to explore photographically. I knew it had great potential. It was a tradition; people came from all over Merseyside to New Brighton for a day out on the beach – if you could call it a beach. It was shabby, but people were still going there. It had an ice-cream parlour, an amusement arcade and funfair rides. I'd been to New Brighton before, and I liked it, and had taken quite a few pictures there in black and white.

I had John Hinde's postcards from Butlin's in the back of my mind. His colours were very strong. When I was a student, working at Butlin's Filey, I'd been disappointed with the black-and-white pictures I was doing for my own projects. I thought they were not as interesting as the colour ones I was doing commercially for Butlin's. I kept working in black and white partly because colour photography wasn't taken seriously in the UK. In the 40s and 50s, colour was almost heresy. It was regarded as commercial and trivial, used for family snapshots because you could get cheap colour cameras. It wasn't high-art photography. Then, in the late 70s, I saw the images from America of serious photography being done in colour: the likes of Stephen Shore, William Eggleston and Joel Meyerowitz were getting shows in the big museums. No longer was colour dismissed. I thought, I must go to colour.

I bought my first colour camera in 1982, and started using colour film. It was a 6x7 Plaubel Makina camera, which had just been introduced into the UK. It was small, with a fixed lens, and I bought a wide-angle one. It was a revelation to use because I could take pictures very quickly. The opportunity to do colour photography in a larger format, and with this new camera, all fell into my lap. Then I had the idea to use flash in daylight.

NEW BRIGHTON, ENGLAND, 1979

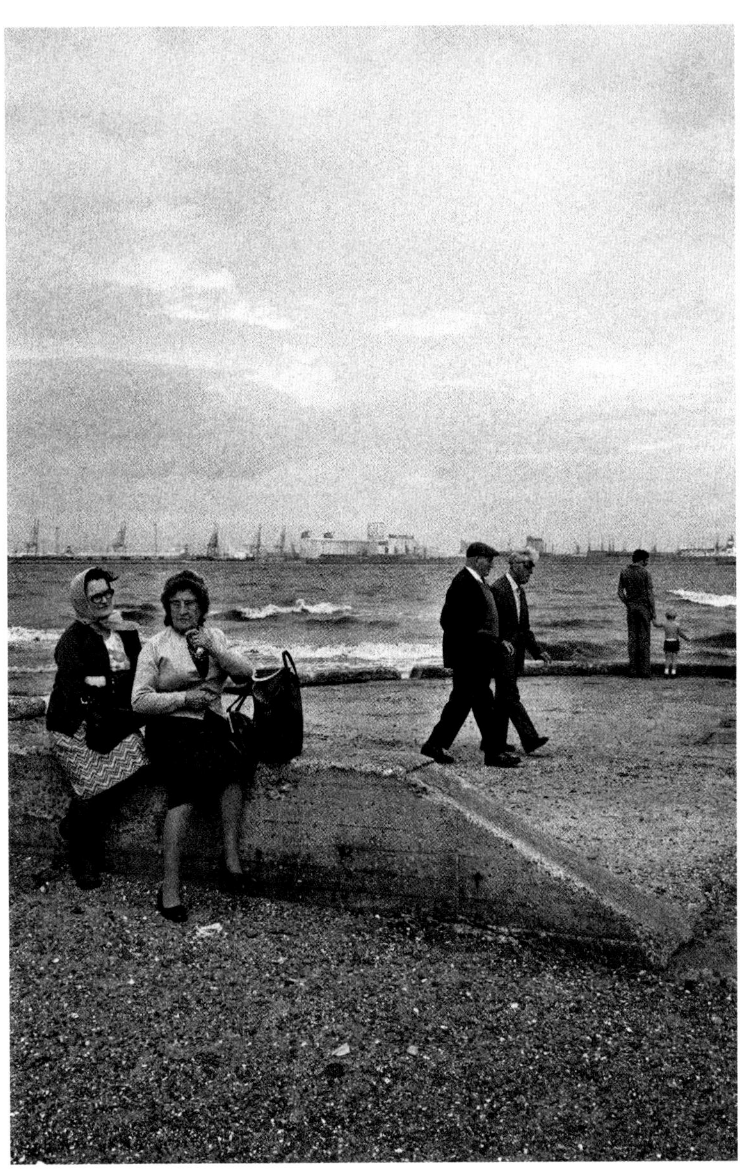

51. Colour and Flash

I knew I was onto something with this combination of colour, flash
and New Brighton. I could tell these were good pictures. It made
me realize that colour really had potential to express my attitude
and subjectivity much more efficiently than anything else. It was
very exciting to do colour photography. Colour is real, isn't it? It's
right in your face. It just looks great. I still love black and white,
but once I moved to colour, I never went back.

FROM *THE LAST RESORT*
NEW BRIGHTON, ENGLAND, 1983–5

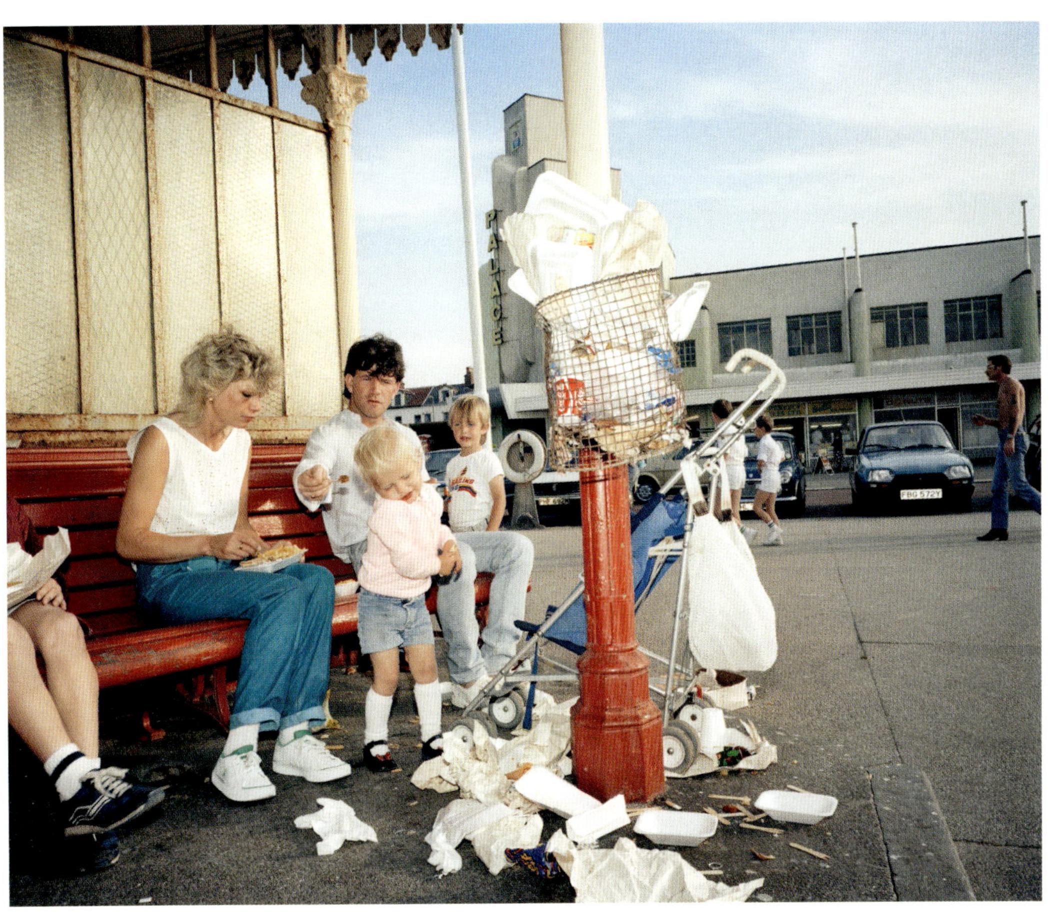

52. The Burger Bar in the Lido

I took many pictures in the Lido in New Brighton. Here, I was behind the counter of the burger bar. People were putting ketchup on the hot dogs – and brown sauce and mustard. Amazingly, no one was looking at the camera. I guess they were so involved with the hot dogs they didn't spot me.

I don't like taking shots when people are in black clothes. I much prefer lighter clothes. Because it was a swimming pool, there was lots of flesh, which is interesting because of the tones.

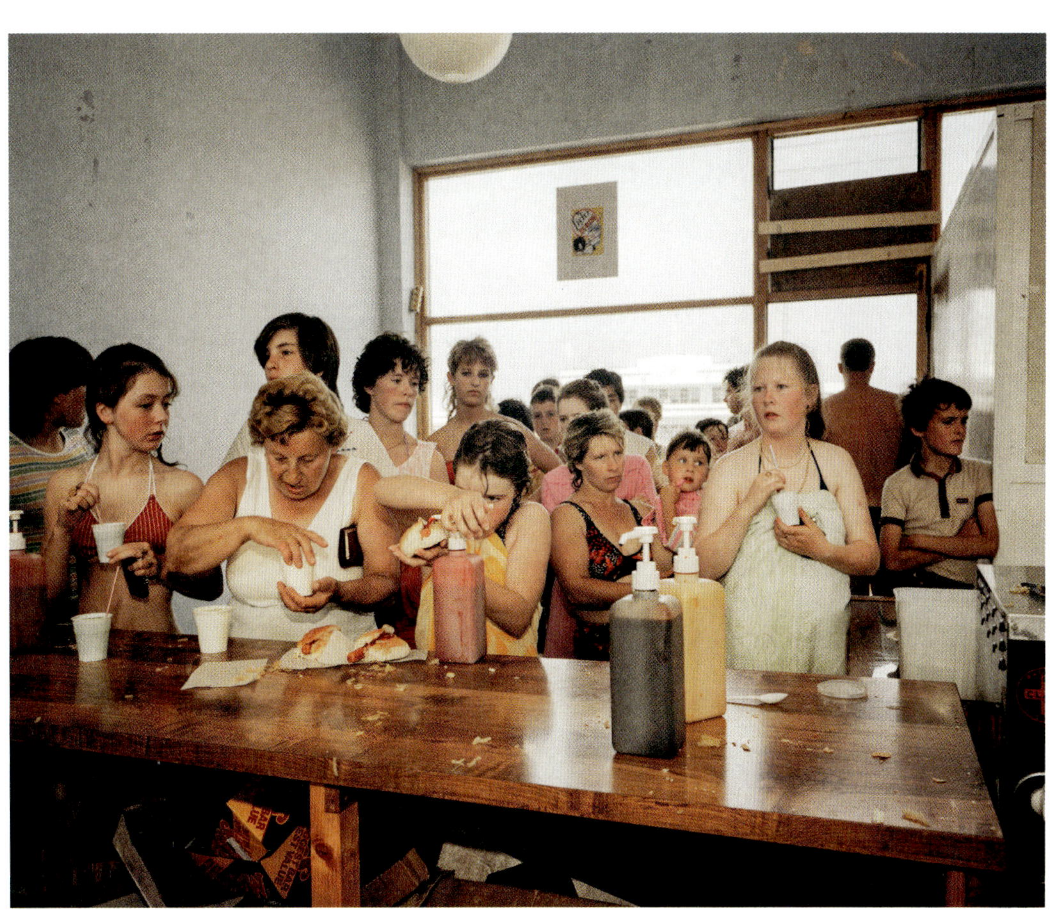

53. The Last Resort

I call this picture *Orange Spade*. There's a baby, the women around him and the orange spade. Nowadays you couldn't take a picture like this, of a kid with no clothes on, but back in the early 80s it wasn't an issue at all. I could photograph freely and no one batted an eyelid. That's the edge of the boating lake, which is gravelly. That's a Milky Way bar being passed along. His mother is in the white top. The women are quite dressed up. It's obviously a day out.

I spent three years shooting these first colour photos, which became a book and a show called *The Last Resort*. The baby in the photo wrote to me a few years ago and said, 'I'm now studying fine art, and I'm doing a thesis on your project *The Last Resort*.' It was so weird to get a request for information from a baby.

FROM *THE LAST RESORT*
NEW BRIGHTON, ENGLAND, 1983–5

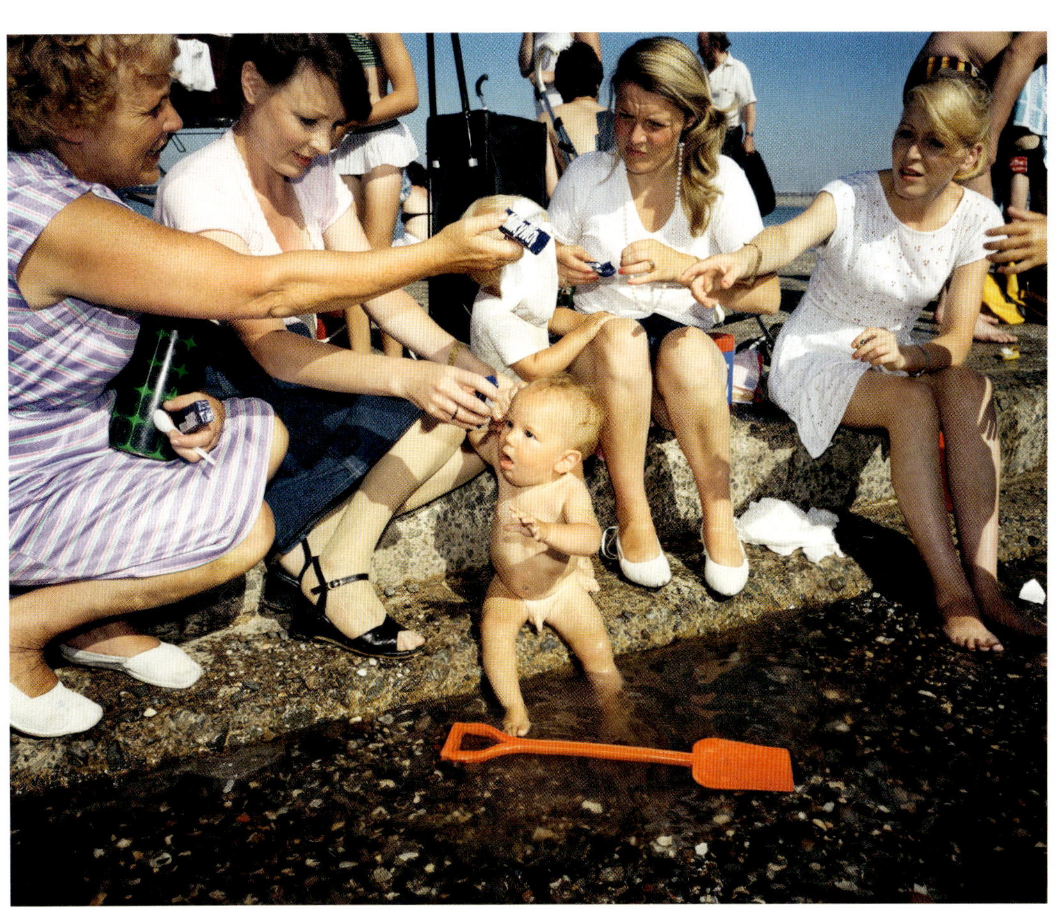

54. The Fairlawn Hotel

The Fairlawn Hotel – what a place! In 1984, Susie and I went to India on a trip. It wasn't a holiday – I don't take holidays. Even though it wasn't a commissioned trip, either, I worked just as hard as if it was.

Although I had moved to colour in 1982, there were a few projects I still shot in black and white. The India trip was one of those. We went to Delhi and Darjeeling, then to Kolkata, where we stayed at the Fairlawn Hotel. It was very basic 1950s deluxe – but this was not the 50s. It was the 80s. Here's Mr and Mrs Smith of the Fairlawn Hotel. They were absolutely classic Raj hangover. He was British and she was Anglo-Indian, and here they are with their two poodles.

They were very, very fond of Britain. Behind them is bedroom number 10 – after 10 Downing Street. They adored Mrs Thatcher. She styled herself like Mrs Thatcher with the pearls, and the pussy-bow blouse, and her hair flicked up in the Thatcher-esque way. And he was like Prince Philip with his safari jacket and cravat. His clothes had been pressed to within an inch of their life. Look at the crease in his trousers. It's not been pressed by him, but by their servants. There are pictures on the wall from the *Telegraph Magazine* of Princess Diana getting married to Prince Charles, of the Queen and a young Prince Philip, and Princess Diana at Prince Charles's feet.

The chairs are beautiful. You can imagine what it was like coming in from the slogging heat of Kolkata and having a gin and tonic in the lush tropical garden in the Fairlawn Hotel. It felt like an oasis.

MR AND MRS SMITH, OWNERS OF THE FAIRLAWN HOTEL
KOLKATA, INDIA, 1984

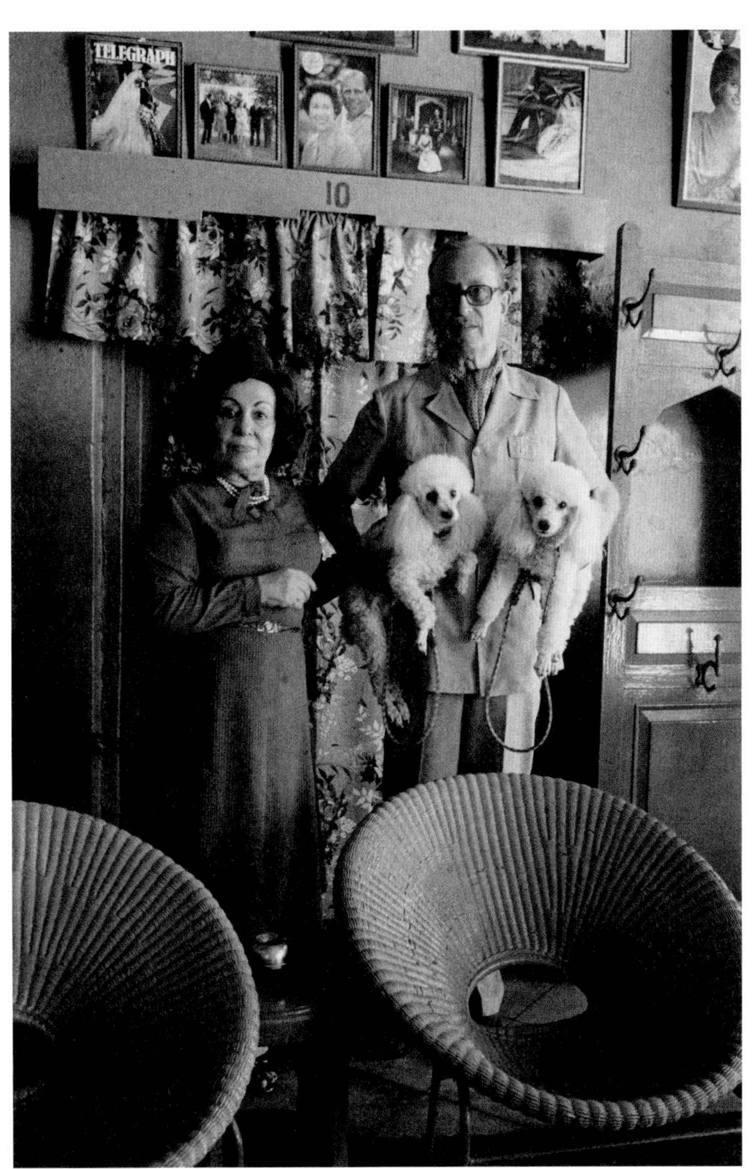

55. Mr and Mrs Smith

This is Mr and Mrs Smith having dinner and being waited on by their servant, who is wearing white gloves. They were very anti all that they considered the low life that surrounded them in Kolkata.

MR AND MRS SMITH, OWNERS OF THE FAIRLAWN HOTEL
KOLKATA, INDIA, 1984

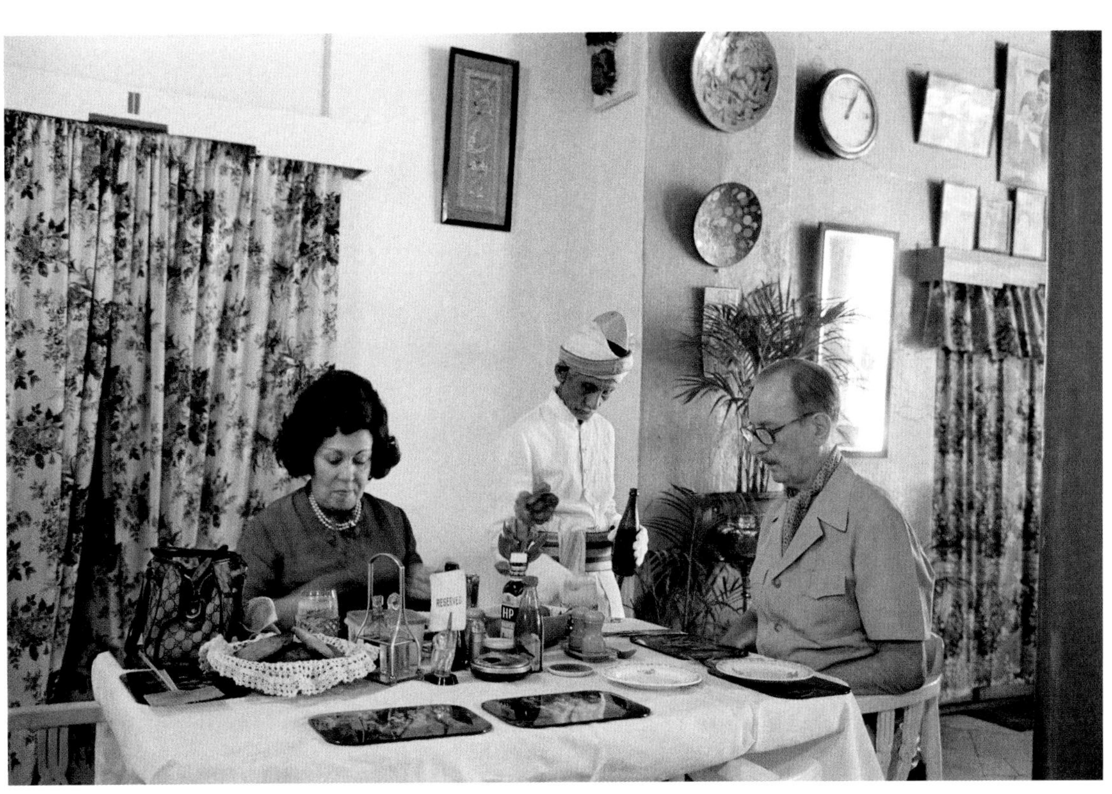

56. Tiananmen Square

In 1985, the Chinese Photographers' Association invited Heather Angel, a wildlife photographer, Jane Bown, the famous *Observer* portrait photographer, and me to China. I was the token up-and-coming young photographer. We went to Shanghai, Guilin – all over China – then we had an exhibition on the third floor of the Geology Museum in Beijing. What a place to have a show! We went to banquet after banquet, and we had all kinds of interesting things to eat like chicken feet – which we found almost inedible and which our hosts loved to suck and chew.

I gave a talk in the Geology Museum and showed colour work from *The Last Resort* – I was two-thirds of the way through shooting it. Two thousand Chinese photographers turned up for the talk, and afterwards I was completely mobbed. I hadn't experienced that before. Even though they didn't know my name, it was exciting for Chinese photographers to hear from a Western photographer.

The last set of black-and-white pictures I ever took was of China. In 1985, there were still portraits of Marx and Lenin in Tiananmen Square, and I homed in on the man holding dumbbells, wanting to incorporate a huge portrait into the photograph, too. I like the young kid on the left in his Communist cap with a star and the kid on the right looking at me. Usually when kids look at you, it doesn't really work, but he has a look of suspicion on his face. He'd probably never seen a very tall Englishman with a camera before. Even though China was austere then, I could see hints of the regeneration that was going to happen and turn China into the second wealthiest country in the world. I was well aware of it. And I'd heard Western music being played. This, though, is old China we're looking at here.

TIANANMEN SQUARE
BEIJING, CHINA, 1985

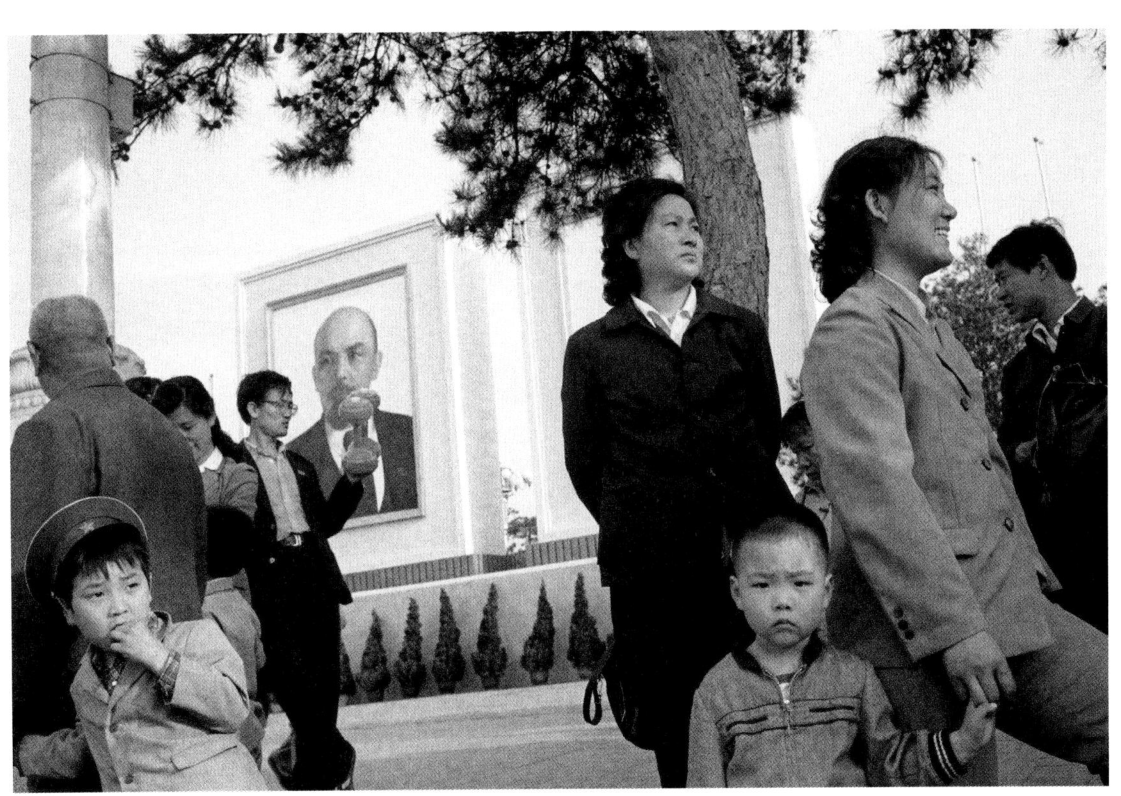

57. Opening Night

I always made a big effort to dress appropriately for openings. That was all part of the fun. Here's Susie and me in 1986 at the opening of *The Last Resort* at Open Eye Gallery in Liverpool. There are photographs of palm trees on my shirt. It was the middle of winter. Susie was expecting Ellen and was in a swimming costume over her tights and T-shirt, and we've got a very good matching lilo and beach bag. I've no idea where that lilo went. Probably went the same way as the stuffed mole.

People in Liverpool came along to the show and, because everyone knew what New Brighton was like, it was no particular shock for them to look at the images. When the very same pictures went down to the Serpentine Gallery in London, people got very angry. All hell broke loose. Middle-class people down south didn't know what the north of England was like. They said, 'How dare this middle-class photographer exploit the working classes? These are patronizing pictures.' *The Last Resort* images were – particularly back then – controversial. We were young. I was thirty-three. I guess you could say I was young to have an exhibition at the Serpentine.

MARTIN AND SUSIE AT THE OPENING OF *THE LAST RESORT*
OPEN EYE GALLERY
LIVERPOOL, ENGLAND, 1985

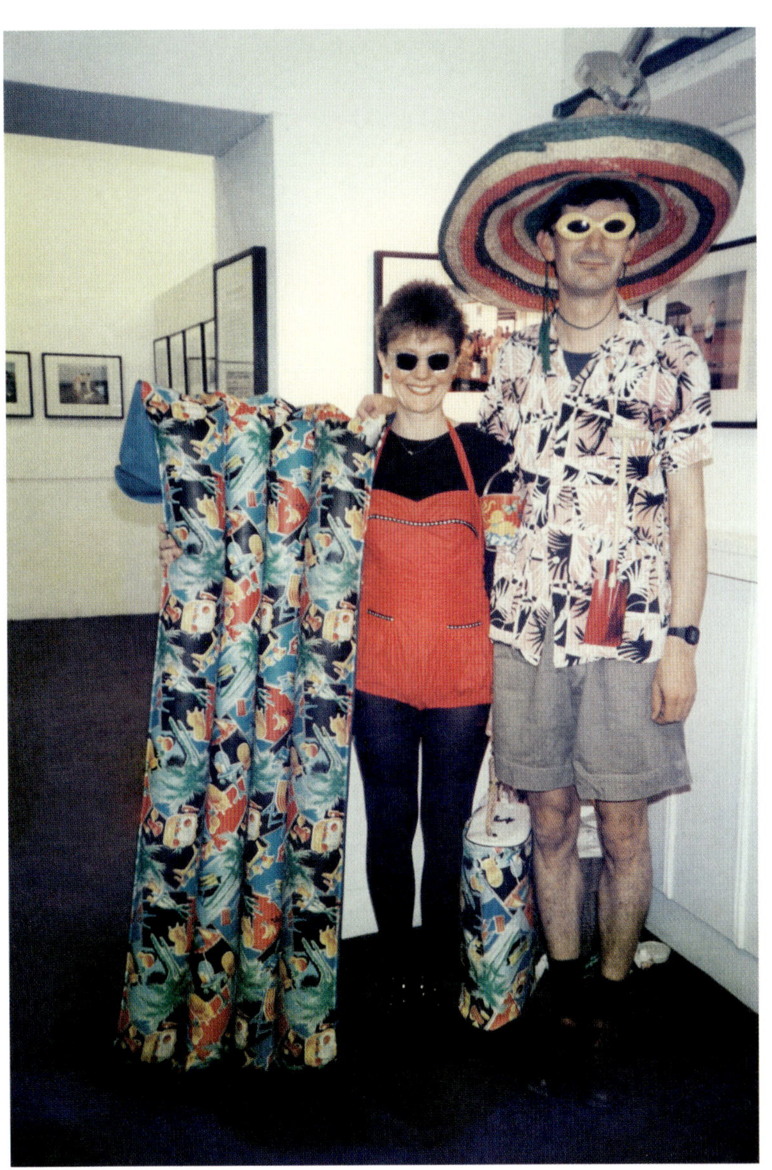

58. Crying

Poor Ellen. Ellen's having a bath. She's very young here, about six weeks old.

Most of the photography we consume around us is a form of propaganda. If we look at the fashion pictures in magazines, everyone looks beautiful. Look at the travel pages; it looks terrific. If we think about our family albums, there's a strong tradition that everyone must be smiling at the camera. Often, when I'm doing portraits, it's very difficult to persuade people not to smile because they're so used to smiling when they're having their photo taken. One of the things I'm interested in is questioning all that. Therefore, I was quite happy when I was taking pictures of our daughter, Ellen, to have her crying, to have her with a pooey nappy, to show life as it really is, rather than a domestic fantasy.

People don't take photographs of crying babies. It's almost a taboo. People don't exactly grab their camera when babies start having a tantrum. We're conditioned to take photographs in certain situations. For example, if people are attending a wedding, they always bring a camera, but if they go to a funeral, they wouldn't dream of taking a camera. These are the unwritten, unspoken rules in society about photography, about what you should and shouldn't photograph. Part of my job is to break these taboos and do things differently.

ELLEN PARR
WALLASEY, ENGLAND, 1986

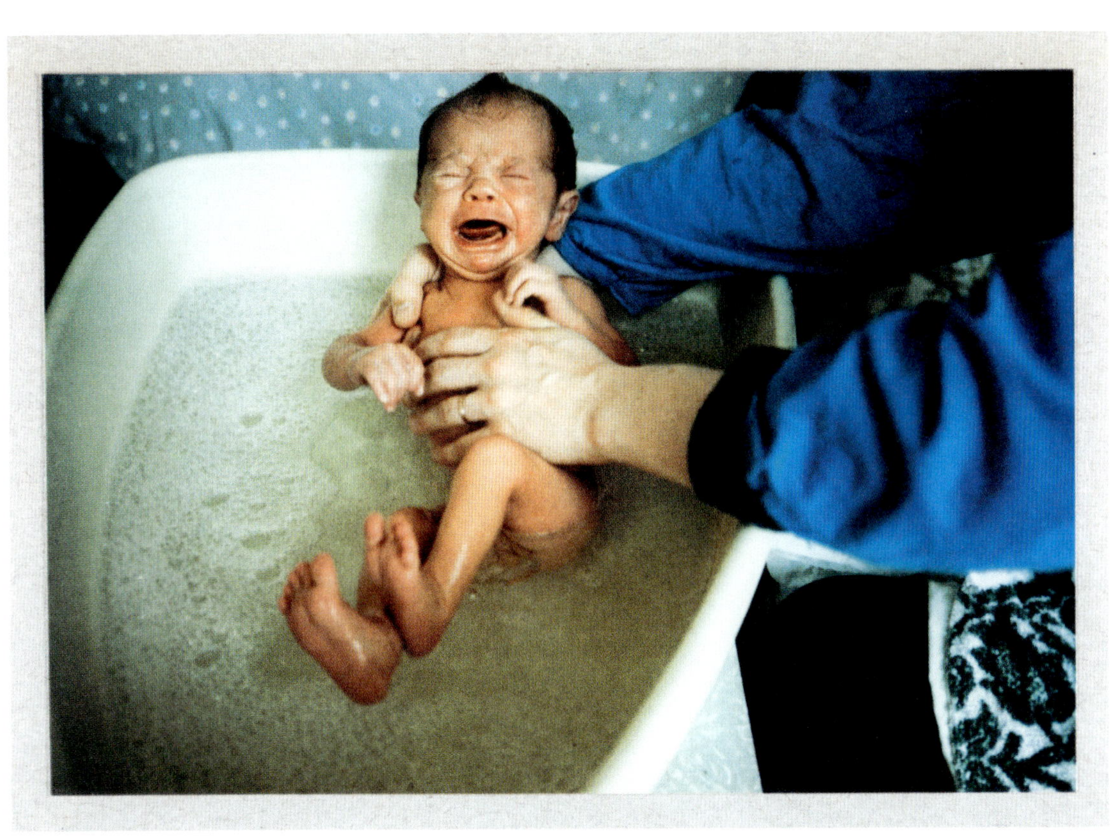

59. With Ellen

Just to show what a beautiful baby Ellen was. That's me with Ellen.

ELLEN AS A BABY ON MARTIN'S LAP
PHOTOGRAPH BY SUSIE PARR
BRISTOL, ENGLAND, 1986

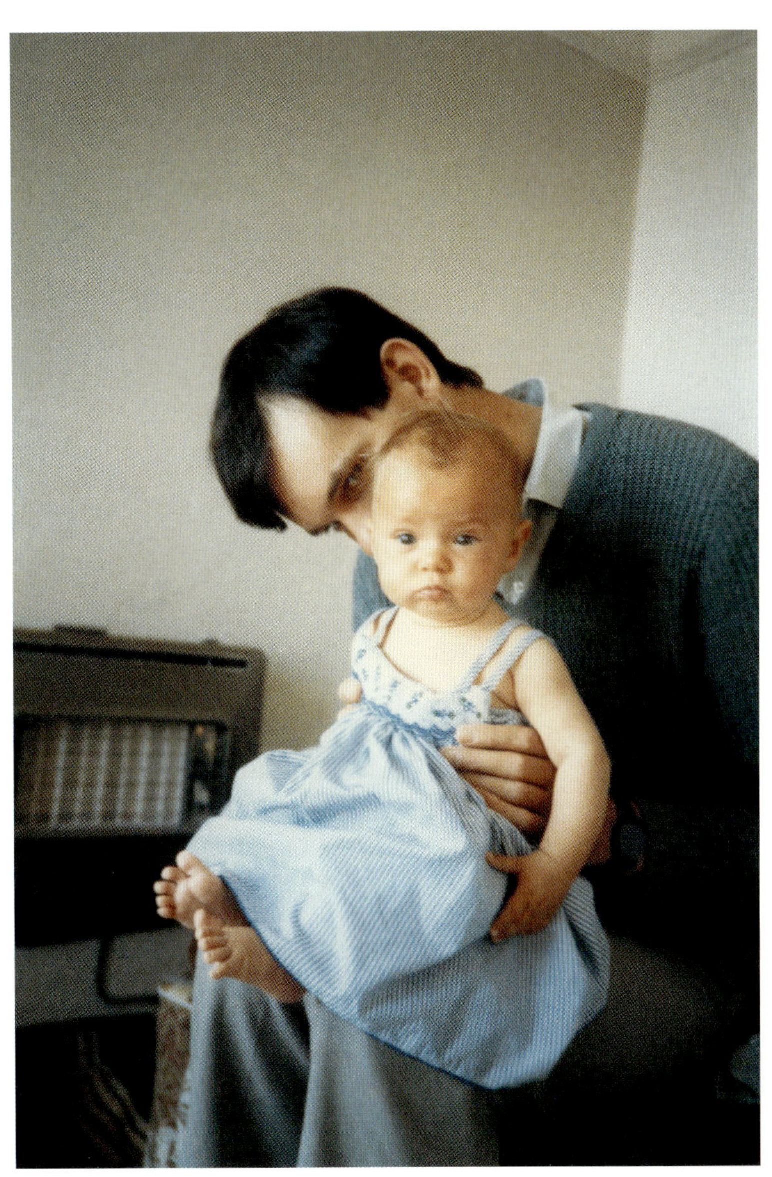

60. Morelli's Milk Bar

I'm obsessed with the seaside. Because my parents were bird-watchers, we didn't go on traditional seaside holidays. I missed out on that, and that's one reason why, for the rest of my life, I've always been keen to go to resorts. I've probably been to every seaside resort of some significance in the country. Broadstairs in Kent is one of my favourites. It's got this fantastic path overlooking the beach, and it has some great cafés, including the wonderful Morelli's Milk Bar. They serve milkshakes, milky coffee, and, of course, they make their own ice cream. You get these amazing ice cream sundaes. You see these two ladies' glasses? They are piled high with ice cream and bananas sticking out, and whipped cream and berries. And there's an Italianesque painting of Venice behind these ladies with their suitably coloured milkshakes. I like the colours of kitsch. I'm like a magpie attracted to colour and glistening things, and seaside resorts are full of the colours of kitsch.

Resorts are meant to be very jolly, but often they're very depressing. The worst poverty in the country can be found in seaside towns, such as Blackpool and Clacton, although some resorts, such as Broadstairs, Southwold and, of course, St Ives, buck the trend because they appeal to the middle classes as well. Britain is defined by class differentials, more than most European countries. I'm middle class, but I photograph all classes. You can read class in images – I'm intuitive about all this, rather than intellectual. We can read class in each other from clothes, hair, accessories and body language. We can tell, can't we?

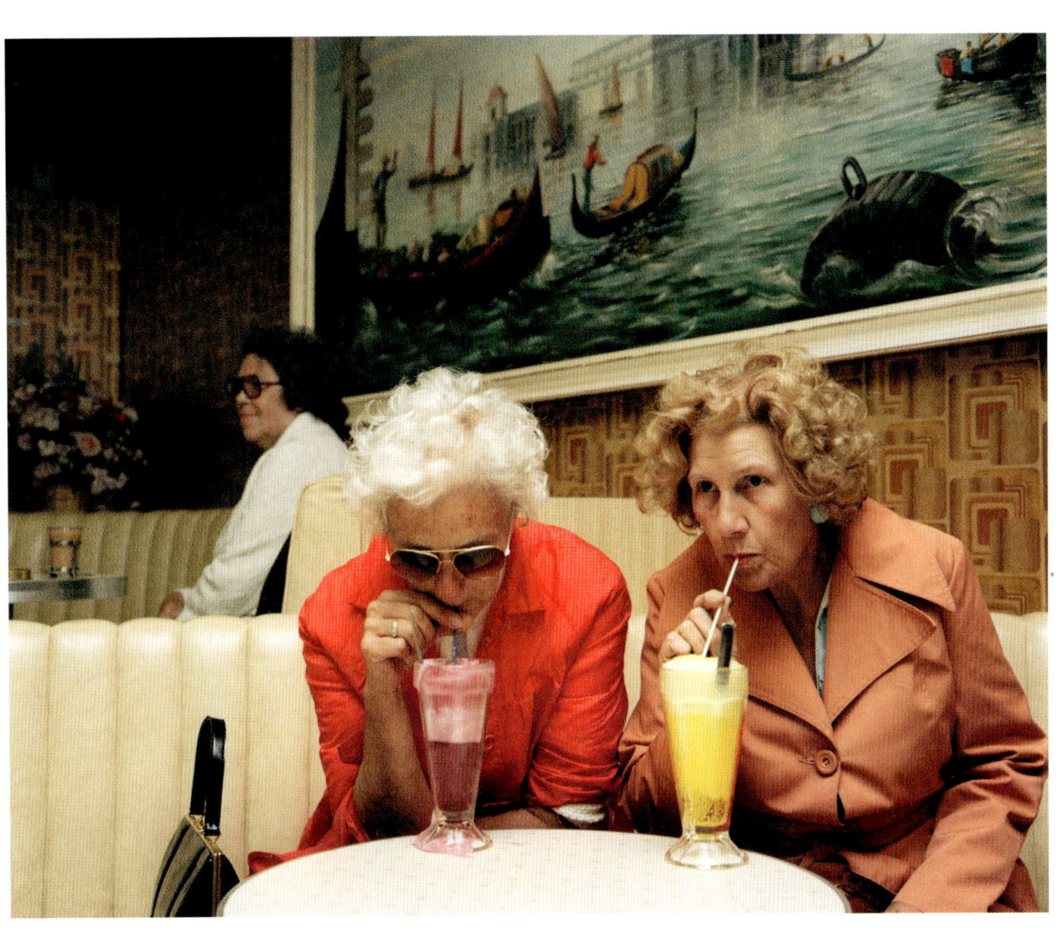

61. Drive-through McDonald's

Whenever I was offered a commission, I said yes, because it was work and money. What was not to like? In 1986, I was commissioned as part of a group of thirty photographers to spend a week taking pictures in Ireland, to produce one of those daily-life type books. The photographers from America and the rest of Europe all trundled to the west coast to look for classic scenes of Irishness – thatched cottages, horse fairs – all the things that, in fact, I had photographed earlier in the 80s. I said to the organizers, 'I'm going to stay in Dublin. I'm going to photograph on the east coast and go to places like supermarkets.'

When the book came out, I was the only photographer who had photographed anything vaguely modern in Ireland. Everybody else was stuck in the past. I was vindicated in trying to represent Ireland in a more interesting way. My thinking was that I've got to represent the times that we live in, the changing times. This, to me, was a symbol of the modernization of Ireland in the mid-80s. It was the very first drive-through McDonald's in the country, in Nutgrove Shopping Centre, in Dublin. This guy was lacking experience of how to function at a drive-through restaurant. He got out of the car when, in fact, he should have driven up closer and just shouted his order. It's humorous. He doesn't know what he's doing. His jumper's bunched up. The machine is so bossy, stating 'ORDER HERE,' and he looks really quite lost. Now I'm sure there are fifty drive-through McDonald's in Ireland and everyone understands how they operate.

NUTGROVE SHOPPING CENTRE
DUBLIN, IRELAND, 1986

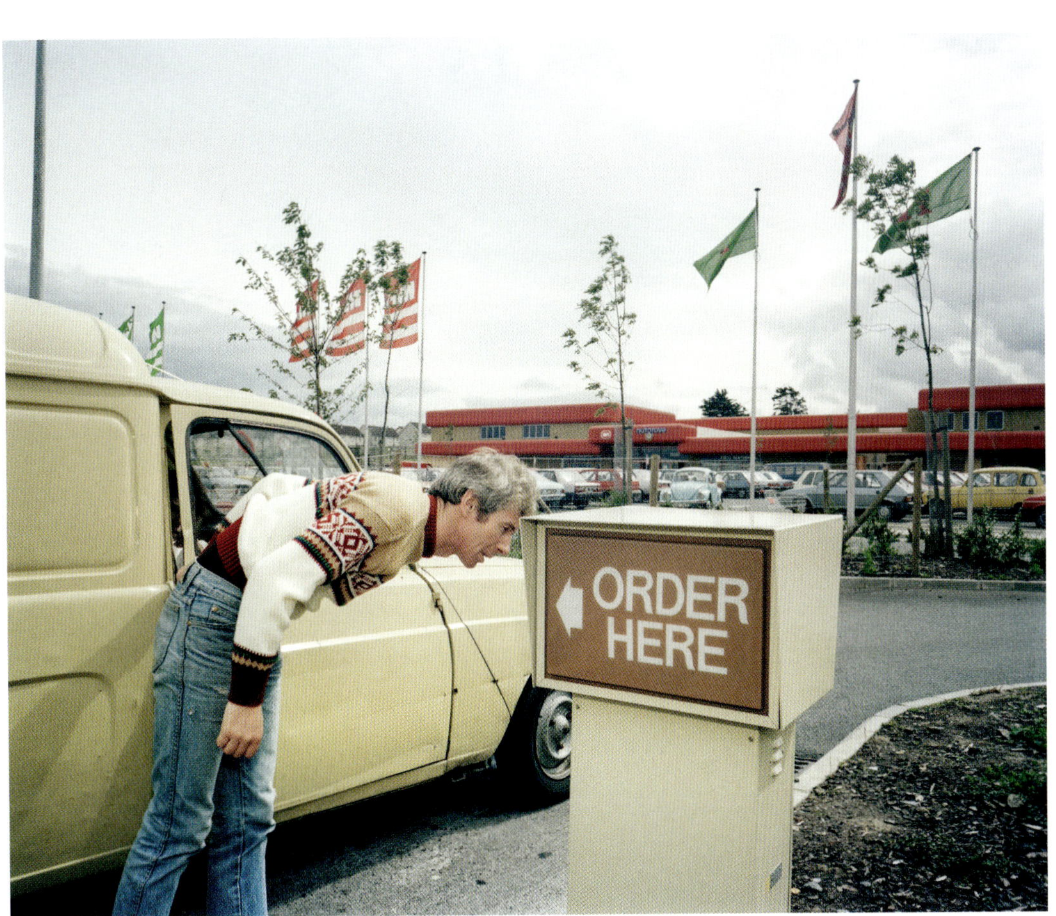

ORDER
HERE

62. Crazy Prices

Here we have a rammed supermarket trolley with a baby stuck on the top. It's as if the baby is a consumer item, and a must-have accessory to your life. This was in the Crazy Prices Supermarket outside Dublin.

I never wanted to photograph war scenes. I had no desire to go to war whatsoever. I went to the local supermarket because, to me, that was the front line.

'CRAZY PRICES' SUPERMARKET
FROM *HOME AND ABROAD*
BALLYMUN, DUBLIN, IRELAND, 1986

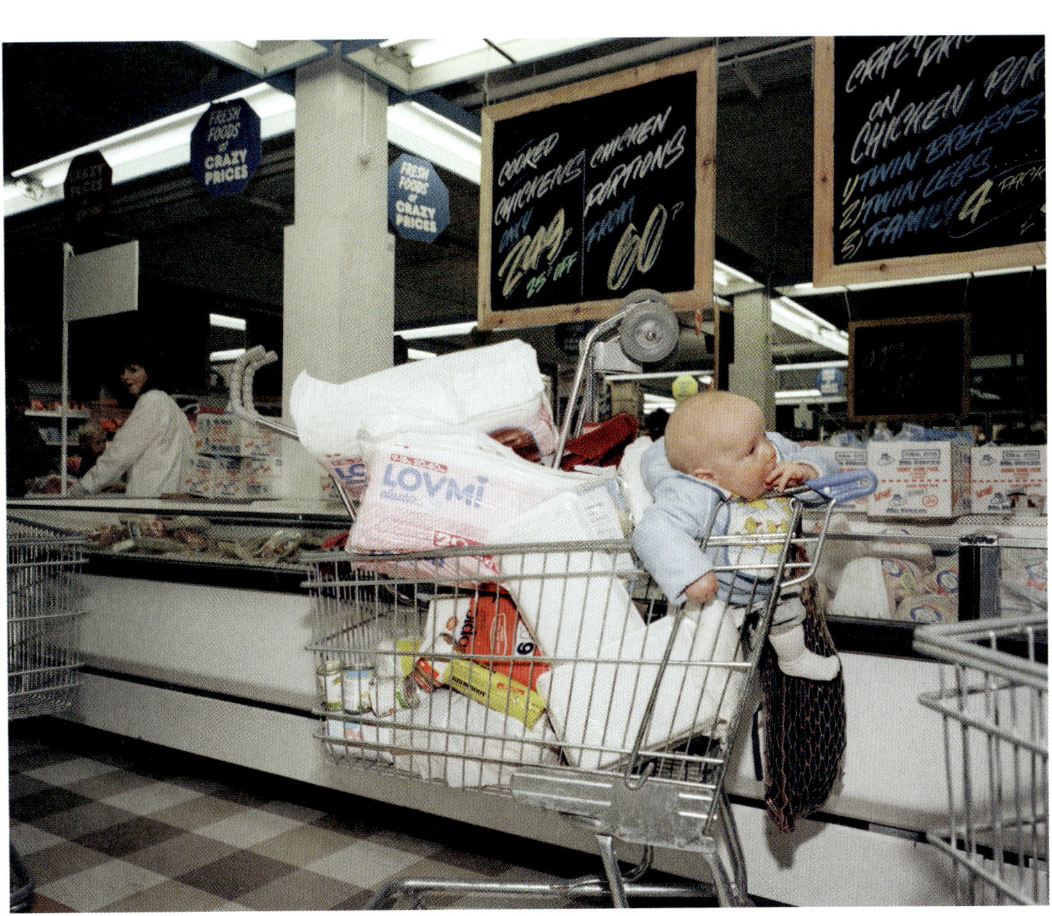

FRESH FOODS at CRAZY PRICES
FRESH FOODS at CRAZY PRICES
COOKED CHICKENS
CHICKEN PORTIONS
FROM 60 P
CHICKEN POR
TWIN BREASTS
TWIN LEGS
FAMILY 4 PACK
LOVM!

63. The Reluctant Wallet

I had some criticism for photographing the working class in *The Last Resort*, and I wanted to answer back. I thought it was important to photograph the middle classes. It struck me that this was a class, and a type of person, that hadn't really been photographed before. Photographers tended to go for the very rich or the very poor. So in 1986, I started *The Cost of Living*, a project about the middle classes. Liverpool, where we were living at the time, was about the least middle-class city in the whole country, so Susie and I said, 'Let's look for a new place to work,' and we came to Bristol.

I went to all the events that I would go to anyway, as a middle-class person, and those I wasn't very keen on – one of which was craft fairs. I've never been a big fan of home-made chunky pottery and bad pots. Any bad pot people can call an ashtray, can't they? And here we have the perfect couple at a craft fair. It's called *The Reluctant Wallet*. I like the way the flash has caught his wallet to make it shine and to bring the foreground up to make it brighter. She's about to pick up a piece of pottery. A purchase is about to be made – hence the reluctant wallet coming out. I don't much like crafts and pottery so this is me trying to put my own attitude into an image.

FROM *THE COST OF LIVING*
LEEDS CASTLE CRAFTS TENT, ENGLAND, 1986–9

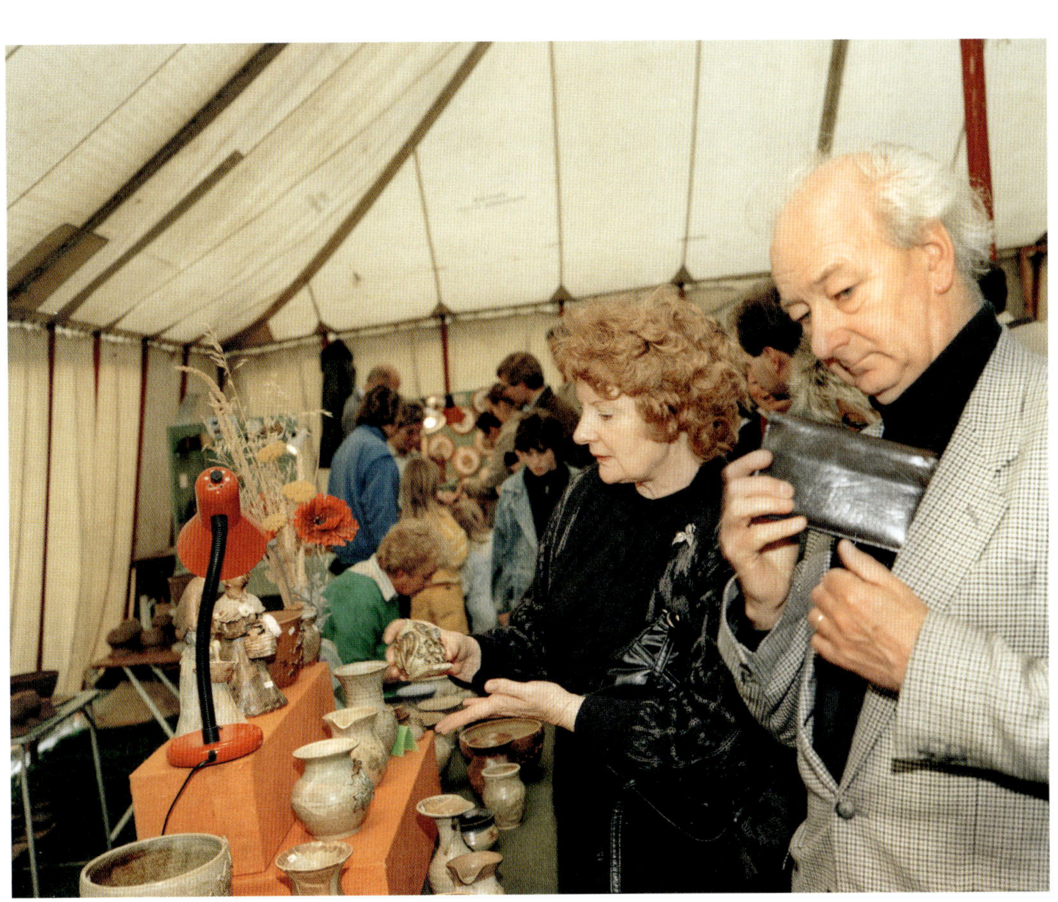

64. The Show Home

To photograph the middle classes, I went to public schools. I went to IKEA. I went to wine tastings. I went to places like this show home. When developers build a new housing estate, they have one house which they do up, to make it look homely, and take prospective buyers around it to try and sell the houses. The show home looks convincing as a real home. It looks lived in. You've got the double beds, the fancy curtains and the miniature car on the windowsill, a Citroen 2CV. Then, in the background, there's a picket fence, the real car bang in the centre of the picture and a building site behind it. This is the guest room. It's a posh guest room with some potpourri. I hope the guests like patterns and flowers.

A 'CALIFORNIAN-STYLE' SHOWHOUSE
FROM *THE COST OF LIVING*
SOMERSET, ENGLAND, 1986–9

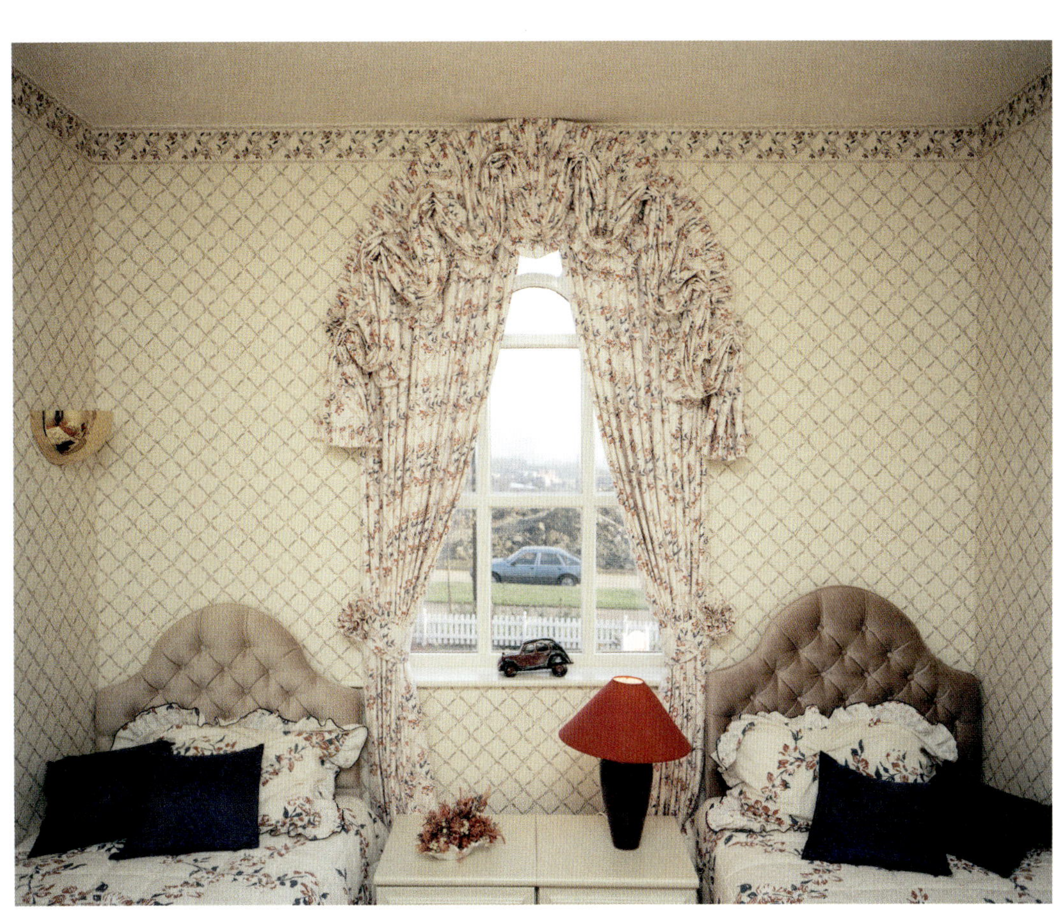

65. Something That Seems Ordinary

I was hanging around a petrol station like a pervert. Photographers at the time would have said this was the craziest place to take a picture. I thought they were all wrong. They would have looked at this photo and thought, this guy is nuts, probably. Because it's a very unglamorous subject matter. Boring. This was taken around the time I was a nominee at Magnum. Part of the purpose of photography at Magnum is to do with the good and the bad of humanity, the big themes, the wars, the drama. There's no drama here. It's not glamorous at all. But there's something very interesting about boring.

If I said to a photographer today, 'Go and photograph people filling their car with petrol,' they would think, 'Well, what's the point of that?' But something which seems very ordinary at the time becomes interesting when you look back at it later, almost forty years later. Here, you see how the pump has changed, the clothes have changed, the car has changed. You realize you're looking at the past, at how things have modernized, and how different it is now to how it was then. It tells us something about consumerism, and how we depend on fuel, oil and petrol. At the time, a scene like this was ignored as a photographic subject, because it was just how everybody lived. But actually, the scene is very specific, historically. This demonstrates the value of documentary photography. There are many things that we don't think are interesting, that we should be photographing, but don't.

FROM *SPENDING TIME*
SALFORD, ENGLAND, 1986

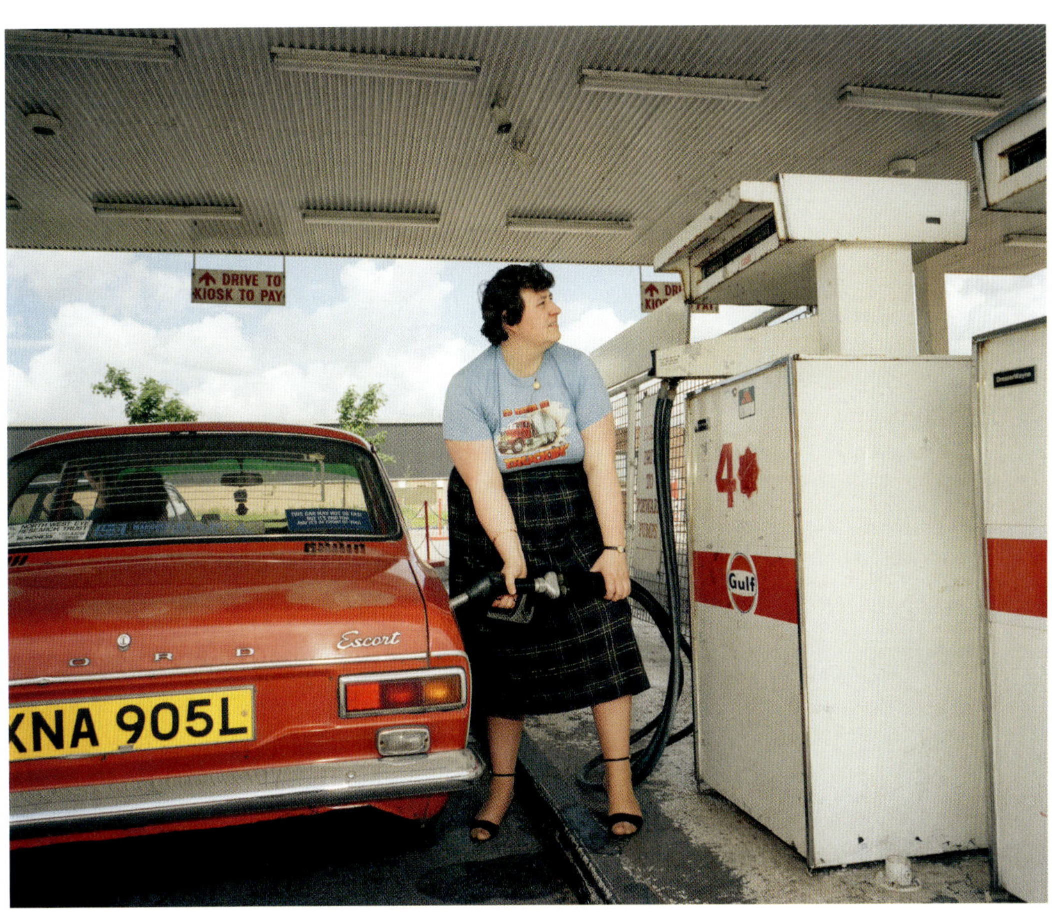

DRIVE TO
KIOSK TO PAY
DRI
KIO
FORD
Escort
KNA 905L
4
Gulf

66. Midsummer Madness

During the 80s, we were all motivated by a dislike of Mrs Thatcher, so when Susie and I moved down to Bristol and I set up *The Cost of Living* project, I decided that one of the things I should photograph was Conservative Party events. I went to the Conservative Party Association in Bath and asked if there was any chance of getting access to these events. They were so very agreeable to that. Access, back in the 80s, was a much easier game to play. I guess now they'd look me up and be horrified by my reputation. I said, 'I'd like to photograph events that are happening in people's gardens and houses.' They said, 'Yes, here's a list.' And up came this one: the Bath Young Conservatives Midsummer Madness Party. I thought, that sounds good, and here is the picture that I took. A few years later, this picture was shown in the Museum of Modern Art in New York in an exhibition called *British Photography from the Thatcher Years*, and they put it on the cover of the catalogue.

They're having a wild time at the Young Conservatives Midsummer Madness Party. I love the guy at the back having his glass of red wine. I like the flowers to the right, and the two guys in the centre of the picture and the woman. Every little component of this picture works – and that's an unusual achievement – including the fence and the house next door, even the lady's pink sandal and the foldable deck chair. The men are dressed up in suits and ties, and they look very smug. This lady's hair is like a helmet. It looks solid. It doesn't look like it would blow in the wind in the Midsummer Madness.

CONSERVATIVE MIDSUMMER MADNESS PARTY
FROM *THE COST OF LIVING*
BATH, ENGLAND, 1988

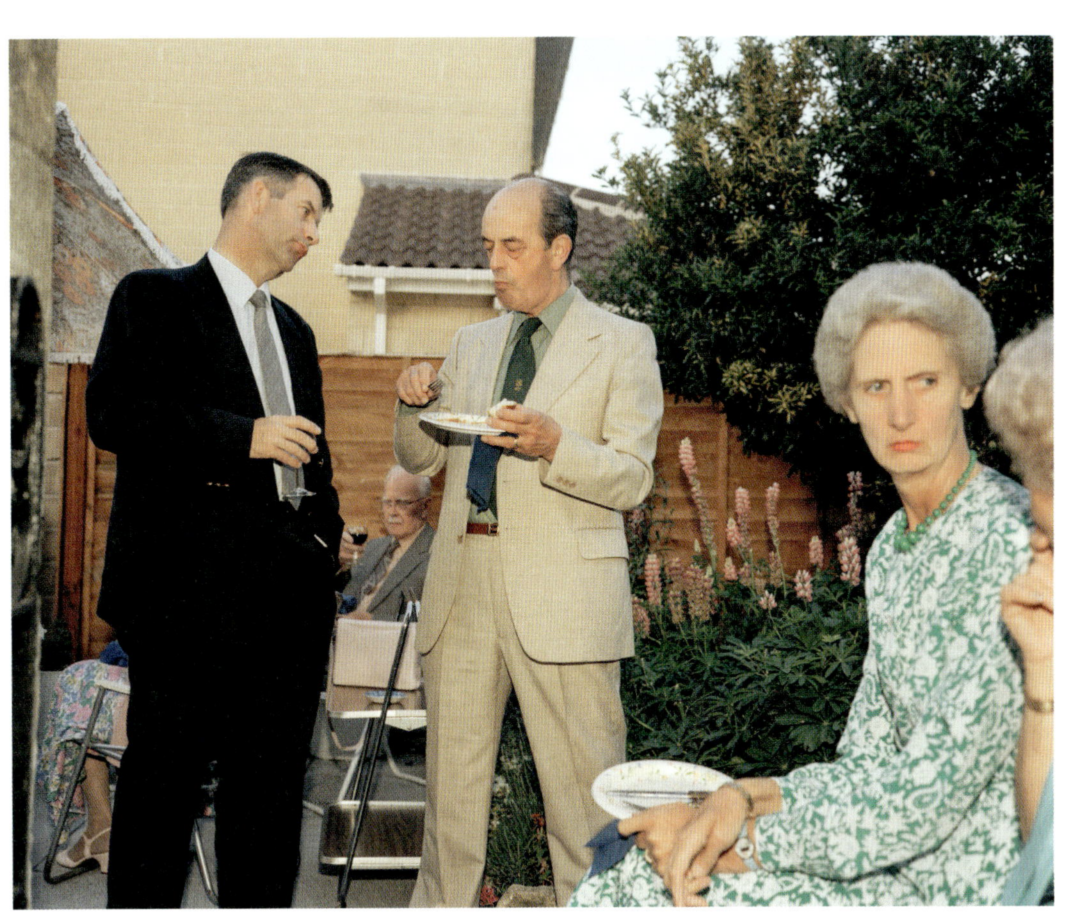

67. The Princess Café

When I was thirty-six, I got a commission for the *Telegraph Magazine*. They asked me to photograph cafés in England for a summer special. I went to all the classic resorts. It was very exciting to suddenly be paid to go around taking pictures while having my expenses covered. It really was a breakthrough for me. It was the first proper editorial commission I got, and it came via Magnum, when I was still just a nominee. This picture of Princess Café in Scarborough is probably the best photo from the series, and the *Telegraph* used it as the lead picture in the spread.

Isn't it amazing how dressed up the *maître d'* is, with her pearls and her dress? She was very friendly, very cheeky. I like the way the red light's coming out of her head. The guy on the left, having his cup of tea, is very relaxed, and there's the beautiful, three-dimensional mural on the wall with the sailing boat. It looks like they're eating fish and chips, the classic British dish.

Photos tend to organize chaos, to define what we're doing here. I often think of what I photograph as a soap opera, where I am waiting for the right cast to fall into place.

THE PRINCESS CAFÉ
SCARBOROUGH, ENGLAND, 1988

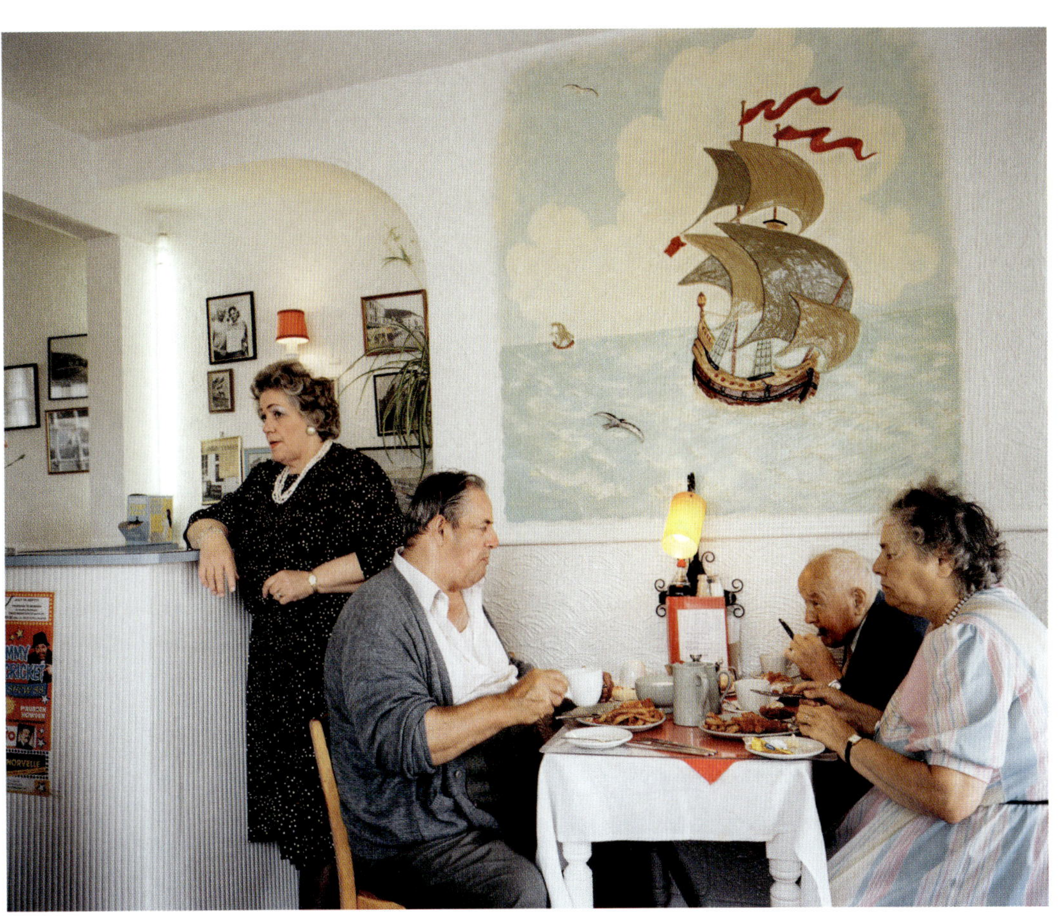

68. An AA Road Sign

The Cost of Living show opened at the Royal Society of Photography in Bath. What was significant about that was that it was the first time – and, in fact, the last time – I've been on an AA road sign. If that's any indication of fame, I don't know. It just tickled me, having that sign. It was another rung on the long ladder upwards. This was at the end of the 80s, when I was slowly and gradually getting better known.

AA SIGN FOR MARTIN PARR EXHIBITION
PHOTOGRAPH BY CHARLIE MEACHAM
BATH, ENGLAND, 1989

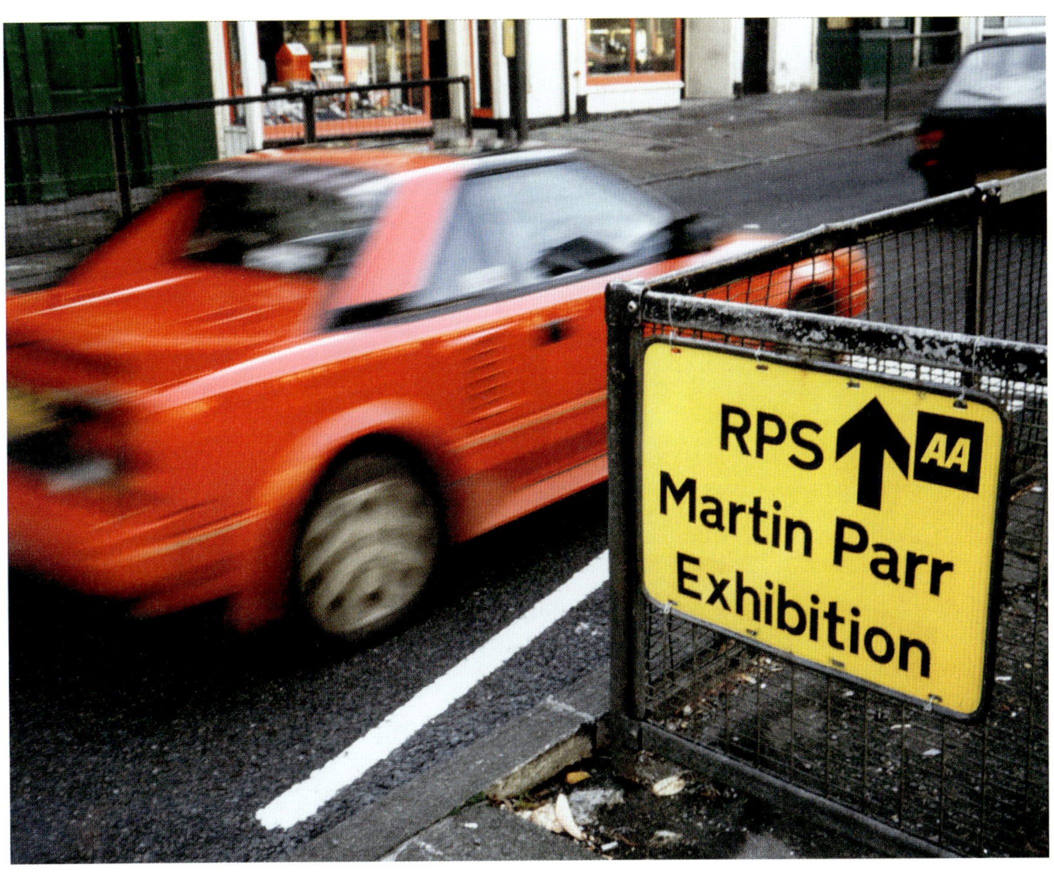
RPS
AA
Martin Parr
Exhibition

69. Arrested in Albania

In 1990, I saw an advertisement for a coach trip around Albania to look at architectural sites, and I decided to book myself onto it. The only way to get into the People's Socialist Republic of Albania was by joining a tour group, as journalists and photographers were barred. When we got on the bus, we realized all of us were from the press: all of us were going there to try and see what was happening, to see if there was any dissent brewing up after the fall of the Berlin Wall in 1989.

We had a tour guide who was very much toeing the Communist Party line. During the day, we had to visit these Roman architectural sites that most of us weren't interested in, but when we got to the hotel in the evening, we'd go out to investigate what was really going on. One of the journalists from the *Observer* managed to find someone who actually articulated the discontent that many people were feeling. It wasn't long after this trip that the regime collapsed.

I would go out and photograph whatever was on the streets to be seen. This was a sports and social club in the city of Saranda, in southern Albania. I like the colours. It's got a Communist feel. I just wandered anywhere I wanted: shops, barbers, and social clubs like this one – and, because I didn't speak Albanian, no one bothered about me coming in, so I could get away with a lot of things. However, one morning I was arrested – but the police didn't speak English, and didn't know what to do with me, so they returned me to the hotel.

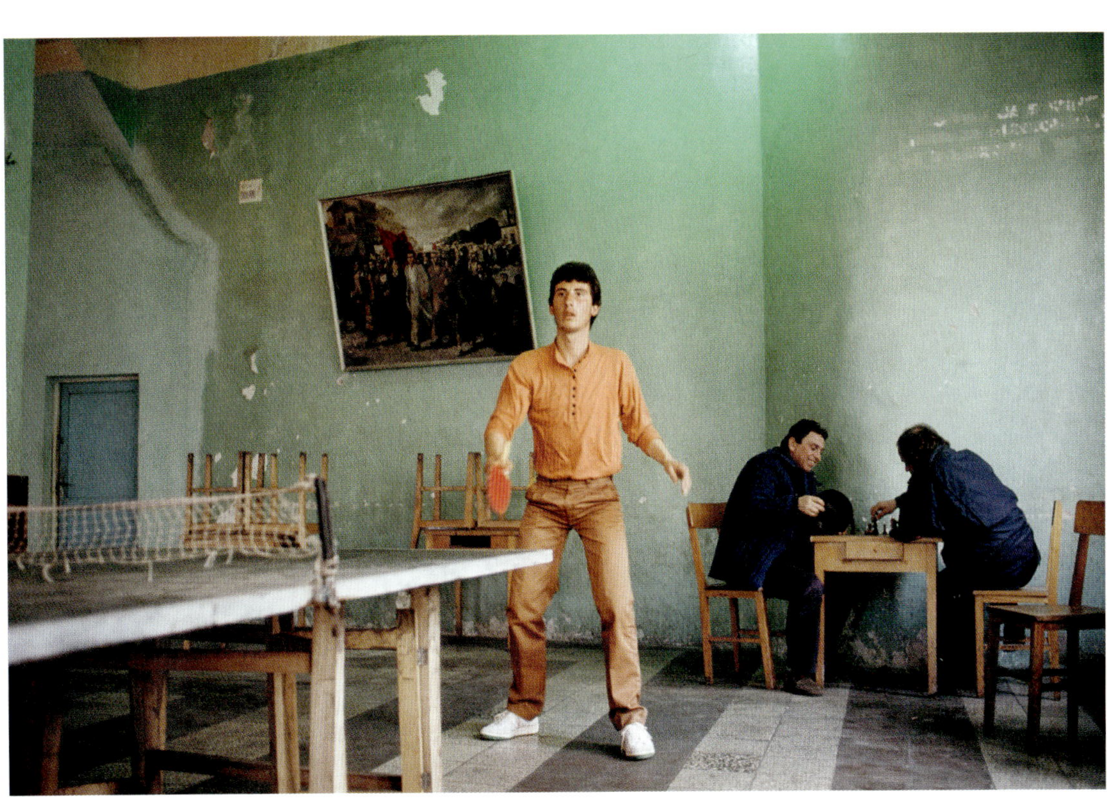

70. The Light-Switch Moment

In 1991, the BBC commissioned a director called Nicholas Barker to make a series called *Signs of the Times* about contemporary British home decor and taste. Nicholas had seen my *Cost of Living* show when it was on at the Photographers' Gallery, got in touch and asked if I would be interested in a collaboration. We agreed that after he'd done the filming, I would take portraits of the people in their houses and still lifes of their things, and then Nicholas would match the images with quotes from their interviews. I must have gone to fifty houses all over the country. The quote for this photo of the light switch is, 'We wanted a cottagey, stately home kind of feel.' I like the fact that one switch is on, one switch is off and that the thing around the switch is so naff and probably unnecessary. The idea of trying to make a cottagey stately home is ridiculous.

Nicholas wanted to make the documentary very deadpan, so it had no music, just people talking, often contradicting each other. The programmes were very provocative and controversial. Some people liked them, some people hated them, which, all in all, made it a good project. Viewers wondered how on earth we got permission to film it, because the people were so revealed. I guess we pushed them into that situation. But they did, in fact, all apply themselves. The people who were chosen were happy with the programmes to a certain degree, although probably not everyone was. I remember Henry, the architect, got fed up.

We had free outdoor exhibitions when the *Signs of the Times* book came out. There were billboard posters, bus shelter posters and an 'Art on the Underground' installation with ten different posters all over the tube. You couldn't avoid it. It's the highest profile exhibition I've had in the UK, because it was seen by millions.

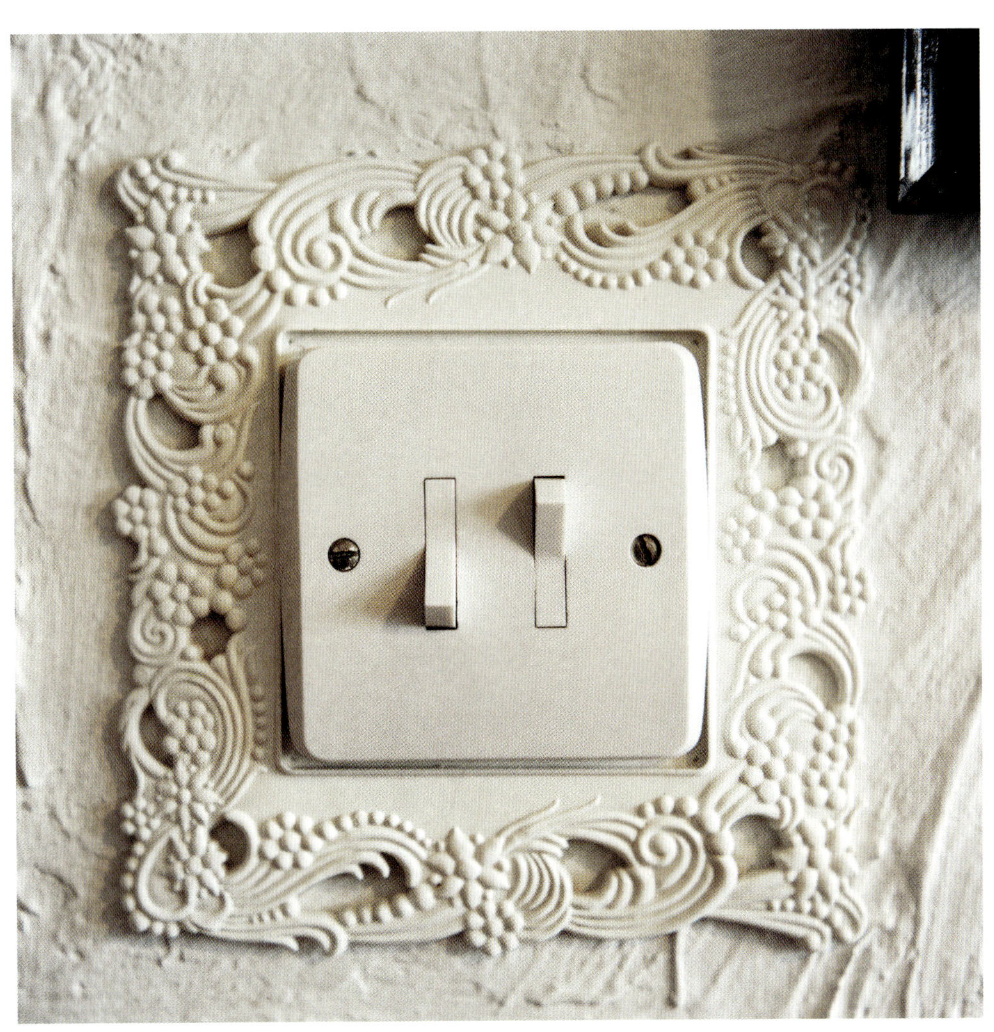

71. Curtains

Certain still-lifes I knew were going to work very well. Often they were very simple. These are just curtains. They're wonderfully silly. I like the quote that goes with the photo: 'I get such pleasure from them every day when I sit in the bath.'

'I GET SUCH PLEASURE FROM THEM
EVERY DAY WHEN I SIT IN THE BATH.'
FROM *SIGNS OF THE TIMES*
ENGLAND, 1991

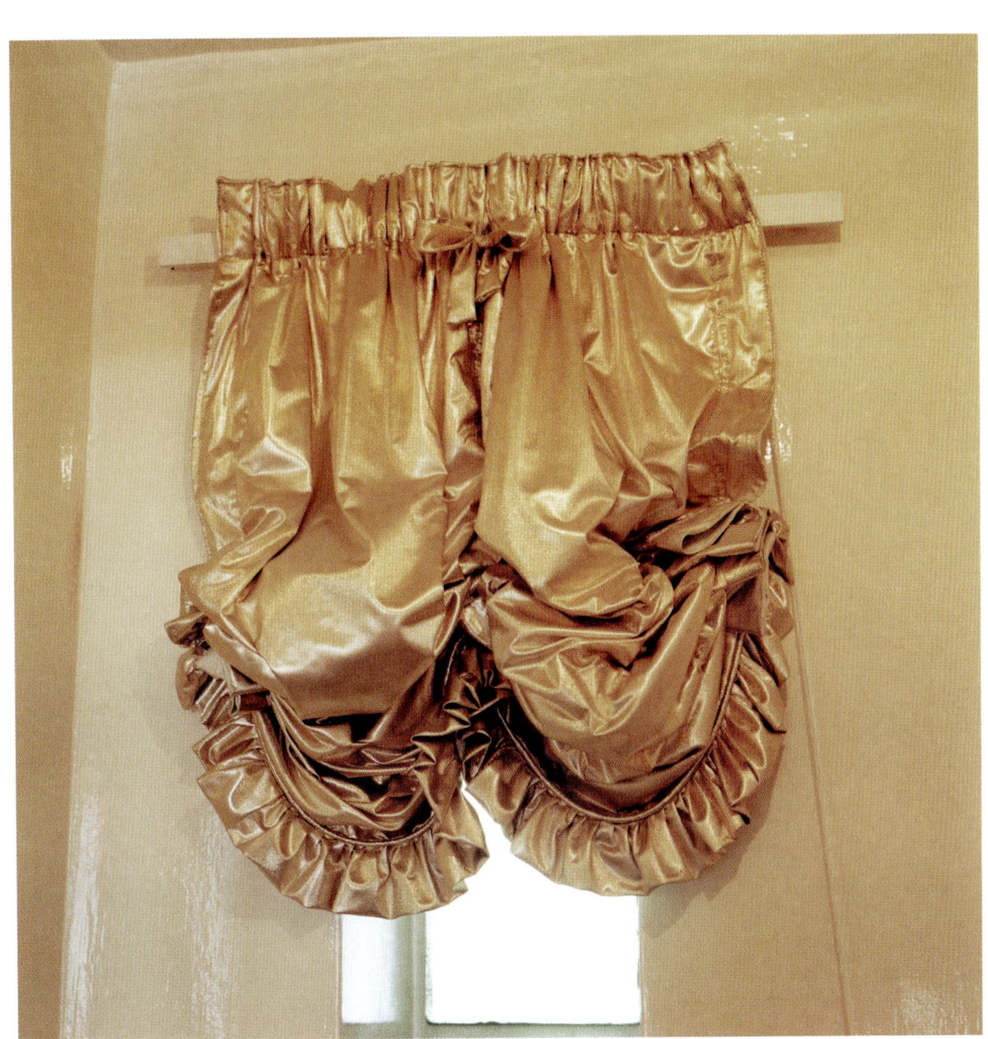

72. Small World

In 1992, I had an exhibition of my ongoing project on tourism, *Small World*, at the Centre National de la Photographie in Paris. One of the guests was Henri Cartier-Bresson, still alive at that time, of course. Cartier-Bresson was probably the most famous photographer in the world, and a founder of Magnum in 1947. He was so annoyed by the exhibition that when he got home he sent me a fax – this was in the days of the fax – saying: 'I don't see your viewpoint. Your work is from a different planet. We belong to two different solar systems.' I thought, oh, this is fantastic. I replied: 'I acknowledge there is a large gap between your celebration of life and my implied criticism of it . . . What I would query with you is, "Why shoot the messenger?"' He was photographing the old style of life; I was photographing modern things. He was shocked that I'd taken these pictures that seemed like a critique of society. Then Martine Franck, Cartier-Bresson's wife, decided to try to wave the white flag. She invited me to lunch at their apartment on Rue de Rivoli. And we got on fine. We recovered from our spat. But that little spat has become quite famous.

This happened when I was an associate member of Magnum. Cartier-Bresson was very against me becoming a full member. He'd retired his membership, so he couldn't vote, but he could be vocal. The debates in Magnum I was not party to, but people would tell me about the arguments. Fierce arguments. They obviously thought I was being a sneering, condescending, patronizing, middle-class photographer, photographing the working classes. It hasn't done me any harm, has it? I usually quite relish criticism and opposition. When I realized that people were against me, I thought, I must be doing something right.

FROM *SMALL WORLD*
KLEINE SCHEIDEGG, SWITZERLAND, 1990

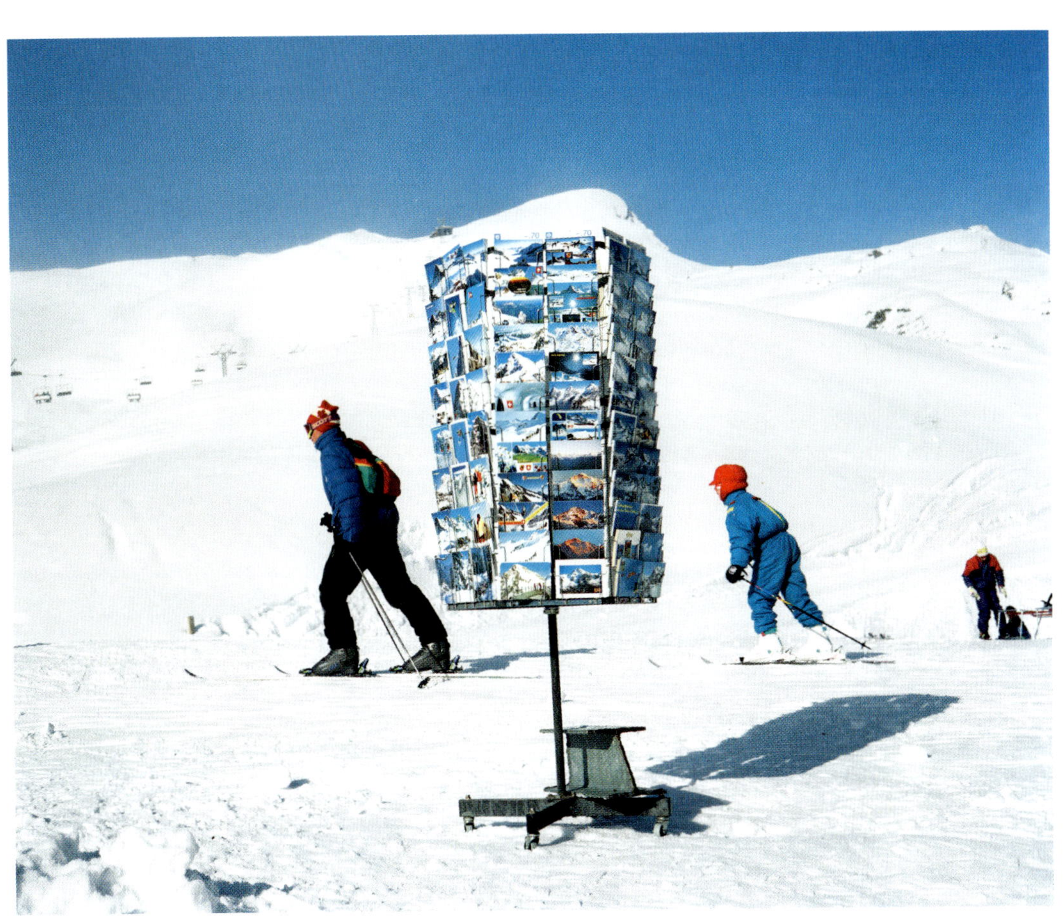

73. McDonald's in Moscow

When the first McDonald's in the USSR opened in Pushkin Square, Moscow, there was a queue of a thousand people trying to get in. I still remember, almost with disbelief, the excitement and thrill of the diners. At the time it was the largest McDonald's in the world, with 600 seats. It was nicknamed 'Bolshoi Mac' and heralded as an amazing advance; because of Gorbachev's glasnost policy, the USSR was letting this icon of America in.

At the time, I was the professor of photography at the University of the Industrial Arts in Helsinki, so I travelled regularly to the Baltics. As there was a direct train from Helsinki to St Petersburg, I'd often have a weekend in St Petersburg, as well as in Moscow.

This was the only time I have been allowed to photograph in a McDonald's. McDonald's don't ever want pictures taken inside, but they were so proud of opening the golden arches in Moscow they actually gave photographers permission. I have often taken pictures in McDonald's without permission. I'll go into a McDonald's and start shooting, someone from the company will throw me out and I'll just move on to another one. Being thrown out by a faintly embarrassed duty manager gives a certain satisfaction.

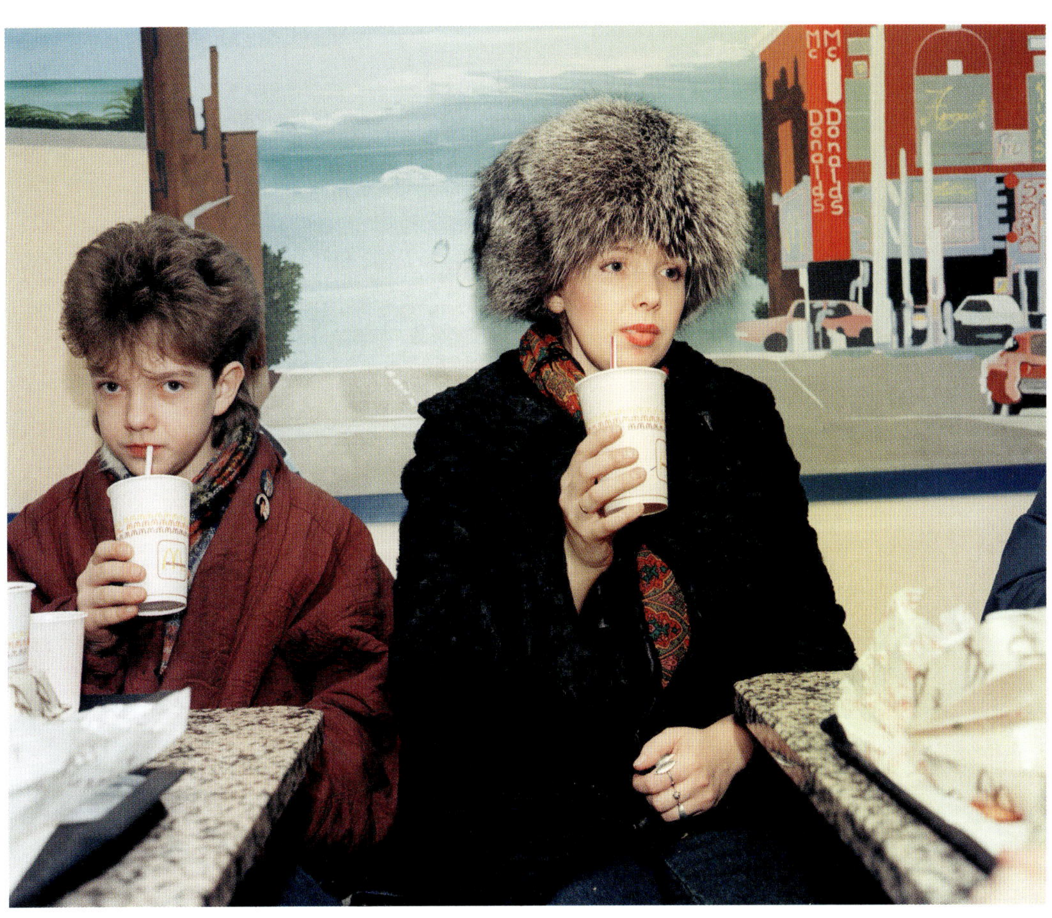

Mc
Mc
Donalds
Donalds

74. Lady on the Till

When I was teaching in Helsinki, I often got the ferry to Tallinn, in Estonia, which was like stepping back in time. Although it had freed itself from Moscow, the country hadn't really changed much since Communism. I would photograph anything and everything, including this supermarket – which wasn't very engaging – where this lady was on the till. It's actually one of my favourite photographs. I love the till roll coming out and the lady's expression. In fact, she looks very beautiful, I would say. I'm struck by how long the till roll is, as there doesn't seem to be anything in the shop to buy, but they've obviously done quite a lot of sales. The figures in the background are slightly murky and slightly ominous.

Nearly thirty years later, in 2019, I was asked to do an exhibition in Tallinn of the images I took back in the 1990s. Tallinn now is like any other Western city – it's modern, it's wealthy, they've got all the brands. It's gone from being a Soviet fossil to the most advanced digital country in the world. Before the exhibition, a journalist at one of the main newspapers said to me, 'We've got good coverage across the whole country, and we're going to see if we can find this lady.' So that's what they did. The newspaper found and re-photographed her holding a print of this picture from 1992, which I had sent her as a gift.

Thirty years makes such a difference. It's always interesting to give people the opportunity to see people they knew, or their society, or even themselves, many years later, when the change is very dramatic. We don't notice change as we live through it. The most interested audience I ever have, for any photographs, is when I show people images of their past.

JELENA ROOP
TALLINN, ESTONIA, 1992

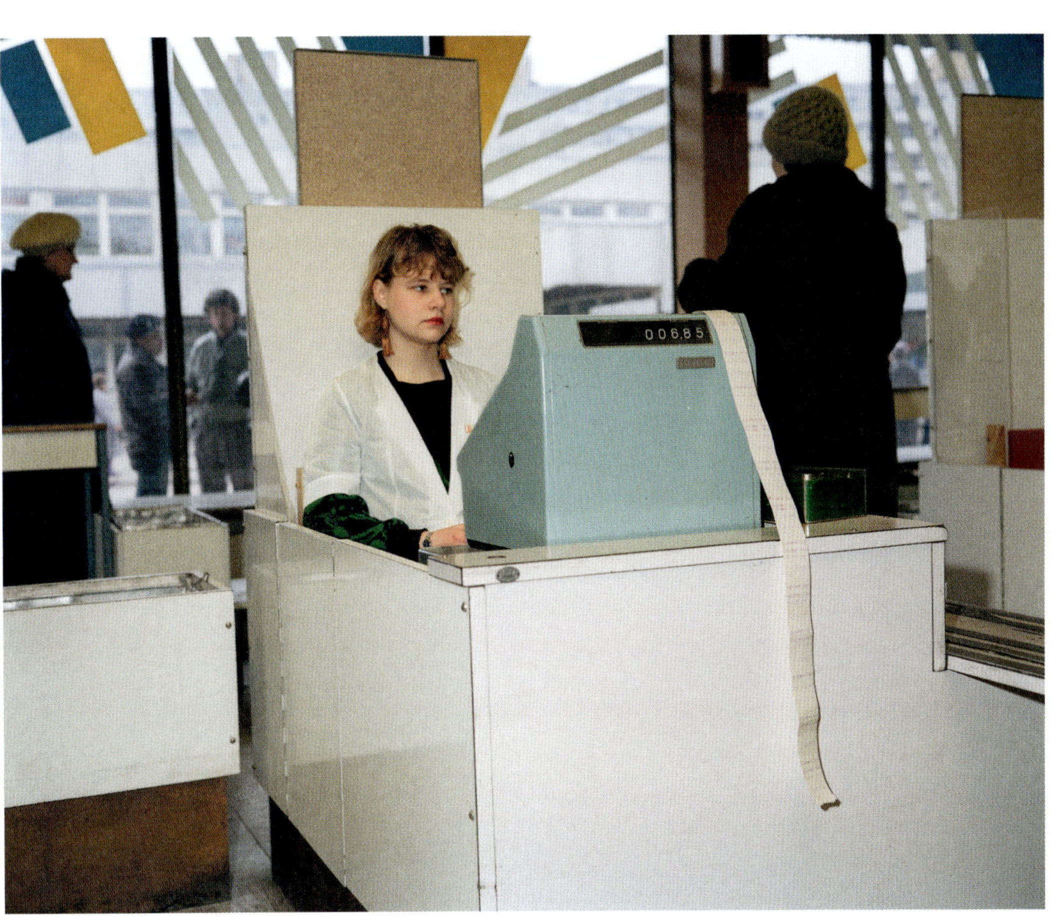

75. An English Village

I started to do a lot of work for the *Telegraph Magazine* in the 90s. It had a very good picture editor called Michael Collins with whom I built up a good relationship. In those days, it was by far the most interesting magazine using photography, although many left-wing people didn't see the images because they wouldn't dream of buying the *Telegraph*.

There was a book from the 1940s by the pioneering British colour photographer, John Hinde, called *Exmoor Village*. Michael and I agreed that I would photograph the same village, and the piece would compare those images with John Hinde's from the 40s. However, this village, Luccombe, was owned by the National Trust and was completely stuck in the past, so Michael said, 'Let's document a village near Bristol over a year.' We drove around and chose Chew Stoke, eight miles south of Bristol. It had a church, a shop, a post office and a vicar – everything you'd expect in an English village. I went to Chew Stoke every couple of weeks through 1992, photographed it extensively and went to all the main events. This is Keith, the vicar. Having Keith's support for the project was important. The lady in her red, white and blue dress looking up to Keith looks quite angelic, whereas the lady in the middle is looking daggers. I like the contrast between the two. The most interesting subject matter I'm ever going to find is people. They are endlessly fascinating.

FROM *CHEW STOKE: A YEAR IN THE LIFE OF AN ENGLISH VILLAGE*
CHEW STOKE, ENGLAND, 1992

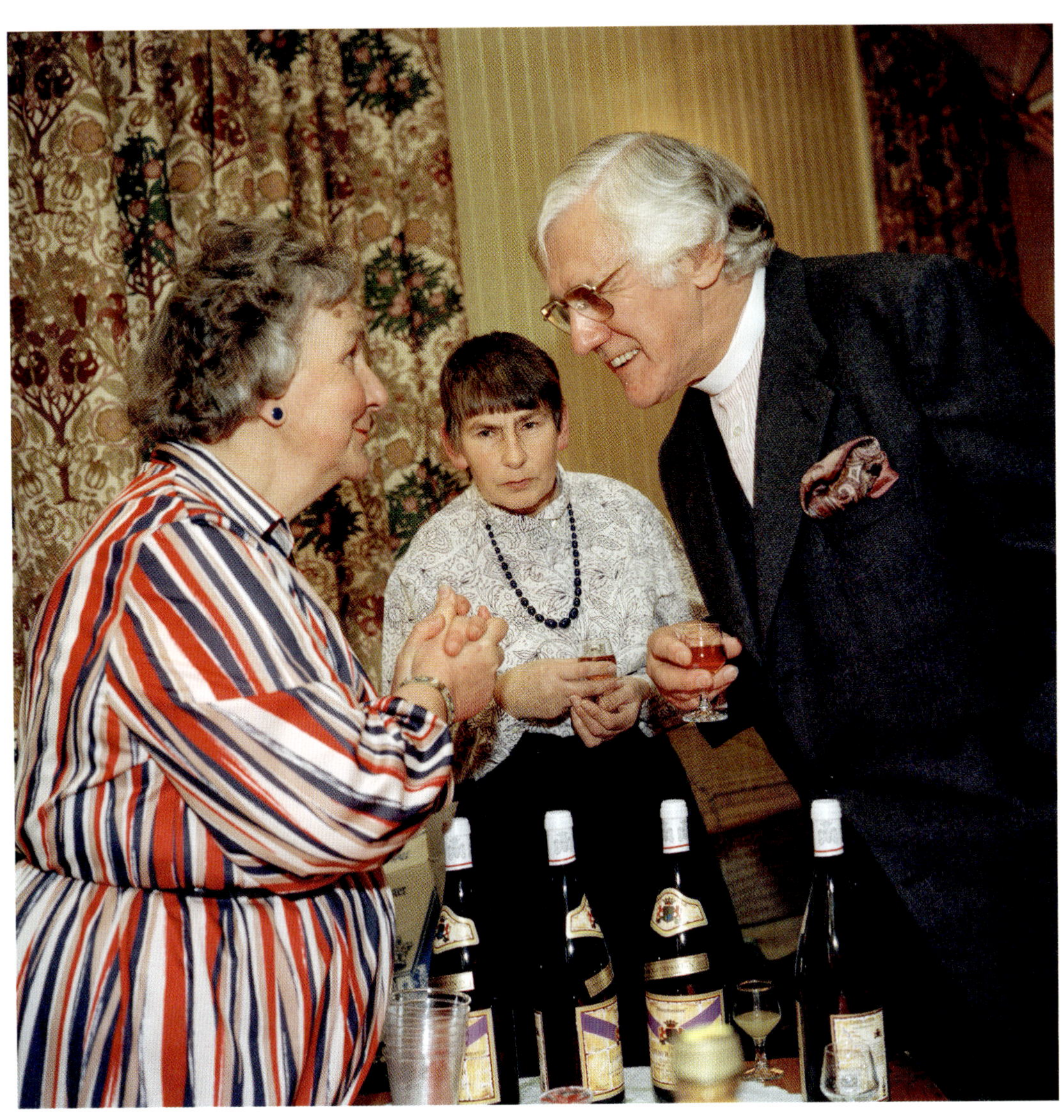

76. Lost Ball

It's called *Lost Ball*. It is what it says on the packet. What can I say? It's a cricket game in Chew Stoke, the ball's gone into the hedge and they're trying to find it. That red stuff must be tarpaulin. It's classic to play a cricket match in the summer in Britain, and yet things can go very badly wrong. It's not a professional match. Everybody's mucking in to try and find the ball so the game can continue.

FROM *CHEW STOKE: A YEAR IN THE LIFE OF AN ENGLISH VILLAGE*
CHEW STOKE, ENGLAND, 1992

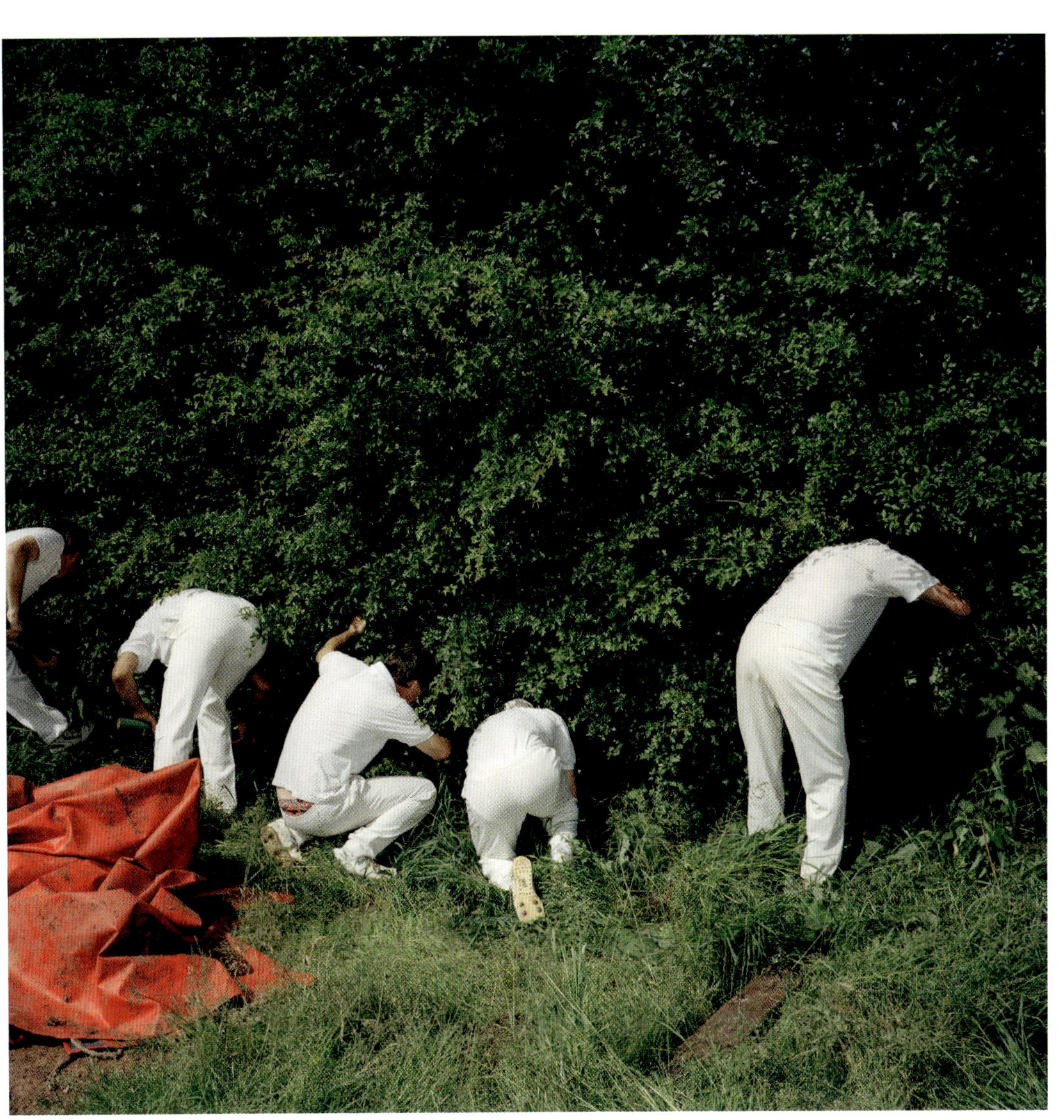

77. Home-Made Lemon Curd

This is the highly competitive world of home-made lemon curd.

FROM *CHEW STOKE: A YEAR IN THE LIFE OF AN ENGLISH VILLAGE*
CHEW STOKE, ENGLAND, 1992

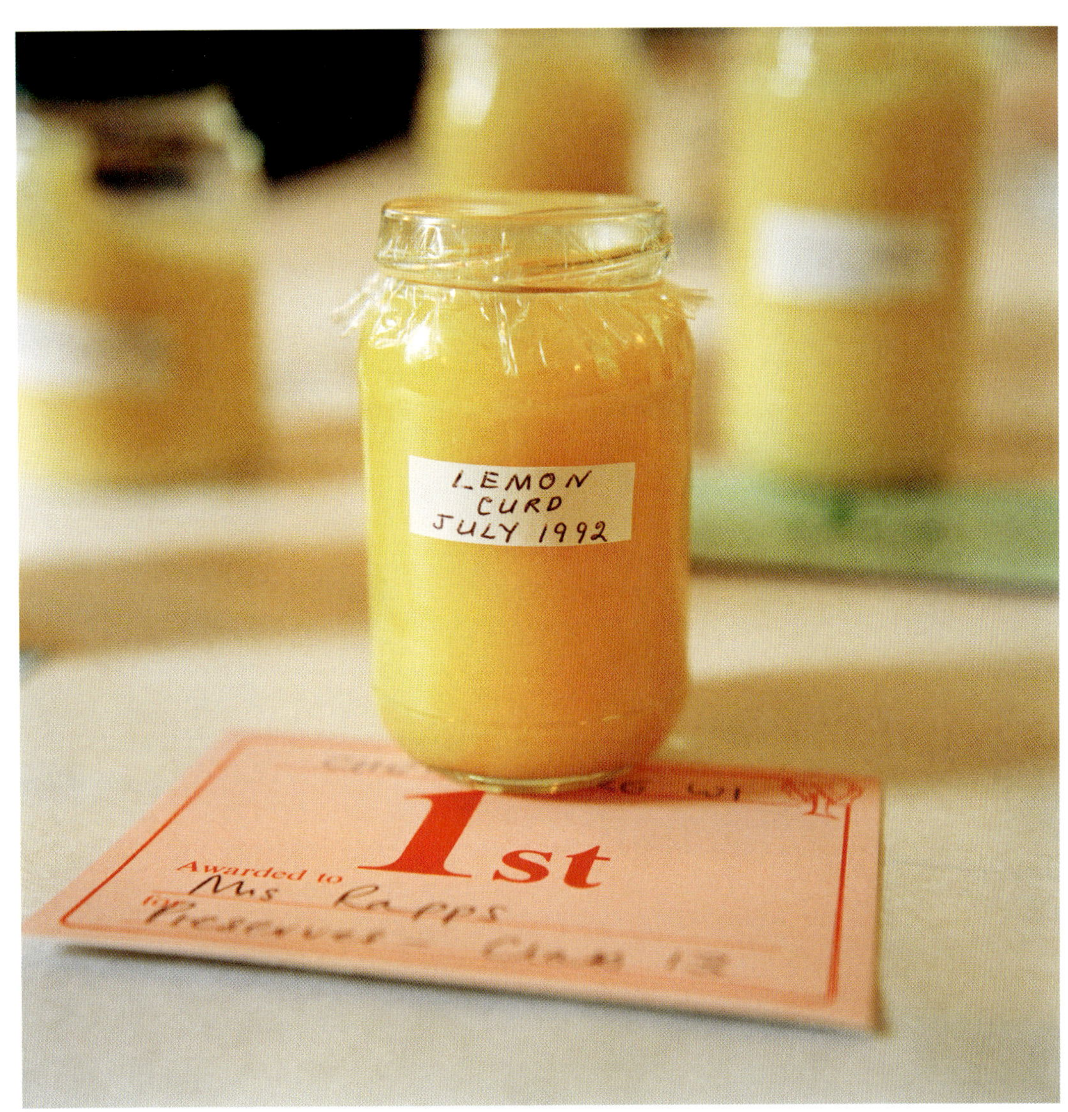
LEMON
CURD
JULY 1992
1st
Awarded to Mrs Rapps
for Preserves - Class 13

78. Day Trip

By default, I am a travel photographer. I continually work on a combination of commissions and personal projects in many countries. In 1993, I flew around the world for *Small World*, my long-running project on mass tourism, which continues to this day. Tourism is one of the biggest industries in the world, and the thing about tourism is that the reality of a place is often quite different from the mythology of it.

At Kuta, a tourist resort in Bali, local people were advertising their services, such as massages and ear cleaning. There was also an advert for a day trip on a minibus to a traditional funeral in a Balinese village. That was something I never thought I'd see: actually inviting tourists to come along and photograph a funeral. The tourists paid the enterprising tour operator – I don't know if the family got money as well – and no one said why they were going. The answer was probably: just out of curiosity. The funeral had a dance, a parade and fireworks, before the coffin was put into the grave. The atmosphere felt more like a carnival. It was a very interesting example of tourism that is in slightly bad taste: fifteen people, including me, showed up to photograph the funeral of someone's family member, and took pictures of the coffin. It's a symbolic photo in terms of the impact of tourism, and how tourism infiltrates even the most private spaces and events. Tourism wins over ritual. The ritual itself becomes monetized.

Part of the cultural history of photography is that people think a loved one's funeral is a private event not to be photographed. There's a great tradition of photographing at weddings, but not at funerals. I have taken pictures at funerals. I photographed my mother's funeral, but that's not surprising. I thought it was worth recording.

FUNERAL
FROM *SMALL WORLD*
BALI, INDONESIA, 1993

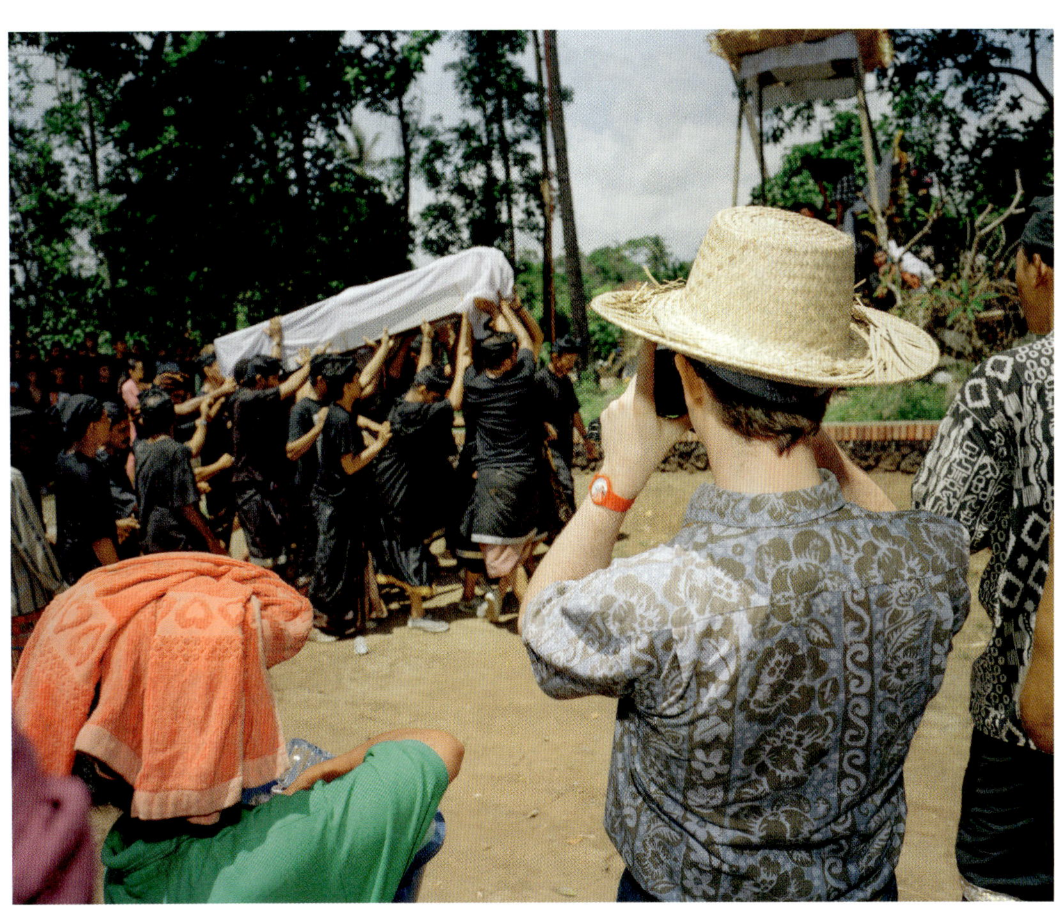

79. Miners

Nearly a decade after the 1984 Miners' Strike, the *Telegraph Magazine* commissioned me to take photos at Tower Colliery in the Cynon Valley, South Wales. I went down a 160-metre shaft in a lift to photograph the miners working. The tunnel wasn't big enough to stand up in in places, and it was hot. Crouching for an eight-hour shift was totally exhausting. I mean, talk about hard work – but the miners were used to it, I guess. And when they came up, they showered.

I went into the shower room, too, but before I could shoot even one picture, I had to wait ten minutes for my camera to warm up. The picture is slightly blurred because the camera was cold compared to the heat of the shower room; there's a hint of condensation on the lens. You can imagine the jokes and rapport that you get in a scenario like this. I was photographing them naked. The miners thought it was absolutely hilarious at first. In a situation like that you have to wait for them to get over it. There was this great system of one miner washing the next miner's back. It took a long time for them to scrub all that grime off. Look at the chap on the right: his head and face are completely covered in coal dust. He's absolutely filthy. It was very hot in the mine, so they wore T-shirts and shorts, which is why the guy in the middle's legs are so dirty. It was an invigorating experience seeing first-hand their camaraderie and friendship, and how hard their work was. My respect grew for what the miners did.

I was a big supporter of the 1984–5 Miners' Strike. During the strike, most mines created their own ceramic plate which they sold to raise money for the strike fund. They also made enamel badges. There are people who collect them very determinedly. People like me.

PLATE FROM 1984/85
MINERS STRIKE (ABOVE)

TOWER COLLIERY
WALES, 1993

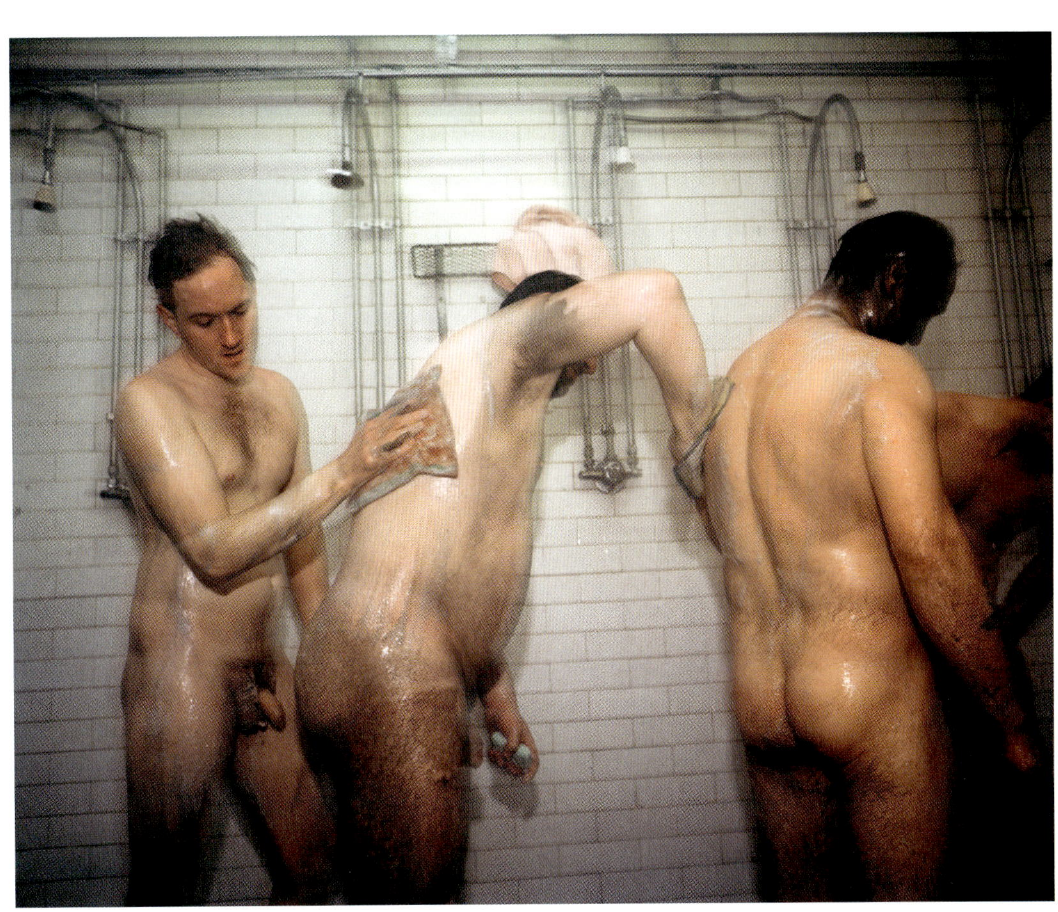

80. Mosney Camp

July 12th is the biggest day in the Protestant calendar in Northern Ireland, because it celebrates the Battle of the Boyne in 1690. And it is quite scary. There are marches with drums, and hundreds of bonfires are lit the night before to burn effigies of the Pope. It's sort of military. You can see why Catholics in Northern Ireland would want to get away: it feels quite sinister. They used to escape to the Republic of Ireland to go on holiday. One of the places they went in the Republic was the Butlin's Holiday Camp in Mosney. In 1994, I went especially to Mosney to photograph the holiday camp in full swing.

I don't know how or why the people are cooped up behind this fence. Why are they all crowded together in that corner? They look like they're in a zoo. It's certainly prison-like, isn't it? That little girl's got her tongue out. It looks like she's licking the fence.

I'm constantly trying to create stories out of images, stories that make you feel something.

BUTLIN'S MOSNEY
COUNTY MEATH, IRELAND, 1994

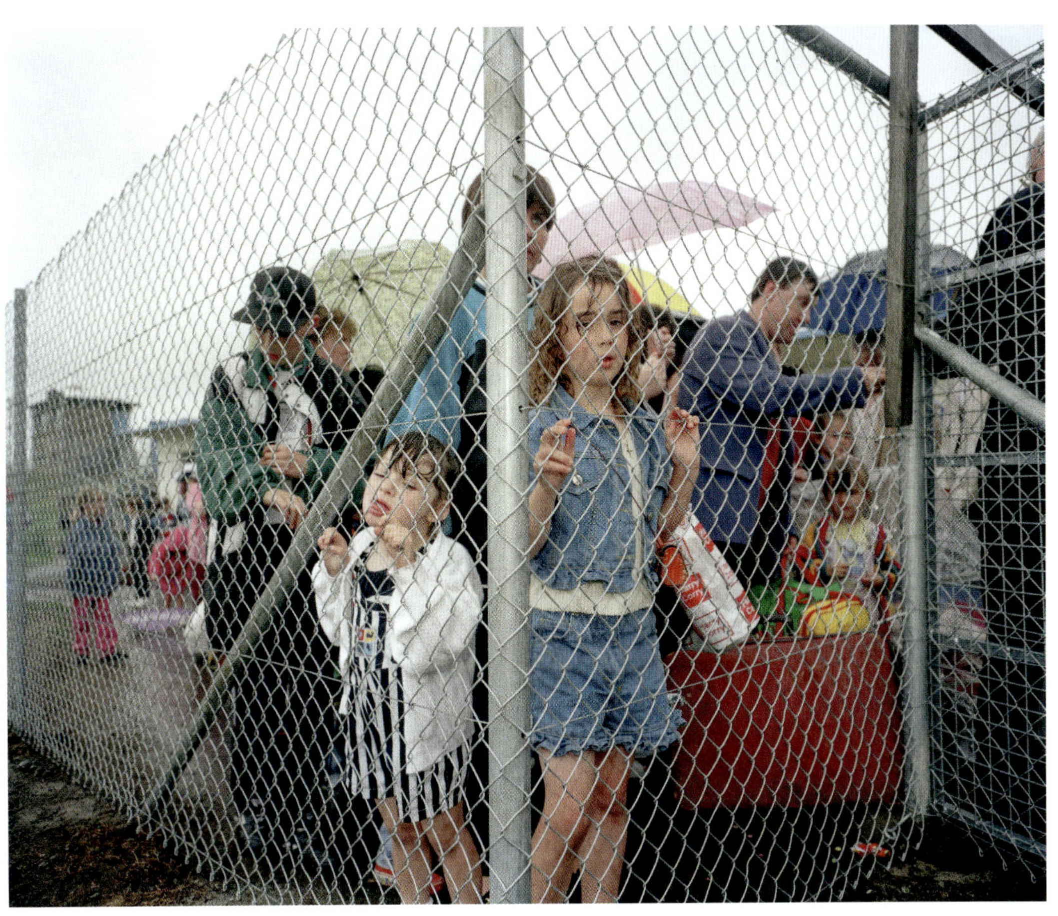

81. From A to B

In 1994, I was photographing cars and drivers for another TV project with Nicholas Barker called *From A to B* about British people's choice of car. At the time, women drivers were becoming more prominent, and more women were buying cars. I was waiting for the right moment to take this photo, and her hand resting there makes it work. The caption was: 'I feel that other women on the road react to me in a nasty hostile sort of way. For some reason this hate comes across. I mean, I give way to them so why don't they give way to me?'

I was still an associate member of Magnum and had applied to be a full member. They held the vote in London. I was in Bristol. I needed 50 per cent of members' votes to get in. The president, Peter Marlow, phoned me mid-morning on the day of the vote and said, 'Good news, Martin, you've become a member.' I thought, Well, that's great. An hour later, Peter phoned to say, 'I'm sorry, you're no longer a member because someone has just come to the meeting and voted against you. The vote was so close that you're out.' Two hours later, some of the members went and got the American photographer, Burt Glinn, who had food poisoning and had been in hospital, wheeled him into the meeting, and he voted for me. Finally, I became a member. I'm the only photographer to have become a member of Magnum twice. I went on to be president of Magnum from 2013 to 2017.

FROM *FROM A TO B*
ENGLAND, 1994

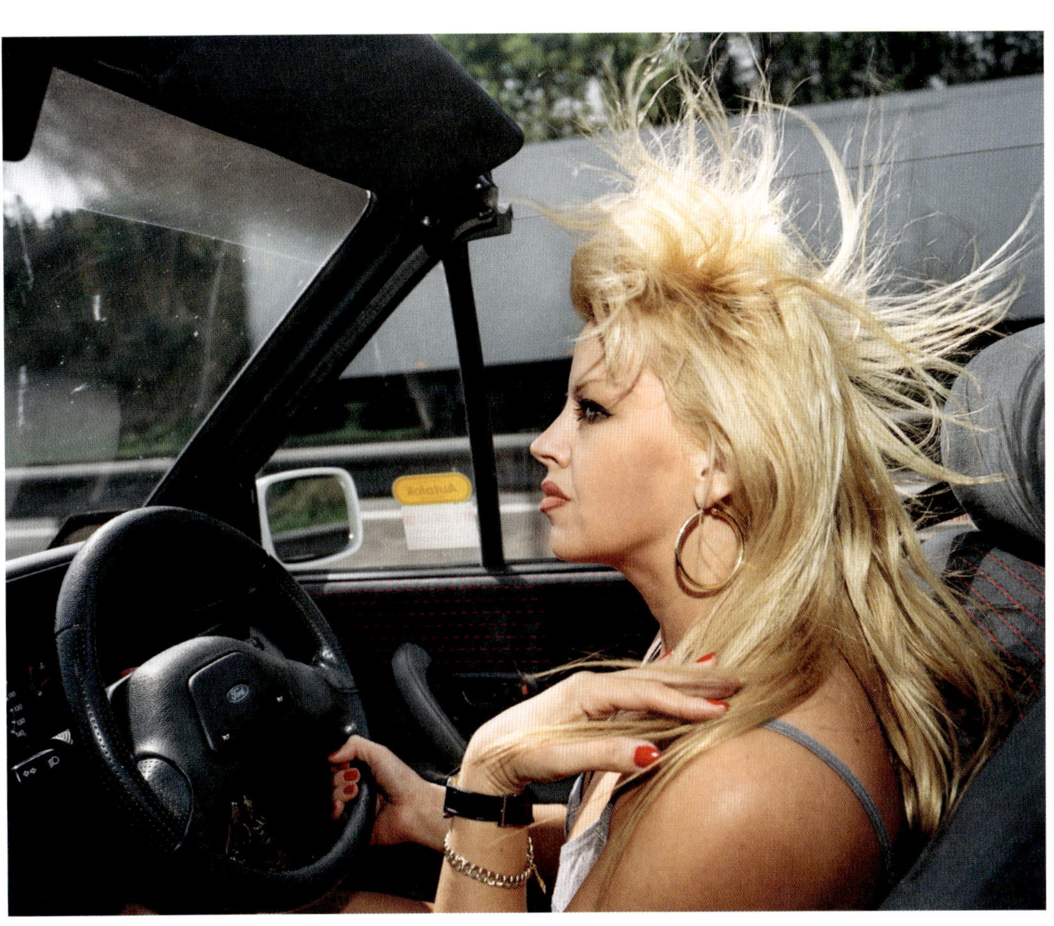

82. Junk Food

Food says a lot about who we are and what we're doing. When I started photographing food back in the late 90s, no one photographed food, but now – particularly if people go to a posh restaurant – everyone takes pictures of every course on their phones. It's part of the ritual of having a posh meal. I don't think that's my influence; it's just that people, when they see beautiful food presented on a plate, want to take a photo of it.

Junk food makes better pictures than posh food. Junk food has bright colours and is a lot more graphic on the plate and in the frame. If the food looks posh, it doesn't look interesting, because it is too reminiscent of the photos we see in magazines where the food is perfect. That's food porn: nice food, beautifully styled and photographed. Stylists paint it and polish it and shine it to make it look even more delicious. A lot of my photographs are really subverting the idea of food porn.

FROM *COMMON SENSE*
RAMSGATE, ENGLAND, 1996

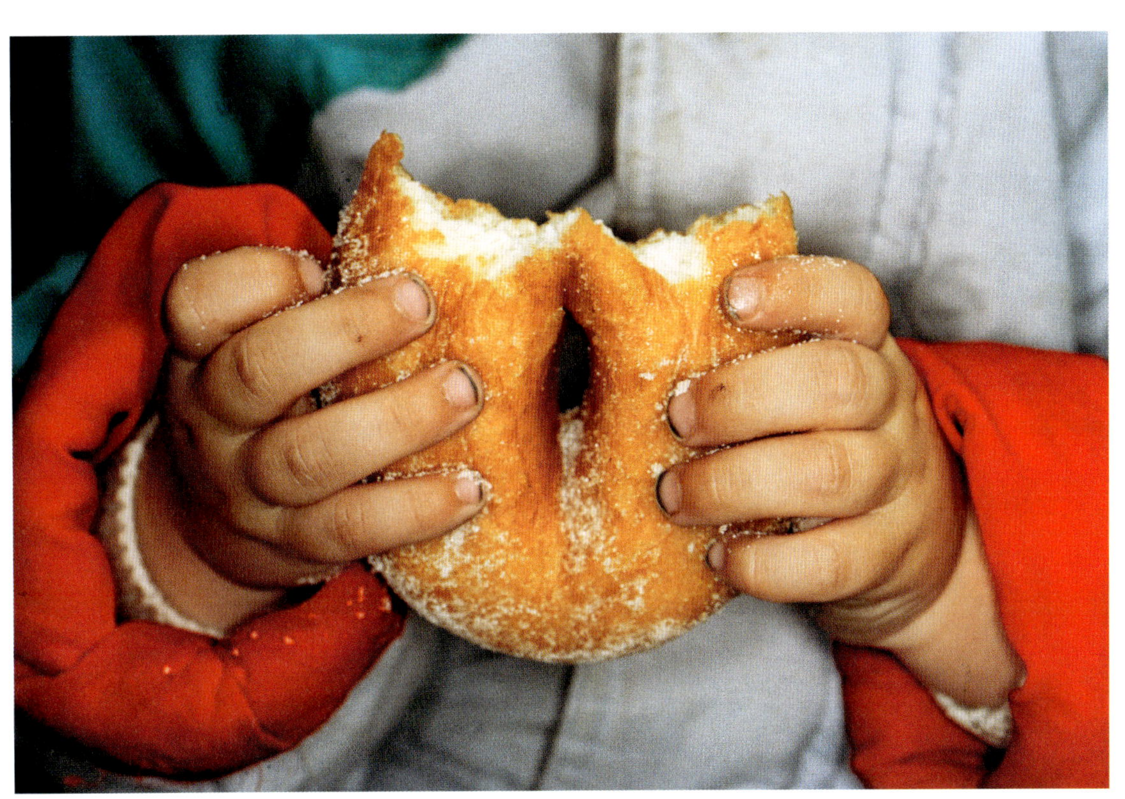

83. Think of England

The best picture is the one that surprises you. The toe is the key element in this photo. I very carefully placed the toe in that gap of the people behind. Sometimes the positioning of a detail like this really can make or break a photograph. I like the radio on the right-hand side, too. I like the woman holding the lilo, maybe she's coming out of the sea. It looks cold in the sea. Well, it's the English seaside, isn't it? But I guess it's warm enough for people to go swimming. And it's a shingle beach, which also isn't ideal.

For four years, I went around shooting pictures for my *Think of England* project, experimenting with the idea of Englishness and looking for English clichés. I spent a lot of time going to agricultural shows, fashion shows, horse racing and the seaside, of course.

FROM *THINK OF ENGLAND*
EASTBOURNE, ENGLAND, 1995–9

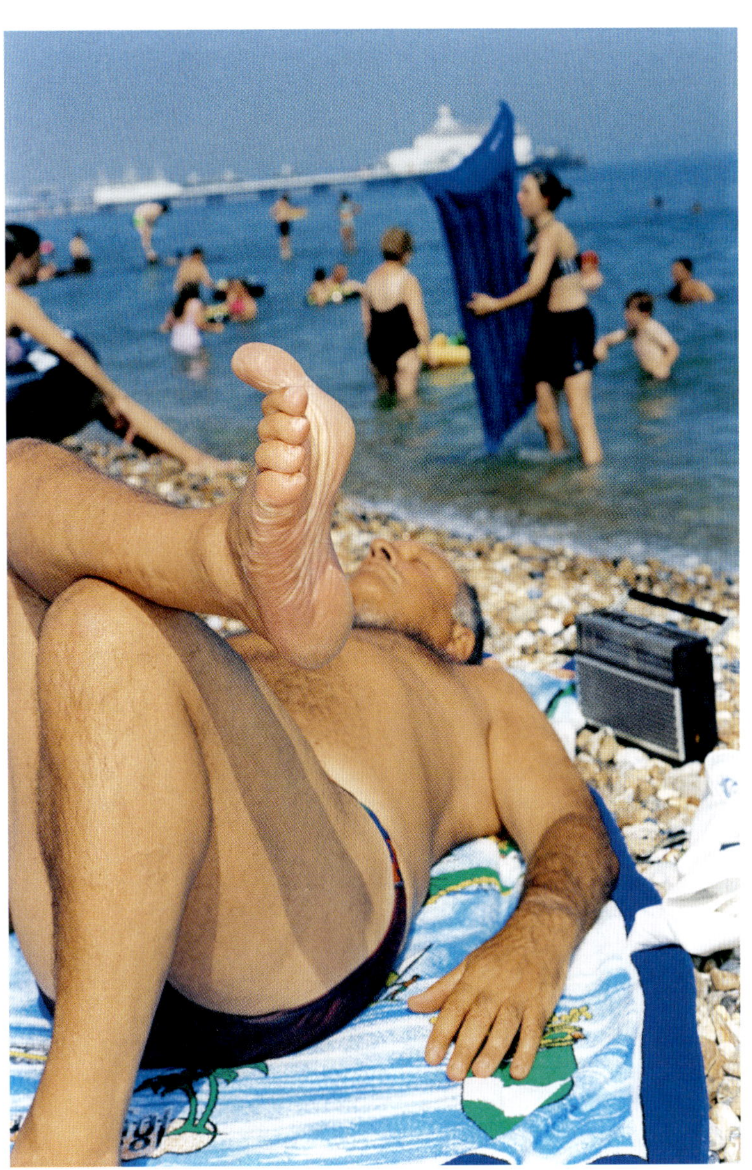

84. Pyongyang

I've always been fascinated by North Korea. Finally, in 1997, I saw an advertisement in *The Times* for a trip that was leaving from Beijing and going to North Korea. I applied and said I was a lecturer – which I was; it wasn't a lie – and they gave me a visa. We were a coachload of twenty people driven around all the propaganda sites, which were like film sets. There were no cars anywhere. We knew that there was a lot of starvation in North Korea, but we didn't see evidence of that. Still, it felt poor.

We were very controlled the whole time, in what we did, where we went, and we had to have an interpreter or a guide with us constantly, so we were very limited. They were okay with me having quite a big camera. They must have realized I was a photographer, but they didn't stop me from photographing anything, because it was all so curated you could only take pleasant photographs, really. It was propaganda of the first order. Occasionally, like here, I had an opportunity to sneak an uncurated picture through the coach window.

North Korea was the most surreal experience of my whole life.

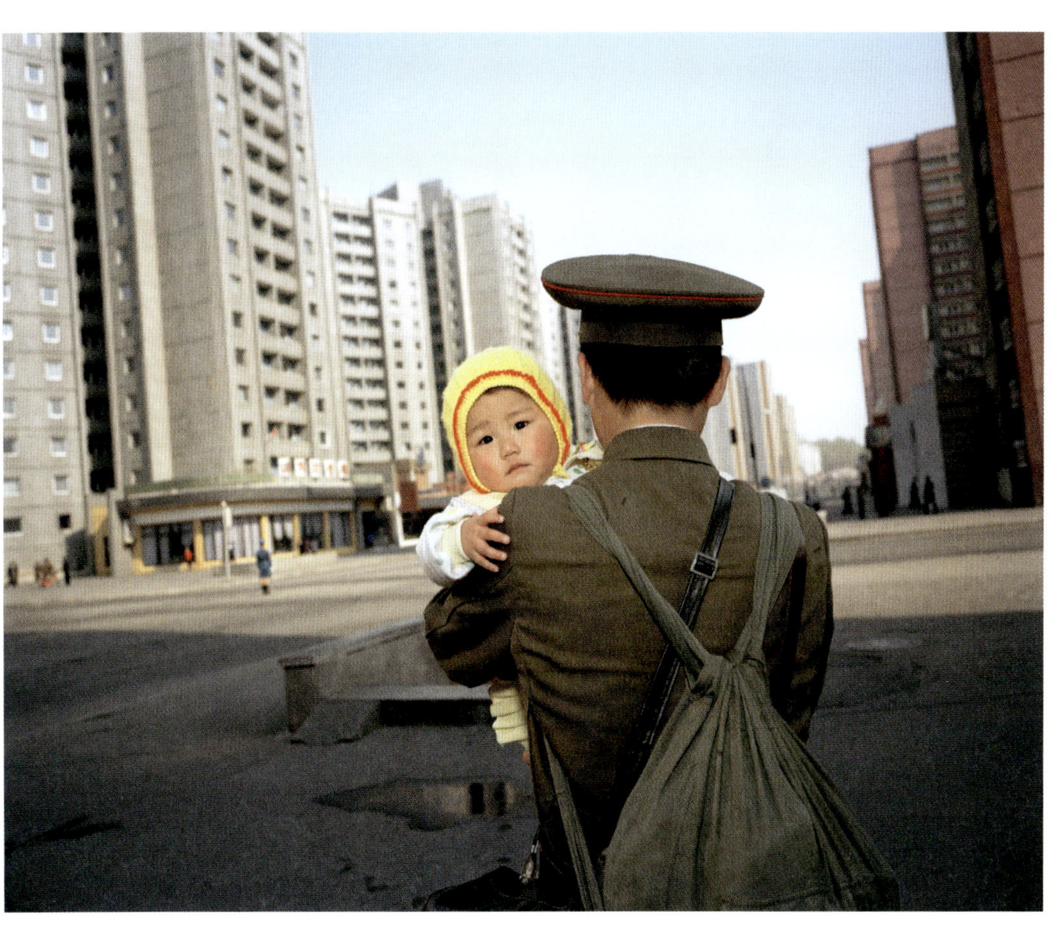

85. Mass Games

My trip to North Korea overlapped with one of their mass games. Here we are in the May Stadium in Pyongyang, the biggest stadium in the world, looking at the mass games, which involve thousands upon thousands of people performing gymnastics and acrobatics. The number of people there – it was just staggering. These mass games were probably the most exciting, exhilarating and unusual and amazing thing I've ever seen.

The spectators in the background have created a picture by holding up cards. The picture changed as the people put different cards up. It must be terrifying to do in case you got it wrong. Execution. Probably.

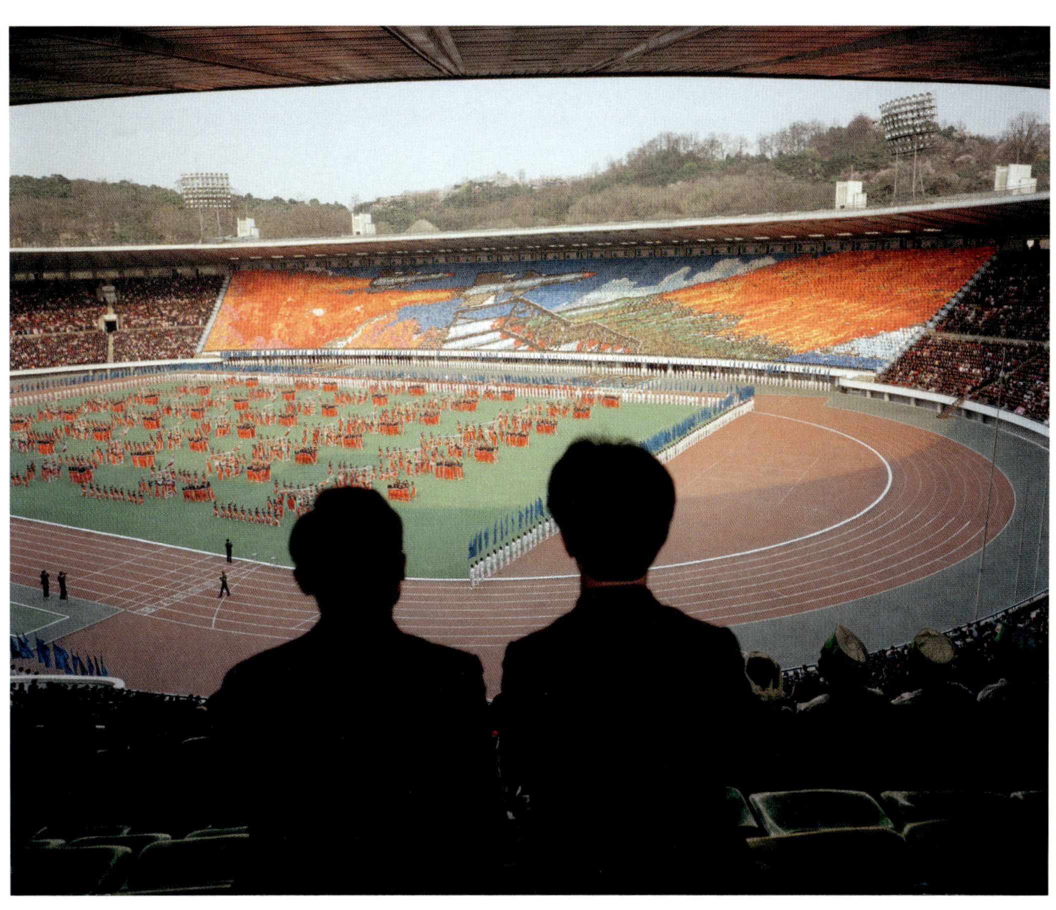

86. Common Sense

From 1995, I started shooting imagery that represented global clichés and everyday excess, highlighting everything from tacky clothes and jewellery to different kinds of junk food, like doughnuts and burgers. Rather than my previous approach of trying to show the whole scene, these photos came in very close and very tight, looking at details of life. They were very garish and over the top; they hurt slightly. The images were taken in Japan, Europe, America – every continent.

By 1999, I had a good selection of images, and published them as a book, *Common Sense*, with 158 pictures. They had a mixture of beauty and ugliness, and by looking at them all together you got an idea about the world. I was using a series of details to try and create a bigger picture. There was not a word of text in the book, to give absolutely no clues whatsoever as to what the book was about. I very much believe that photography has ambiguity built into it, and I wanted to maintain that ambiguity.

I liked the idea of this very global project being shot – and seen – everywhere, so to accompany the book, a set of laser prints were sent to forty-one different galleries in seventeen countries across the globe. The *Common Sense* exhibition was the largest ever exhibition held by one artist, and I got a *Guinness Book of Records* record for this achievement. This is how the show looked in Rome.

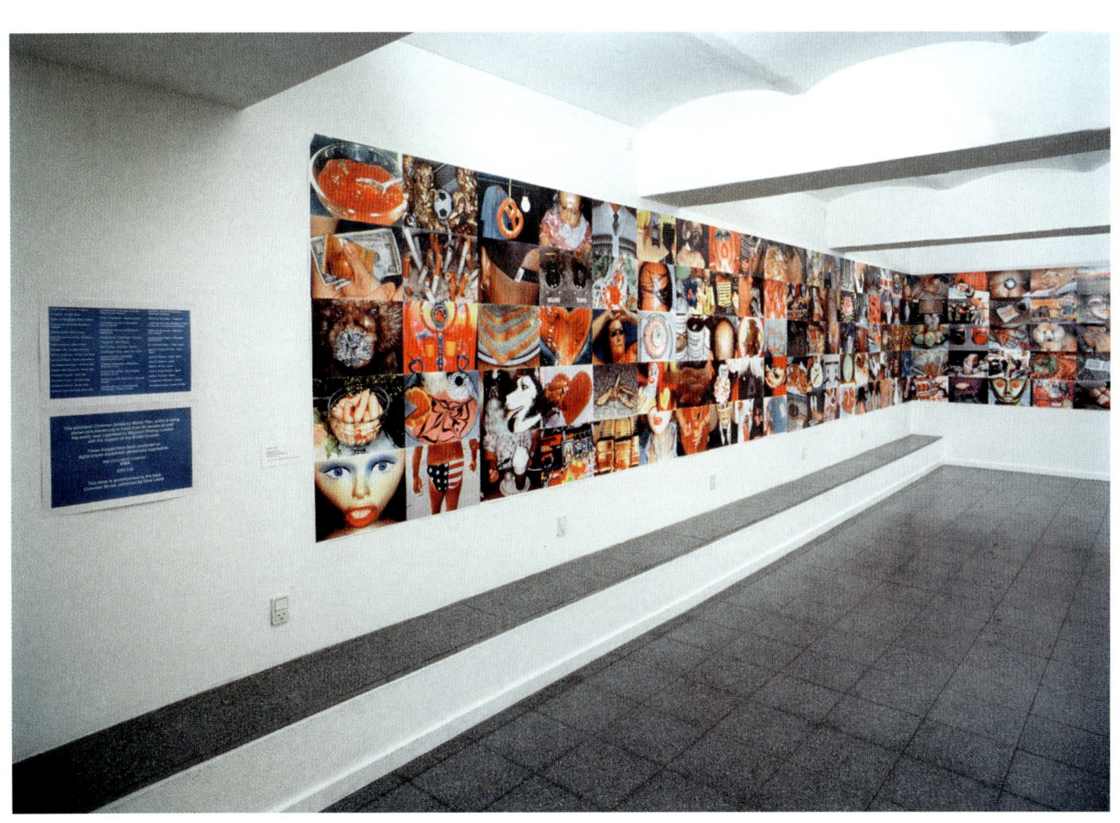

87. A Perfect Cup of Tea

A cup of tea. It could not be more British, could it? I've done many other pictures of cups of tea but this is the best: every component is correct. It's a perfect cup of tea in a perfect Wedgwood cup and saucer on a perfect red gingham tablecloth.

I didn't set this shot up; it was just there. It was taken in a café near Weston-super-Mare that Susie and I used to frequent, called Monk's Rest, on a hill overlooking the sea. Sometimes we'd have poached eggs on toast, and sometimes sardines on toast, and one day someone put this cup of tea on the table and I took a photo of it. It's a simple picture that's become very well known, licensed and used many, many times.

It's very rewarding to take an iconic image. It doesn't happen often. I take so many pictures that aren't iconic that are, basically, not very good. Bad pictures, I guess. I have to take lots of bad pictures to get a good one. I have to be in the right place, at the right time, with the right momentum, then something good may happen. I wake up every day when I'm going out to shoot and think, 'Today, I might take an iconic picture,' but it's unlikely. I have taken millions of photos, and I'm always looking to take an iconic image, one that will survive on its own without context, without the narrative.

FROM COMMON SENSE
SAND BAY, ENGLAND, 1997

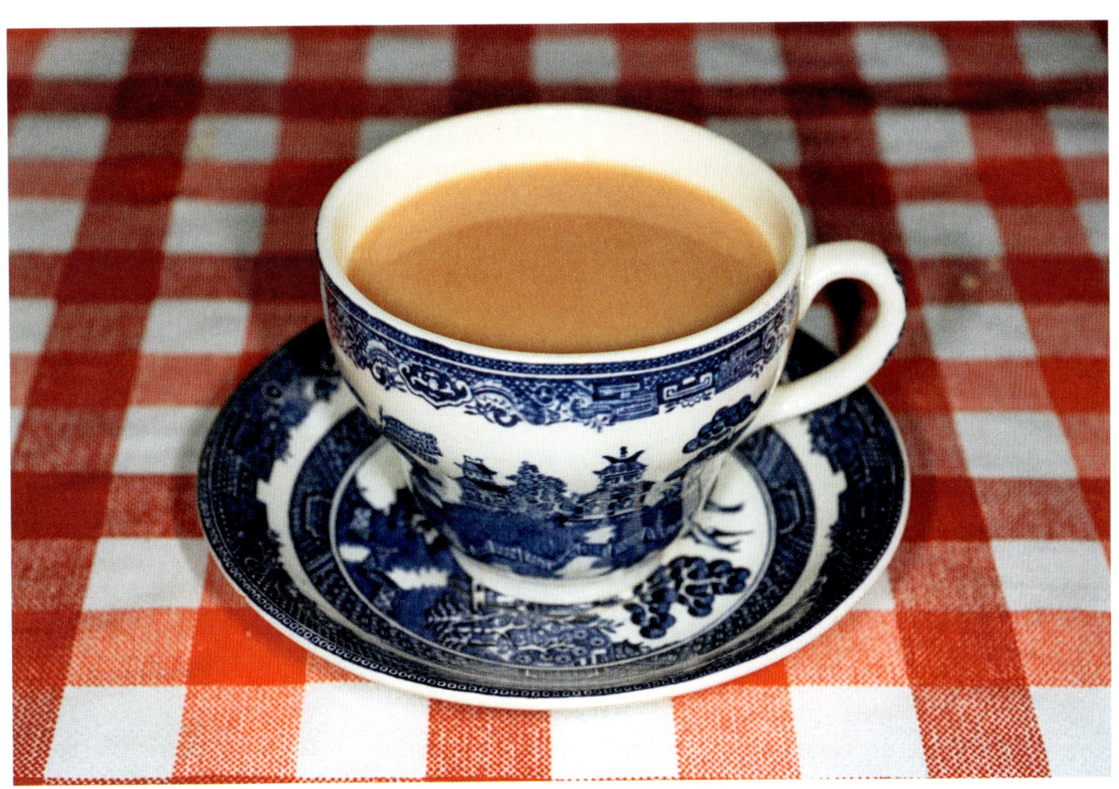

88. Benidorm

I've always used the beach as a creative lab to explore what's possible. I was very excited about going to Benidorm with a macro lens for the first time, because it meant I could take photos at close range. And the scale of the beach in Benidorm is quite amazing. It's huge. It must be three miles long, with three different beaches, and there's this long path by the water where the Spanish go promenading during the day, particularly in the morning. It's quite an event. I call it the motorway.

I took the picture of this woman very quickly. She was fast asleep. Those blue things on her eyes are eye shields. It was one of those rare moments when everything fell into place. I was very close to her. With the combination of the macro lens, the ring flash – a circular light that goes around the lens – and a slow 100 ISO film which lets in more light, I got very saturated colours. I didn't pump the colours up; this is how it looked on the negative. I only took one frame and then moved on. I had a hunch that this would be a good photo, and it is now one of my most famous pictures. I had no idea that it would be one of my iconic images when I took it and that it would live on. I just thought, this is potentially going to be interesting.

I've since had two people write to me and say, 'That's a photo of my grandmother.' They were both trying to get a picture out of me for free. I asked them, 'Where was it taken?' and they both said, 'I can't remember.' They weren't able to prove it was their grandmother. The woman hasn't ever come forward.

FROM *COMMON SENSE*
BENIDORM, SPAIN, 1997

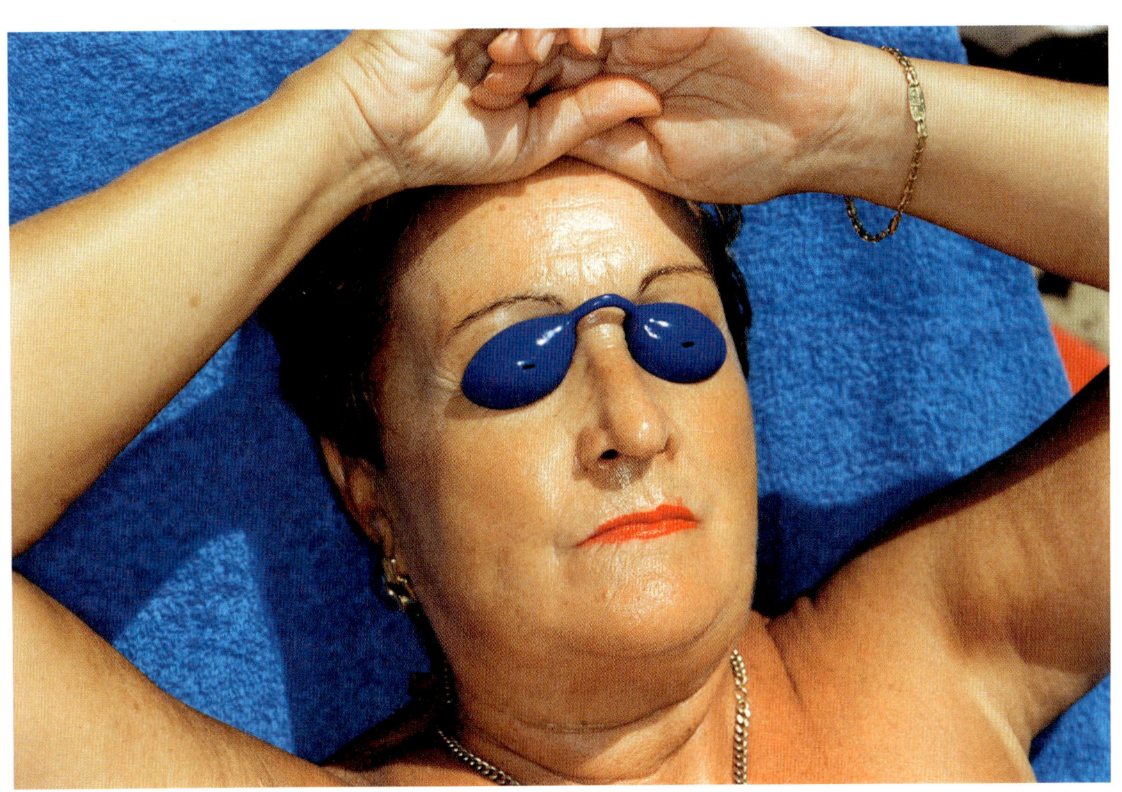

89. Sleeping Commuters

The Japanese are brilliant at sleeping on trains, then waking up just as their stop comes along. In the late 90s, I was going to Japan regularly, to collect Japanese photobooks for *The Photobook: A History*, which I co-authored with Gerry Badger. Japan's a very easy country to photograph in. While I was there I decided to do a project on sleeping commuters. I would go out from seven till nine o'clock in the morning, walking down the trains on the Tokyo metro, and maybe one in three people would be asleep. When people were bowing their heads in sleep, I photographed them from above. If their heads weren't bowed in the right direction, it didn't work. I'd focus on the hair, as you can see here, and the rest of the image fades away and gradually goes out of focus by the time we get to the mouth. The hair has no shadows to it because the photo is taken with a macro camera with a ring flash. I'd only take one picture of a commuter, and if they ever did wake up, I'd be well gone by the time they looked around and wondered what was going on. When I want a photo, I become somewhat fearless, and that helps a lot. Most people in the train in the morning were in their own little worlds. They weren't interested in this huge, lanky Englishman coming along with a camera and a flash gun.

FROM *JAPONAIS ENDORMIS*
TOKYO, JAPAN, 1998

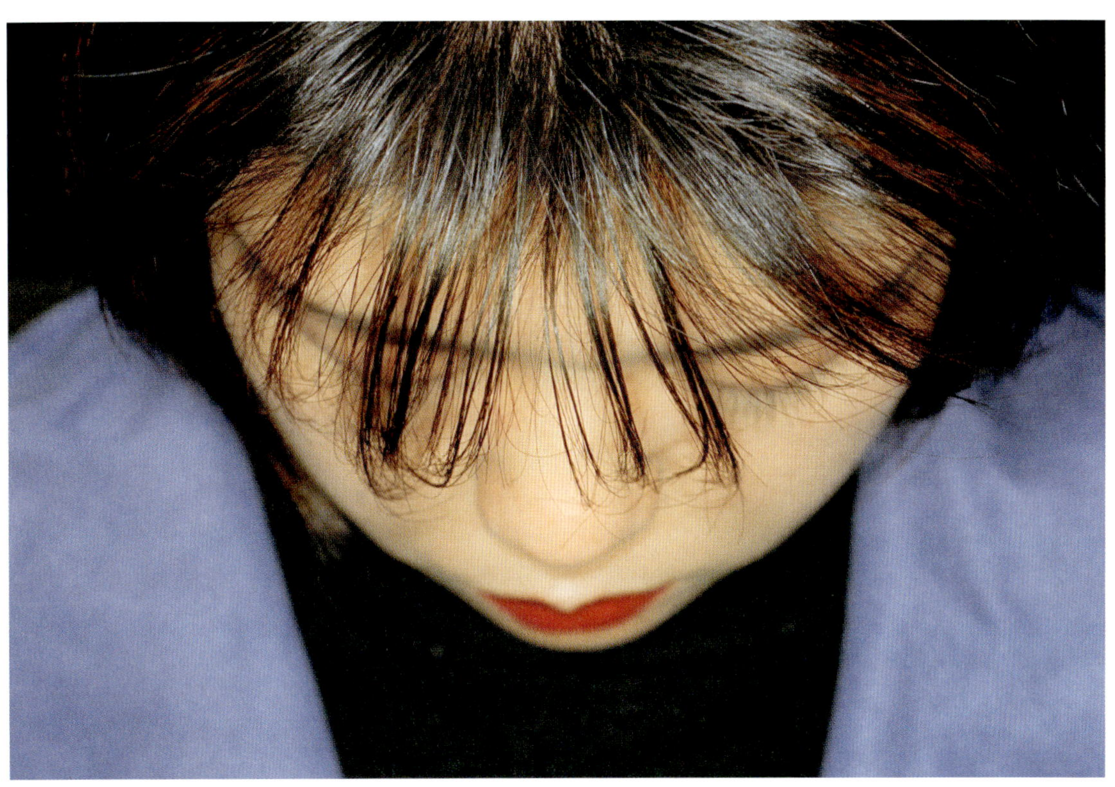

90. First Fashion Shoot

In 1999, I was invited by *Amica*, an Italian magazine, to do some fashion shots on the beach in Rimini. Even though as a student, I had been against commercial photography, when I was asked by *Amica*, I thought, Why not? I'll give it a try. And this was my first fashion shoot.

You've got the two models – the models look really miserable. The guy on the left is not a model, he just showed up and spontaneously did this muscle man pose. You've got the two older ladies in swimming costumes walking through, looking on. They're wondering what on earth's going on. The picture's not quite straight, because pictures don't need to be straight. The slight tilt helps the guy with his arms out to balance the picture. I like the way the models have been incorporated into the beach scene, with real people. This is the photo that really ignited my fashion career.

FASHION SHOOT FOR *AMICA* MAGAZINE
RIMINI, ITALY, 1999

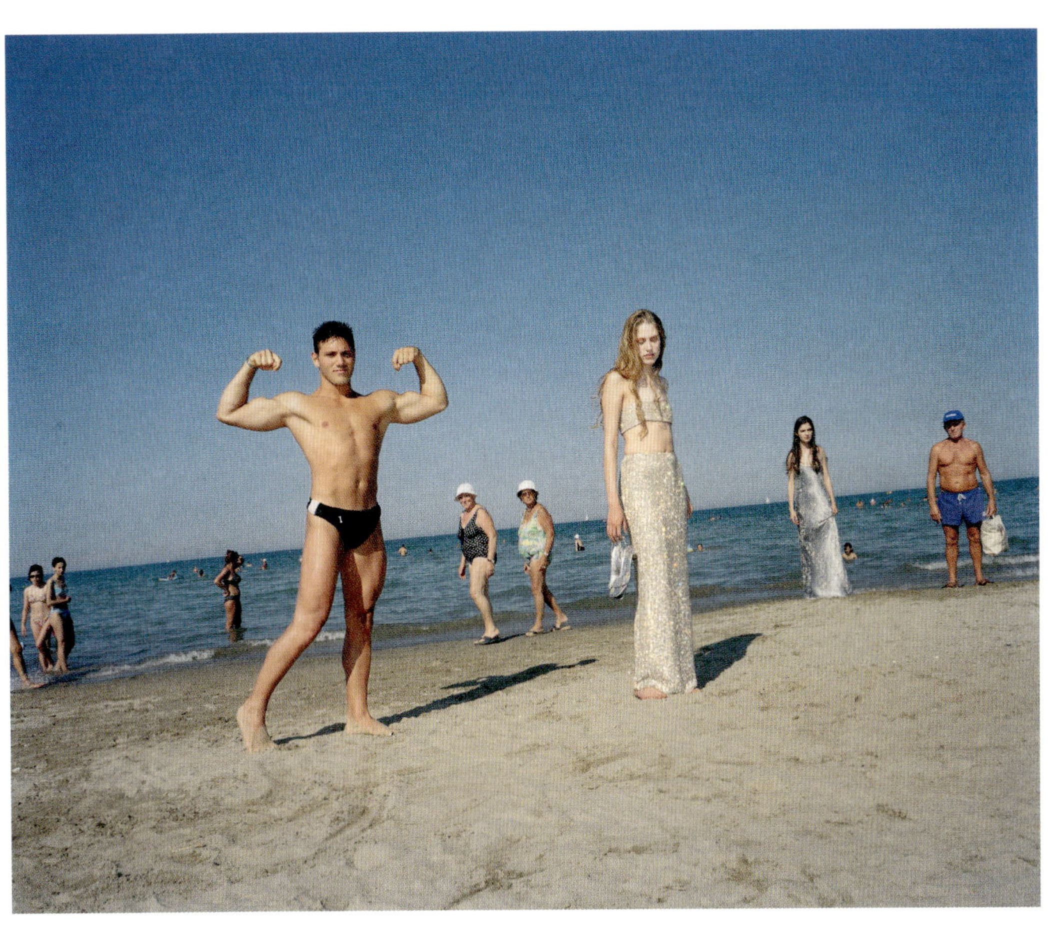

91. Boring Sewage Treatment Facility

I went out for a drive one day in Portland, Oregon – I was there for the opening of an exhibition of my work at the Blue Sky Gallery – and I came across the town of Boring. I thought that was very exciting, so I organized a return trip. I went to Boring, stayed in Boring and photographed everything in Boring. I looked for any notice that had the word 'Boring' in it and took pictures of anything and everything. There's only one set of traffic lights in the town, right in the middle. I photographed those. It has a church, a bank and a sewage treatment facility. What more do you want? It is quite boring in Boring. It's a very dull town. There's nothing much to commend it, apart from having an interesting name.

Sewage treatment works are boring anyway, so the fact that it's officially boring is quite interesting. Someone's got a little bit of a garden going on there. What an effort that is. I doubt whether that garden is maintained still, but it's absolutely at its best here, with pansies, little lilac flowers and primulas. I like the way the writing on the notice stands out because it's been flashed. I took snapshots – small prints of 6x4 inches – of Boring, which I put into albums that held 240 images and called it *Boring Photographs*.

The town must be called Boring because it had some mining history, which would explain how the name came into existence. I don't know if the people in Boring find it funny that their town is called Boring. They must be used to people taking the piss out of them because of the name.

FROM BORING OREGON
OREGON, USA, 2000

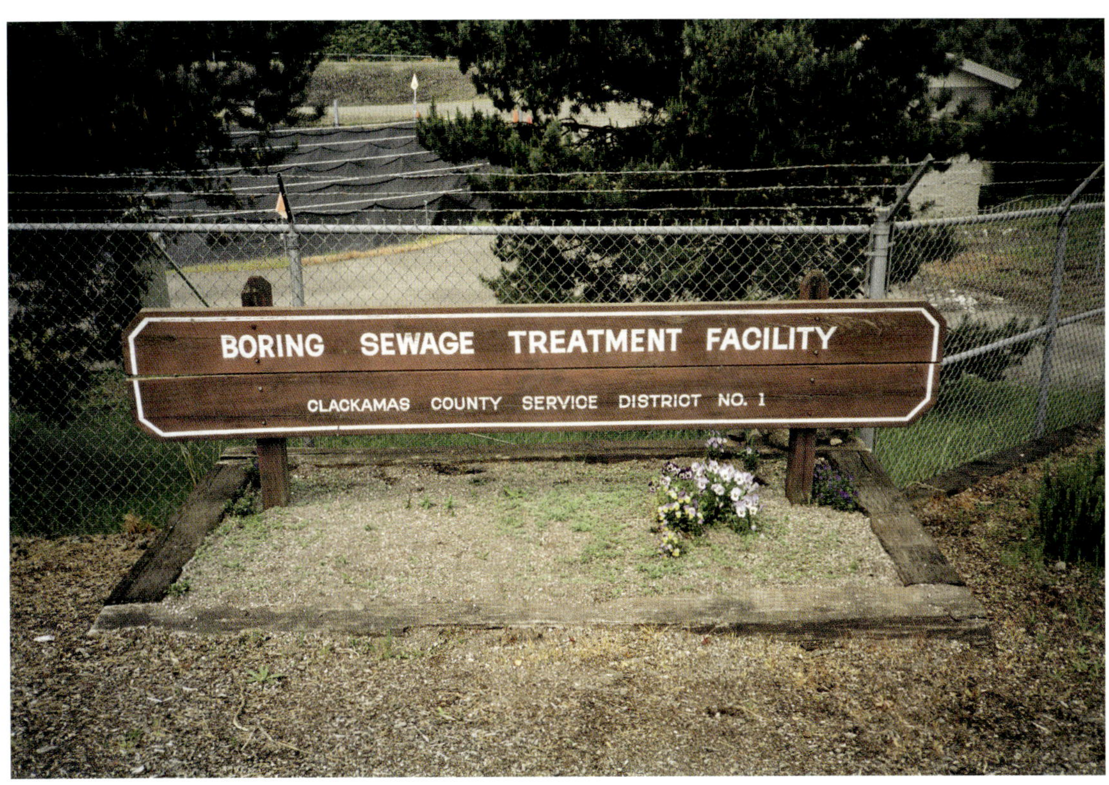

BORING SEWAGE TREATMENT FACILITY
CLACKAMAS COUNTY SERVICE DISTRICT NO. 1

92. Cherry Blossom Time

I went to Tokyo in April 2000, and had in mind to photograph the cherry blossom and the parties the Japanese have underneath it. In fact, that year the cherry blossom was late, so I couldn't photograph it – but what I hadn't realized until I got there was that they have cherry blossom festivals in the shops, too. They do displays of everything from necklaces to the latest electrical gadgets and put fake cherry blossom around them all, so I went about photographing as many of these set-ups as I could possibly find. And, of course, I was delighted when I came across this Spam selection. I assume Japanese people must like Spam, which is processed ham; otherwise, it wouldn't be such a big display.

The photographs became a very beautiful, limited-edition album of twenty pictures called *Cherry Blossom Time in Tokyo* of cherry blossom displays in different stores. The album came in a special hand-made box covered with pink silk – I have a fondness for paying attention to the presentation of my work. Making a beautiful box for what are essentially kitsch photos of completely fake cherry blossom was a kind of joke.

FROM *CHERRY BLOSSOM TIME IN TOKYO*
TOKYO, JAPAN, 2000

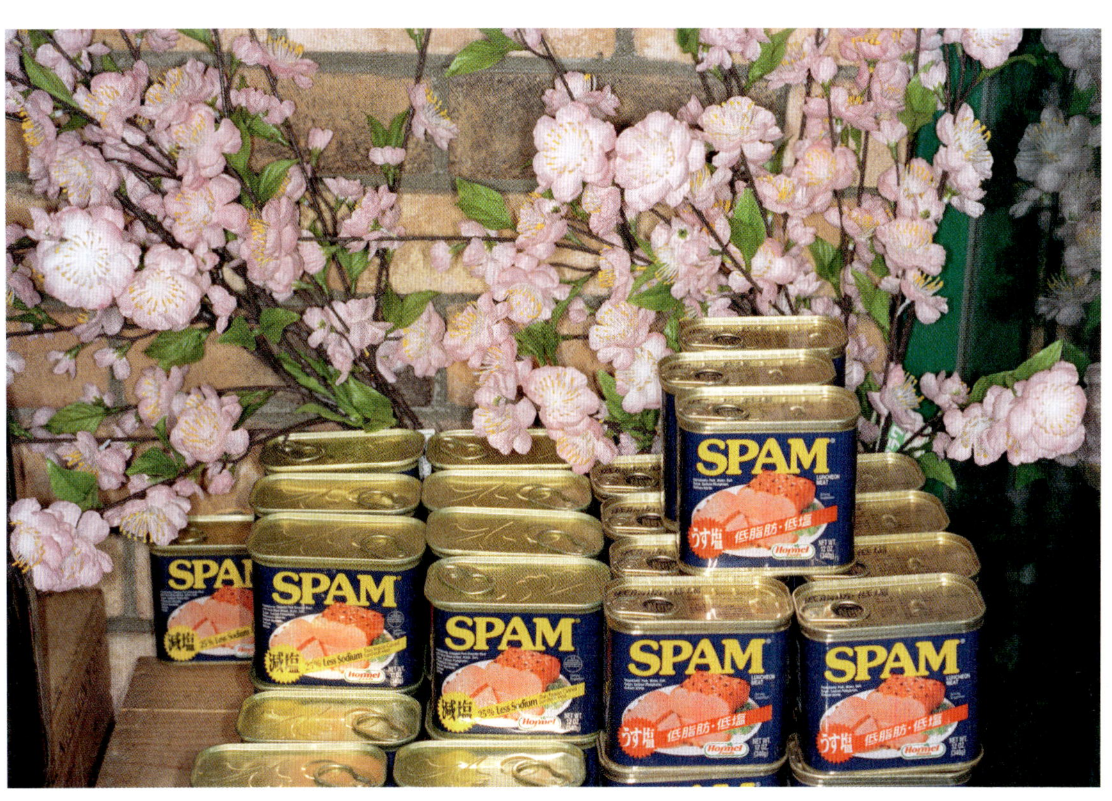
SPAM
減塩 25% Less Sodium
Hormel
SPAM
LUNCHEON MEAT
うす塩 低脂肪・低塩
Hormel
SPAM
LUNCHEON MEAT
うす塩 低脂肪・低塩
Hormel

93. The Masonic Lodge Headquarters

The Freemasons are very wealthy; they own a lot of buildings. They must own their huge headquarters, which is in Covent Garden, in London. It's predominantly white men who are Freemasons. Once accepted into a Masonic lodge, a new member can take eight to ten years working his way through the offices, starting as a Steward, then an Inner Guard, then a Senior Deacon, all the way up to the Master of the Lodge. They accept women now, but only into two of their seven thousand lodges. God, they're so liberal, aren't they?

There's a lot of secrecy and a lot of very strange traditions that the Freemasons uphold, so I found it really interesting to go inside the Masonic headquarters. I met the Freemasons' PR people, who were very keen to have a more open remit, and they gave me a commission to photograph this. It was quite extraordinary, really, to have this access to a secret organization.

THE FREEMASONS' PRESS OFFICER (FAR LEFT) WITH OTHER MEMBERS
LONDON, ENGLAND, 2001

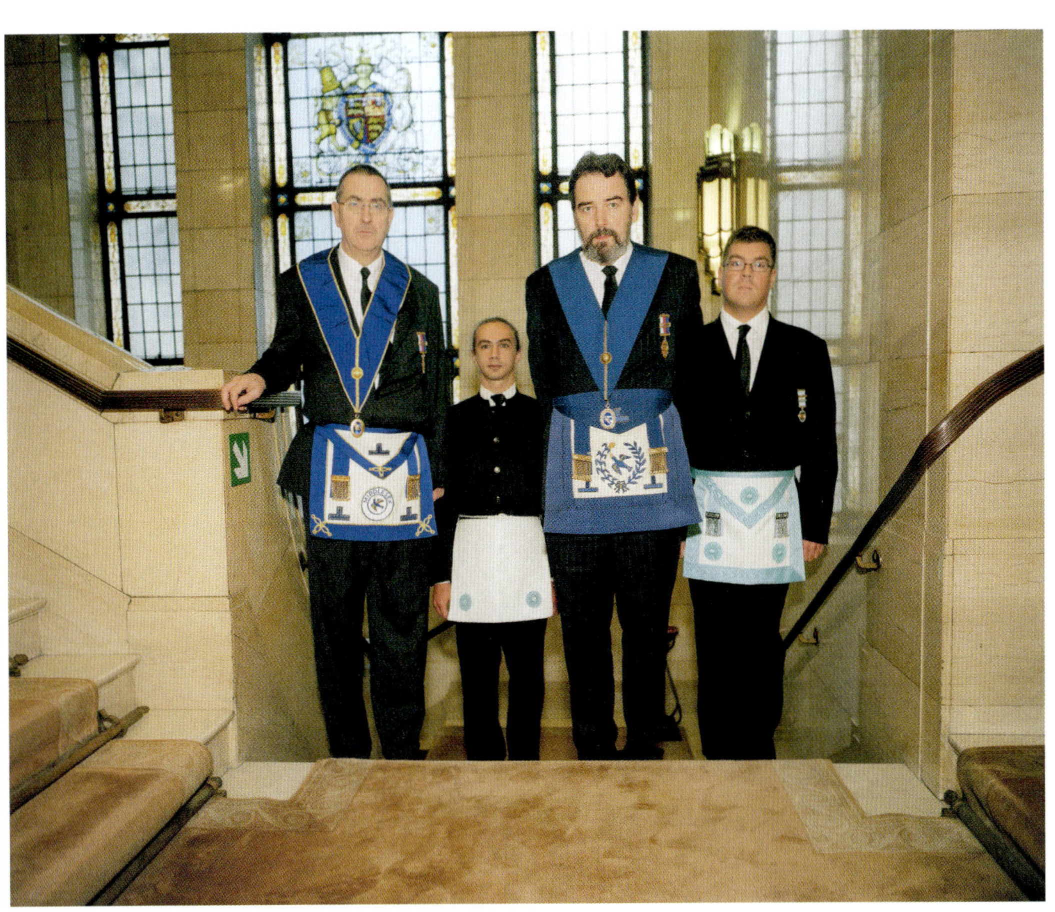

94. A Nice Row of Sinks

This is the toilet block in the Freemasons' headquarters. I went in there with the express intention of taking photographs. There's a nice row of sinks, a nice row of pissoirs. A couple of Freemasons are knocking around – perhaps having a secret conversation. Who knows? Probably doing a business deal, which, of course, is what the Freemasons are famous for.

INSIDE THE MASONIC LODGE HEADQUARTERS
LONDON, ENGLAND, 2001

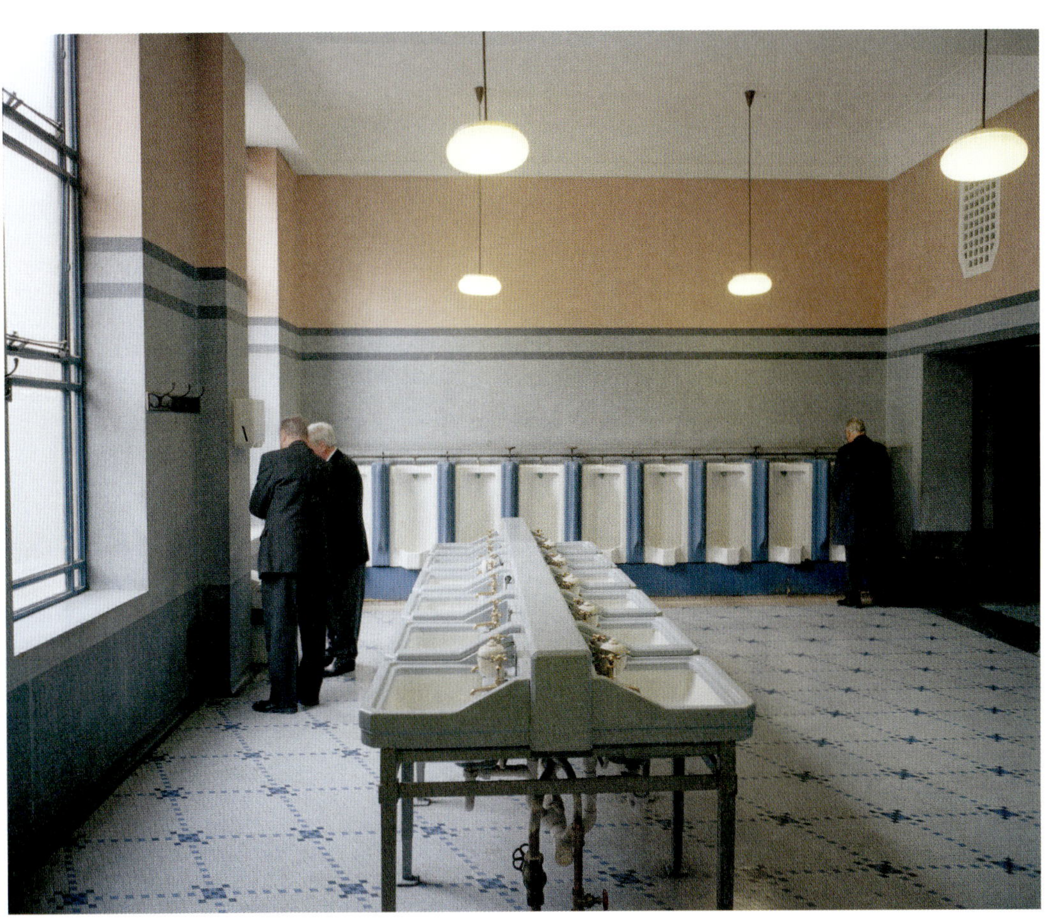

95. Senegalese Street Seller

In 2001, I went to Dakar, Senegal, for a fashion shoot for *Rebel*, a French fashion magazine. I had accessories to photograph – handbags, sunglasses and a Louis Vuitton cigarette case – the silver square in the front row. Fashion photography gives me a chance to arrange objects and get people to stand where I want them. Every fashion picture is about solving a problem: how to make the picture look good while showing the item of clothing. This guy was selling his wares on the street for two or three dollars. I negotiated to pay him to take his photo – I can't remember how much – and I placed the cigarette case into the tray. And Bob's your uncle.

His display of things is nice. It's colourful. There's an extension lead, an alarm clock, a spring and batteries. It's all cheap stuff, apart from the Louis Vuitton cigarette case, which is an expensive French luxury good. It's a very direct image. In this context, it looks as if you could buy the cigarette case for $10. It devalues it. It's ironic, isn't it, really? I put it there as a form of subversion, because everything else on that tray would be worth under $10. And that Louis Vuitton cigarette case is going to be worth $1,000. Minimum.

FROM *FASHION MAGAZINE*
DAKAR, SENEGAL, 2001

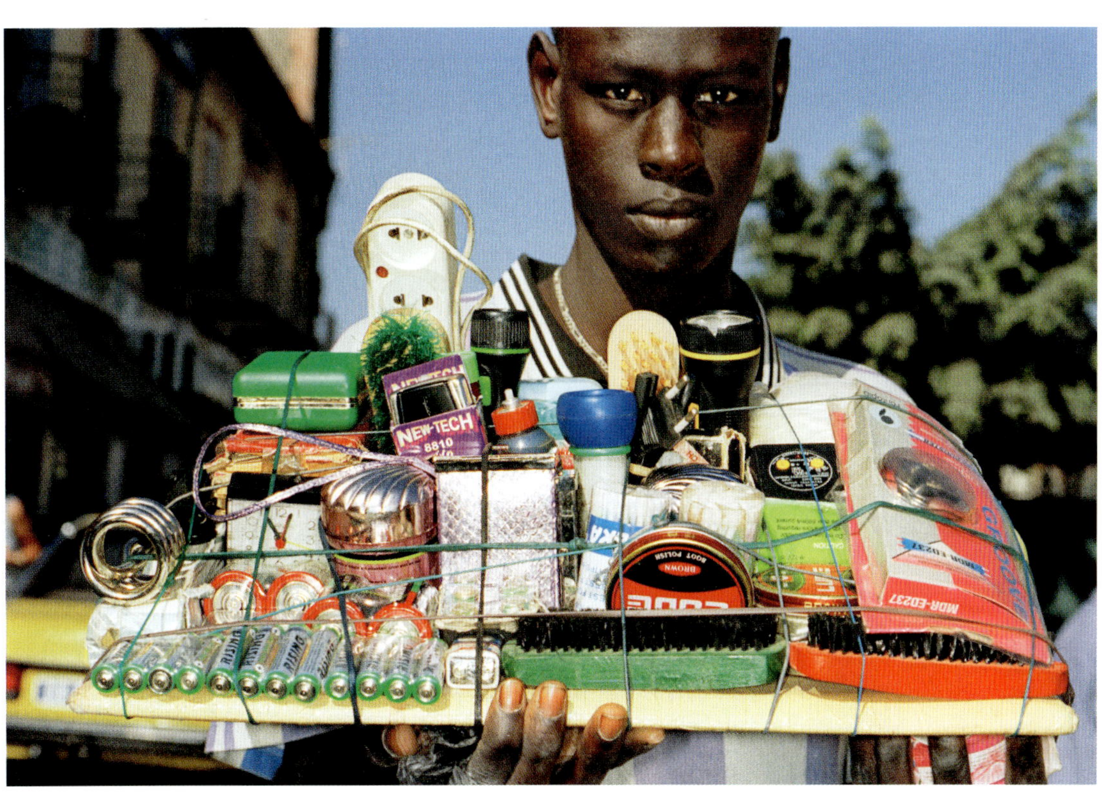

96. Autoportrait

My autoportrait project has run over a forty-year period. The aim is to demonstrate the different ways in which you can have your portrait done in a studio or public space, as well as to show off the different techniques photographers employ to sell their images. The only reason I use myself as the subject is because I'm the one person who's consistently there.

Hanoi Studio in Havana took five black-and-white shots of me in different poses, and in the middle one they gave me naff sunglasses. They then did a montage, making the five negatives into one image. It was printed in black and white, then hand-coloured. You can see the unevenness of the green dye applied to the picture, and in the flesh-colour added to my face. My hair is slightly different colours in each one, and very dark in the middle picture. It's not quite accurate, but who cares? My hair is brown here as opposed to how it is now, which is white. The autoportrait project also demonstrates my ageing process. It's a great picture because the colours are good, the poses are good, and it is a good likeness.

I'm completely uninterested in how I look, as long as I'm presentable. I look in the mirror once a day – I have no choice, as I've got to comb my hair. I guess that's interesting given that I do fashion photography. I'm not interested in clothes or buying expensive brands, I just wear what's comfortable, and what's there. In the spring, I wear socks with sandals as it's a good combination before it gets to the hottest part of the year. I guess you could call it my 'spring look'.

FROM *AUTOPORTRAIT*
HANOI STUDIO, HAVANA, CUBA, 2001

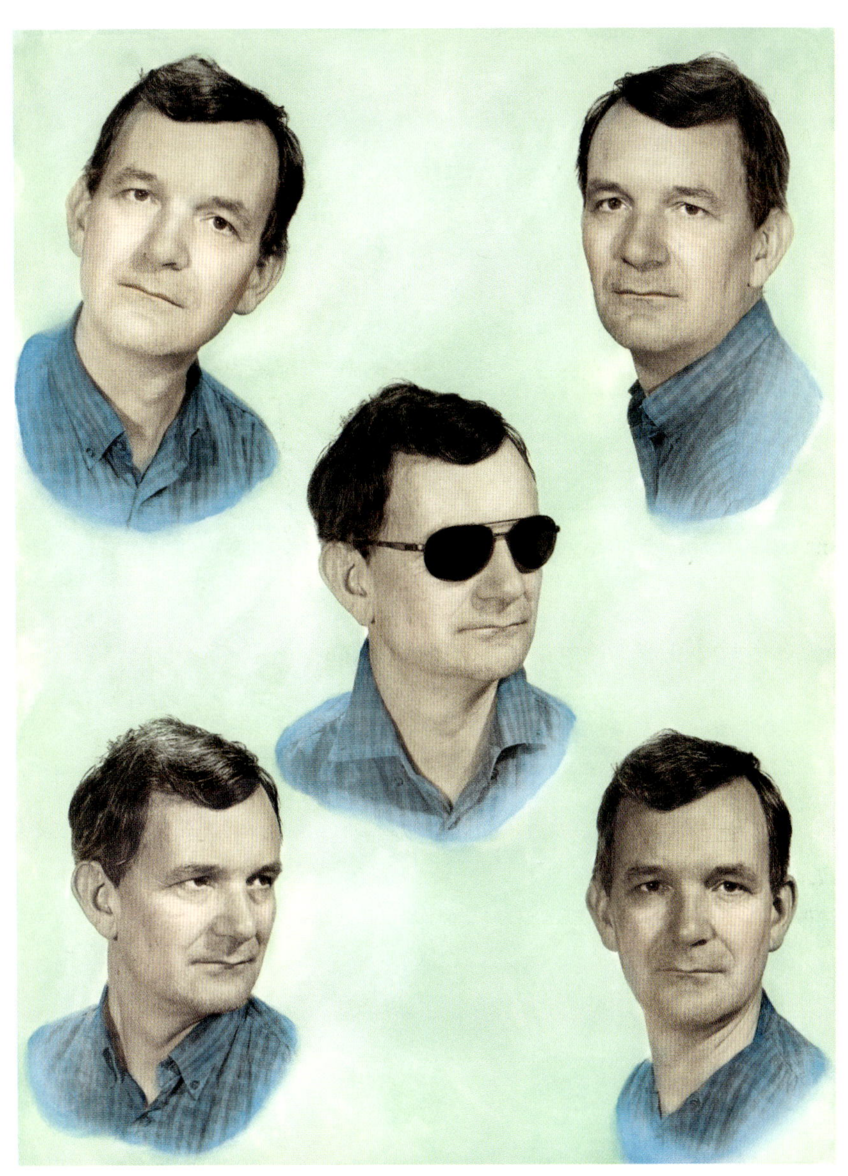

97. Gourock Lido

In 2004, the architect who redesigned King's Cross station, John McAslan, commissioned me to photograph the A8, which runs from Glasgow to Dunoon. He said, 'Here's a fee. Go and take pictures along the A8.' So I did. I accept most of the commissions I'm offered because if people pay me to take photos, what's not to like? I photographed all the conurbations along the road over a week. And here we are passing Gourock Lido. The sky was dark and grey. The bright blue of the salt-water lido made a good contrast with that grey sky – so familiar in Scotland in the summer – and bang in the middle of this picture is someone swimming along. That's what's really striking. The colours were very luminous, and the contrast between the two was perfect. I stood there waiting for maybe half an hour, waiting for the swimmer to be in the right position. This image has become famous because the rock band, Blur, selected it for the cover of their album, *The Ballad of Darren*. It has turned out to be one of the most popular pictures I have ever taken.

GOUROCK LIDO
FROM *A8*
INVERCLYDE, SCOTLAND, 2004

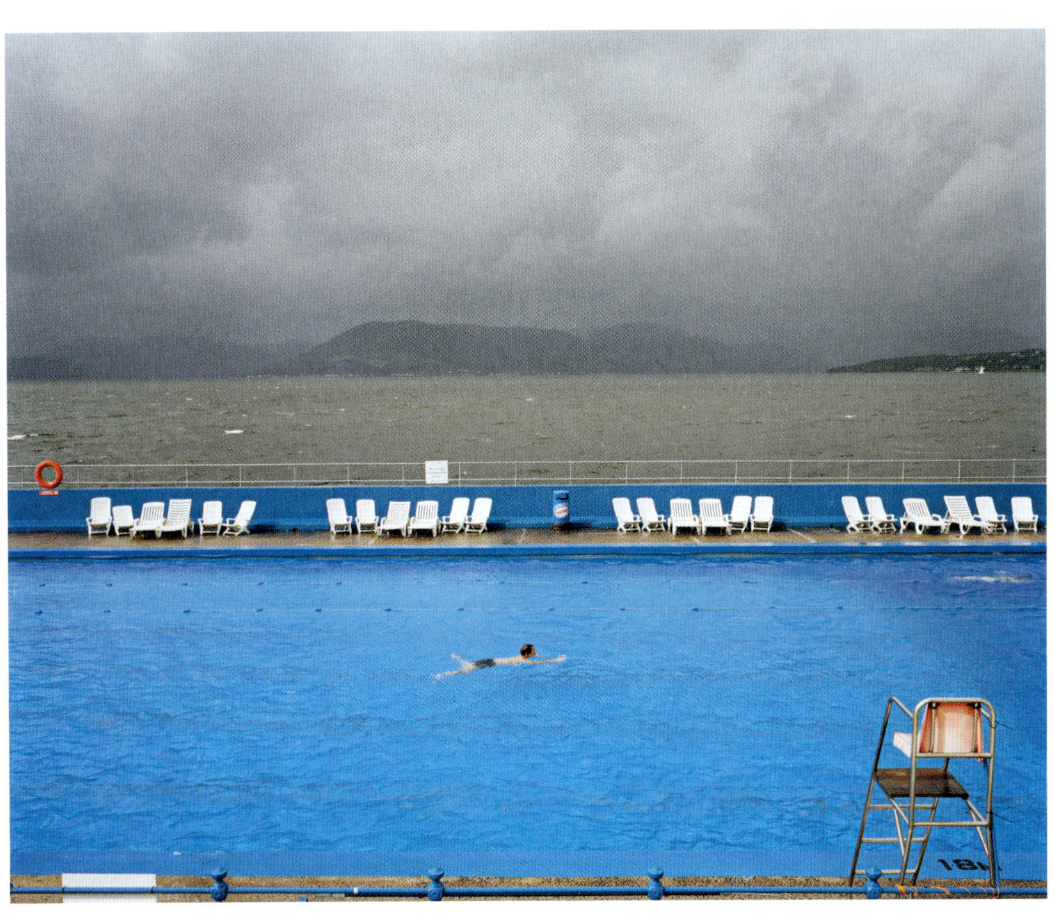

98. Almost Believable

People don't like dentists particularly. This is a girl at the dentist. You wouldn't know it was a fashion shot unless you were told. It's for a German children's fashion magazine, *kid's wear*, and the idea was to put fashion into everyday circumstances to make it look almost believable. I suggested to the magazine that we fix up with a dentist, a dental nurse and the girl's mother, so that it would look as if she were having her teeth done, thinking, to my knowledge, no one's ever done a fashion shoot in a dental surgery. All the dental stuff is completely pretend, but completely convincing.

Over the years, I've done fashion shoots in places like pubs and car boot sales – I go to places that are as mundane as possible to get my backdrops. I'm interested in bringing the world of fashion and the ordinary together. I guess it is one of my hallmarks. The more mundane the scenario, the more interesting a fashion shot becomes, because no one would expect to do a fashion shoot there. Does it sell the clothes? Do people think, 'Oh, I'll buy that skirt for my daughter.' I guess they do. I don't look into that; it's not my role. I'm interested in a slight subversion of the whole idea of fashion.

FROM *FASHION MAGAZINE*
GERMANY, 2004

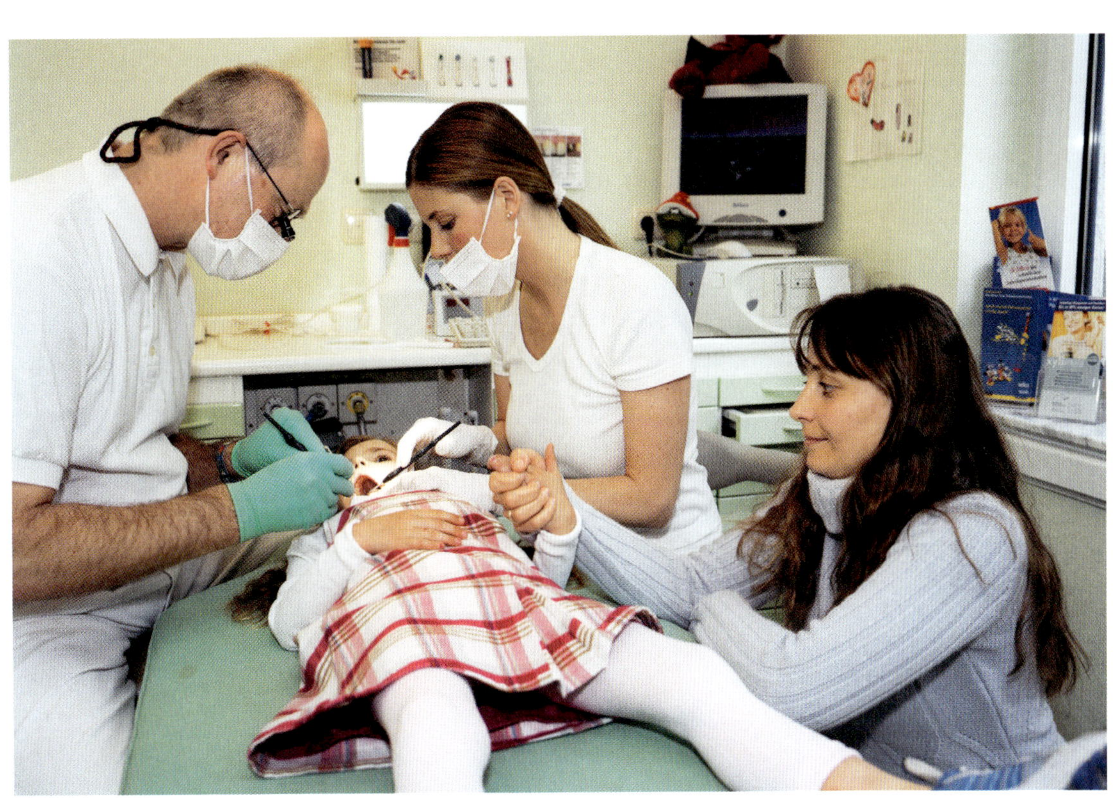

99. Boring Postcards

I've been collecting postcards, boring and interesting, since my twenties. In 1999, I did a book called *Boring Postcards* which became very successful. But I thought the postcards in the book weren't boring at all, because they showed the aspirations of people in the 60s and 70s. They were postcards of new supermarkets, motorways, bus stations, housing estates and factories, which, at the time, were exciting and heralded a new age in postwar Britain. When I was twelve or thirteen, I was taken onto the M1 as a treat. People would send postcards of things that summed up modernization, all the things we take for granted now, but when they were first built they were celebrated with postcards. Nowadays, you wouldn't be able to get a single postcard of the M1 or the M6.

FROM *BORING POSTCARDS*
PUBLISHED BY PHAIDON, 1999

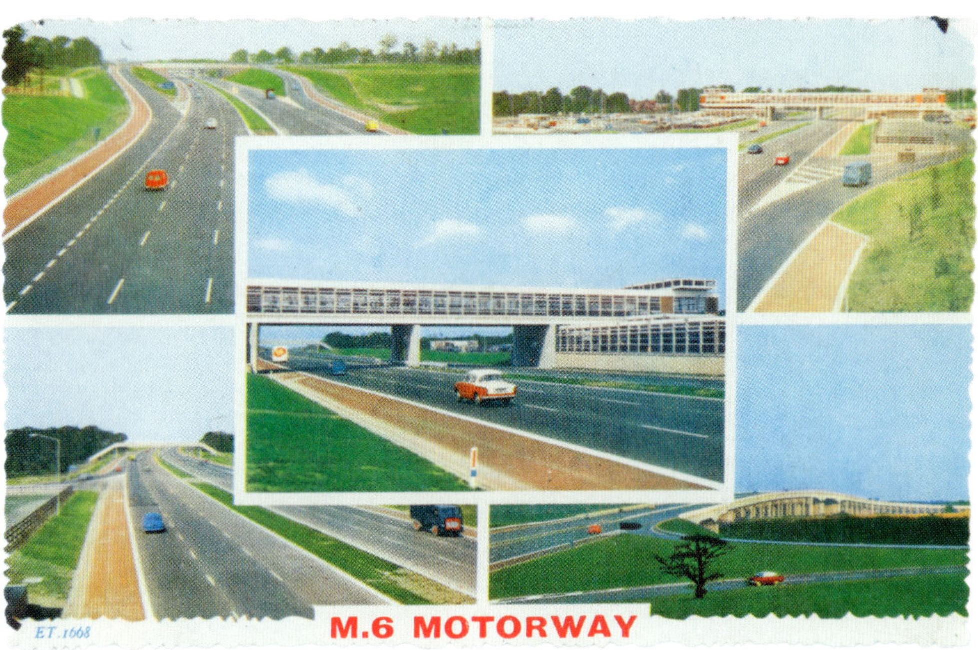

M.6 MOTORWAY

ET. 1668

100. Indian Cakes

I'm fascinated by India, which is now a very wealthy country, although it has a lot of poverty as well. I like Indian cakes. They're the most colourful, most interesting cakes, and often quite funny. This is a close-up of 'HAPPY'. I like that it's just got 'HAPPY' here. We don't know what sort of happiness it is, but it is probably for a birthday. And the icing is in happy colours. I mean, it contains nasty sugar, but nonetheless, the cake looks good in the photograph.

KOLKATA, INDIA, 2005

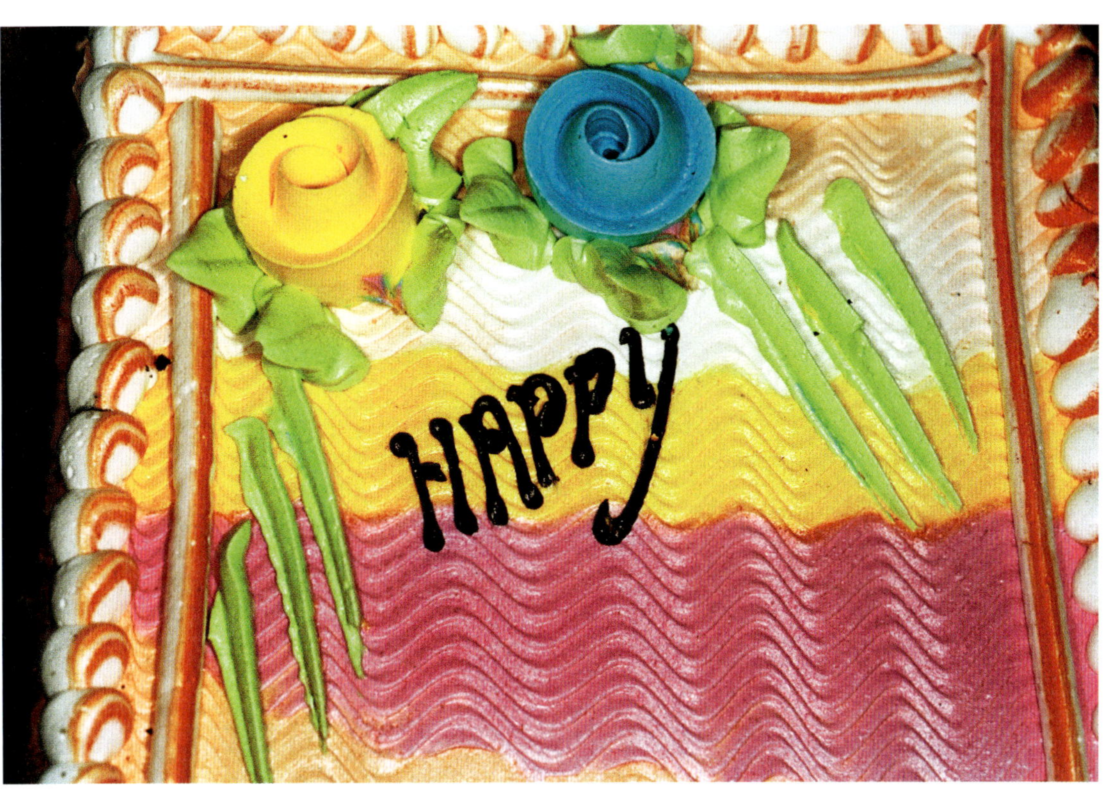

HAPPY

101. The Durban July

Poverty has been the front line for the socially concerned photographer. I have been happy to reverse that and photograph the wealthy. I'm very democratic in terms of covering different classes. I photographed the working class at New Brighton with *The Last Resort* and the middle class in southern England with *The Cost of Living*. *Luxury*, which I began in 2003, looks at the richer side of society.

I went all the way to South Africa especially to attend this race, the Durban July – the biggest race meeting in South Africa. It only takes place over one day, unlike a lot of other race meetings like the Derby or the Melbourne Cup. It's pretty intense. I wanted to go because I wanted to see wealthy South Africans enjoying themselves, and, sure enough, that was what was there. It turned out to be a very fruitful engagement. This was long after apartheid, and the wealth of some Black Africans had increased. Places change all the time, and the type of people who live in a place changes.

It's not a fashion shot. This lady is a real person. I don't know which brand created the *FETISH* handbag, but it's perfect in this situation. The background's good with the other lady, she looks quite trendy, too. And there's the lady right at the back with the polka dot dress. They are the new class of wealthy South Africans in 2005. You can always tell the date by the state of the phones. This is a very old-fashioned Samsung phone, but it is in good condition and was new at the time.

JULY RACES
FROM *LUXURY*
DURBAN, SOUTH AFRICA, 2005

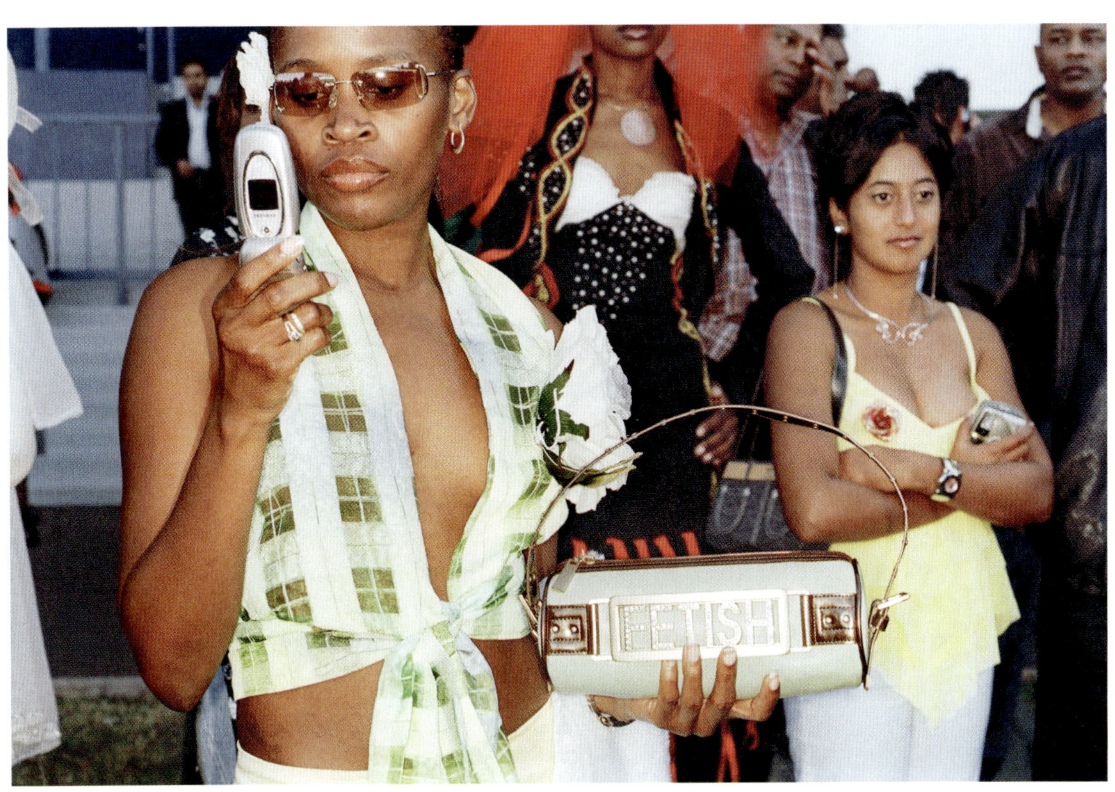

FETISH

102. A Free Tomato

I have been to so many country fêtes over the years. I can't get enough of them. The summer season isn't the same without going to, in particular, church fêtes, ideally in the vicar's garden. This is a good example of one on the Isle of Wight. It's like stepping back in time to the 1950s. You can't help but admire the notice here: '*Do take ONE cherry tomato with your roll.*' It's a shame that in agricultural shows and fêtes these days the food is often covered in clingfilm. I can sometimes get an interesting photo with cling film when I'm using flash, sometimes the reflections are quite interesting, but clingfilm just annoys me. You don't need clingfilm. The food's only going to be in the open air for a couple of hours before it's eaten. It's health and safety gone mad.

SHALFLEET CHURCH FÊTE
ISLE OF WIGHT, ENGLAND, 2007

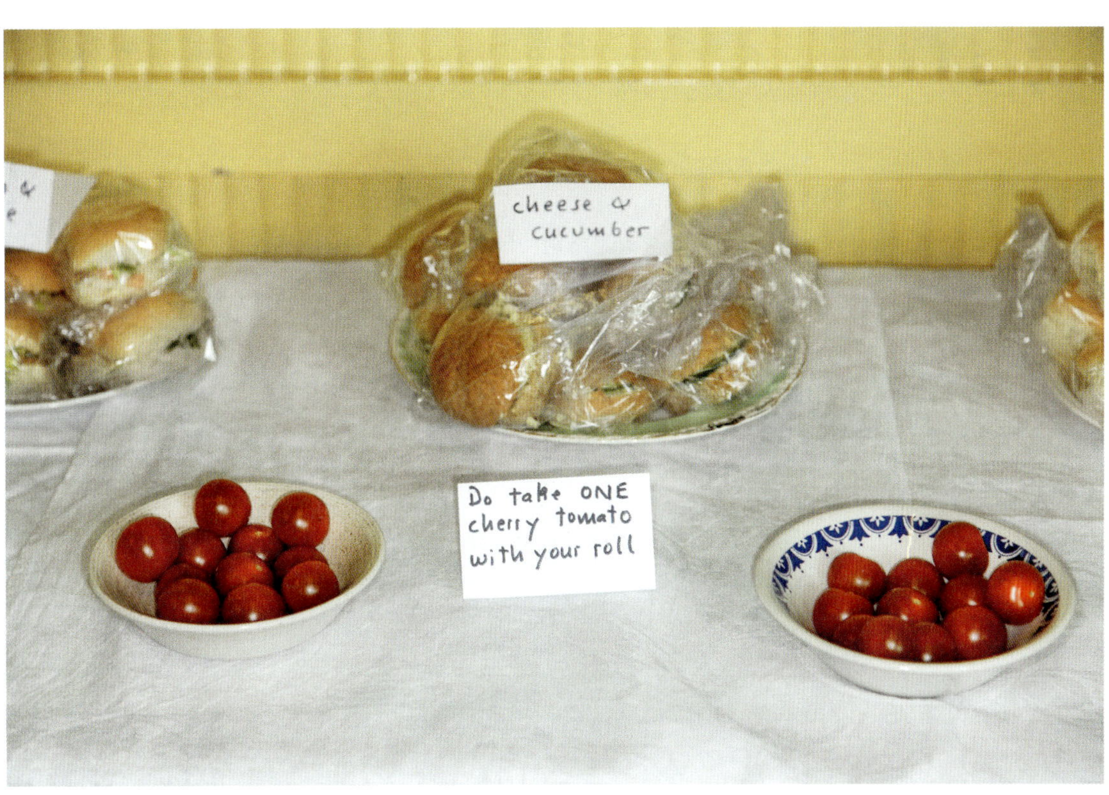
cheese &
cucumber
Do take ONE
cherry tomato
with your roll

103. Remote Scottish Postboxes

For Susie and me, going to the Scottish islands was almost an obsession. Every summer we would go to a different one. There are hundreds of islands, of which maybe eighty or ninety are inhabited, and we spent some years trying to visit them all, or as many as we could. We explored them together; Susie went swimming, and I took photos.

I began to notice these remote postboxes and, over three or four summers, I started shooting them. I just liked them. Susie said that I would screech the car to a halt when I saw a postbox and take a picture – you can't miss them because they're big and red. Sometimes I had to come back to a postbox later on the same day, or another day, because the light wasn't right, or perhaps there wasn't any sunshine, or the postbox was going against the sun. What I liked about the postboxes was that they were in the middle of nowhere. People must drive to them to post their letters – I don't think anyone would walk, because they are very remote indeed. They would often be at junctions on the islands, and there would be a telephone box nearby. The postboxes are from different islands – the Outer Hebrides, Skye, Orkney, Shetland, Barra, Lewis and Islay – as well as a few from the mainland. It's the only time I've ever done a landscape project.

FROM *REMOTE SCOTTISH POSTBOXES*
DEERNESS, ORKNEY, SCOTLAND, 2007

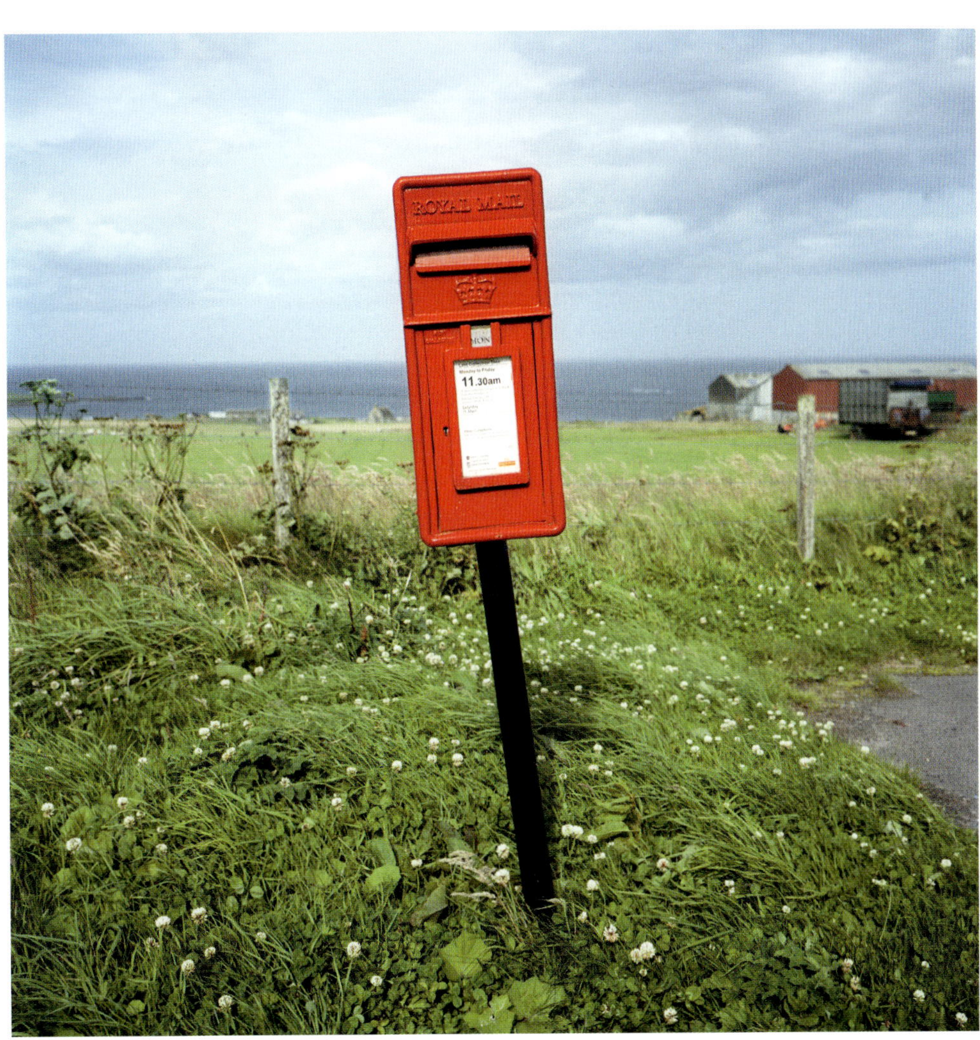

104. The Millionaire Fair

One event I wanted to attend as part of my *Luxury* series was the Second Moscow Millionaire Fair. At the Millionaire Fair, everything was very expensive. You can buy a helicopter or an expensive car, an apartment in Dubai or a mobile phone encrusted with diamonds. It was a great shoot – perfect – and worth going all the way to Moscow. I like this woman here on the phone. And I like the other woman holding her cigar, and in the background there's a luxury car. The attendees are not all actually millionaires but aspiring to be millionaires. The Fair was selling aspirations, really. The Muscovites have no hesitation in showing off their wealth. Talk about bling! When I photographed the Gucci store in Moscow, I was told that the store took more money than any other Gucci store on the planet. I like photographing the wealthy, although I am convinced that the nonstop drive for growth and consumerism has many problems associated with it.

THE MILLIONAIRE FAIR
FROM *LUXURY*
MOSCOW, RUSSIA, 2007

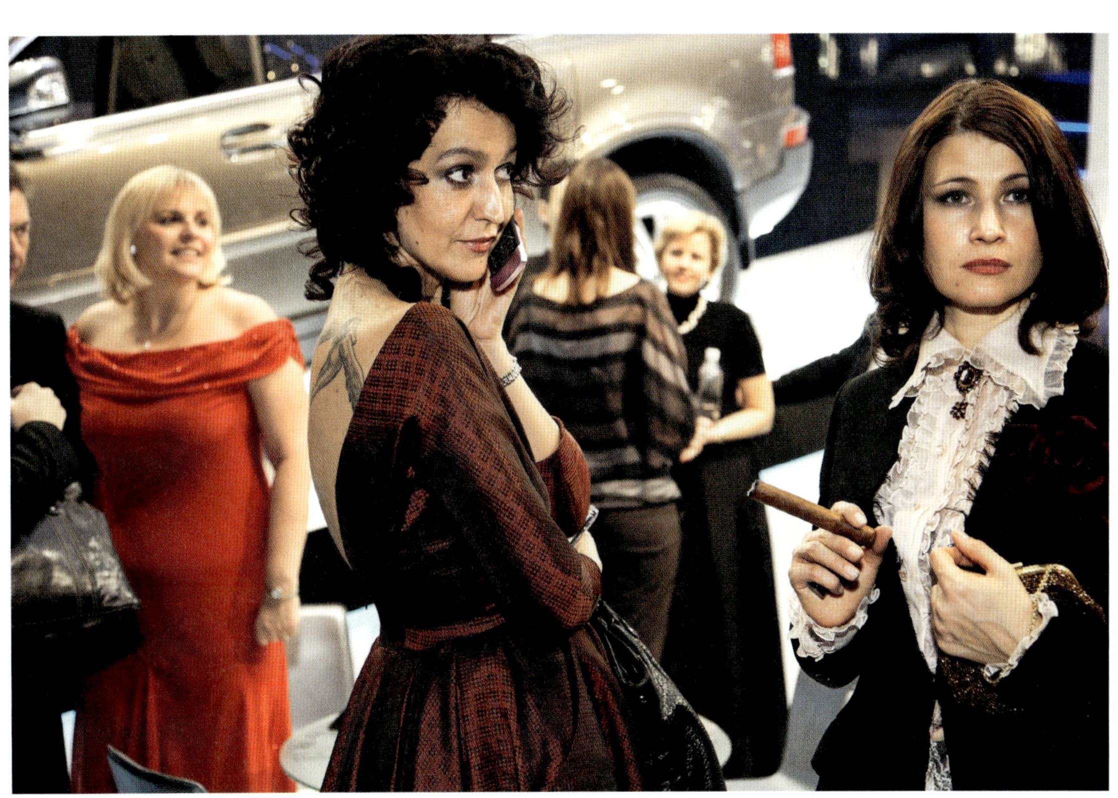

105. Chain-Makers

I have visited, and photographed, most major cities in Britain, but one blind spot for me was the Black Country, so when I was asked if I might be interested in doing a commission on the Black Country, I could not say yes fast enough.

The Black Country, near Birmingham, was once heavily industrialized. People travelling through in the early nineteenth century would describe the iron smelting fires and the toxic air. Chain-making used to be a major industry but, like most traditional industries in the region, it has declined. Whereas forty years ago there might have been fifty people working in Griffin-Woodhouse Ltd, now it's only a father and son. Chains aren't made like this any more; there are more large-scale ways to make them – but they still get chain-making orders and work three days a week. They've got the Union Jack in the background – that makes the photo.

Despite the inevitable sense of decline in the Black Country, you could sense that the area was being revitalized, too, because it has been a major area for immigration, and the new people coming in were reviving the economy and revitalizing the area. There was a very vibrant multicultural feel, with Sikh temples, Hindu temples and mosques. It was an incredibly friendly place with a strong sense of community.

The work came together with a book called *Black Country Stories* and an exhibition in Wolverhampton. We showed the films I did, alongside a big selection of 10x8 prints on a wall, which we offered to local people at a very reasonable price. I don't ever hear back about what people do with their prints. In the Black Country, nobody had a clue I was a photographer. They weren't coming up to me and saying, 'Are you Martin Parr?' – apart from the photography students.

FATHER & SON, BRIAN & ROSS CARTWRIGHT,
CHAIN-MAKERS AT GRIFFIN-WOODHOUSE
FROM *BLACK COUNTRY STORIES*
SANDWELL, ENGLAND, 2010

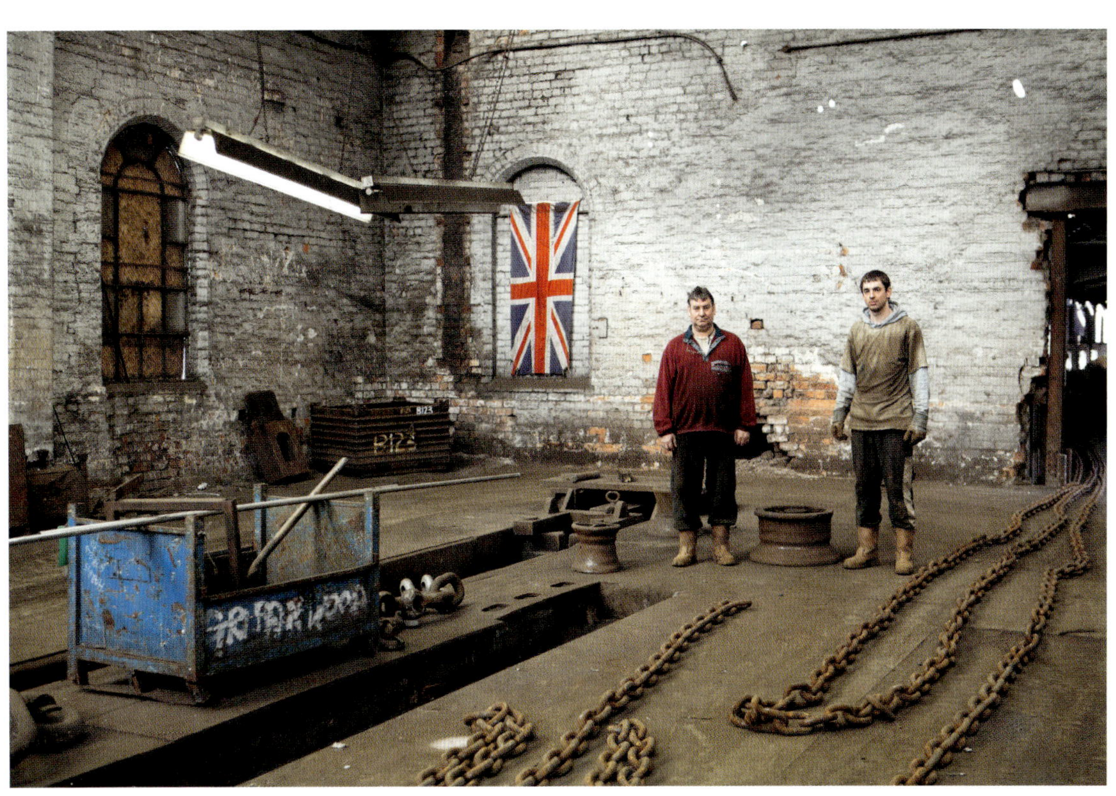

106. Christ's Hospital School

I met, at some conference somewhere, the head of art at Christ's Hospital School. He was very friendly, and I told him I knew about Christ's Hospital. It is a tremendously old-fashioned public school, yet quite modern at the same time. I said I'd love to come and take some photos in the school, so he asked the headmaster, and the headmaster gave me clearance. I visited ten times, took photos, then produced a zine – because there weren't enough photos for a book – and held an exhibition of my pictures in the school's art department. This is the Grecians' ball, when the sixth formers leave.

The school is in West Sussex on the main line going down to Worthing. It actually has its own station. I thought Christ's Hospital was interesting because it has more public scholarship places than any other public school. The City of London subsidizes it, so that at least 70 per cent of places are given to deprived families in London. That's why you'll find that it has more Black kids, and that it's more socially diverse than any other public school. Interestingly, Tony Ray-Jones, my photographic hero, went to Christ's Hospital, and he hated it.

The school was founded in 1552 and has a Tudor-inspired uniform and, surprisingly, even though the pupils are regularly asked through a referendum, 'Would you like to change your uniform?' they always vote to keep it. Four days a week at lunchtime, the school band stand outside, then march into the refectory, playing their instruments. At that point the pupils can start eating. It's quite amazing that this tradition is kept up.

CHRIST'S HOSPITAL SCHOOL LEAVERS' BALL (TOP)
WEST SUSSEX, ENGLAND, 2011

THE CHRIST'S HOSPITAL BAND
PLAYING ON THE DAILY PARADE (BELOW)
WEST SUSSEX, ENGLAND, 2010

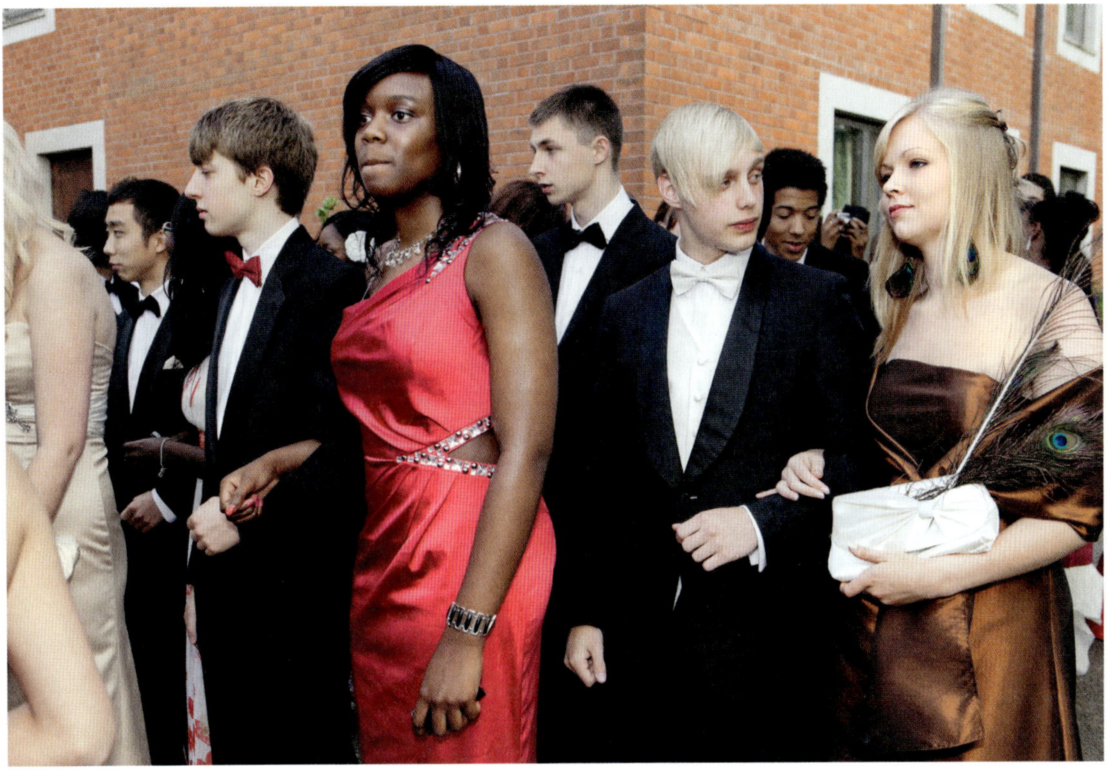

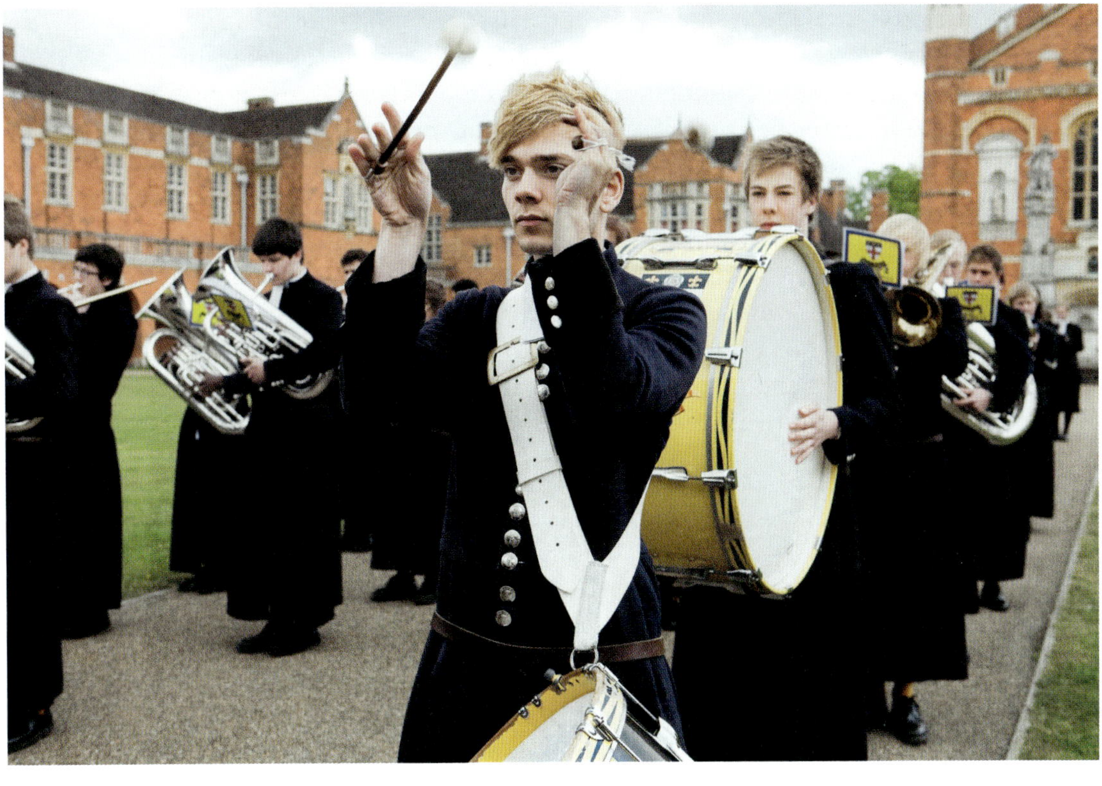

107. Hen Party

Most hen parties seem to have blown-up penises as part of their armoury. Hen parties are great, but I usually have this big problem: everyone's looking at me, posing, as if it's a Facebook picture. All they want to do is smile and laugh. Luckily, I've got around that in this picture. One of my techniques is to hang around for a long time. And they get used to me. They just get bored with me. I took this in a Yates's Wine Lodge, the one in Wolverhampton. The child on the T-shirts must be the bride's child. Or maybe it's the groom as a boy. Or the bride.

Is this photo Parr-esque? What does Parr-esque mean? Colourful, funny, I suppose. Small. Small scale. It's not the big event. It's not the Queen being crowned, it's the people in the crowd watching the Queen being crowned. It's the small person's perspective on the big event. The scale is more important than the colour. Colour does come into it, although that's not exactly right because of my black-and-white photos of Hebden Bridge, and all my early photographs until China. That work is less Parr-esque, partly because it's not colourful, but mostly because it's more old-school, old fashioned, humanistic photography. The black-and-white work had humour, but it was gentler.

Some of my colour work has been characterized as being in your face, but it's not confrontational. Sometimes people say that I sneer in my photographs. I don't think I do, but people are entitled to say that if they want, of course. I like people, basically.

HEN PARTY AT YATES'S WINE LODGE
FROM *BLACK COUNTRY STORIES*
WOLVERHAMPTON, ENGLAND, 2011

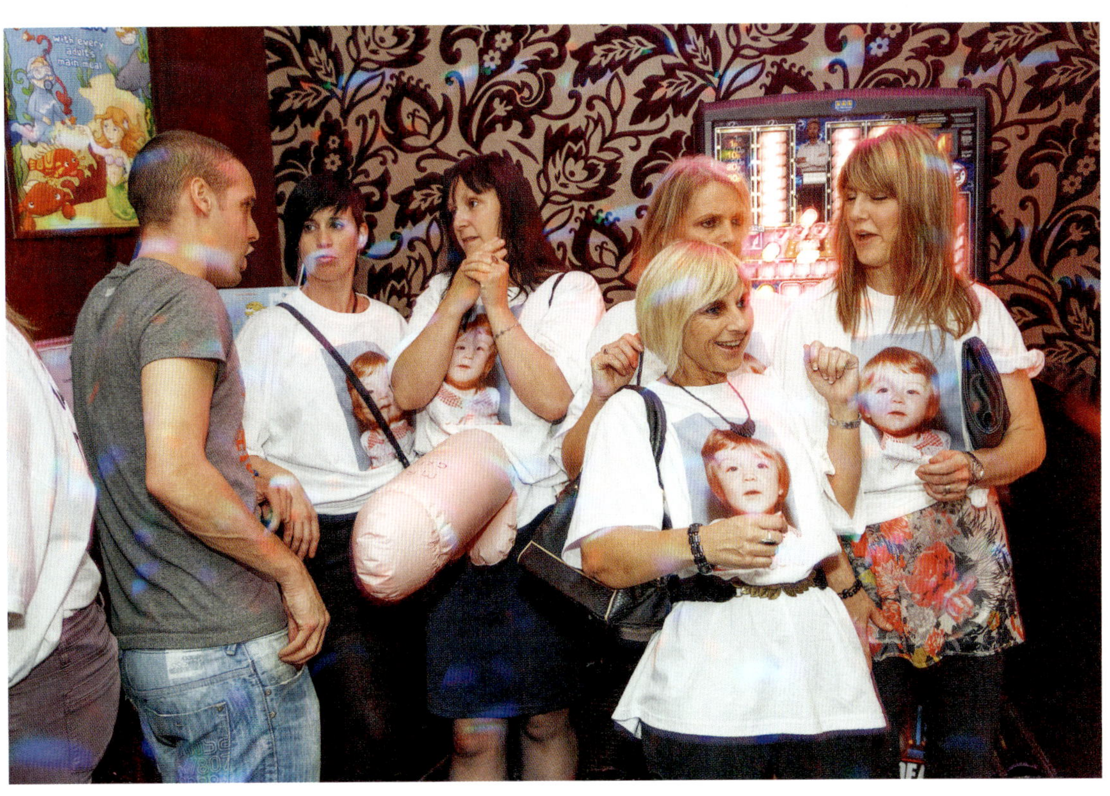

108. The Zion Tabernacle Fire Baptized Holiness Church

When I was commissioned by the High Museum of Art to document Atlanta, I got permission to go to the Tabernacle Baptist Church where Martin Luther King preached. Then I looked around for smaller Presbyterian chapels, such as this one: the Zion Tabernacle Fire Baptized Holiness Church. They were holding a service on Palm Sunday, and they literally got these palm leaves out and started waving them about. And, of course, I was very excited to see this. It's quite surreal, the way that the woman in the front reading the Bible or singing – she must be singing – looks like she's got two arms coming out of her back.

This was a very small congregation of about twelve people, and they were all singing and praying and waving their palm leaves. They didn't seem to notice me, and I was there for the duration – maybe over an hour. It's an example of why it's good to hang around in private spaces, or spaces which are used for a particular purpose. I couldn't believe it when they got these leaves out.

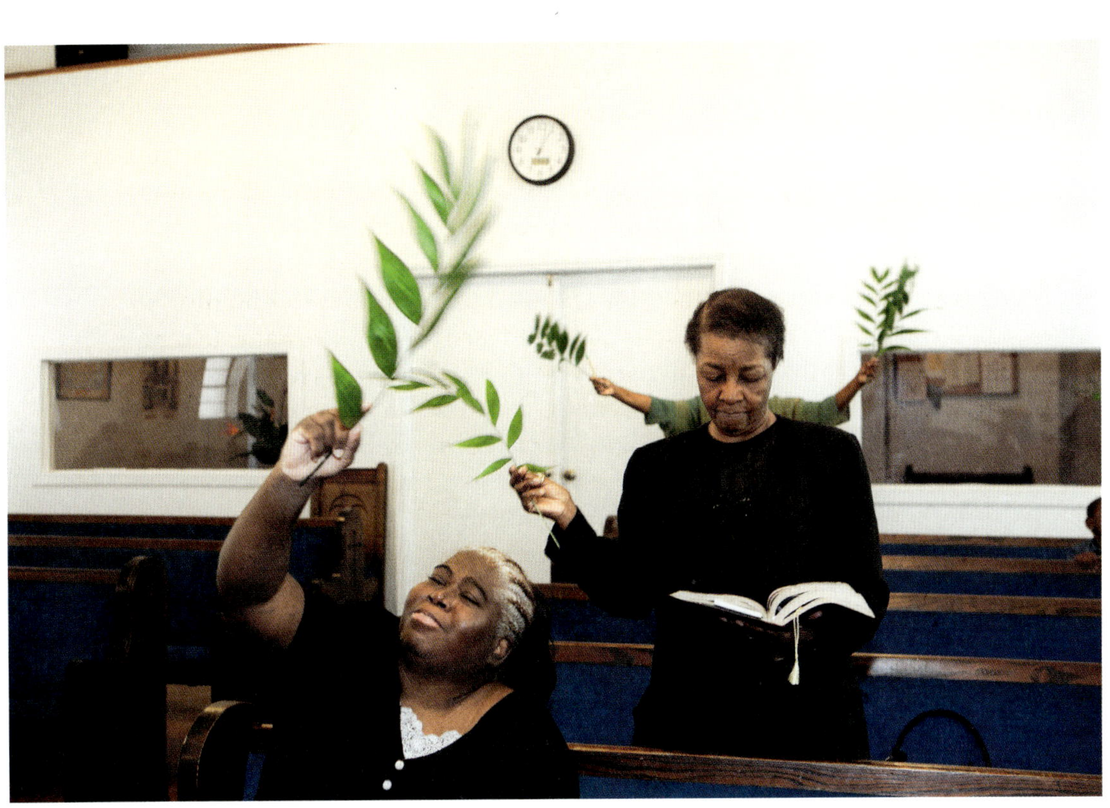

109. I Love My Gay Sons

One of the things I love is people who make their own placards. I was lucky to find a very plain background for this photo from the Pride March in Atlanta. The danger with marches is that there's too much noise behind the person I'm photographing and the placard they're holding, so it's always good to try and isolate them.

In Atlanta, they had people from religious groups really taunting the Pride parade, saying that they were all going to go straight to hell, so Pride is quite controversial there. I've photographed many Prides, but I've never seen people heckling before. I just love this mum and her home-made banner with the pictures of her two kids, who are gay. I actually took a picture of someone with exactly the same placard at Bristol Pride this year that said: 'I love my two gay sons.' So that's nice.

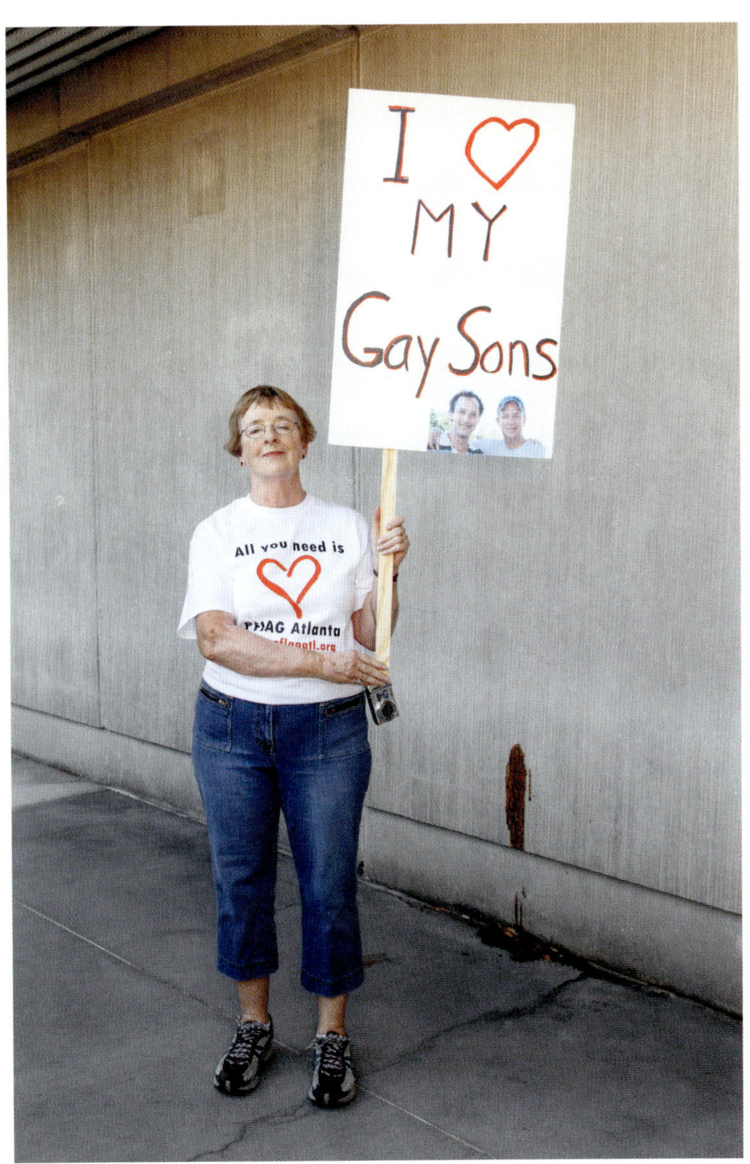

I ♥ MY Gay Sons
All you need is ♥ PFLAG Atlanta

110. World of Coca-Cola

Coca-Cola has its world headquarters in Atlanta. In their museum, World of Coca-Cola, you can try all the different Cokes from around the world – because in each country it has a different taste. So you can taste what Coca-Cola is like in India, in Japan and, of course, in America.

This is one of my favourites from the *Autoportrait* series in which I have my photo taken in different studios, or theme parks, often with different gimmicks. The polar bear is what the Coca-Cola Museum uses as a gimmick for people to have their photograph taken with. I match the bear very well with my red checked shirt – that's just an accident of good colouring.

In Atlanta, I saw Gay Pride, churches, a Coca-Cola museum. It's an interesting city, I liked it.

WORLD OF COCA-COLA
FROM *AUTOPORTRAIT*
ATLANTA, USA, 2010

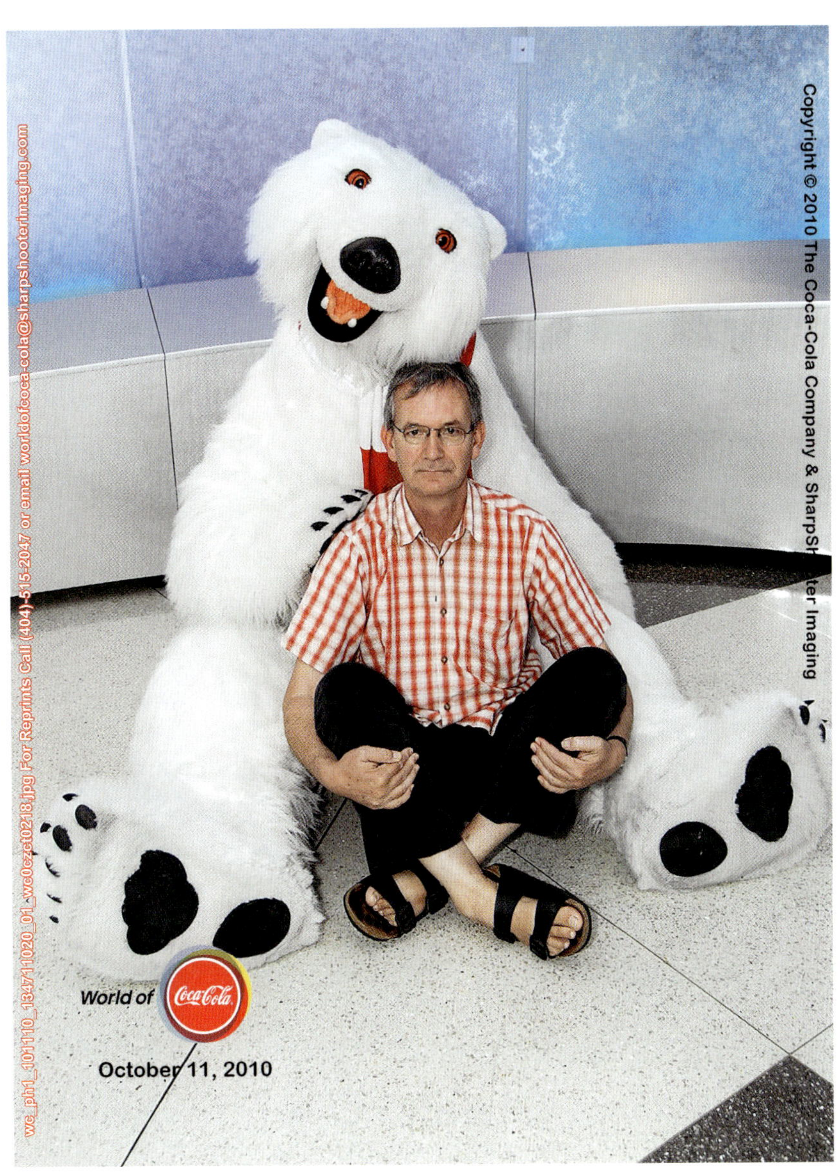

World of Coca-Cola
October 11, 2010
Copyright © 2010 The Coca-Cola Company & SharpShooter Imaging
wc_ph1_101110_134711020_01_wc0czct0218.jpg For Reprints Call (404)-515-2047 or email worldofcoca-cola@sharpshooterimaging.com

111. The Snow Polo World Cup

Thank God for *The New York Times.* They gave me a press pass to get into this scenario – the Snow Polo World Cup on the frozen lake in St Moritz, Switzerland. When the matches were on, photographers weren't let in. This was a big problem for me. Access is everything. Access is more difficult now than it was when I started as a photographer, because now I have to deal with public relations people. They may already know me from my work, but they also could look up my work and think, 'We're not going to let this guy in. It's too dangerous,' because they'll be exposed. At that time, I was in touch with the *New York Times Magazine.* I asked them, 'Would it be possible for you to commission me to do a shot here?' They said, 'Yes, go ahead.' They got a letter to the PR person for the Polo Cup, and they finally let me in when the World Cup match was being played. That's how I was able to photograph this array of wealthy Swiss people watching polo. I wasn't interested in the polo. I wanted the spectators. And they're very much spectating. They're very, very attentive. Everyone is wearing their sunglasses and watching the match very intently. The way the dog is integrated into the fur works well. It is, in fact, a real dog as opposed to a coat, and I like the other terrier-like dog, also paying attention to the match.

SPECTATORS IN SWITZERLAND WATCHING POLO
FROM *LUXURY*
ST MORITZ, SWITZERLAND, 2011

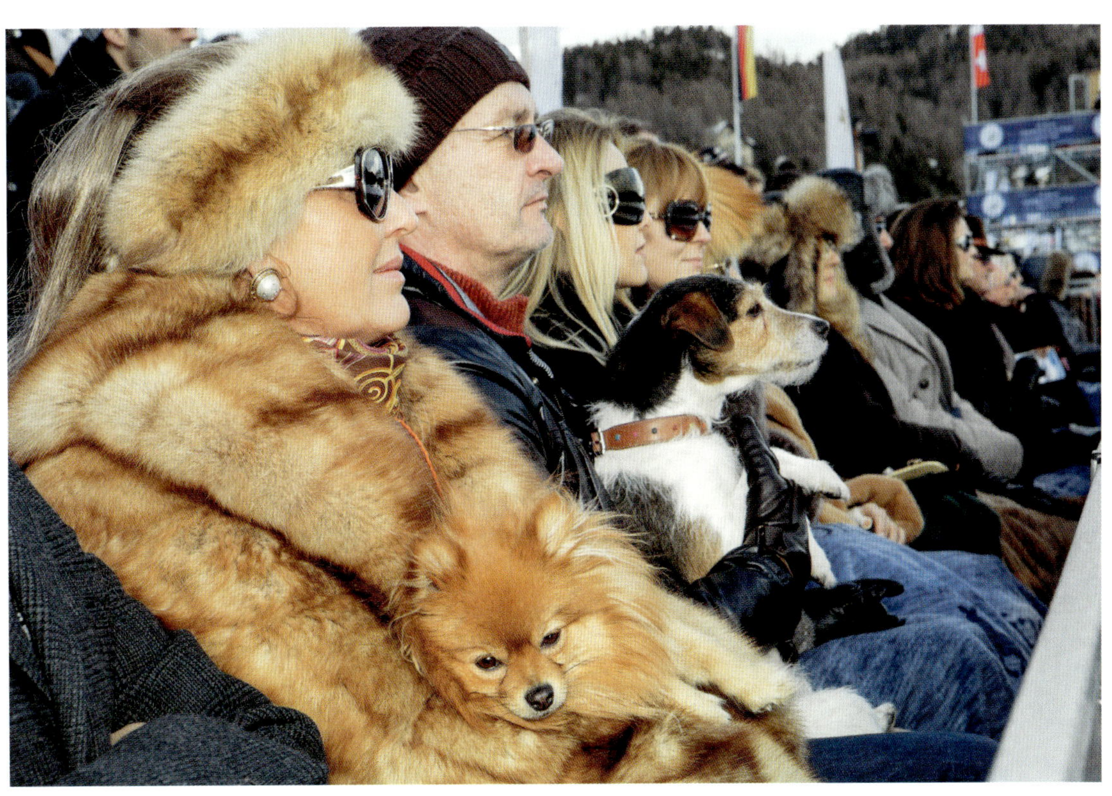

112. The Polar Bears Club

Port Beach Polar Bears Club on Port Beach go swimming in the sea all year round. I met them when I was commissioned to take photos of port cities in Western Australia. We came down to the sea early in the morning. I got them all together, sent them in – although it was winter in Fremantle, it wasn't cold at all – and photographed them. At one point I got them to cheer. When I looked later, that was the best picture, which I was very surprised about because I don't normally get people to cheer and shout and smile. That really took me aback.

This picture appeared on the front cover of my book of Western Australia pictures, called *No Worries*. There had been loads of shark attacks around Fremantle; apparently, a shark can take you in a metre of water. The swimmers called sharks 'the men in grey suits'. When Susie went swimming there, she was darting in and out very nervously, looking around for the shadow of a shark, but these swimmers all look very confident in the water. After all, they are in the sea every day. I don't swim. I don't particularly like water or immersing myself in it. I had a swimming accident back in my childhood: I fell into the River Severn, which I didn't much like. I've always been slightly haunted by that.

PORT BEACH POLAR BEARS SWIMMING CLUB
FROM *NO WORRIES*
FREMANTLE, AUSTRALIA, 2011

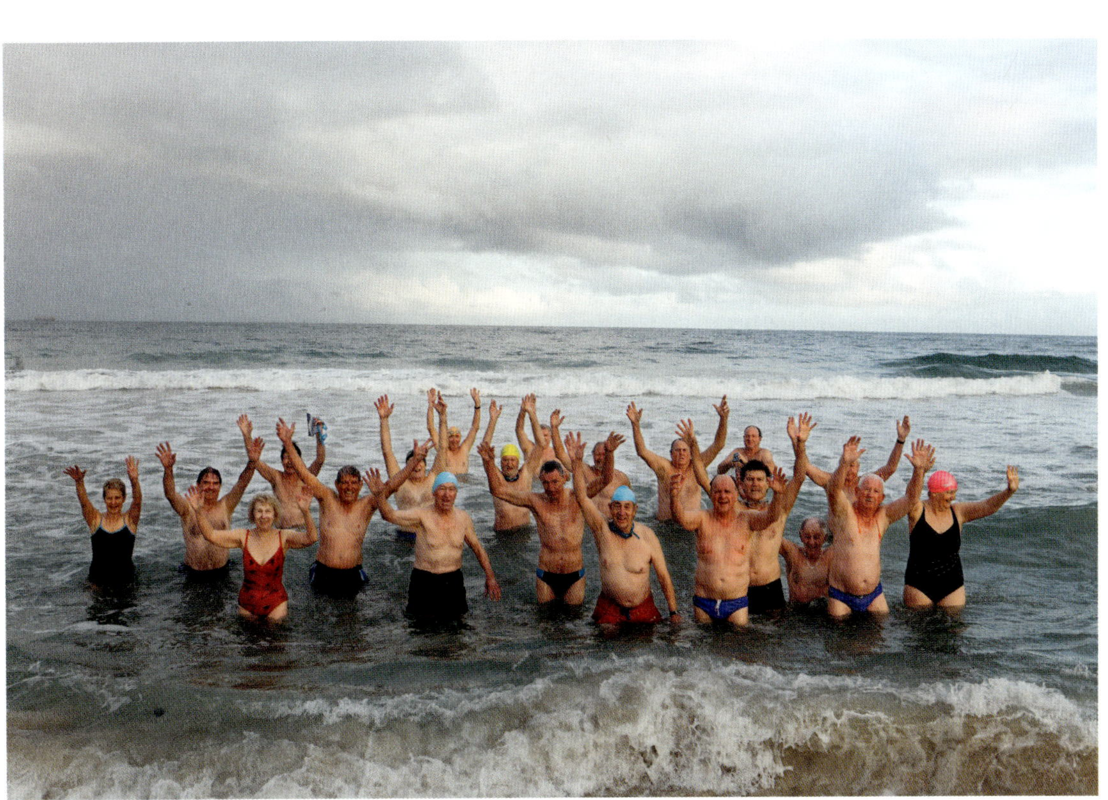

113. Employee of the Month

In 2012, Magnum initiated a project called *Postcards from America*, in which a group of photographers were sent to different towns in the US for ten days. I was sent to Rochester, New York, where I came across Tim Montondo. I just love the idea of the Employee of the Month. The sign tells the story: he's Employee of the Month. It's his sixth time. I love the fact that he's holding his Employee of the Month cup, the way it's held in one hand and the other hand just drops down. He's by the parking space for Employee of the Month. It's very near the front of the building because if you're Employee of the Month, you get a few perks: for example, you don't have to walk so far to get into work.

This is a portrait, a very proud portrait. I wanted him to look very proud of the fact that he's Employee of the Month. I had to tell him not to smile. I didn't want him to smile because I wanted to take it seriously. I want to make sure people can read that he's proud of this achievement. Getting people to stop smiling is always a big task. People assume when you do a portrait you should smile. The opposite is the case. I want the subject to show dignity.

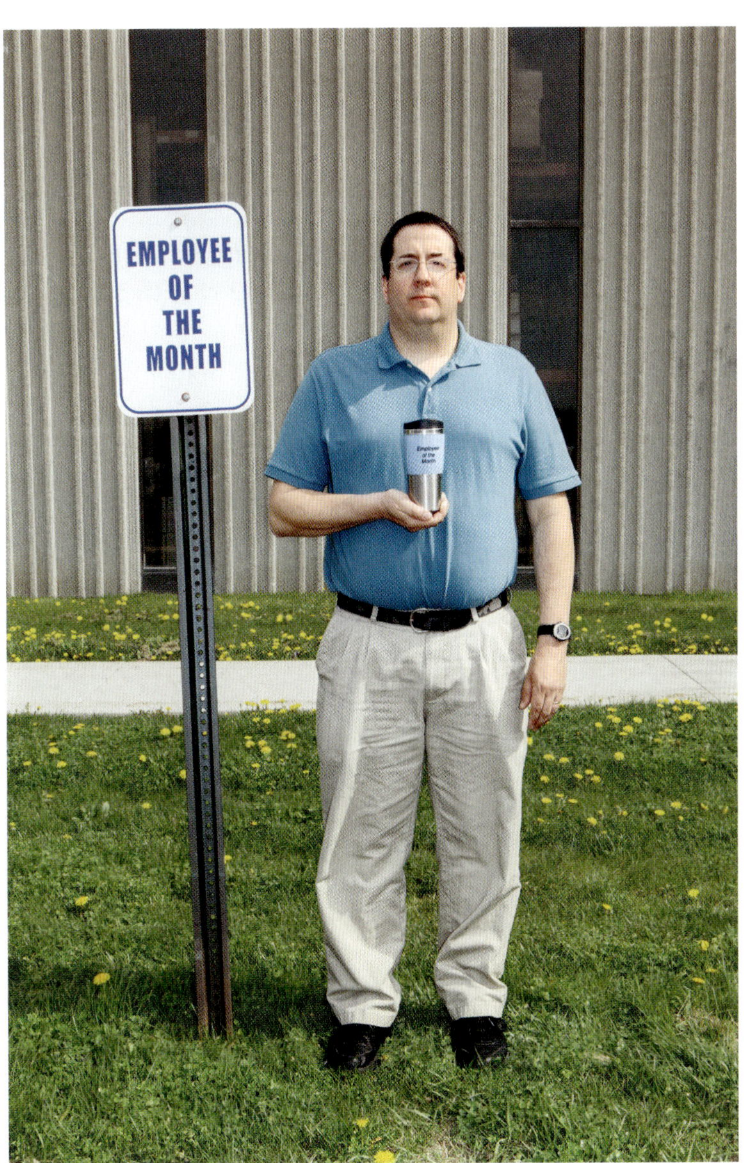
EMPLOYEE
OF
THE
MONTH
Employee
of the
Month

114. The Queen

When the Drapers' Livery company had their 650th birthday, they said to me, 'We've got the Queen coming to lunch to celebrate our 650th birthday. Would you be happy to take the pictures of the event?' and I immediately said yes. The livery companies in London are trade guilds, or professional associations, and they are famously very wealthy through property they've purchased over the centuries. They are also typically very male, very white and very old. They really are part of the old Establishment. But still they go on. Still rich. Still giving out money. Still having their dinners. Or, indeed, their lunches. With wine, of course.

As opposed to most of the times I've photographed the Queen at public events, this time I was the only photographer, and I followed her around. After lunch, the Queen had a room of fifteen or so people to meet. I asked the person with the Queen – her bridesmaid or her manager or whatever it was: I mean lady-in-waiting, not bridesmaid – I said, 'How long will it take her to go around the room?' She looked at the room and said, 'Twenty minutes.' I glanced at my watch. The Queen went around, said hello to everyone, indulged in small talk, everyone bowed, and she was in and out of there in twenty minutes exactly.

Here she is leaving the event. By this time, a good few pedestrians had twigged that the Queen was in the building. Hence, you see people with their phones trying to take pictures of her. The trouble with all the photos they've taken is they'll have me in them, with my camera. Sorry about that, folks. This has become a very popular image. It's interesting in that the Queen is perhaps the only person who's recognisable from behind. She's got that classic hat and a slight hunch on her back. I'm sure she was photographed from behind many times, but here, it really works.

THE QUEEN VISITING DRAPERS' HALL ON THEIR
650TH ANNIVERSARY DURING THE LORD MAYOR'S YEAR
FROM *UNSEEN CITY*
LONDON, ENGLAND, 2014

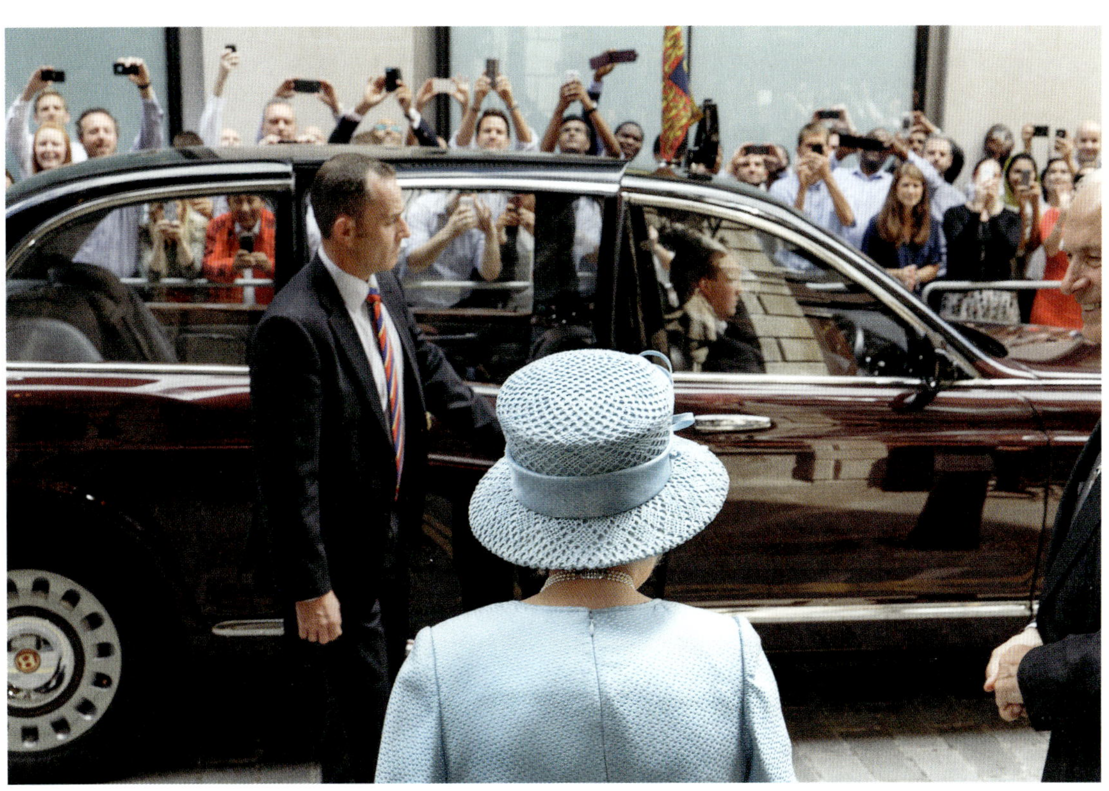

115. Space Dogs

Belka and Strelka were Soviet space dogs who went up into space together, then came back down together and became national heroes. The Soviets sent up thirteen space dogs. There was Laika. Laika was the first dog to orbit the planet. Laika, sadly, died on re-entry. The Soviet authorities did not inform the public of her demise. Belka and Strelka were really the biggest space dogs of all. In fact, they gave a puppy of Strelka's to President Kennedy's wife, Jackie, during the Cold War, when the USSR was ahead of America in the space race. They recruited these dogs from strays they captured on the streets of Moscow, because they thought strays would be stronger, then trained them. I'm not sure quite how you train a space dog.

The Soviets produced a lot of this space dog ephemera as a way of celebrating their achievement in the space race. This is a cigarette case with Belka and Strelka on the front. One of my obsessional collections – one of many – is space dog ephemera. I found a very good dealer on eBay who specialized in it and was able to buy a lot of the stuff from her. But it's quite expensive: this cigarette case was about £100. It's real leather with enamel dogs stuck on the front. There is a load of people who collect space dog ephemera. There's one woman in Belgium I have a lot of conversations with. I find out what she's got, and I might tell her what I've got. I'm part of a club.

BELKA AND STRELKA
SOVIET SPACE DOG EPHEMERA
PHOTOGRAPHS BY LOUIS LITTLE

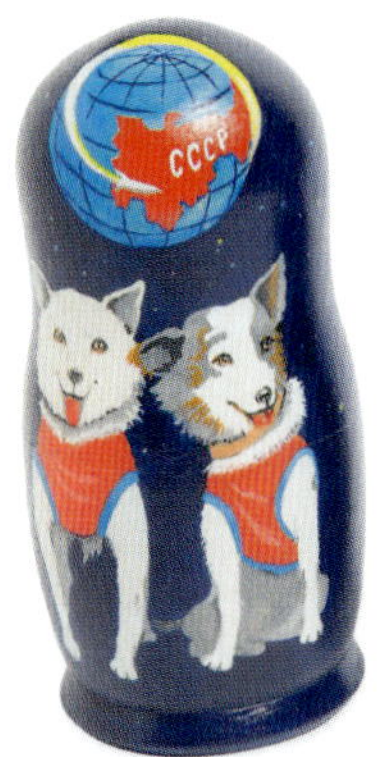
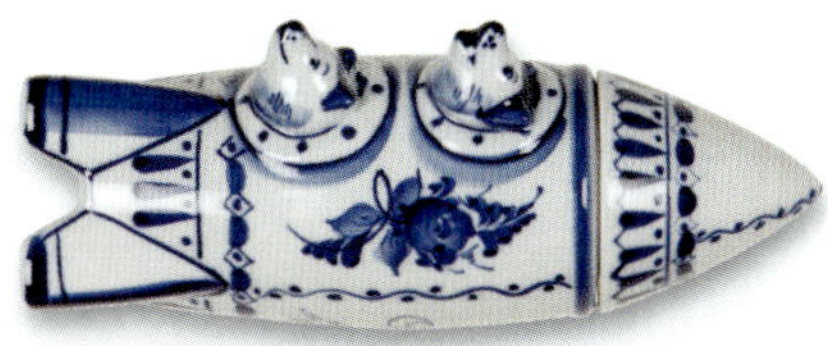
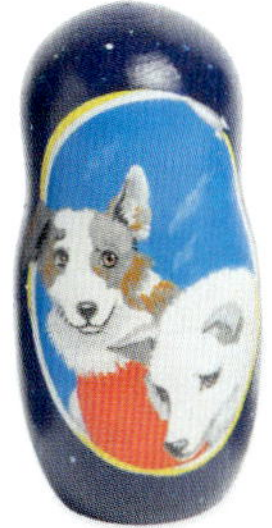
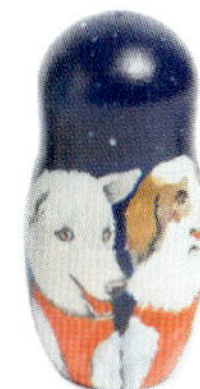
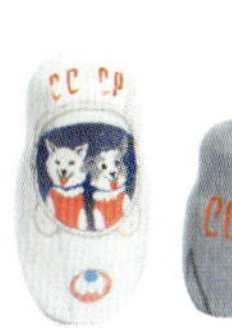
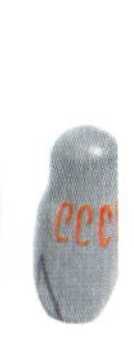
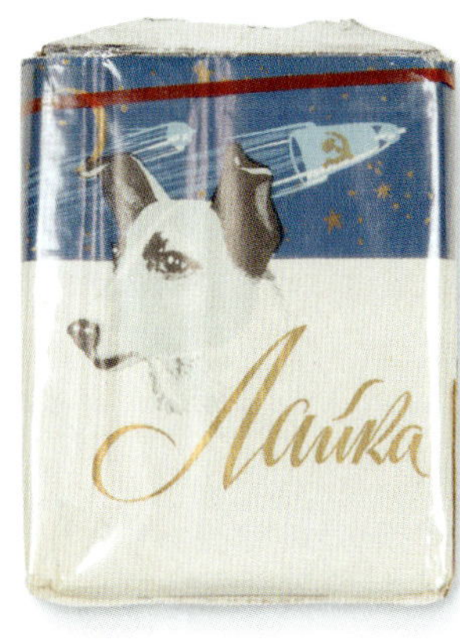

Лайка

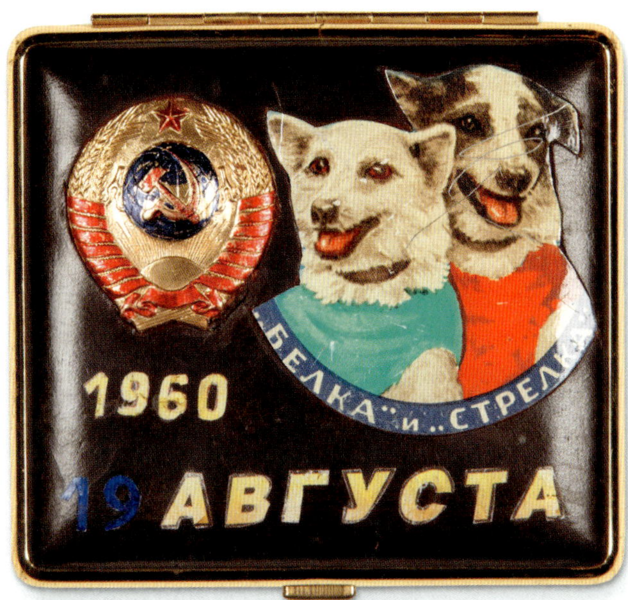

1960
19 АВГУСТА
БЕЛКА и СТРЕЛКА

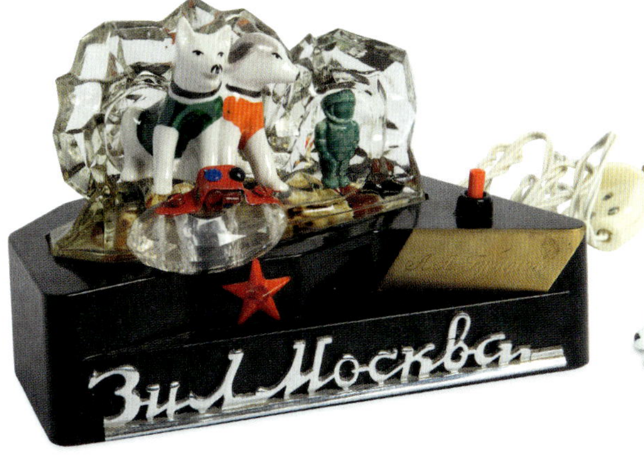

ЗиЛ Москва

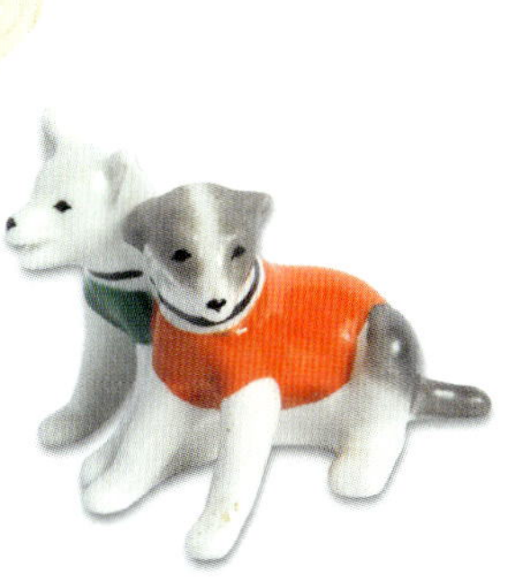
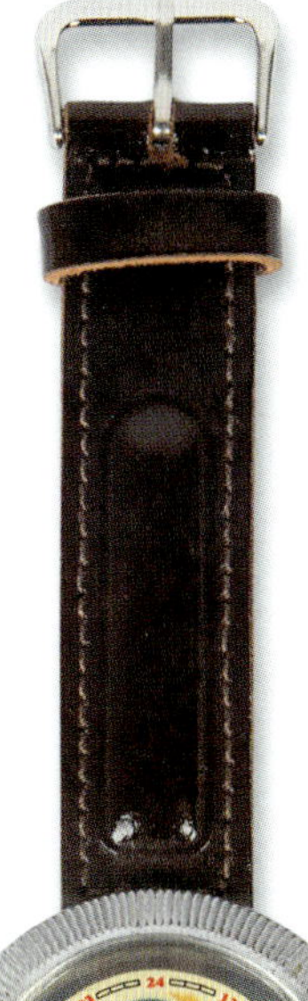
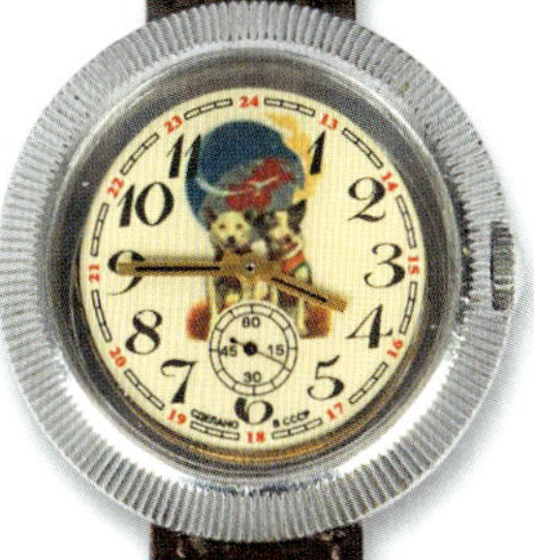

116. Mar del Plata

I've been to most big tourist resorts in the world, and Mar del Plata beach is the resort with the most energy, and the best crowds, and it has to be one of the biggest. It's absolutely massive. If you ask anyone from Argentina, 'Have you been to Mar del Plata?' they always say yes. Mar del Plata is ten miles long, has thousands of hotels, and eight million visitors a year, and is by far the biggest seaside resort in Argentina. They have twelve different beaches for different sorts of clientele. This is obviously the young beach. In fact, the main beach there is called Bristol Beach, which makes me feel at home, and when I'm there I take great pride in telling people that I actually live in the original Bristol. Quite how it was named Bristol is beyond me, but it is something to behold. You will never see a better collection of sun hats, one-piece costumes and beach umbrellas in one location.

Over the years, whenever I've bought a new piece of camera kit, I've gone to the seaside to experiment with it. It's a way of looking at the same place but with different technology. I started by using colour and a 6x7 wide-angle lens in New Brighton in the 80s, a more standard lens on the south coast of Britain, the macro in Benidorm and the telephoto lens in Mar del Plata in 2014. This is an example where the telephoto lens really pays off. You can see how it has compressed the people slightly and that helps make the picture.

I guess I'm in the top 1 per cent of most travelled people in the world. By travelling so much I accumulate images, and I accumulate a view of the world. Don't ask me what that view is. I can't tell you what that is in words, because I express it through photography.

GRANDÉ BEACH
FROM *BEACH THERAPY*
MAR DEL PLATA, ARGENTINA, 2014

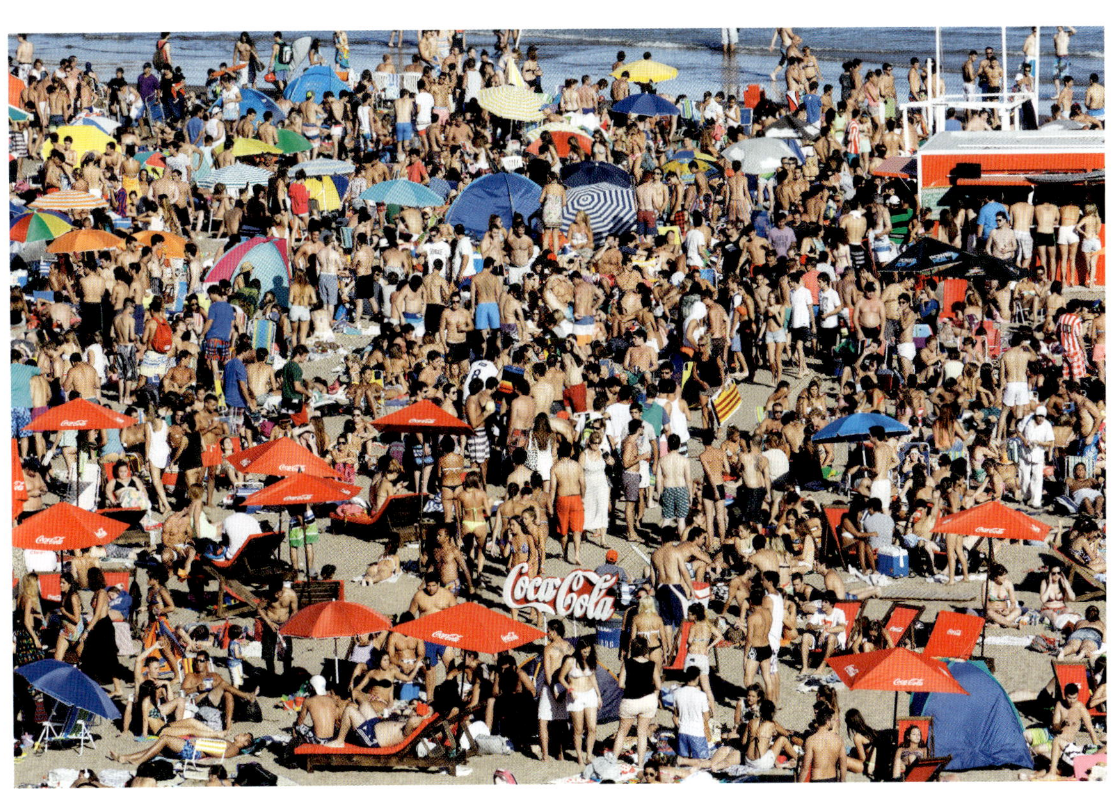

117. The Rhubarb Triangle

Britain is the world's biggest consumer of rhubarb. In 2015, I was commissioned by the Hepworth Wakefield Gallery to go and take pictures of the Rhubarb Triangle, which I've always been intrigued by. The Rhubarb Triangle is an area defined by the towns of Wakefield, Morley and Rothwell in West Yorkshire, which was historically considered the ideal location to grow forced rhubarb. The coal from the nearby mines was used to heat the rhubarb sheds; they covered the soil with old sheep's wool, called shoddy, from the nearby mills.

In the past, there were many family-run rhubarb farms. This one belongs to the Newton Brothers and is one of the fifteen or so farms left. The two Newton brothers are picking the rhubarb in the forcing shed. Rhubarb has to be grown in darkness to make it grow straight, and stay sweet and tender, then it's harvested by candlelight. You can see the candle. My problem was, how do I photograph in candlelight and get a decent exposure? The faces are slightly blurred because it's a long exposure, as that's the only way to capture candlelight. On a quick exposure, you'd see the candle but wouldn't see anything else.

January and February are the months where they force rhubarb to grow because the tubers need sub-zero temperatures to get going. Traditionally, this meant there was fruit in the winter. Forced rhubarb is pink and sweet, whereas in the summer, you get garden rhubarb, which is green and bitter. There used to be express trains called 'Rhubarb Specials' that would take the forced rhubarb overnight from Yorkshire to Covent Garden Market in London, where it'd be sold and sent all around the country, as well as to Paris.

NEWTON BROS
FROM *THE RHUBARB TRIANGLE*
WAKEFIELD, ENGLAND, 2015

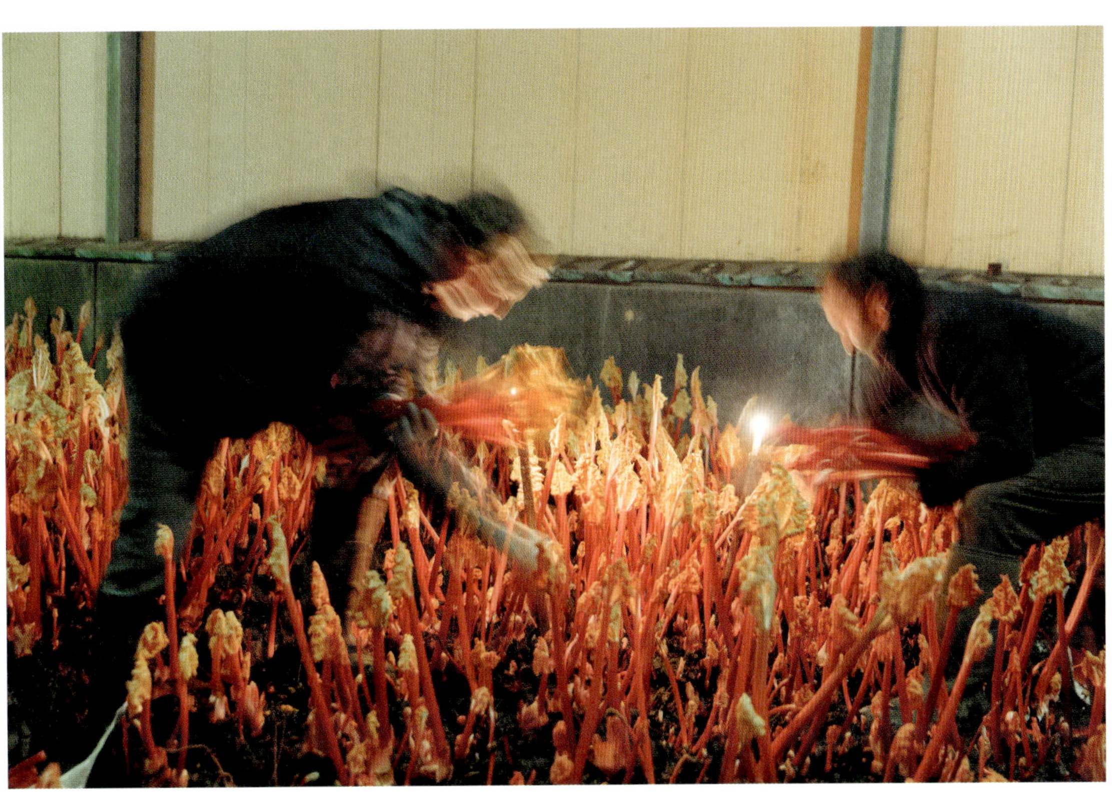

118. The Magic Hour

The Rothesay Pavilion on the Isle of Bute in Scotland is one of two great art deco buildings in the UK. The other is the De La Warr Pavilion in Bexhill. Both of them I like very much. Just by this hint of it on the right-hand side, you can see how beautiful the Rothsay Pavilion is. The curve is amazing, and so is the straight line. This was the magic hour, as the light was fading. I tried to get that perfect balance of the light from the interior with the outdoor light. You can even see the moon. I like the little person walking along on the left-hand side.

ROTHESAY PAVILION
FROM *THINK OF SCOTLAND*
ISLE OF BUTE, SCOTLAND, 2015

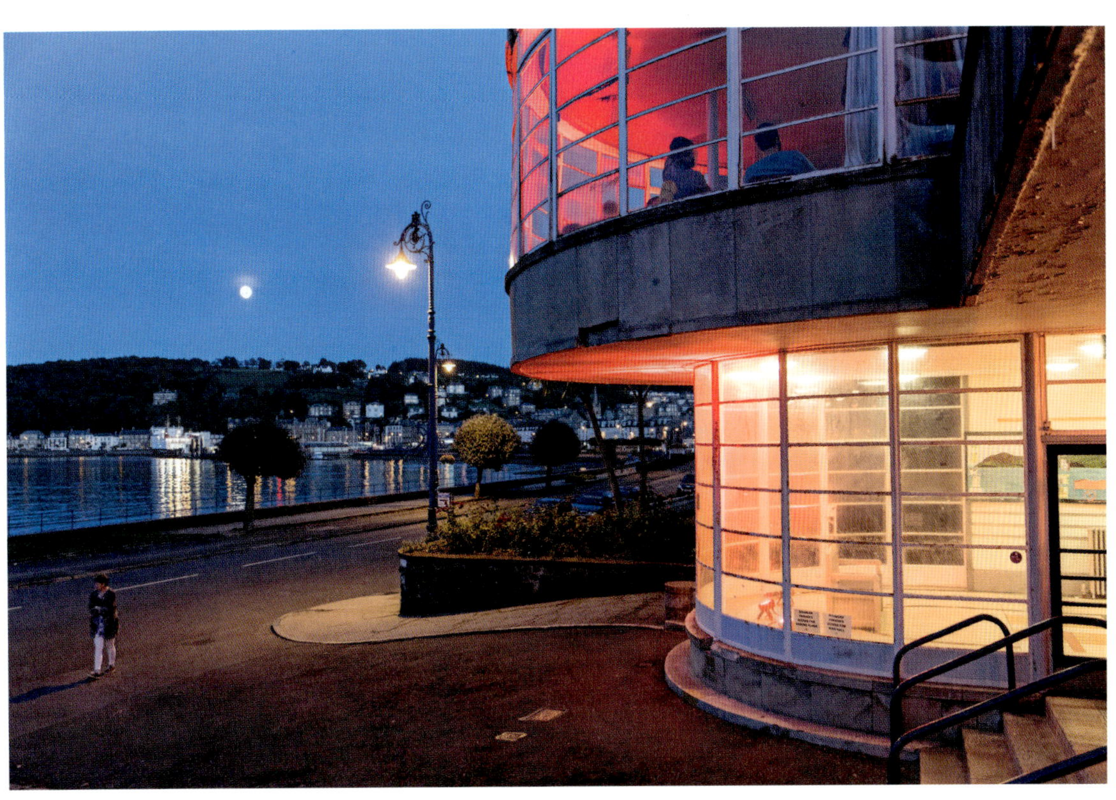

119. Scottish Line Dancing

These people inside the Rothesay Pavilion look like they are having a good time. They're probably Scottish line dancing, I guess, as it's in Scotland. Over the years, I have perfected the art of dancing and photographing at the same time.

ROTHESAY PAVILION
FROM *THINK OF SCOTLAND*
ISLE OF BUTE, SCOTLAND, 2015

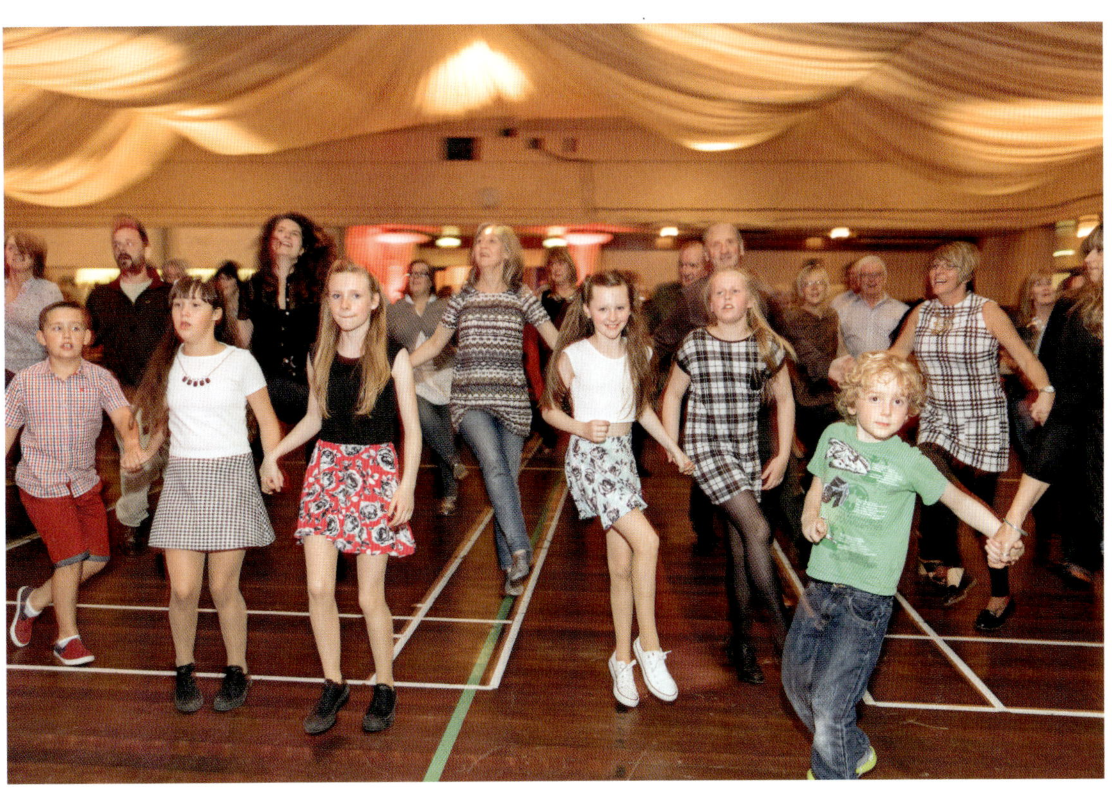

120. Swan Upping

The Queen – now the King – owns all the mute swans in the country. The monarch is allowed to eat swans, although I don't think they ever have. Certainly King Charles wouldn't. No one else in the country is allowed to do so, with the exception of the fellows of St John's College, Cambridge. Every year, in the third week in July, the Queen's Swan Marker sends out two livery companies – the Vintners and the Dyers – to spend five days rowing the Thames to catch every cygnet and ring them. They put these little metal rings around their legs, and that's how they know the total number of swans and how many have hatched that year. It relates to what my dad used to do, going off with the Surrey Bird Club and ringing birds. At five o'clock, when they've finished, the two livery companies stand up, they take a drink and they toast the King. It's a classic tradition, which still continues today. At the back, you can see the Swan Marker in red – he's one of the two men with a swan's feather in his hat – and someone on the bank holding a flag with a swan on it.

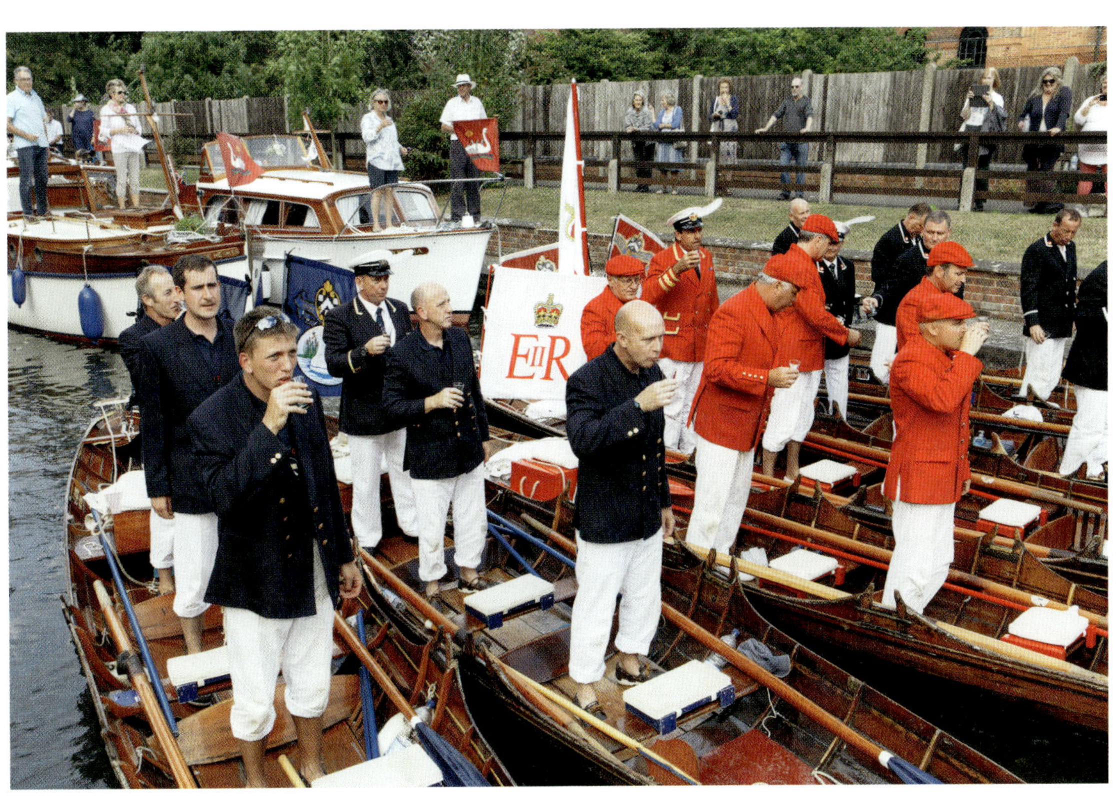

121. Trump Doll

In 2016, I was commissioned by CNN to photograph both the Democratic and the Republican National Conventions. It was an amazing job. The Republican Convention was first, and Republicans were by far the most photogenic because you got all these old ladies with Trump hats, Trump this, that and the other. They were really dressed up. And, of course, they were selling the Trump doll. I managed to snap this woman here holding – fondling is the word, perhaps – her statuette of Trump. It almost looks like a religious painting. She looks in love with him, doesn't she? I can't imagine what you'd do with a Trump doll. Do you keep it in a box and put it on the mantelpiece? Well, if I had one, I'd put it in the bin, so I wouldn't have it. Many different people were at the Republican Convention. The Bushes were there, and then Trump made a rambling speech, which went on for over an hour and was pretty repetitive, but I could see that everyone loved him.

Then I went to the Democratic Convention, which was dominated by people like Bernie Sanders, even though he had been wiped off the shortlist of presidential nominees. And then, of course, we heard Obama speak, who was brilliant, and Michelle Obama, who was also very good and carried the crowd with her. Although the Democrat Convention was less interesting photographically, it was a lot easier to digest because, inevitably, if I was American, I'd be voting Democrat. Unbelievably, watching Trump in 2016, yes, I did think he would get in.

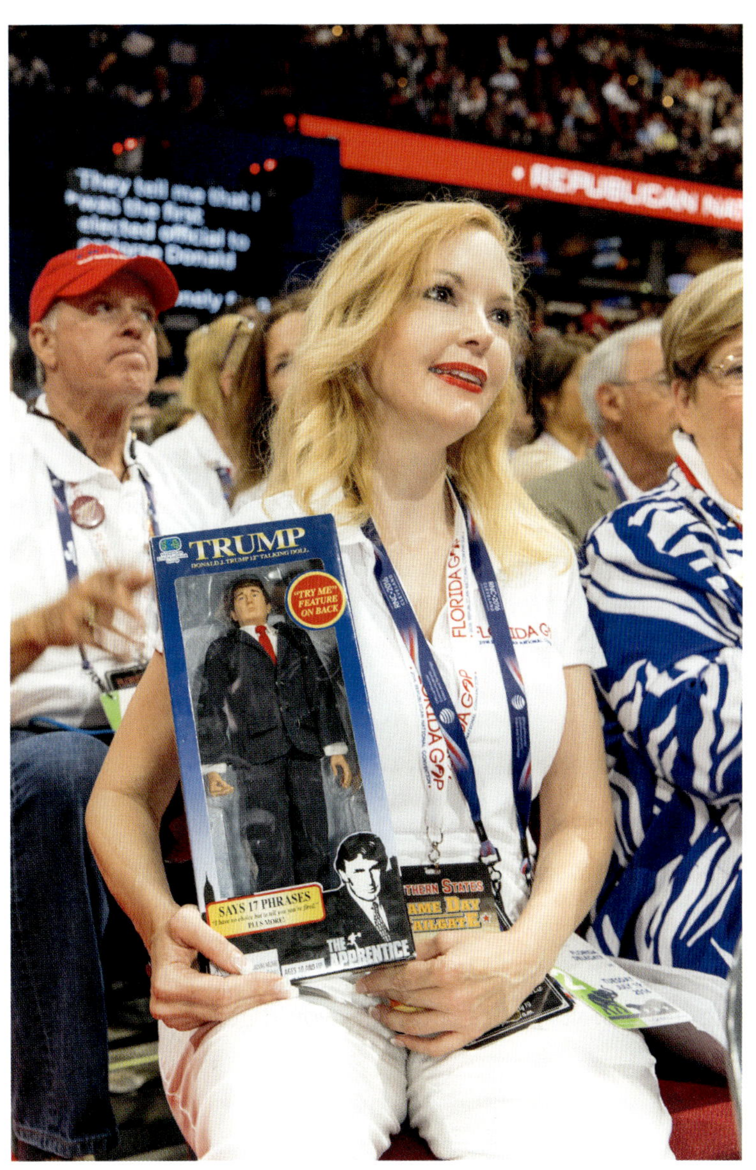
They tell me that I
was the first
elected official to
endorse Donald
...only #...
REPUBLICAN
TRUMP
DONALD J. TRUMP 12" TALKING DOLL
"TRY ME" FEATURE ON BACK
SAYS 17 PHRASES
THE APPRENTICE
FLORIDA GOP

122. Trashing

In order to do exams at Oxford, students have to wear a black gown, and they're encouraged to pin a carnation on it. Traditionally, it's a white carnation for the first exam, pink for ongoing exams, then, when they do the final exam, it's a red carnation. When the students are let out of the back of the examination hall after their final exam, their friends will be waiting there to 'trash' them. That's spraying them with Prosecco and foam, drinking Prosecco, basically going pretty mad.

I like Britain, but there's always a contradiction. There are many traditions in Britain – like this one – which are interesting, quaint or hugely hidden away. Yet we also have Fascist marches and violence. I'm not particularly fond of those. So I have a love–hate relationship with Britain, which I can express through documentary photography. Part of the aim is to create an inventory of life in Britain in my time living here as a photographer.

'TRASHING' AFTER FINAL EXAMS AT THE UNIVERSITY OF OXFORD
OXFORD, ENGLAND, 2016

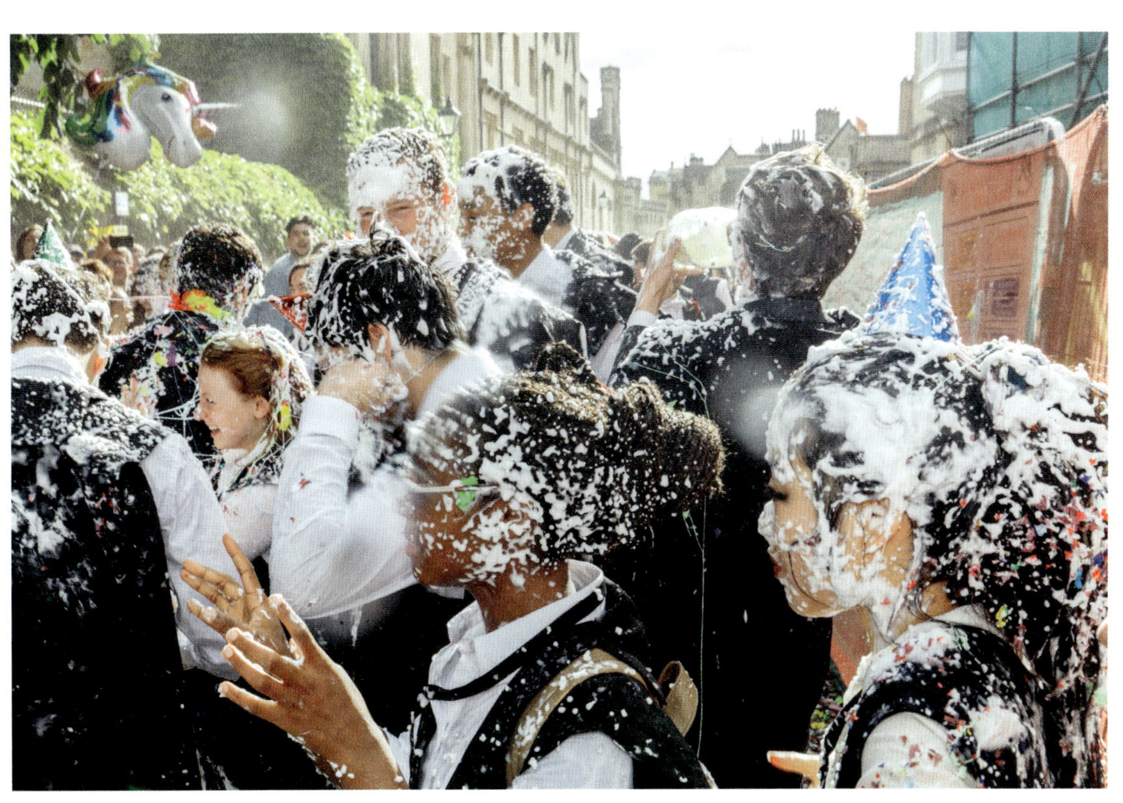

123. Henley Regatta

Of all the summer sporting events that are part of what's called 'the Season', Henley Regatta is my favourite. I've been to Henley Regatta three times now. What I like about it is that its sponsorship is very subtle. All the other events like the Derby and Royal Ascot are sponsored by huge companies, while the Henley Regatta feels pure because there aren't loads of ads around.

No photographers are allowed in the Stewards' Enclosure. They don't want to be interrupted by, or corrupted by, press photographers at a rowing regatta. The first time I went I bought a VIP ticket to the hospitality enclosure where you can get all the food and the drink you want for three hundred quid. Quite expensive. Then, if you paid fifty quid extra you got into the Stewards' Enclosure. So I got in that way. I thought I might be thrown out, and I was asked what I was doing there a few times but I managed to get away with it.

Most of the people who go to the regatta are ex-rowers. It's six days of rowing, and everyone goes and watches and has tea. It's a great event. They're queuing here for afternoon tea. I like that I managed to get that sign – 'BADGE OFFICE' – in isolation. It's got its own little gap. And it's raining. Look, umbrellas are out. Men are wearing sportingly striped jackets. Those stripy blazers make great photographs.

HENLEY ROYAL REGATTA
HENLEY-ON-THAMES, ENGLAND, 2016

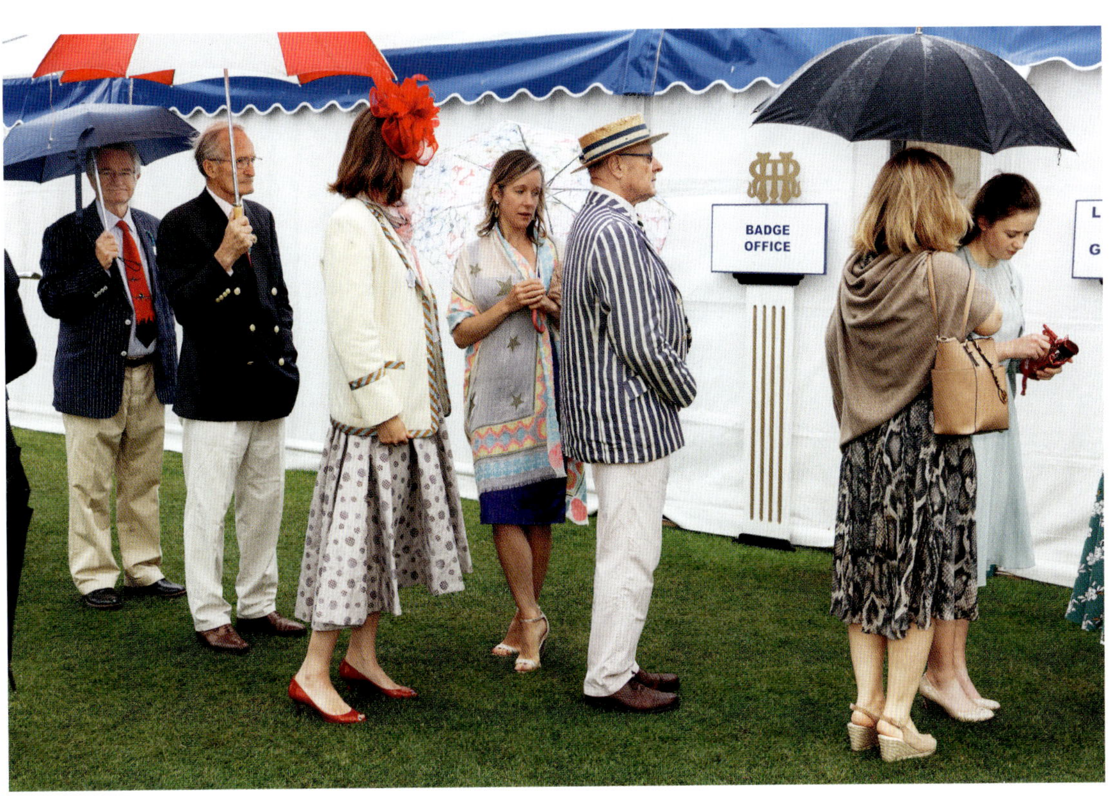
BADGE
OFFICE

124. Crisp & Fry

People don't take photos in chip shops very much, although I have over the years. Chip shops are part of the scene in Britain and unique to the UK, fish and chips being typical British food. I found this fish and chip shop called Crisp & Fry, in Hull, and I couldn't believe that two Muslim women were running it. I've never seen another fish and chip shop run by Muslim women, and the lady on the right has got a lovely, checked scarf on as well. I asked them if I could take a picture. I was very nervous that they would say no – in my experience, Muslim ladies sometimes don't want to have their picture taken – and then I would think that this was a great opportunity that I'd have missed. Luckily, they agreed to the picture. I had to stop them smiling too much, but there's just enough of a smile for it to be okay.

Crisp & Fry is an archetypal fish and chip shop. You've got the battered fish, you've got the Specials, you've got the salt and pepper and vinegar, and the tomato ketchup sachets in the back, and the Coca-Cola. It's exactly your average chip shop.

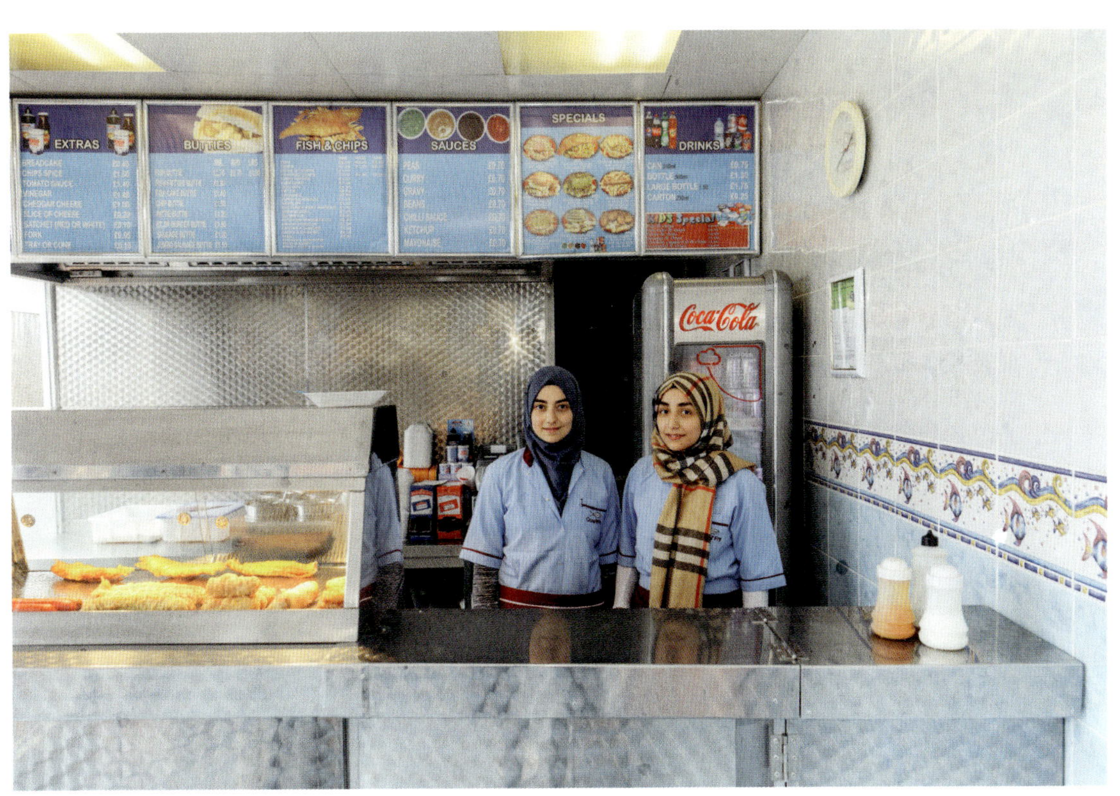

125. Royal Bath and West

I'm always on the lookout for agricultural shows. I like the contrast between the very small agricultural shows like the ones in Orkney, and the big ones like the Royal Bath and West.

The Royal Bath and West in Shepton Mallet is a very big agricultural show. It goes on for three days. Here they are judging the sheep. Look how they're so neatly lined up. Quite fantastic. And look at the five people kneeling down. The judge is about to start examining, I assume, the anuses of the sheep. Perhaps she lifts up the tail. That's a quick look. Are they not looking at their tails? I don't know if they're males. Could be girls. I think they are girls because I can't see any pockets of bollocks. They don't have horns, so I think these are girls.

Just look at their neatness. It's quite something. I love the white coats everybody's wearing. Amazing. It's very formal. You can tell the Royal Bath and West is a very high-class agricultural show. You can see people are taking it very seriously. There's no doubt about that. It just makes my heart sing when I see pictures like this with all those sheep, and the people in their neat rows. It feels like all's right with the world.

ROYAL BATH AND WEST SHOW
SHEPTON MALLET, ENGLAND, 2017

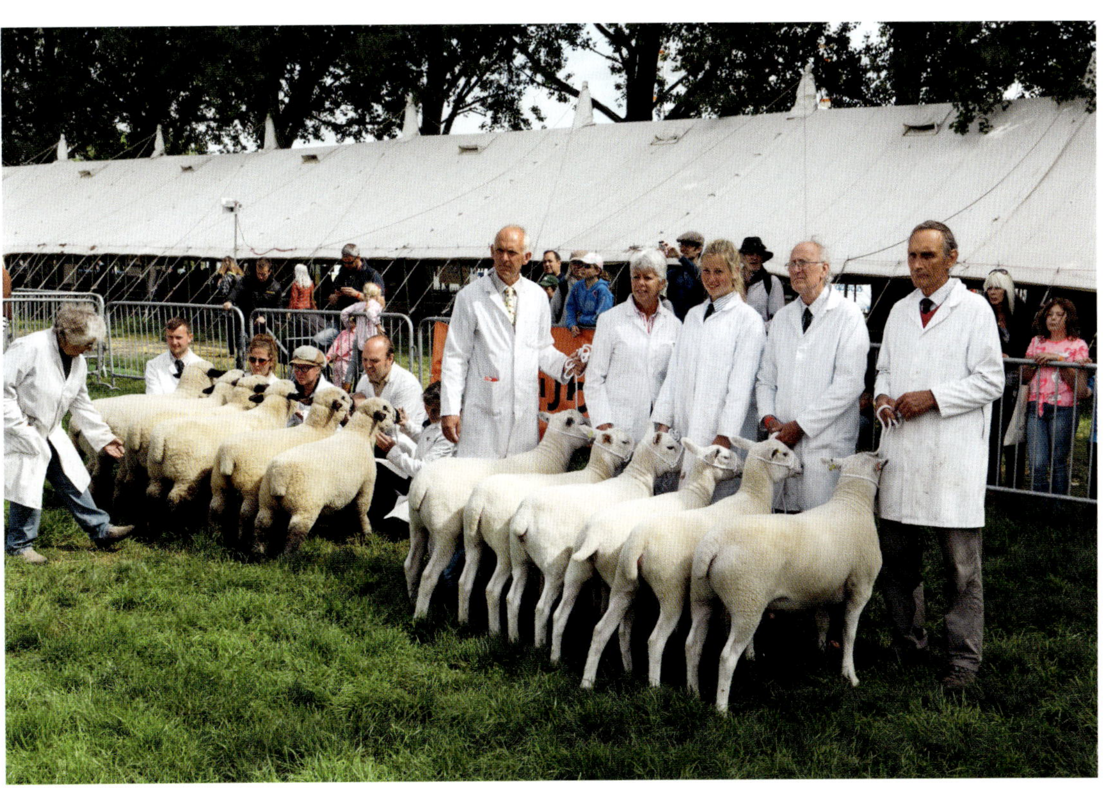

126. Clacton in the Rain

I'm like a migrating bird; I always go back to the beach. This is Clacton in the rain. I like it when it rains on the beach because it means people do interesting things. They try to cover themselves. They try to avoid the rain. They rush around. They have to adjust their parasols, head in or, in this case, shelter under a big ground mat.

CLACTON BEACH
CLACTON, ENGLAND, 2017

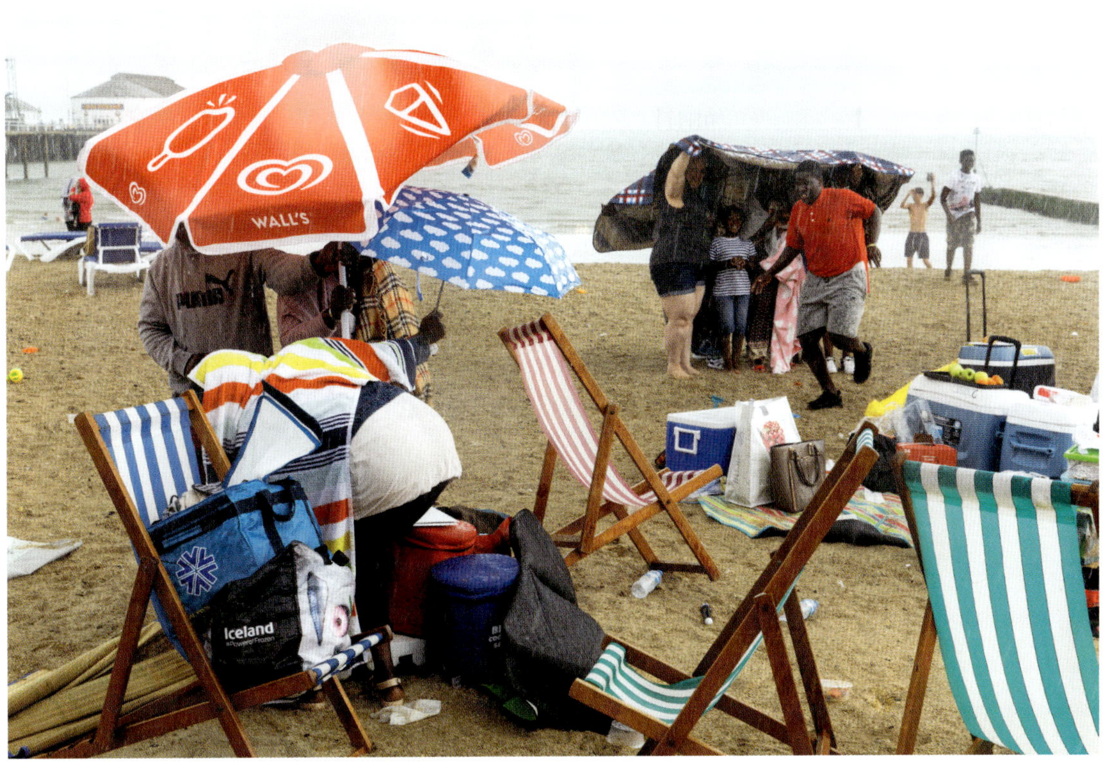

WALL'S
Iceland

127. Three Photographers

This is the only known image of these three photographers together – Don McCullin, David Bailey and, on the right, me. When David Bailey and Don McCullin first started, I didn't have the respect for them that I do now. It was one of those things where I only realized later what they'd achieved and how brilliant they've been in doing that. McCullin is nearly ninety. He worked as a photojournalist, and he always says that he failed as a war photographer because there are more wars now than ever before, so it makes him think, what was the point of doing it all? And David Bailey is probably the best-known photographer in Britain. I often hear, when I take a picture, people saying, 'Who do you think you are, David Bailey?' He does portraits, he does fashion, he does landscape, he does everything. He's a very cheeky working-class kid and he's a lot of fun.

DON MCCULLIN, DAVID BAILEY AND MARTIN AT PHOTO LONDON
LONDON, ENGLAND, 2017

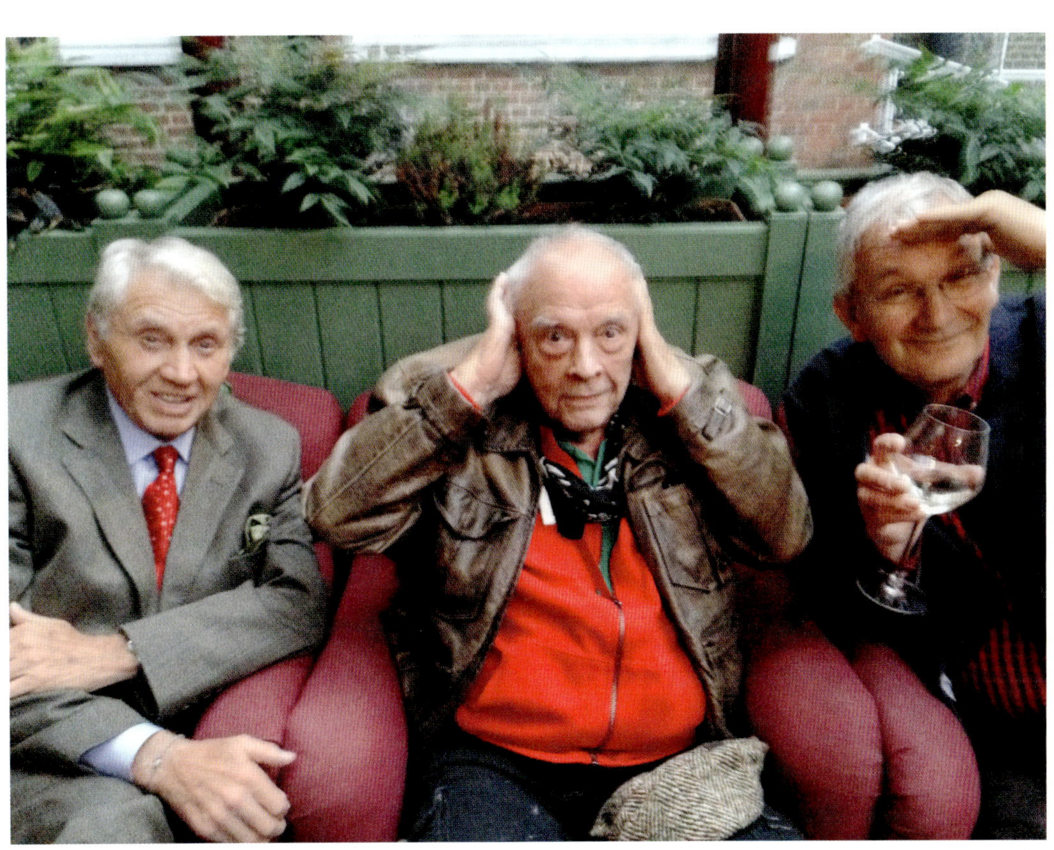

128. St George's Day

In West Bromwich, on the Sunday after St George's Day, they used to hold the biggest, and maybe the only, St George's Day parade in the whole country. This was taken in 2018. In the Brexit vote, West Bromwich very strongly voted to leave the EU. What's weird is that it's such a multicultural town. The parade went around the town – of about ten thousand people – starting at the Stone Cross outside the town and then going through the streets. They also had a sing-song at the Tipton Club on St George's Day itself.

St George's Day doesn't have a national public holiday. I don't even know when St George's Day is. I think it's April 23rd, isn't it? They celebrate St David's Day a lot in Wales. There's a St Patrick's Day, of course, traditionally for the Catholics in Ireland. I don't know if St Andrew's Day is a public holiday in Scotland. Anyway, the point is, they went to town for St George's Day in West Bromwich, and it was unique. You got a flavour of how patriotic they were.

ST GEORGE'S DAY STONE CROSS PARADE
WEST BROMWICH, ENGLAND, 2017

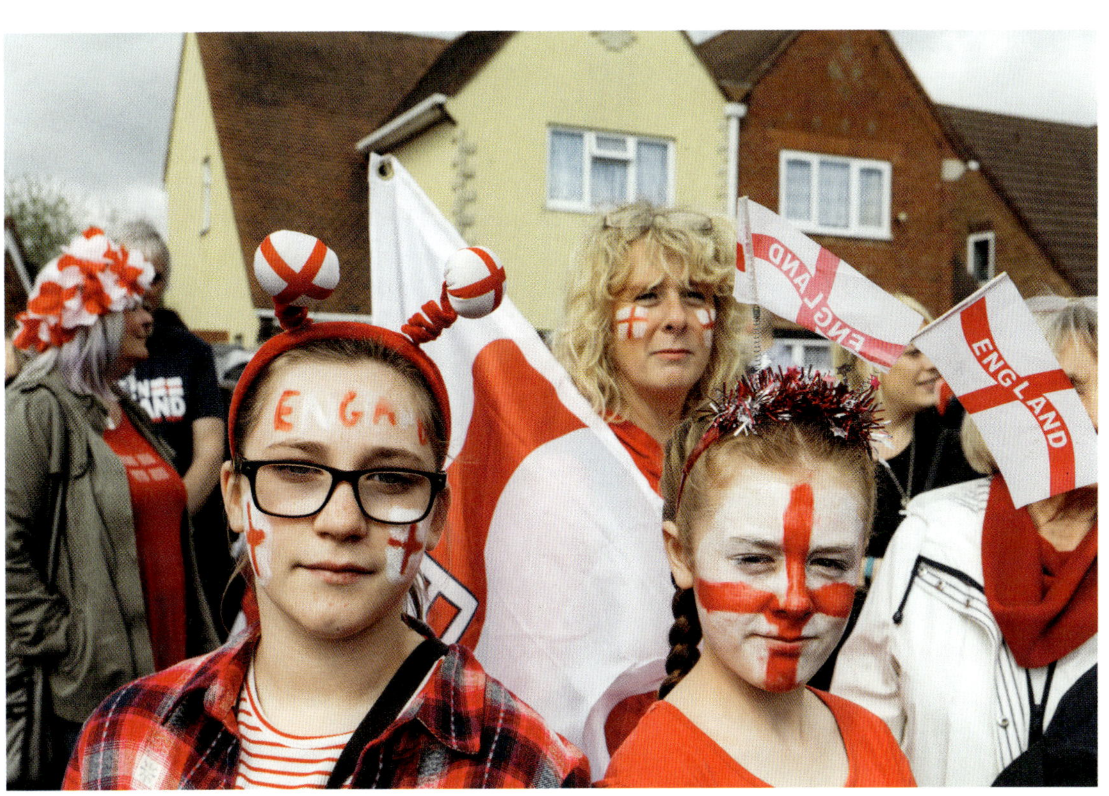

129. Fans

In 2018, I went to the big four tennis Grand Slams: Roland-Garros in Paris, Wimbledon in the UK, Flushing Meadows in the US and Melbourne in Australia, for a book called *Match Point*. I was photographing anything but the actual tennis. I was photographing people walking around, people drinking, people lying down. I turned my back on the actual sport.

The Australian Open takes place in January in the middle of summer, and it is very hot. That year, it got to 40°C or 104°F. Oh, it was very hot. They had these fans that sprayed cold water so spectators could cool themselves down briefly during the huge heat we had to contend with. People just loved them. I knew something was going to happen by that fan. It was one of those occasions where I pinned down a place that had something to reveal, and I waited there until I got the right picture. It's called fishing. Basically, I stayed there until I got my fish. I might not have got my fish; I might have been unlucky. Here I was lucky. She's enjoying the damp, enjoying the spray. She's just very expressive. It's sort of a weather photograph. And a climate change photograph. You can see I've used flash here. That's why the two hands on the right are so well lit. I used flash in the middle of a sunny day because I wanted to have the clarity of the person immediately in front of me. They didn't notice me. They were too busy enjoying the water. They were really oblivious to me. That's what I like.

AUSTRALIAN OPEN
FROM *MATCH POINT*
MELBOURNE, AUSTRALIA, 2018

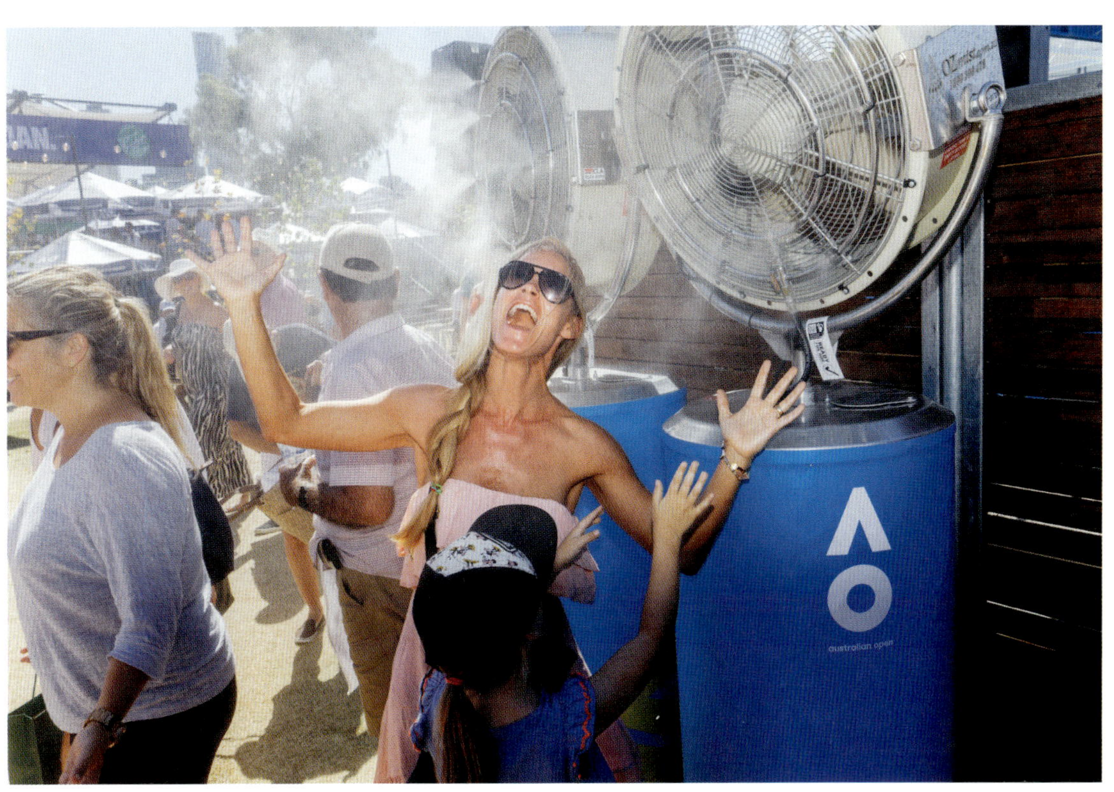

AO
australian open

130. Chelsea Flower Show

On the last day of the Chelsea Flower Show, at around four o'clock, there's 'The Great Sell-Off', where they sell off the plants at bargain prices. This creates a fantastic opportunity to photograph, because from four o'clock to five o'clock people are streaming out of the Chelsea Flower Show clutching huge quantities of plants, often with great difficulty. It's a hilarious occasion. The trouble with it is that there are lots of other photographers there – I'm not the only one, by any means. The other trouble is that most of the people carrying plants start laughing because they know how ridiculous they look. This is one person who's made it to Sloane Square Station and is waiting for a tube. Here it doesn't matter whether she's laughing or not because we can't see her face. She's exulted by flowers, isn't she? It's a terrific event, one of the key photographic opportunities presented to us throughout the calendar year. Give me a crowd, give me an event, I'm happy.

THE SATURDAY SELL-OFF AT THE CHELSEA FLOWER SHOW
LONDON, ENGLAND, 2018

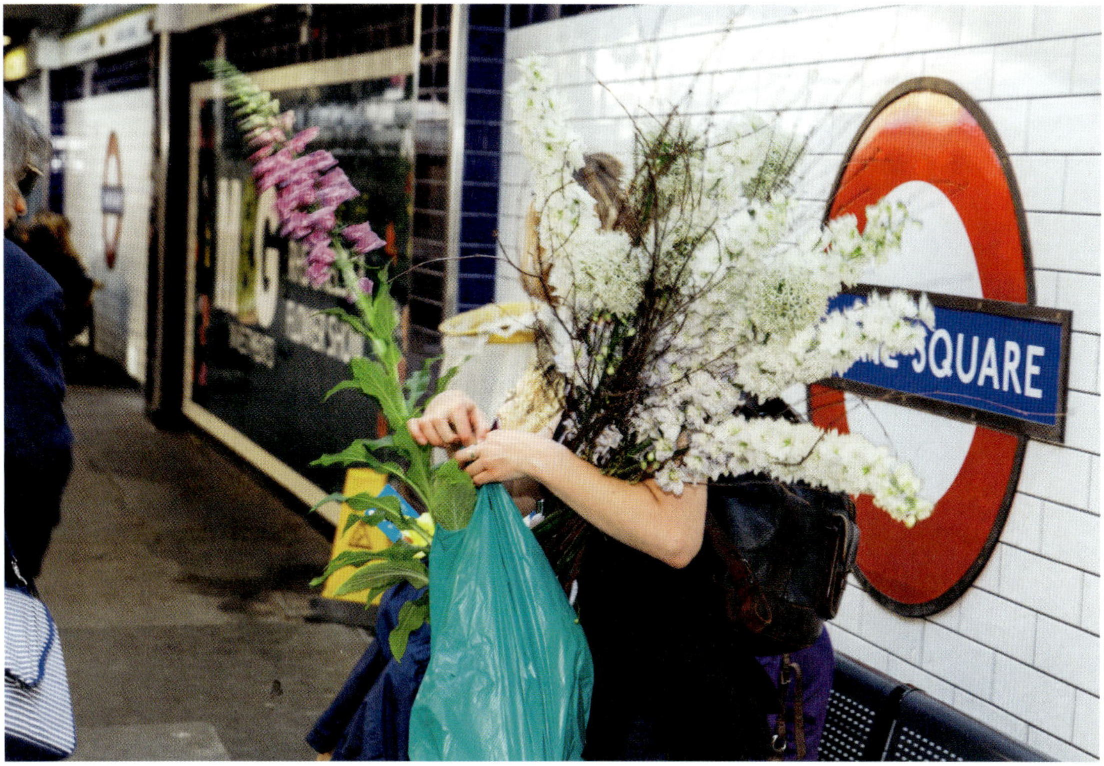

SQUARE

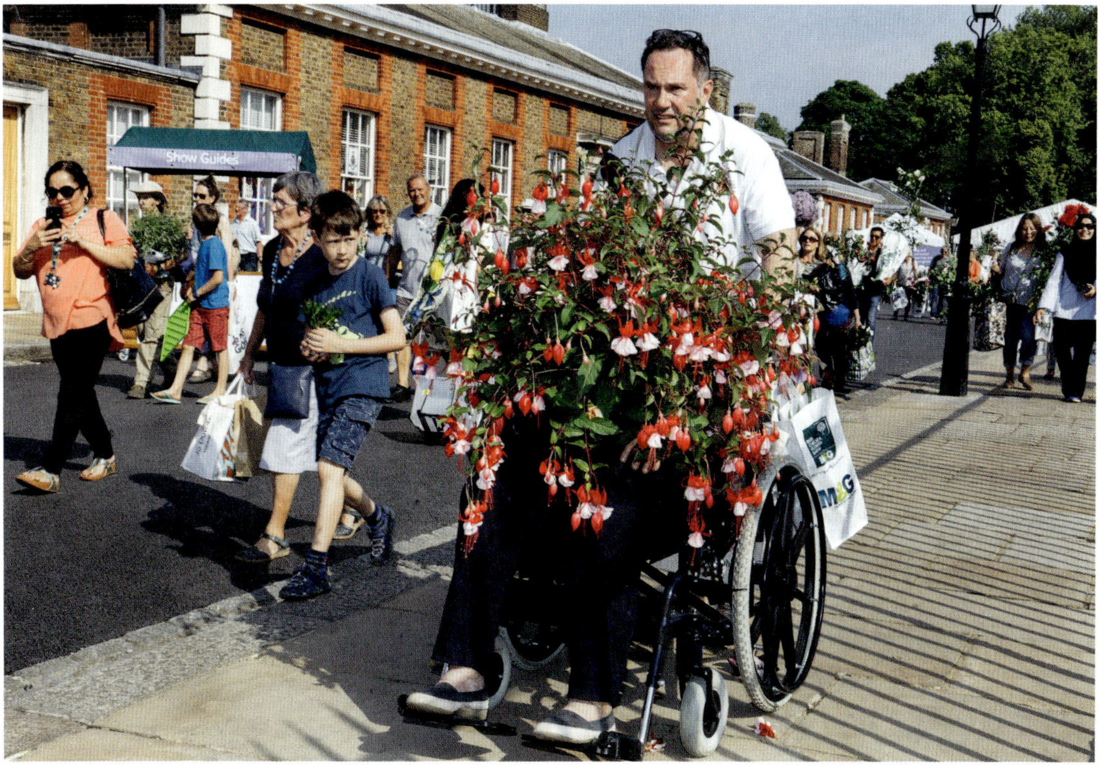

Show Guides

131. The Martin Parr Foundation

In 2015, we established a charity, the Martin Parr Foundation, to look after my archive and my collection of work by British and Irish photographers. Then, in 2017, we bought a building in Bristol, funded from the sale to the Tate Gallery of the very large photographic book collection I'd built up over the years. We fitted the building out with a gallery, an archive, a library and workspaces, because it is combined with my ongoing photography business as well. We've since built a substantial library of about six thousand books by British photographers, mainly since the Second World War – we have more prints by British photographers than the Tate. We have a membership scheme, a lively bookshop, a very interesting programme of events and we hold four exhibitions a year of emerging photographers, alongside established and overlooked photographers. The purpose of the Foundation is to collect and give a platform to British and Irish photographers, as well as photographers who have come to Britain and Ireland and taken photographs.

We had Martin the donkey visit the Foundation in 2018. Adam Lee and his donkey were walking the length of the UK in aid of Centrepoint, the homeless charity. Adam had named his donkey, Martin, after me. Susie and I invited them to camp in our garden en route down south. They walked to the MPF, where Martin the donkey went into the gallery. He actually did a massive poo.

The MPF has worked out very well, so I'm very happy with it. I guess I've contributed to documentary photography being taken more seriously, but I haven't personally changed it. I'm simply trying to put back into British photography culture, having benefitted from it myself.

MARTIN THE DONKEY WITH ADAM LEE
AT THE MARTIN PARR FOUNDATION
BRISTOL, ENGLAND, 2018

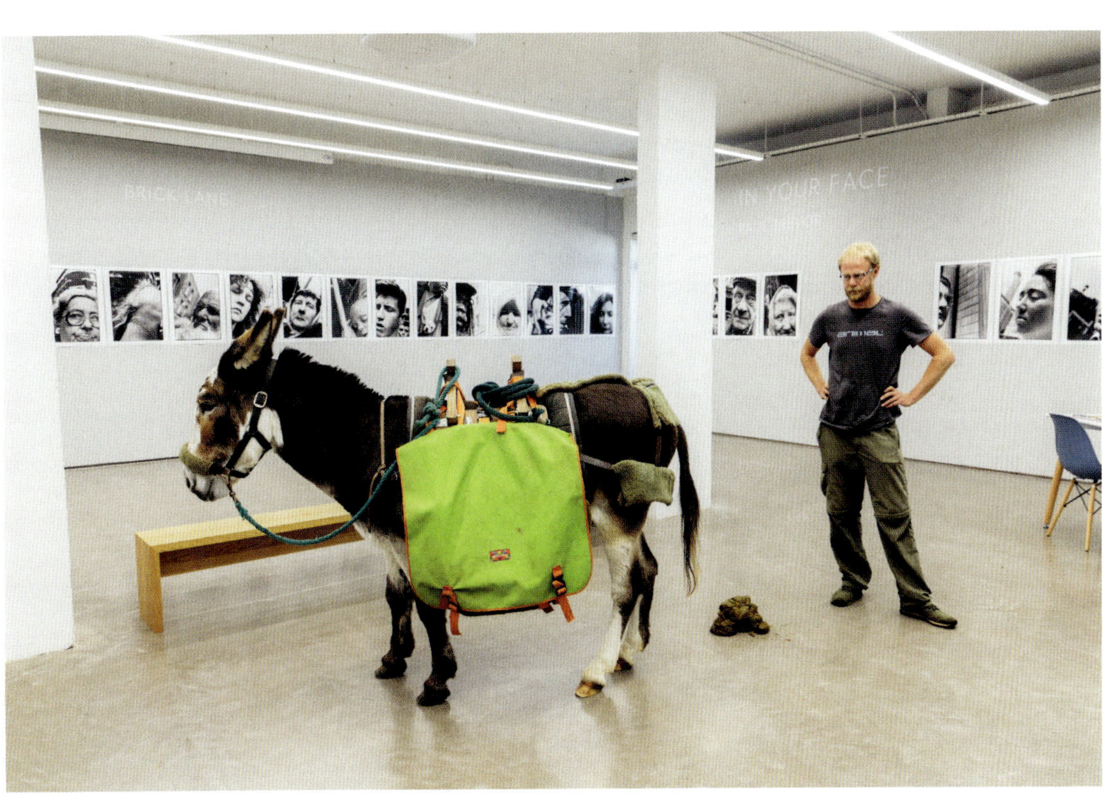

132. Orange Lady

I was on a Gucci shoot in Cannes, doing a look book where I photographed every new outfit that Gucci was launching that season. As well as the models, they also brought along another ten or so extras – older women, young men – whom I could at any given time just pop into the picture. Gucci were a bit different: they liked the idea of older people being in their ads. I saw this lady. I said, 'Can I take a picture of you lying on the deck chair?' I frizzed out her hair because it was neat, got a pair of Gucci sunglasses and put them on her and, Bob's your uncle, here's the shot. It's a good stab of subversion.

The sun glare in the left-hand lens is very attractive. There's a hint of it on the right. It's messy. It's also very straightforward. It's strong and punchy. One of the things I was interested in demonstrating is that it's often only older, wealthy people who can afford to buy Gucci. I like photographing older women when I'm doing fashion shoots. They can't wear the dresses – they wouldn't fit in them because all the models are very skinny – but they can wear the accessories.

GUCCI CRUISE
CANNES, FRANCE, 2018

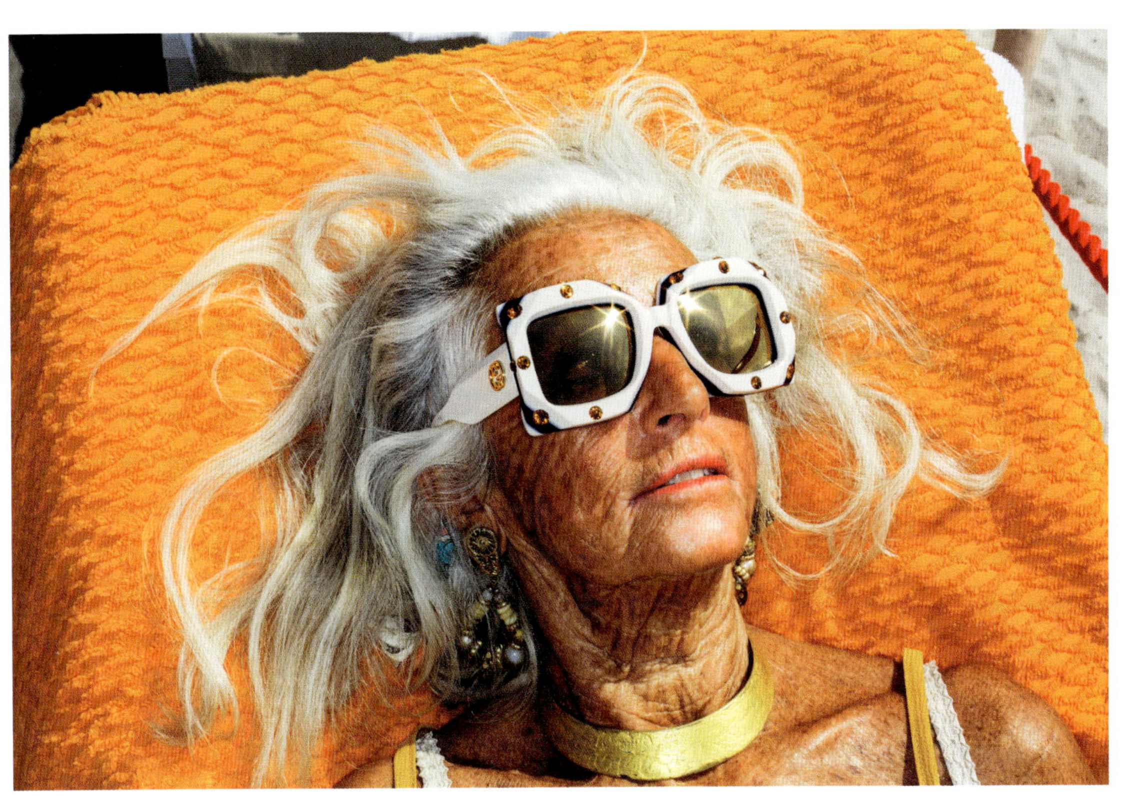

133. Death by Selfie

I'm fascinated by people taking selfies. If you look up the death by selfie statistics on Wikipedia, the country where the most people have died taking selfies is India, so I decided to include many pictures of people taking selfies in India in my book *Death by Selfie*. It's the same shape as an iPhone, and it has an Apple-like logo on the back. People die from taking selfies because they walk backwards and fall off a cliff or into an oncoming train. They're distracted, basically.

Selfies serve a purpose. Selfies are what tourists do at tourist locations. It is impossible to look around at a tourist location without seeing a selfie being taken. You have to have the picture of yourself in front of the thing you've come to view. You don't stand there and enjoy the scene. I guess it's like a pilgrimage, getting the photos of family and friends in front of X, Y or Z. Having yourself in front of the monument proves you're part of the world. It's a confirmation of your existence. It's so normal now – everyone taking a picture on a selfie stick – but in thirty years' time, people will look back and think, Look at them all, with those selfie sticks and old-fashioned phones. The selfie stick is going into decline. I don't know why. Maybe people's arms have got longer.

Selfies are such an important part of photography at the moment. People taking selfies are good to photograph because they often have their back to whatever site they're visiting. I get the benefits of both angles – I can photograph the site of interest and the person taking the selfie in front of it. I get a double whammy. Previously, people were facing the monument or whatever it was, and I only got their backs. Now people have turned around. That's helped me enormously.

DEATH BY SELFIE BOOK COVER
PUBLISHED BY SUPER LABO, 2019

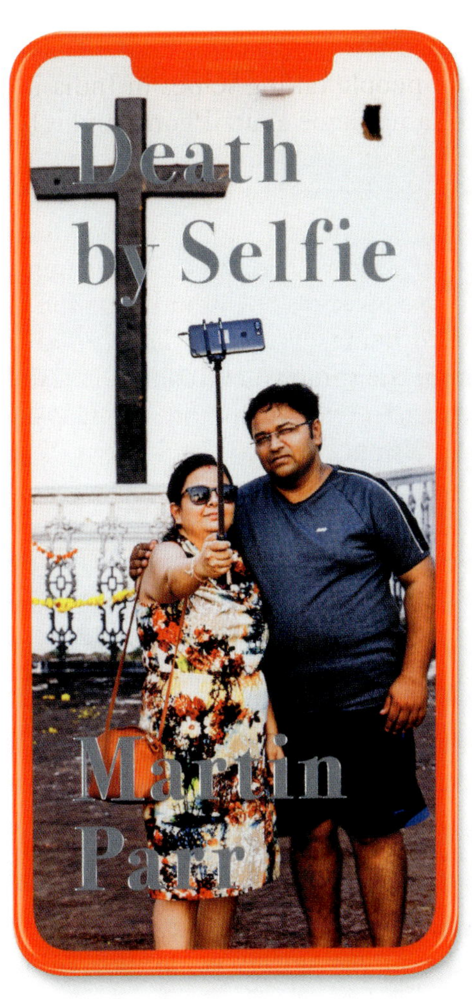

Death
by Selfie
Martin
Parr

134. Banksy

I've lived in Bristol for a long time now, and I photographed around the city a lot during the pandemic, when we weren't allowed to travel. This is a Banksy mural, which I photographed in 2020. It's of an old woman, a handbag and a stick. It's called *Aachoo!!* See, look – she loses her false teeth. Some nursery kids have come to visit it, and an old guy, too. So it's a photo of people looking at art, not just the art itself. It's on a very steep road, called Vale Street, next to the steepest street in England. Banksy was born in Bristol and brought up here, and there's a lot of his – what would you call them? – spray paintings around. This one didn't last very long, probably two days, then it went. It must be hard to take the plaster, but they do. When you see a new Banksy, first it's got to be confirmed on his Instagram – he will confirm that it is his – well, not him, his organization. Whoever owns the house owns the Banksy, and probably the house is worth less than the Banksy on their wall. This one would have been worth hundreds of thousands. It was moved in broad daylight, very officially. The people who owned the house would have done a deal with the people who bought it.

TOTTERDOWN BANKSY MURAL
BRISTOL, ENGLAND, 2020

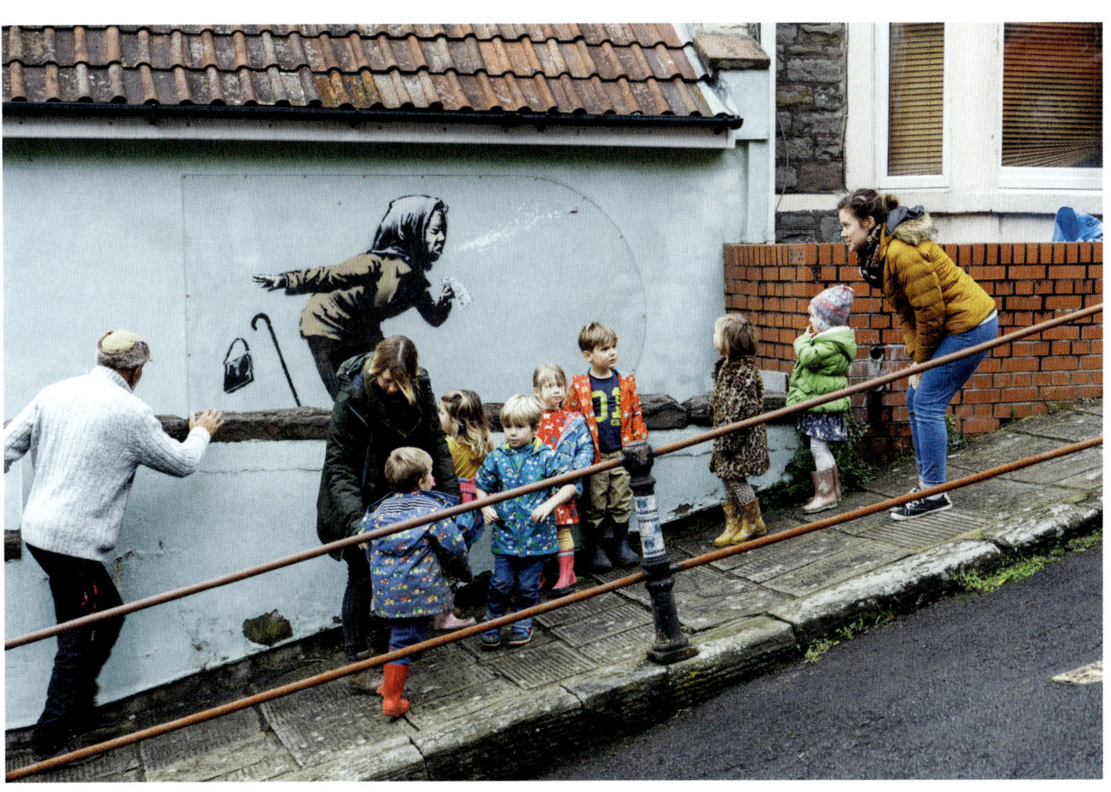

135. Collecting

It's quite nice that the Queen's got the same outfit on as when I took the portrait of her from behind. The doll behind the poor Queen is an Albanian doll from my trip to Communist Albania. These are part of the collection which my dear wife despises so heavily, which she managed to tell the whole audience at a talk recently. She pushed my cabinet of collections out of the house, where they were my pride and joy, and into the Foundation. She said, 'I've got my house back and my kitchen back from the Spice Girls crisps.' What an outrage! I had many visitors come to see my cabinet in our kitchen before the collection went to the Foundation. But more people come and see my cabinet in the Foundation. My other collections in the cabinet include Saddam Hussein watches, Martin Luther King pendants, Communist crockery, and Spice Girl crisp packets. Sadly, the crisp packets deteriorated so much that eventually I had to throw them away. My choice of what to collect is an intuitive thing, really. I can't explain it. I think it's a desire to bring things together. I would drown in objects if I didn't have the ability to photograph them.

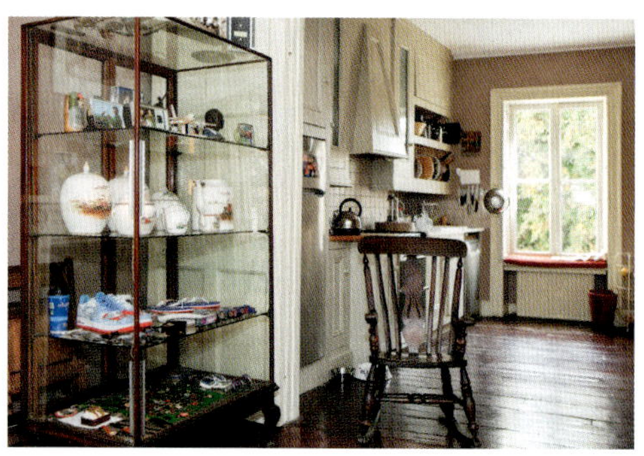

THE CABINET AT MARTIN'S HOME
BRISTOL, ENGLAND, 2020

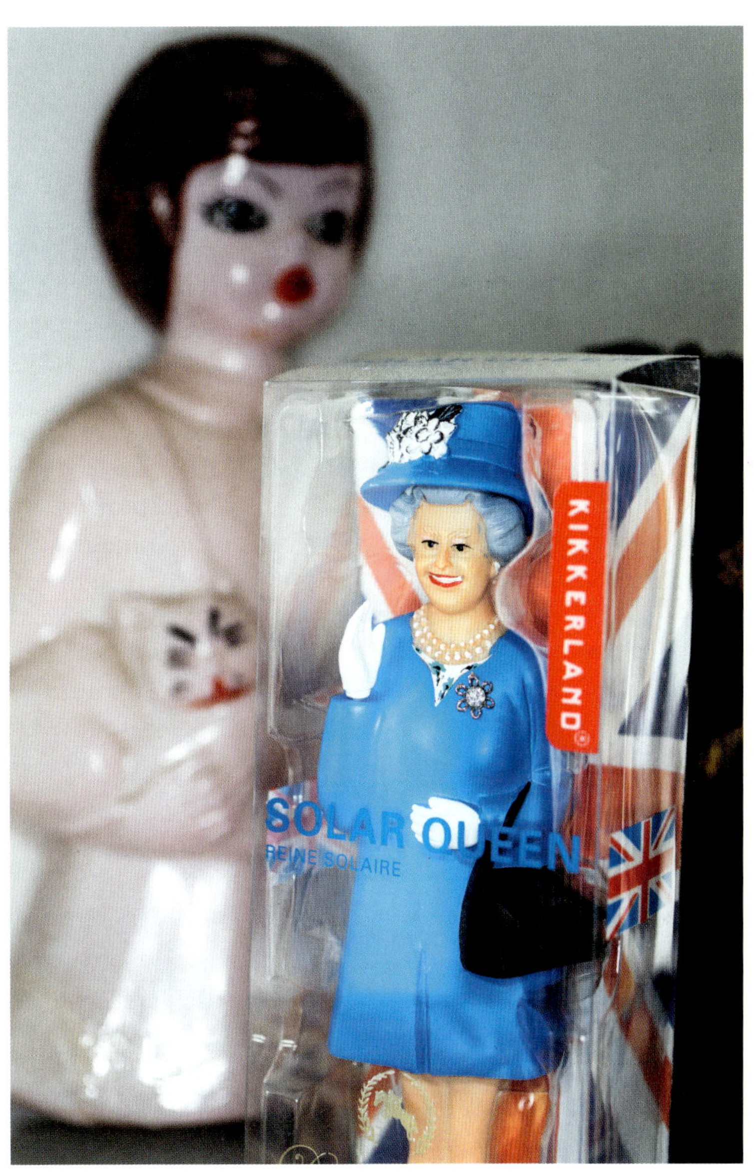

KIKKERLAND®
SOLAR QUEEN
REINE SOLAIRE

136. Black Lives Matter

This event haunts me. It's the remains of the plinth of the notorious Colston statue that was thrown into Bristol Harbour on 7 June 2020, during the Black Lives Matter march. I was at the march photographing all the banners and I got as far as the statue and thought, 'Well, there's nothing more happening now, I will go home.' By the time I got home I learnt on the news that the statue had been pulled over and pushed into the harbour. If I had stayed just five minutes longer I would have been able to photograph the statue coming down, being rolled along, then thrown into the water.

It was a global news story. Edward Colston was a Bristol philanthropist in the seventeenth century who made his money from the slave trade, and the question of whether his statue should be taken down had been discussed many times before. It had been simmering away as an issue, but I hadn't the sense to put two and two together and to think that this particular day and this particular march would be the occasion when they came equipped with the rope and tools to actually take it down and get rid of it. There were at least a couple of thousand people at the march, and there must have been a good few hundred that were part of the whole event of ripping it down and putting it in the water.

It's my big regret in my photography career. I have thought about it so many times. I would have so liked to have been there to witness it; to photograph the statue being torn down and tossed into the harbour, because it was such a significant event during the Black Lives Matter protests. I did go down the following morning. By then, you can see, the council had cleared up these surrounds. They'd taken the banners away, it was all neat and sanitized, and all that was left was the plinth for the statue.

BLACK LIVES MATTER PROTEST:
THE REMAINING PLINTH OF THE EDWARD COLSTON
STATUE THAT WAS THROWN INTO BRISTOL HARBOUR
BRISTOL, ENGLAND, 2020

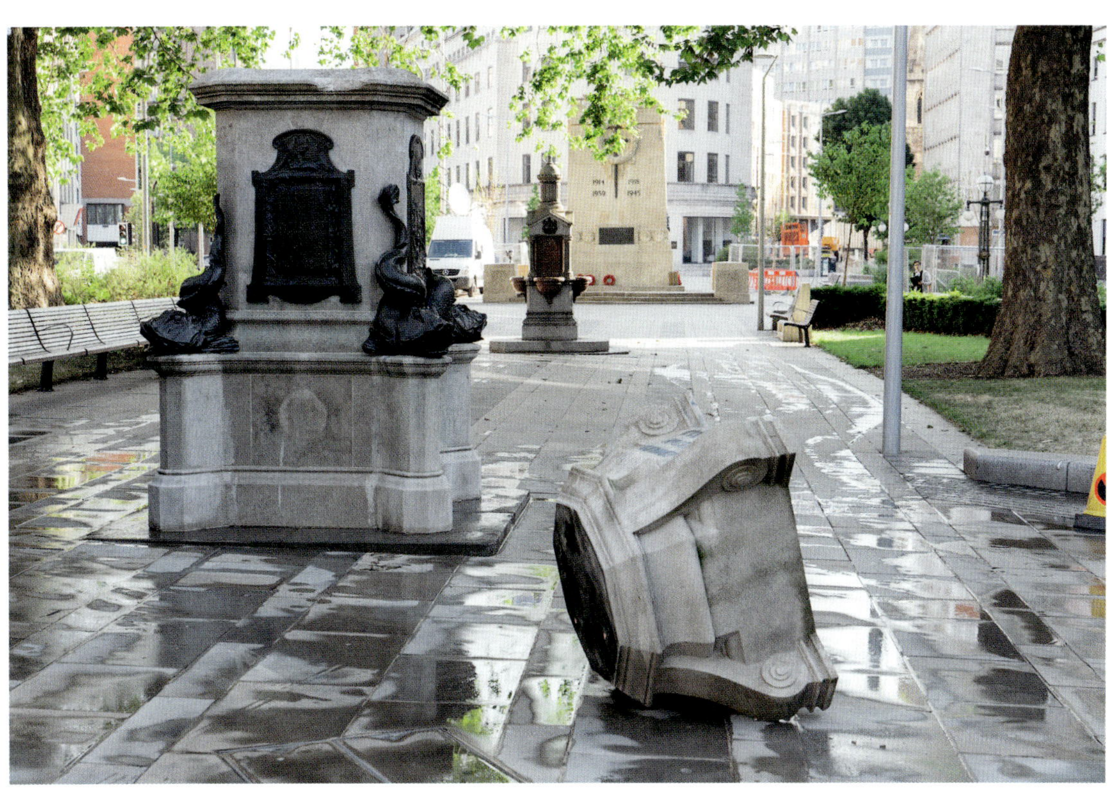

137. Ambulance

This is a selfie of me in an ambulance. I'm waiting in the ambulance, just waiting, waiting, to get a bed in A&E in the Bristol Royal Infirmary. These paramedics came to pick me up from home because I was vomiting and there was something wrong with my stomach. I had tests all night, then the following day they noticed that I had a blockage. I had to have an emergency stomach operation because something had come loose – I'm not sure exactly what happened. Anyway, by pure coincidence, when they were doing the scans for that they found the myeloma. Well, they called it 'nodules on the spine'. And when they say that it means it's cancer. But they didn't say to me, 'You've got cancer.' They just said, 'You've got nodules on the spine.' So I said, 'Is that potentially cancerous?' They said, 'Yes.'

PARAMEDICS TAKE MARTIN TO BRISTOL ROYAL INFIRMARY
BRISTOL, ENGLAND, 2021

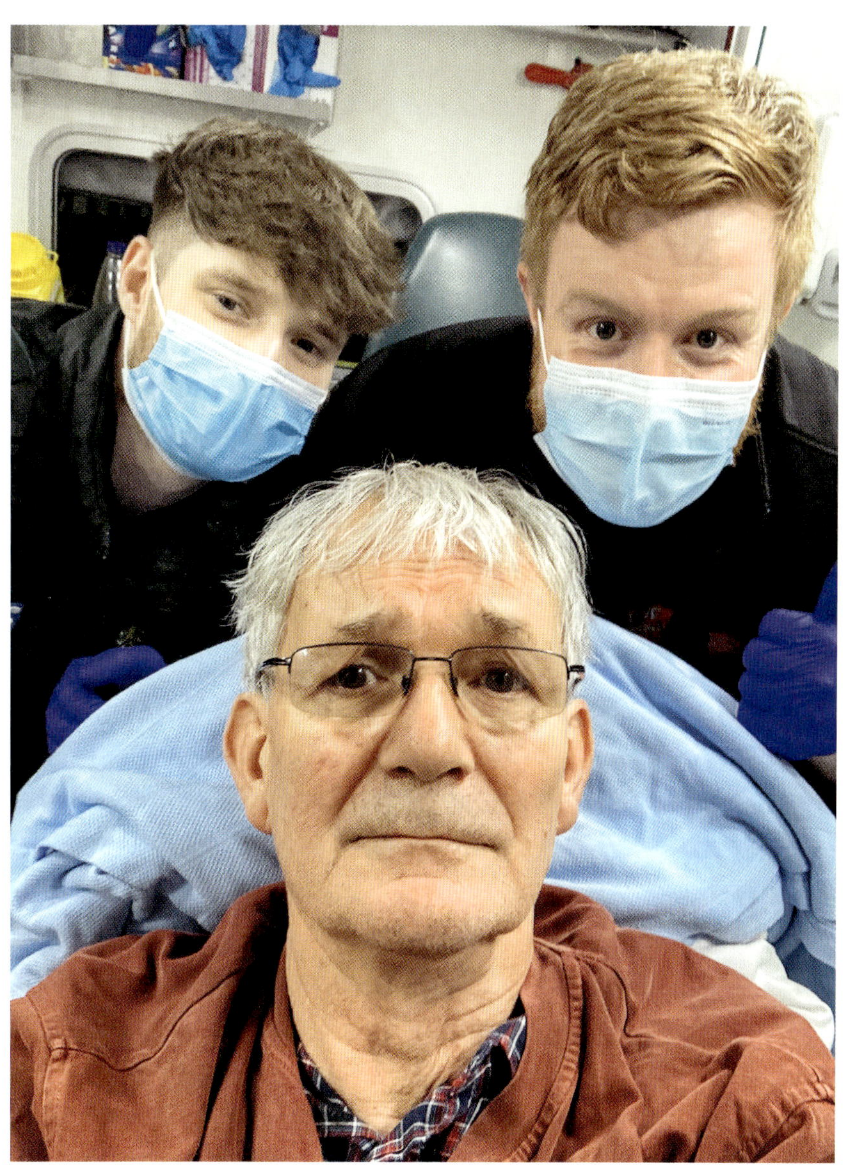

138. Tomato Soup

They removed my stem cells, gave me a blast of chemo, and put the stem cells back in. Then I had to remain in a highly controlled room for another two weeks while my immune system was maintained. The only person allowed in was Susie, who came every day, God bless her.

After that, I was in the ward. I can't remember the name of the ward now. Gastro Ward? It took a long time for my bowel to start working again, I literally didn't go for three weeks. I had to have food pumped in to me to keep me alive, it was nil by mouth. Then at some point they decided I was ready to eat. The first food I had in three weeks was tomato soup – I think it was Heinz tomato soup – orange juice and an ice cream. NHS ice cream was very good. Surprisingly good. It was quite delicious. During those three weeks I could only drink sips of water. I remember getting my first cup of tea, that was a great moment. It was the best cup of tea I had ever drunk.

BRISTOL ROYAL INFIRMARY
BRISTOL, ENGLAND, 2021

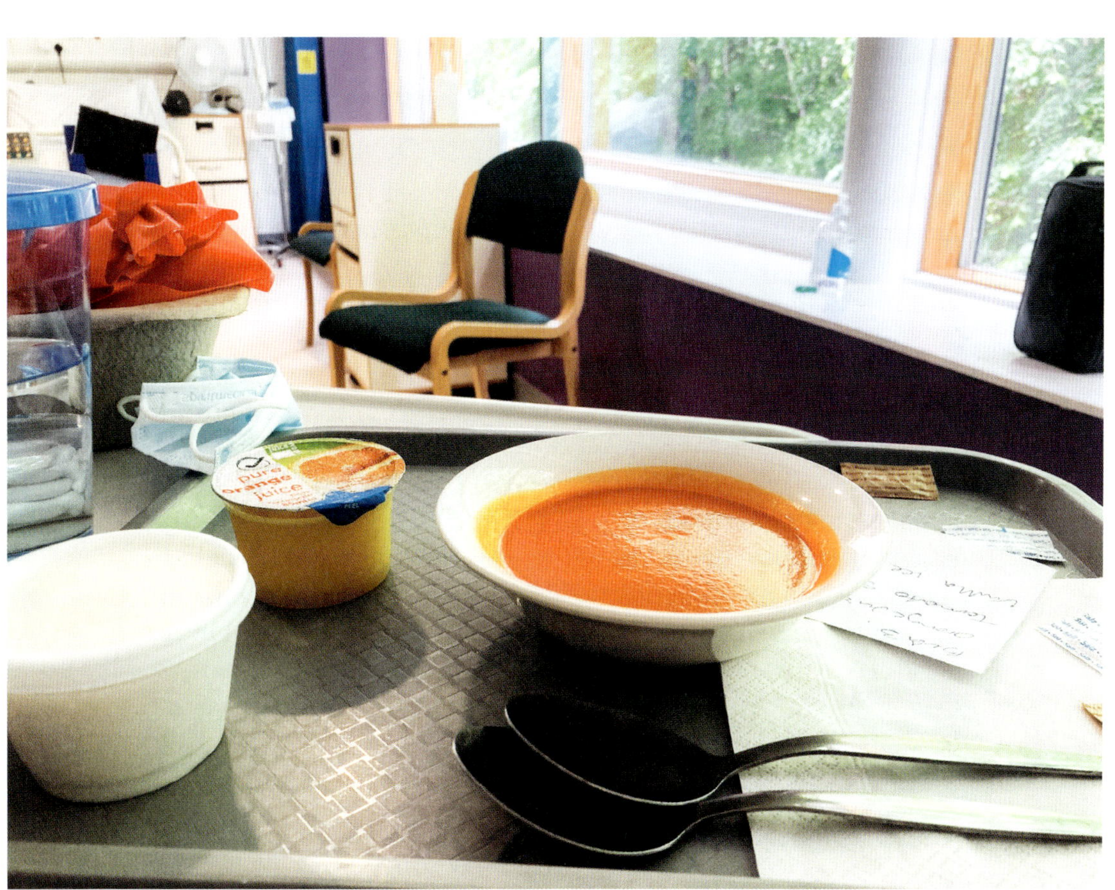

139. Blue Gloves

I went to see Annie, my dentist, after I got out of hospital. She was still working, but she was completely kitted out in this gear. She's dressed like someone who works on a nuclear submarine. The other lady is her dental assistant. They're all so wrapped up, they're like nuclear scientists.

I have to visit my dentist frequently because my teeth are absolutely appalling, so I know Annie very well. Annie is on the right, the one with the blue gloves. Well, hang on, maybe it's her on the left. I don't even recognize her. That's Annie on the left. Annie's excellent and takes really good care of me. I decided I would take not only a picture of my dentist but also my – what do you call the people who do feet? Paediatrician? I got my paediatrician also in his uniform. No, no, podiatrist. Paediatrician looks after children. Podiatrist – so I've got a portrait of him as well.

CLIFTON DOWN DENTAL PRACTICE: MARTIN'S DENTIST
BRISTOL, ENGLAND, 2021

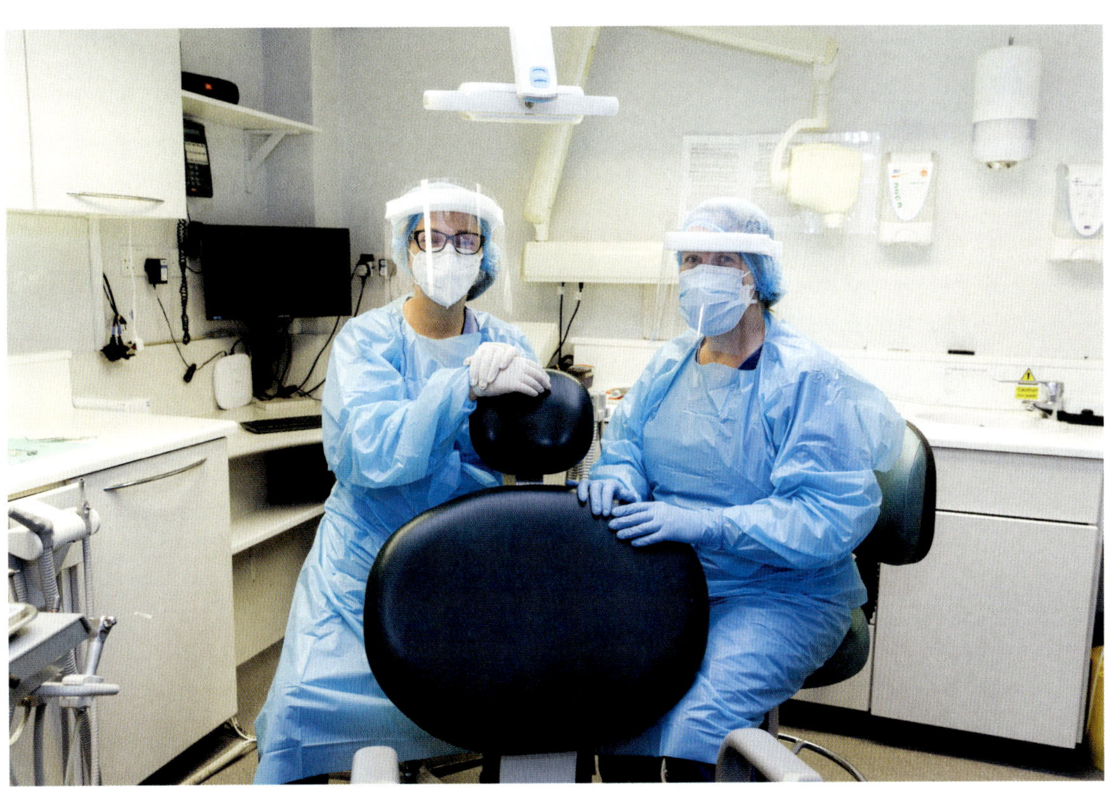

140. A Revelation

François Hébel, the director of the Cartier-Bresson Foundation, discovered that in 1963 Cartier-Bresson did a film about the English, which had been hidden away. Cartier-Bresson had photographed Blackpool – at that time the biggest seaside resort in the country – and industrial communities in the north and put them into a twenty-minute film of still pictures called *Stop Laughing, This Is England*. François invited me to get my pictures of Blackpool and northern industry out from my archive, and we put both of our sets of pictures together. They appeared first as an exhibition at the Cartier-Bresson Foundation, and second, as a book called *The English / Les Anglais*. What was interesting was that our subject matter was very similar. We had gone to the same factories and the same beaches and looked, though we were working twenty years apart, so the exhibition was quite a revelation. You couldn't really tell the difference between the photographs, apart from that mine were in colour, his were in black and white.

THE ENGLISH / LES ANGLAIS
BY MARTIN PARR AND HENRI CARTIER-BRESSON
PUBLISHED BY DELPIRE & CO., 2022

The English

Martin Parr   Henri Cartier-Bresson

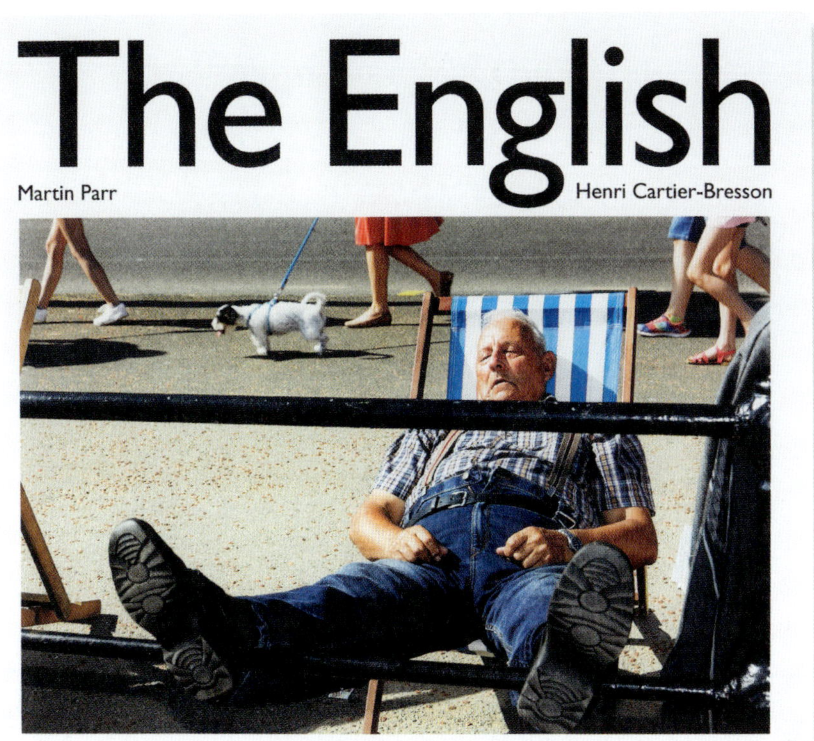

Les Anglais

Henri Cartier-Bresson   Martin Parr

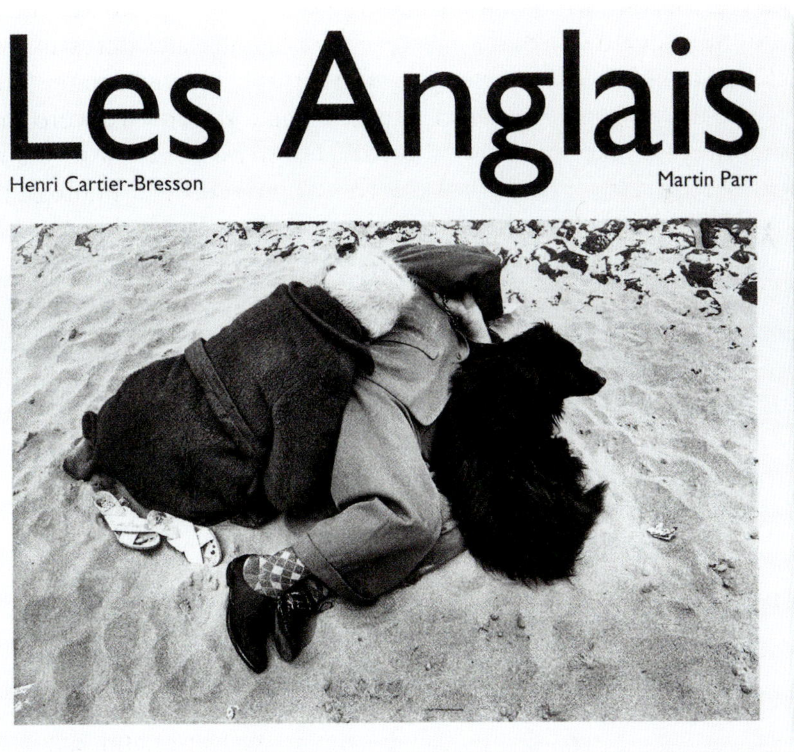

141. The Queen's Garden Party

Photographing the Queen's Garden Party was on my bucket list, but I didn't know how I'd ever get an opportunity to do so. Then I was awarded a CBE, which was very nice. I guess my CBE was awarded for services to photography. The Palace wrote and said: 'We've had to delay giving out honours because of Covid; as compensation, we can offer four tickets to our garden party.' I immediately said yes, so Susie and I, our daughter Ellen, and her partner, Holly, all went along. This photo was taken by my daughter. It's a family snapshot, but it's come in handy to explain this. Is it a good photo? It does the job.

Before we went, I looked up the rules for the garden party, which said you can bring in a small camera, but not a big one. I thought, this is great; I'll take my small camera. No problem. I was shooting away all afternoon and got some quite good pictures. I imagined the garden party would be attended by five hundred people, but there were seven thousand. The queues for cake and tea – no alcohol was served – were massive. The gardens were spectacular. There were photographs to be taken everywhere. I was almost overwhelmed. Afterwards I wrote to the Palace and said: 'Can I publish these?' They said no. That was a big disappointment. What it has meant is that, when I give a talk, I show the censored pictures from the Garden Party, and people are excited, because there's no way they could see these photos otherwise.

Susie had met the Queen and Prince Philip a few years before. She received an award from the Royal Academy of Arts on my behalf because I was away. Prince Philip asked Susie, 'Where is he? Gallivanting about the world?' Susie said, 'Yes.' I was in Ireland, because I'd said I'd give a talk that day to a community centre in Roscommon. When I told the audience in Roscommon they loved it. I didn't cancel the event for the Queen. I'm not a republican – it's quite simple: I had a very complicated schedule and didn't want to put it out.

MARTIN AND SUSIE AT THE QUEEN'S GARDEN PARTY
PHOTOGRAPH BY ELLEN PARR
LONDON, ENGLAND, 2022

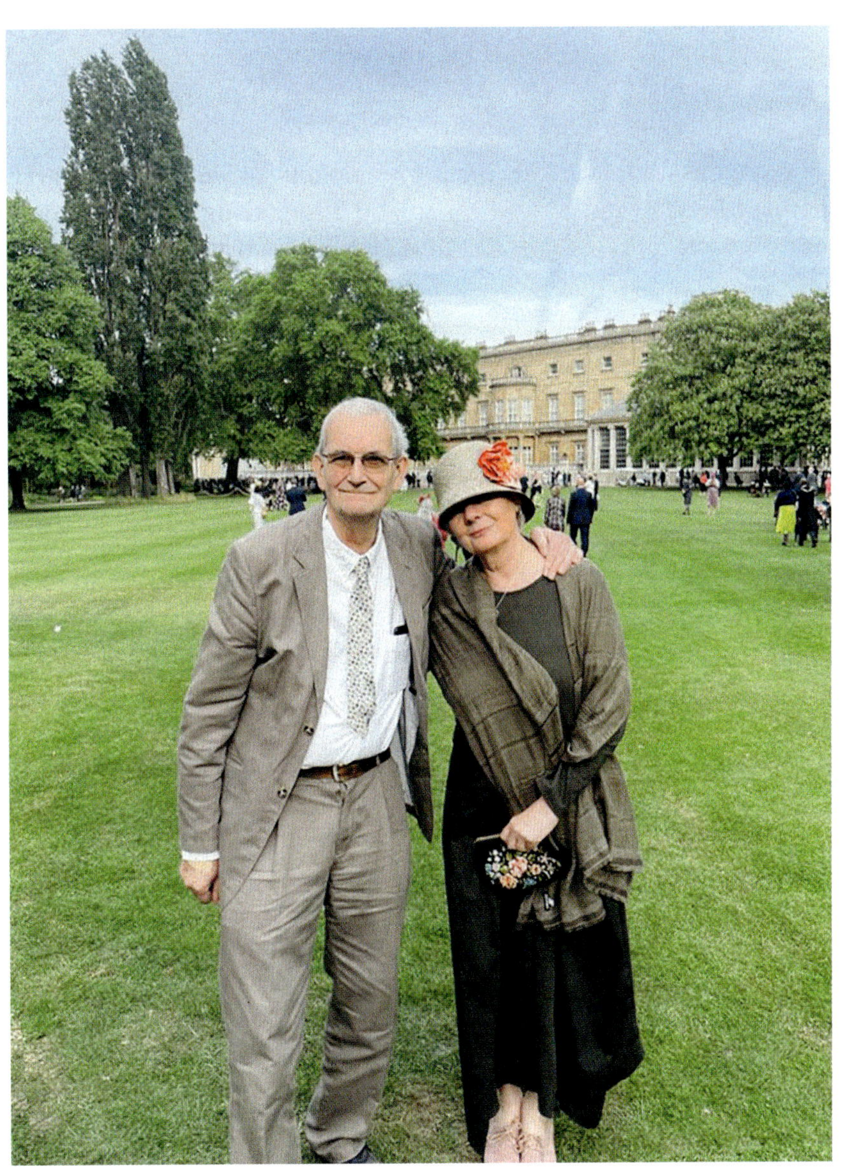

142. Refreshments

Steam fairs are one of the great discoveries I've made since lock-down ended. I've always seen adverts for steam fairs: I never thought to go to one. The Great Dorset Steam Fair is the biggest in the country and, in 2022, I decided to give it a go. It was a fantastic event. There were all these old men tinkering away with gadgets and their steam tractors. It was quite fantastic to see that particular generation of enthusiasts for steam engines, and to see steam cars, tractors being pulled by steam engines and all kinds of machines to do with steam. It was a complete revelation. I was very excited. It's very rare now that I go to a new event which I think is fantastic.

So here we are at the Great Dorset Steam Fair in the church tent. Going in, we have this scenario. The lady on the right is washing up. The dog is obviously greatly in love with his owner – who's got a cup of tea, of course. Look at the dog. Isn't that a great gesture? And I love the big 'REFRESHMENTS' sign. The man looks in need of refreshment; he looks tired, doesn't he? I look at this photo, and it brings back how brilliant it was – it really was like stepping back in time. I worry about being only attracted to things that feel as if they come from another generation, but I can't help but be attracted to them, really. I do try, and have tried throughout my career, to photograph shopping malls, petrol stations, motorway service stations, all the things that are very modern and rather ugly, as well as chasing beautiful scenes like this.

REFRESHMENTS AT THE GREAT DORSET STEAM FAIR CHURCH TENT
DORSET, ENGLAND, 2022

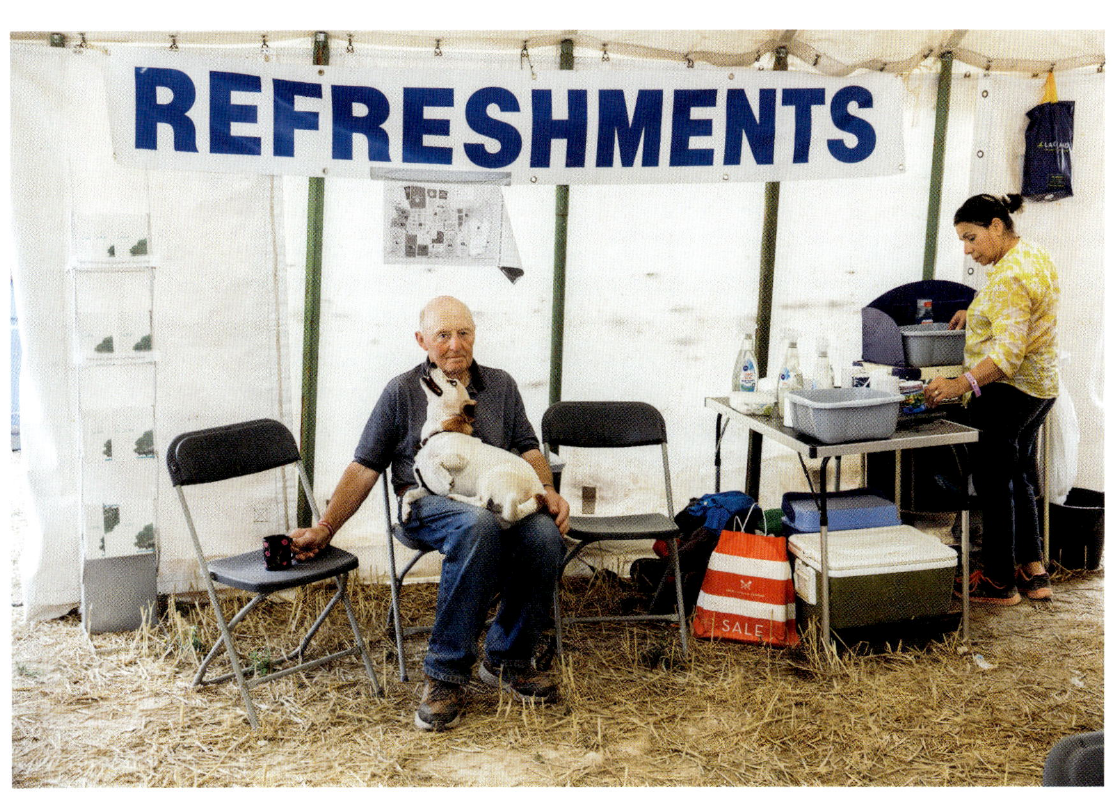

REFRESHMENTS
SALE

143. Elmhurst Hospital Ball

Elmhurst Hospital in New York is unusual because it's a public hospital. Anyone can go there to be treated. During the pandemic, it was very early on the scene to help. In 2020, they curated a photo sale to raise money. Photographers, including myself, donated an unsigned image. These were sold for $100 each and raised a phenomenal amount, over $300,000 in total.

In 2023, Elmhurst Hospital sent a circular saying: 'We have our hospital ball in October.' I wrote and asked, 'Can I attend the ball and take some pictures?' and they said yes. The ball was held in the Natural History Museum in New York, and at the cocktail party beforehand there were a lot of wealthy people. These are three well-dressed women talking with each other, getting on very well.

With many people, to put them at their ease, I chat to them before I photograph them; I didn't need to do that with these ladies because they were so engaged with each other. At an event like this there are lots of people with cameras, so it's less threatening to take photos. Besides, everyone's got a phone, and they're all taking pictures of each other, too. This photo was taken with a wide-angle lens, so I was standing near to them. I have a technique: I'll put the camera towards the subject, I'll be focused, ready to shoot, but my body will be facing the other way. My body's not pointing towards the subject. Then I just turn around and take the photo. I don't do that all the time, but that's a trick I have up my sleeve if need be.

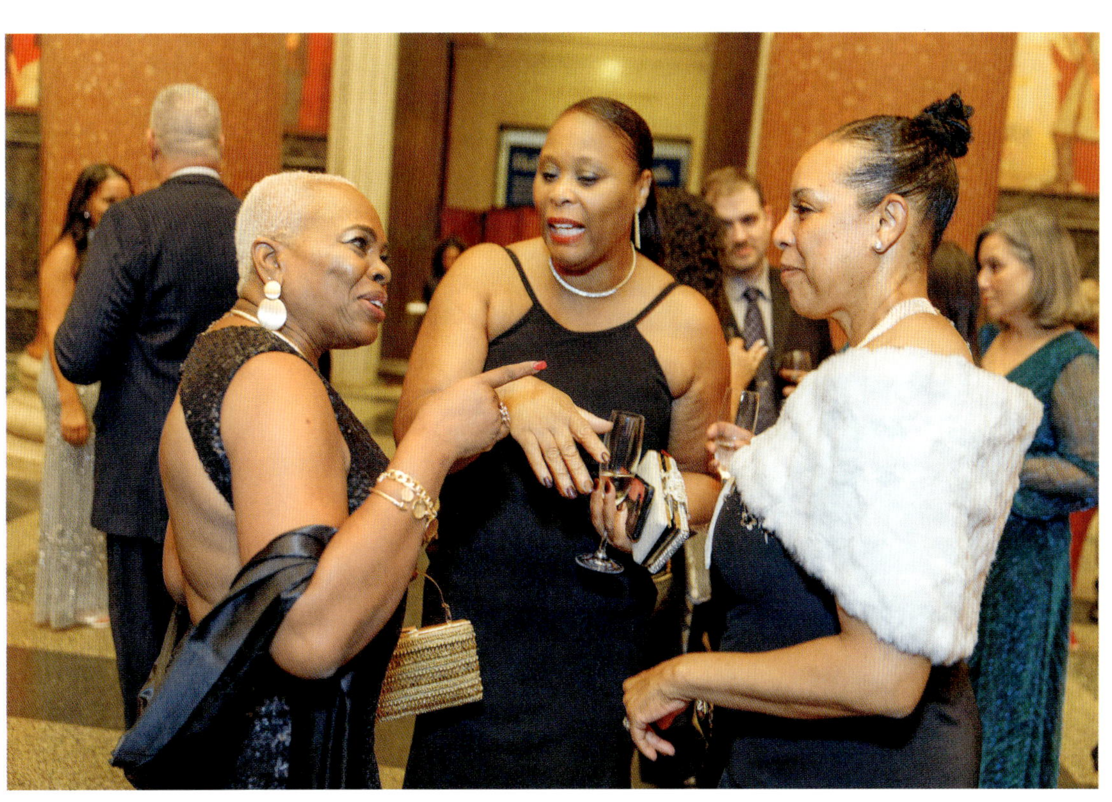

144. Glastonbury

I'd always wanted to go to Glastonbury Festival, but because it's always on the same weekend as the Magnum AGM it's been very difficult for me to attend. Then, in 2021, the *Guardian* commissioned me to photograph the site, to show what it is like when there isn't a festival on. While I was there I had a very good reception from Emily Eavis, who runs the festival. She was very keen on the idea of me photographing the festival, so I then went two years on the trot: 2022 and 2023.

A guy called Haggis offered me a caravan to stay in, which was very nice and very luxurious because it had electricity, so I was able to charge my camera batteries. Luckily it didn't rain, so I didn't have the whole muddy scene. My assistant Nathan came with me, and he camped by the caravan. I went round and photographed everything and anything I found. It was a fantastic experience. I just love this guy, who was called Paul Ford. He was making spatulas for ten quid. You couldn't have someone looking better. This was in the Green Futures field, although it looks more like the past than the future.

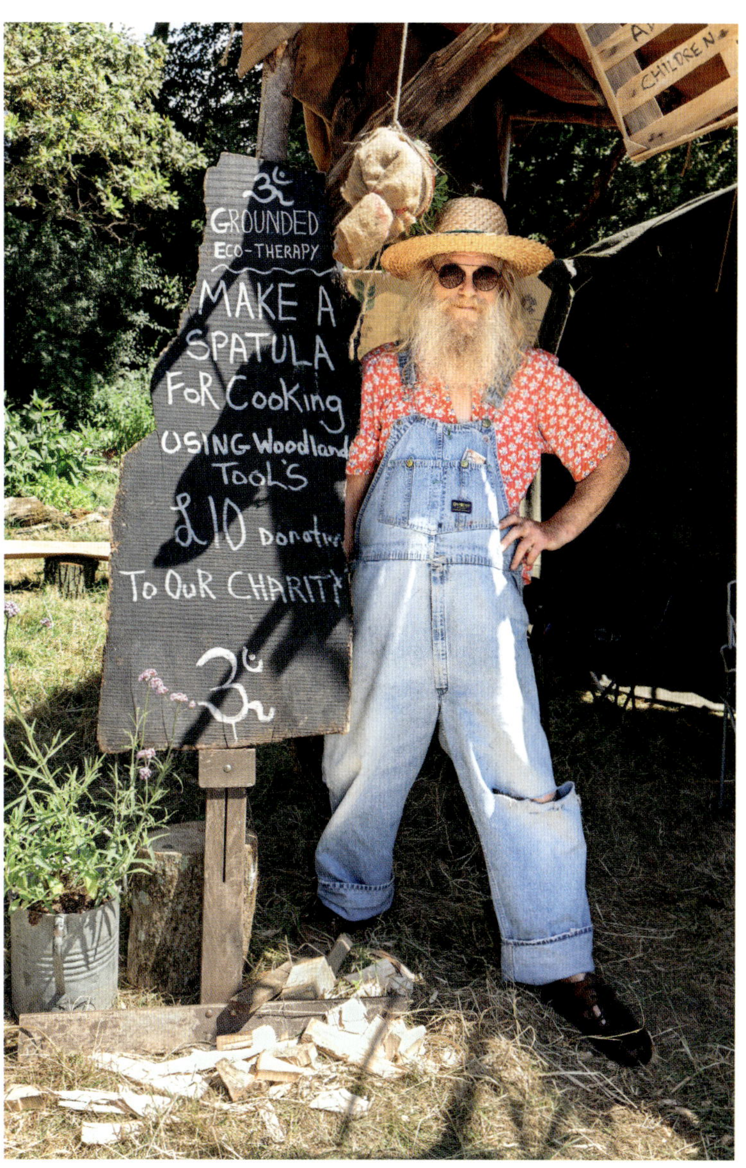
GROUNDED
ECO-THERAPY
MAKE A
SPATULA
FOR Cooking
USING Woodland
TOOL'S
£10 Donation
To OUR CHARITY
CHILDREN

145. Amusement Arcade

I was back in New Brighton in 2023, and I saw this mother with her five kids in their green outfits in the amusement arcade. I just said, 'Is there any chance I can take your picture?' She agreed and didn't ask why. She must have been very proud of her brood so it made sense to her that I'd want to take their photo. I never know if people think I'm an amateur or a professional photographer. I haven't got a particularly fancy camera that says 'professional photographer'.

I love the matching dresses of the two girls and the T-shirts of the two boys; the boy at the back doesn't seem to have anything green on. Mum has got a very classy dress as well. They look quite subdued for an amusement arcade, which is great. The little girl looks like she's struggling not to smile, which is quite nice, really. It's a very structured, formal, painting-like picture.

New Brighton has changed, probably for the better. It's virtually litter-free now, and there's actually a beach, properly laid out. The amusement arcade hasn't changed much, though: like all amusement arcades it's brash, noisy and good fun. New Brighton was very shabby in the 80s. Altogether, it's much tidier. It's the *new* New Brighton. Gentrification is the name of the game.

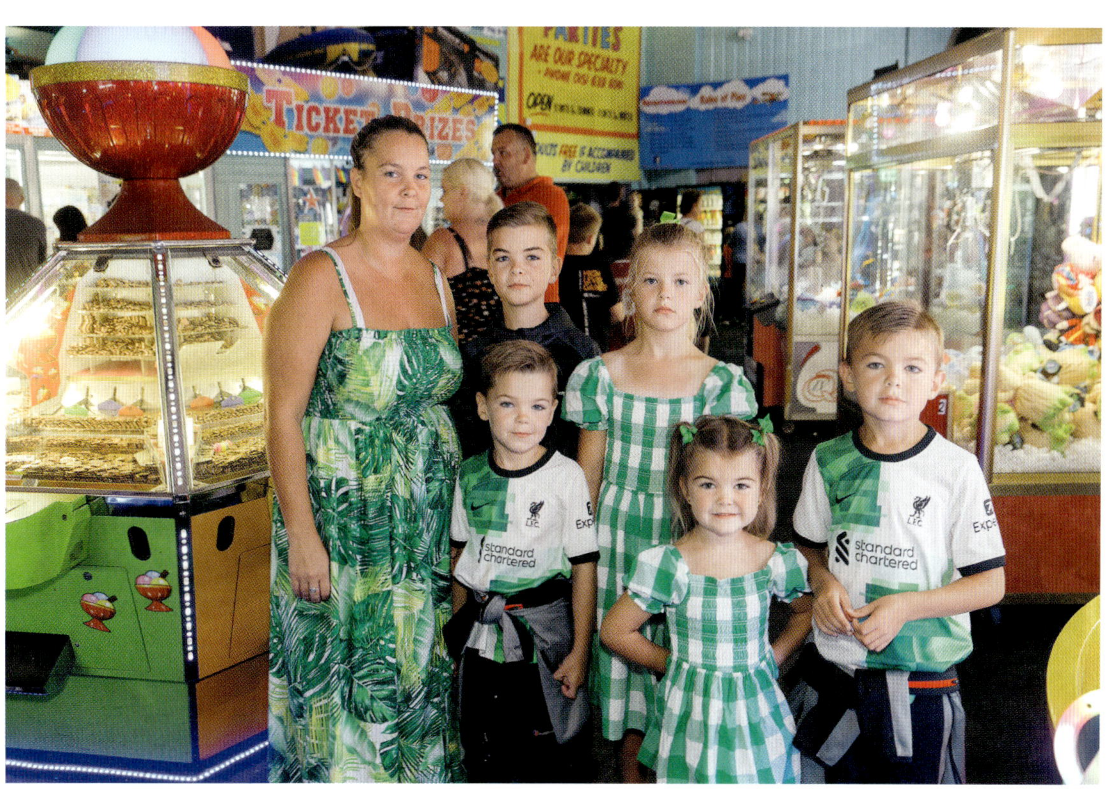

TICKET PRIZES
PARTIES
ARE OUR SPECIALTY
OPEN
standard
chartered
standard
chartered

146. Tesla Showroom

One of the things I'm always thinking about is, 'How can I record current trends, moods and fashions?' Tesla are a huge player in terms of electric cars, and this is a Tesla showroom in New York. You see different images in the photo. You see that big Apple computer on the left. You see the guy in the red tracksuit showing the woman his phone, and on the end you've got three people discussing the purchase, obviously, of a Tesla car. You've got the picture of the car boot. And you've got the woman on the left who's in control of that computer. In the background you see the cars themselves. In fifty years' time, will Tesla still be around? Will we still have electric cars? We don't know, do we? It looks like a non-event now, but when we look back at this in fifty years, it will be incredibly old-fashioned. I would urge everyone to start looking at the world in a different way. Spend some time looking at everyday objects, at their design, their shape, their individual characteristics. Think ahead and imagine their significance.

TESLA SHOWROOM
NEW YORK, USA, 2023

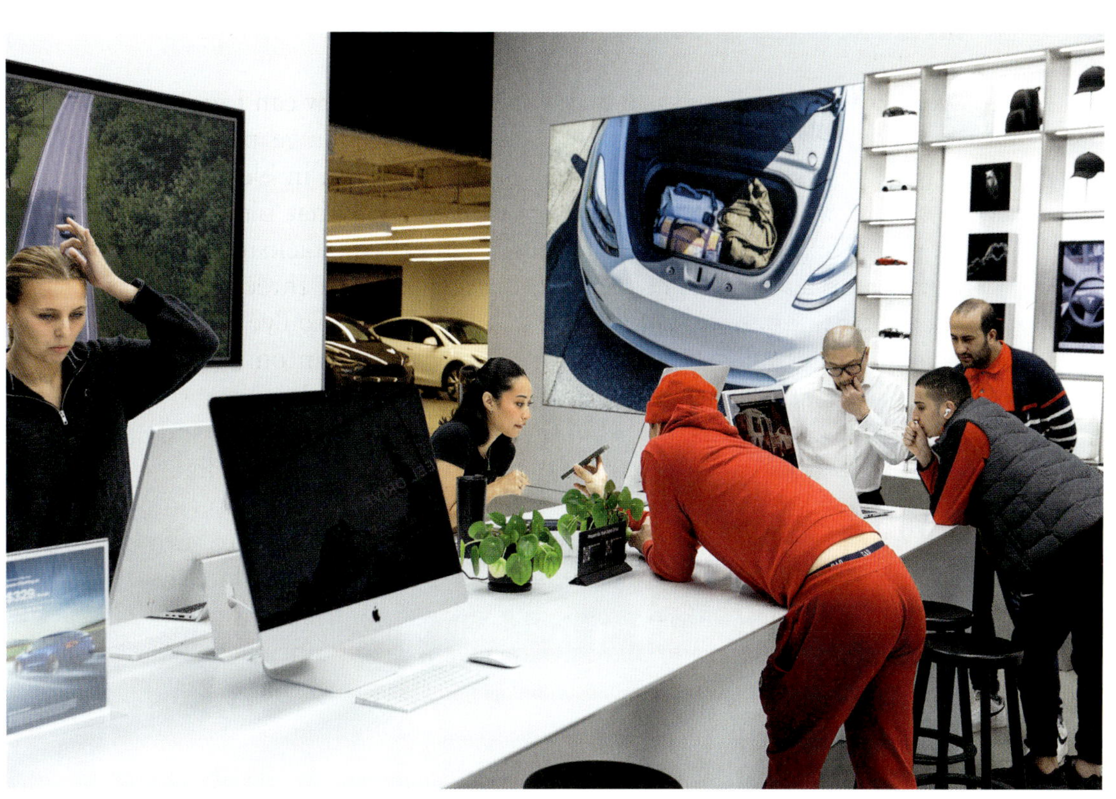

147. The Trevi Fountain

Finally, after years of trying, I got a half-decent picture of the Trevi Fountain, one of the great sights in Rome. It was taken in April. You can see people have got coats on. It was not yet the height of the tourist season and still you could hardly get anywhere near the Trevi Fountain, let alone photograph it with your friends or family in front of it. I've been to both Venice and Rome since the pandemic, and both places have been completely mobbed. This photo is a demonstration of the number of people who are at the Trevi Fountain. Post-Covid tourism has just gone completely mad. I suppose people are catching up with what they've missed out on. Chinese tourists are pushing the numbers up hugely because there's an emerging Chinese middle class with money to burn. Let's face it, a lot of people have got a lot of money to burn, and tourism is one of the things that they burn it on. The planes are packed, hotels are packed, everything's packed. We're meant to be aiming for net zero but it's impossible because everyone wants more things all the time. More flights are being scheduled. Ryanair has got three hundred new planes on order. There's no chance of doing anything near net zero by 2030. Tourist destinations are suffering because of Airbnb and the resulting lack of accommodation for local people. We have anti-tourism marches in Barcelona, Majorca and Venice, which is something that started post-Covid. I didn't see this coming to the extent it has. It's gone insane. People like me contribute to it, because I'm out there, travelling to places like Rome.

I was back in Rome recently, in the summer. It was thirty-seven degrees, so it was hard work being a tourist in that temperature. Thirty-seven degrees Celsius is a lot, isn't it? Much better off in Wales.

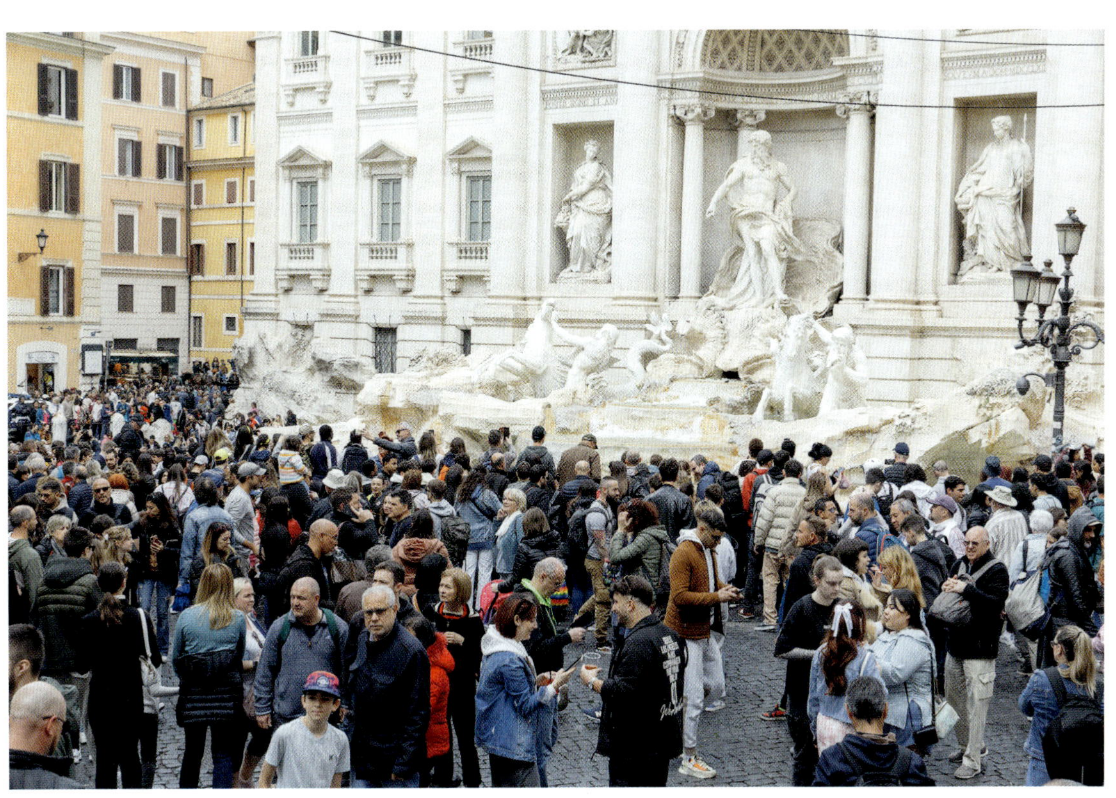

148. Ronnie Scott's

How many photos do I think I've taken? Oh God, millions. The basic theory is: the more rubbish you take, the better the chances of a good photo emerging, so I keep on taking the rubbish. In my archive, there are about 250 boxes, all full of 10x8 black-and-white and colour prints. Now, we do the edits of digital files on the computer; then the production department sends the high-res scans to a lab in Manchester; they do the prints, and send them back. I don't print out every photo I've taken, only the ones I want to double-check and edit. These are then loaded onto the Magnum site.

Do I take photos every day? It depends, really. It doesn't feel strange not to have a camera with me. I took this image at Ronnie Scott's using an iPhone. These days, there are many trips I go on where I don't take my camera. I can't be bothered. I mean, either I'm taking photos seriously or I'm doing something else, so I might just go to a festival for fun and not take a camera. I'm not going to retire from taking photographs. I will just drop dead first. Then I'll have to retire. Then I'll have no choice.

GARY WILLIAMS PERFORMING AT RONNIE SCOTT'S
LONDON, ENGLAND, 2024

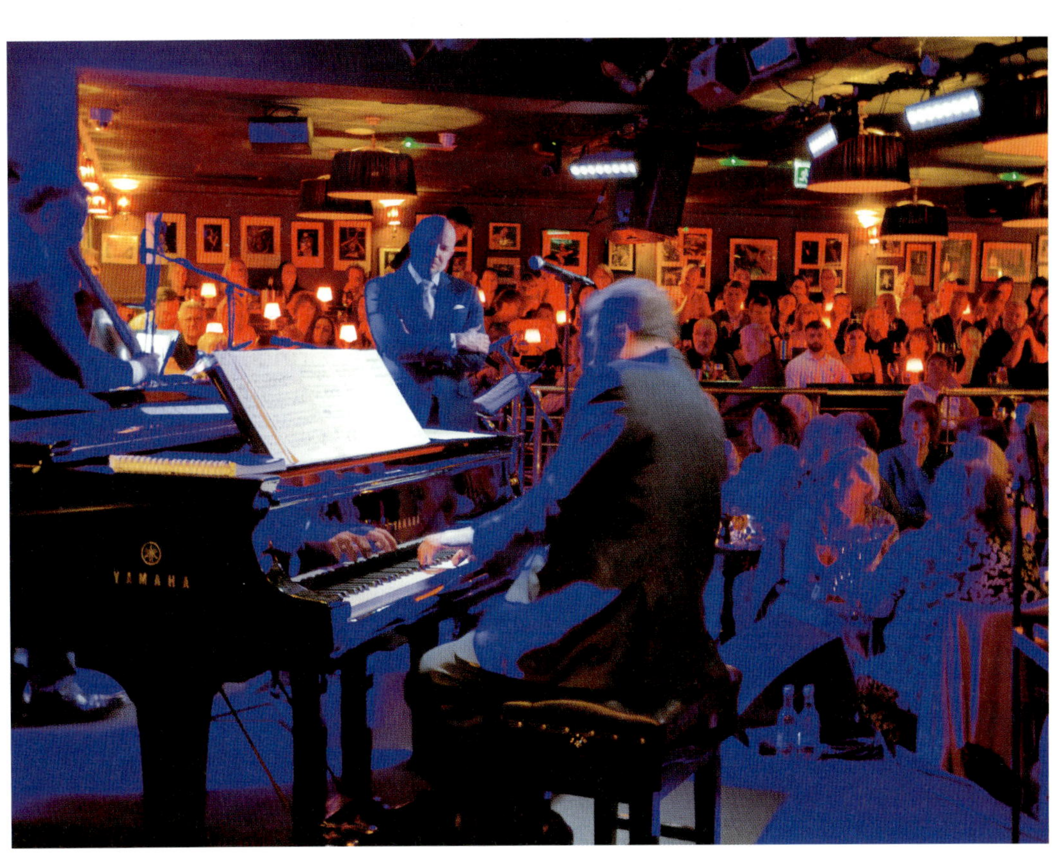

149. Iftar

When the sun goes down on any day during Ramadan, you can hold an iftar festival. That's what happens on St Mark's Road in Bristol, which has many Muslim shops, curry houses and supermarkets. Anybody is invited to come to an iftar, sit and get ready for when the sun sets – on this night in 2024, it was 8.56 p.m. – then they feed everybody. Here there are two or three hundred guests, but I've seen it busier. The iftar is an act of generosity by the Muslim community. They emphasize the hospitality that is integral to Islam, where you can go into any mosque and be fed for free. In fact, you can be given free food in a Sikh temple as well. It's quite extraordinary that they offer a meal to anyone who comes. You get a nice vegetable curry, you get fruit, you get a bottle of water, and it's always moving to see so many people enjoying the iftar.

This photo was shot on an iPhone 15. When the light is low, it's an absolutely brilliant camera: it can actually see more things than the human eye. It makes me wonder if in future phones will be so phenomenal that we'll just drop our main cameras and use phones instead. I can shoot a lot more anonymously with an iPhone than with a big DSLR. Most people now shoot everything on their phones. Unless you're a serious photographer, you don't need a bigger camera than that. Compact cameras are no good to anyone now because the technology on phone cameras is better. Nikon and Canon are fine, because they make professional cameras with much bigger files than even an iPhone, but phones are hot on the heels of these big camera manufacturers.

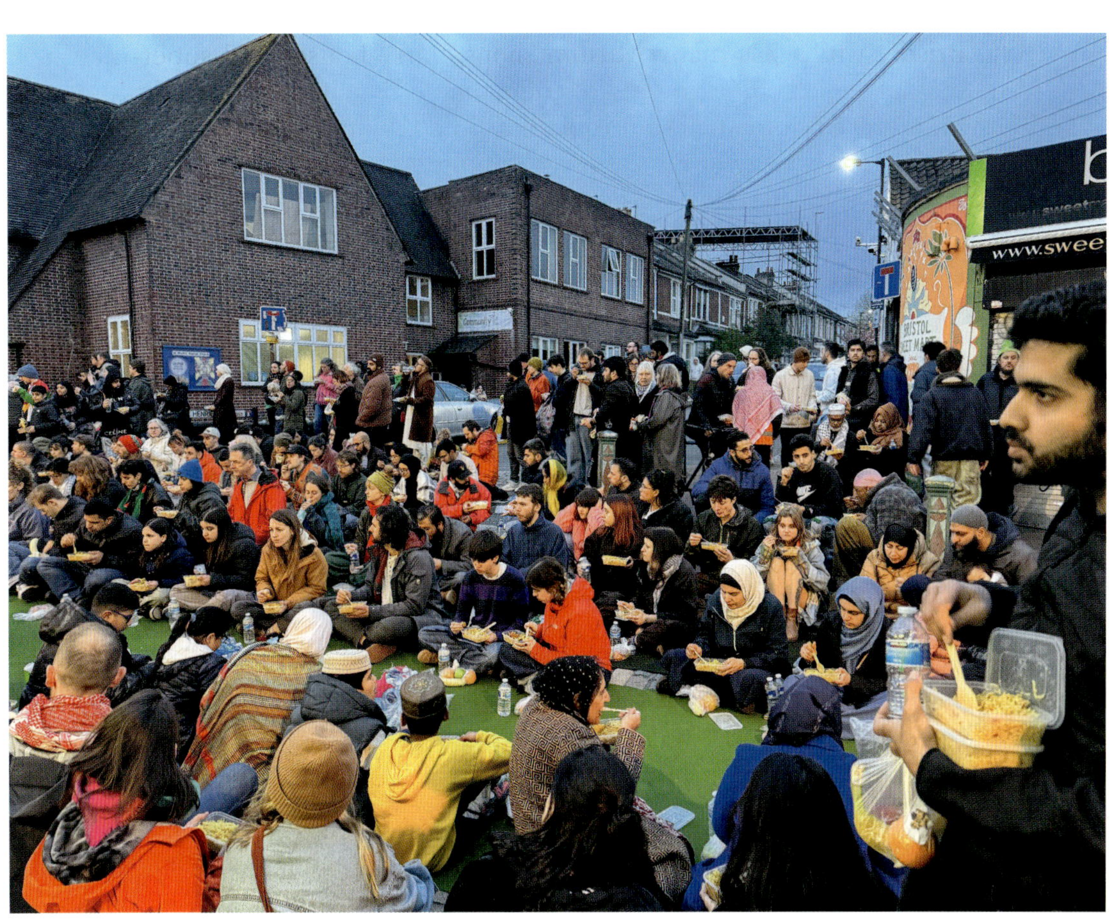

150. Like Martin Parr?

I have had a wonderful life with photography. I have travelled the world. From visiting amazing North Korea, to a vicar's garden party in Somerset, or shooting Mar del Plata beach in Argentina – what a privilege it has been to see the world and record my response with photography. I had a funny one in Morecambe last summer. I was taking photos, and I had my wheelchair – my rollator – with me. This couple came up and said, 'Oh. That's a nice camera.' They asked, 'What are you doing around here?' I replied, 'Well, I'm just documenting Morecambe.' They said, 'You mean like Martin Parr?' I said, 'I am Martin Parr.' They were rather surprised.

I've been taking photos for almost seventy years, and two things have happened in that time: we've witnessed the amazing transformation from analogue film to the digital era, and I've got a lot older. I was taking photographs only last week, in Greece, and I photographed something crazy, called *bouzouki*. It was almost unbelievable. It's a tradition of throwing flowers at singers of traditional ballads. I went to a nightclub, and at 2 a.m. a singer came on. As a sign of appreciation people threw trays of carnations at him. All around the club young ladies were holding piles of ten flower-laden trays at a time. These would be replaced as soon as the carnations were thrown, because the best clients are serial throwers. Each tray cost €100, and at the end of each singer's performance, the thrower was given a bill. By the end of the evening, there were so many trays on the ground it was quite staggering. It is the maddest thing I have witnessed, and it is all thanks to the natural curiosity that being a photographer can bring. We live in a difficult but inspiring world, and there is so much out there I want to photograph.

Okay. Next photo. Which one?

GIORGOS MAZONAKIS AT FANTASIA
ATHENS, GREECE, 2024

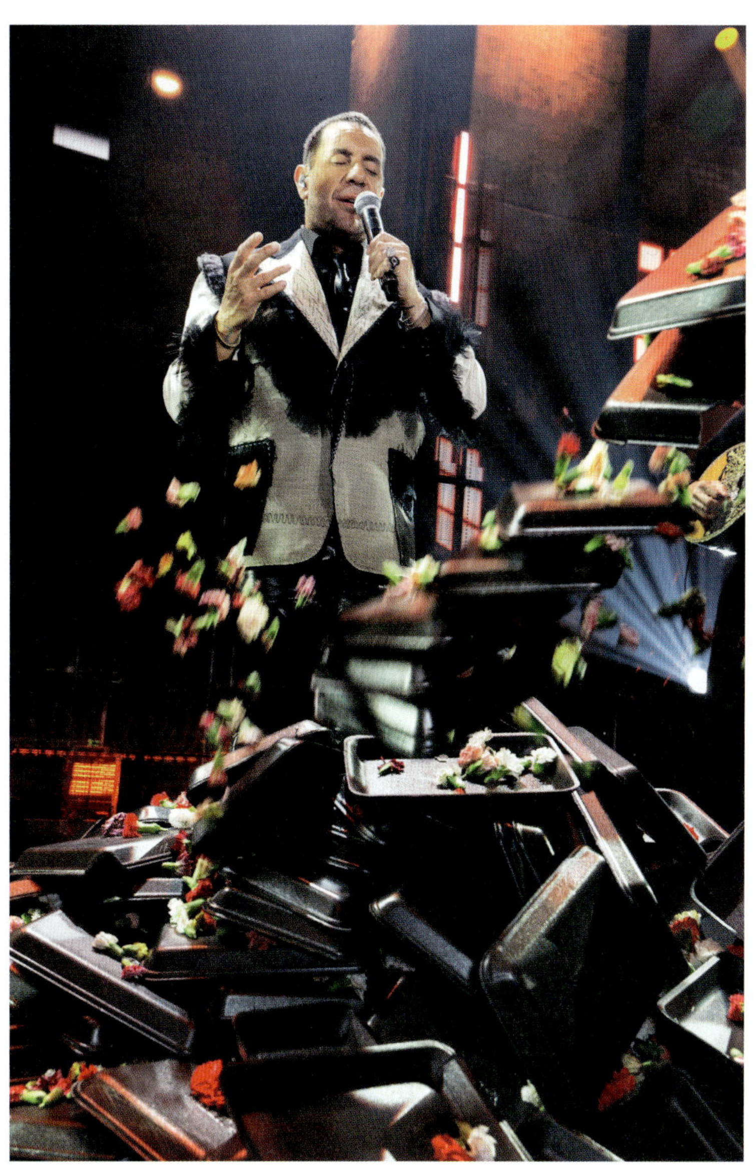

Acknowledgements

Thank you to Susie and Ellen Parr. Susie has written very accomplished texts to accompany my photos in several of my photobooks, including the work on Crimsworth Dean, *The Rhubarb Triangle* and *The Non-Conformists*. Thank you to my team, past and present: Jenni Smith, Louis Little, Charlotte King, Nathan Vidler, Mike Hale, Alex Parkyn-Smith, Jon McCall, Isaac Blease, Chris Hoare, Izzy de Wattripont, Millie Ferguson, Ilayda Akarca, Beatrice Gillies, Tom Groves, Conor Kilroe and Steve Joyce, as well as everyone else who has been involved in the studio over the years. Thank you to Alan Murgatroyd, my photography tutor at Manchester Poly. When I had a big show at Manchester Art Gallery in 2018, I contacted Alan Murgatroyd and invited him to open the exhibition. It was a vindication. MP

Thank you to Will Archer, Matt Stuart, the team at MPF: Ilayda Akarca, Isaac Blease, Millie Ferguson, Beatrice Gillies, Mike Hale, Louis Little, Jon McCall, Alex Parkyn-Smith, Jenni Smith, Nathan Vidler; the team at Penguin: Thi Dinh, Jodie Lewis, Ingrid Matts, Stefan McGrath, Liz Parsons, Imogen Scott, Jim Stoddart, Anna Tuck, Thea Tuck, Jo Whitehead. I owe particular thanks for their guidance, hard work, kindness and skill to Ruth Cairns, Chloe Currens, Charlotte King, Susie Parr and Joanna Scanlan. Thank you to Solly. And thank you to Martin, for trusting me. WJ

PARTICULAR BOOKS

UK | USA | Canada | Ireland | Australia
India | New Zealand | South Africa
Particular Books is part of the Penguin
Random House group of companies
whose addresses can be found at
global.penguinrandomhouse.com

Penguin Random House UK,
One Embassy Gardens,
8 Viaduct Gardens, London SW11 7BW

penguin.co.uk
global.penguinrandomhouse.com

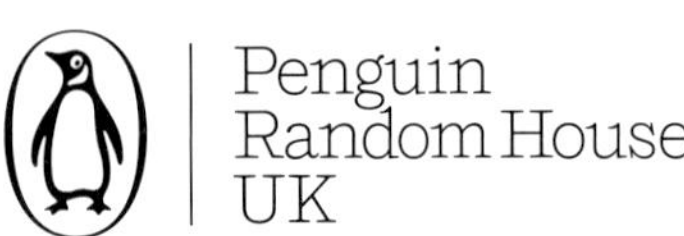

First published in Great Britain 2025
002

The moral rights of the authors have been asserted
Design by Jim Stoddart.
Printed and bound in Italy by Printer Trento
The authorized representative in the EEA is
Penguin Random House Ireland,
Morrison Chambers, 32 Nassau Street,
Dublin D02 YH68
A CIP catalogue record for this book is available
from the British Library.

ISBN: 978-0-241-74082-8

Penguin Random House is committed to a sustainable future for our business, our readers and our planet. This book is made from Forest Stewardship Council® certified paper.

www.greenpenguin.co.uk

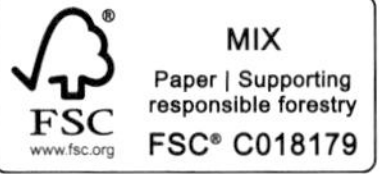

Penguin Random House is committed to a sustainable future for our business, our readers and our planet. This book is made from Forest Stewardship Council® certified paper.